THE SEX OF CLASS

DATE DUE

BRODART, CO.   Cat. No. 23-221-003

THE SEX OF CLASS

WOMEN TRANSFORMING AMERICAN LABOR

Edited by Dorothy Sue Cobble

ILR Press

AN IMPRINT OF

Cornell University Press

Ithaca and London

First published 2007 by Cornell University Press
First printing, Cornell Paperbacks, 2007

Printed in the United States of America

Library of Congress Cataloging-in-Publication Data

The Sex of class : women transforming American labor / edited by Dorothy Sue Cobble.
    p. cm.
  Includes bibliographical references and index.
  ISBN 978-0-8014-4322-0 (cloth : alk. paper) — ISBN 978-0-8014-8943-3 (pbk. : alk. paper)
  1. Women in the labor movement—United States.   2. Women labor union members—United
States.   3. Women—Employment—United States.   I. Cobble, Dorothy Sue.   II. Title.

  HD6079.2.U5S49 2007
  331.40973—dc22

2006036018

Cloth printing   10 9 8 7 6 5 4 3 2 1
Paperback printing   10 9 8 7 6 5 4 3 2 1

CONTENTS

ACKNOWLEDGMENTS

This volume has been simmering since 2001, when the Rutgers University Institute for Research on Women (IRW), which I directed at the time, chose Reconfiguring Class and Gender: Identities, Rights, and Social Movements as its theme. A number of wonderful women and men from the IRW helped me keep the fires stoked and the project moving along. I thank Marlene Importico, IRW's office manager, and Beth Hutchison, IRW's associate director, who worked with me in the first stages of this project. They helped me mount a number of IRW programs in which contributors from this volume presented their works-in-progress: the 2002 spring colloquium on Unions and Worktime; the 2002–2003 Thinking about Women/Thinking about Class Distinguished Lecture Series; the June 2003 roundtable, Immigrant Women Organizing; and the 2004 spring conference on Labor, Class, and Sexuality. They also helped secure crucial funding for these programs from the Offices of the Vice President for Academic Affairs and the Dean of the Faculty of Arts and Sciences at Rutgers University, New Brunswick; the Rockefeller Foundation; and the Sexuality Fellowship Research Program of the Social Science Research Council.

In the later stages of the project, the encouragement and intellectual support of Nancy Hewitt, whose tenure as IRW director began in 2004, proved invaluable, as did the superb research assistance of two graduate students in women's and gender studies, Anique Halliday and Andrew Mazzaschi. The enthusiasm and good sense of Fran Benson at Cornell University Press helped smooth the way forward. I also thank the many other Cornell University Press staff who steered the production process along with such alacrity. In particular, Candace Akins and Julie F. Nemer did a superb job with the copy editing.

Last, the nineteen contributors to this volume have my heartfelt thanks for their eye-opening, meticulous research; their patience through the long book production process; and their thoughtful comments on the overall framing of the project. I am so pleased we took this journey together and hope that our work in this volume can contribute in some small measure to making the world a more humane and just place.

Dorothy Sue Cobble

ABBREVIATIONS

ANA	American Nurses Association
ACLU	American Civil Liberties Union
ACORN	Association of Community Organizations for Reform Now
ACTWU	Amalgamated Clothing and Textile Workers Union
AFDC	Aid to Families with Dependent Children
AFL-CIO	American Federation of Labor–Congress of Industrial Organizations
AFSCME	American Federation of State, County, and Municipal Employees
AFT	American Federation of Teachers
AIWA	Asian Immigrant Women's Advocates
ATU	Amalgamated Transit Union
BSOIW	International Association of Bridge, Structural, Ornamental and Reinforcing Iron Workers
CAAAV	Committee Against Anti-Asian Violence
CAFÉ	Carolina Alliance for Fair Employment
Cal-OSHA	California Occupational Safety and Health Administration
CAW	Committee for Asian Women
CCPOA	California Correctional Peace Officers Association
CCTWC	Child Care That Works Campaign
CEAL	Labor Studies and Support Center [El Salvador]
CFRA	California Family Rights Act

CHAOS	Create Havoc Around Our System
CIOAC	Central Independiente de Obreros Agricolas y Campesinos
CIW	Coalition of Immokalee Workers
CLUW	Coalition of Labor Union Women
CNA	California Nurses Association
CRLA	California Rural Legal Assistance
CSEA	California School Employees Association
CSL	California Senior Legislature
CTA	California Teachers Association
CTW	Change to Win Federation
CWA	Communications Workers of America
CWE	Consortium for Worker Education
DWU	Domestic Workers Union
EEOC	Equal Employment Opportunity Commission
ENDA	Employment Nondiscrimination Act
ETWF	European Transport Workers Federation
FAT	Frente Autentico del Trabajo
FLF	Fuerza Laboral Feminina
FLOC	Farm Labor Organizing Committee (AFL-CIO)
FMLA	Family and Medical Leave Act
FNV	Federatie Nederlandse Vakbeweging
FOG	Focus on Globalization
FTUWKC	Free Trade Union of the Workers of the Kingdom of Cambodia
HERE	Hotel Employees and Restaurant Employees Union
HUCTW	Harvard Union of Clerical and Technical Workers
IAFF	International Association of Firefighters
IAM	International Association of Machinists
IATSE	International Association of Theatrical Stage Employees
IBEW	International Brotherhood of Electrical Workers
IBT	International Brotherhood of Teamsters
ICFTU	International Confederation of Free Trade Unions (disbanded as of November 1, 2006)
IDEPSCA	Instituto de Educacion Popular del Sur de California
IHSS	In-Home Supportive Services
ILA	International Longshoremen's Association
ILC	International Labour Conference
ILGWU	International Ladies' Garment Workers' Union
ILO	International Labour Organisation
INS	Immigration and Naturalization Service
IRW	Institute for Research on Women

ITUC	International Trade Union Confederation (formed when ICFTU joined with the World Federation of Trade Unions)
IUD	Industrial Union Department (AFL-CIO)
IUE	International Union of Electrical Workers
IUF	International Union of Food, Agriculture, Hotel, Restaurant, Catering, Tobacco and Allied Workers' Associations
IUOE	International Union of Operating Engineers
IUPA	International Union of Police Associations
JFREJ	Jews for Racial and Economic Justice
LIUNA	Laborers' International Union of North America
LMO	La Mujer Obrera
MCSU	Marine Cooks and Stewards Union
NAACP	National Association for the Advancement of Colored People
NAALC	North American Agreement on Labor Cooperation
NAFTA	North American Free Trade Agreement
NCHE	National Committee on Household Employment
NEA	National Education Association
NLRA	National Labor Relations Act
NLRB	National Labor Relations Board
NWRO	National Welfare Rights Organization
OFCCP	Office of Federal Contract Compliance Programs (U.S. Department of Labor)
OPEIU	Office and Professional Employees International Union
OSHA	Occupational Safety and Health Act
OTOC	Omaha Together One Community
PAW	Pride at Work
P-FLAG	Parents and Friends of Lesbians and Gays
POWER	People Organized to Win Employment Rights
RWDSU	Retail, Wholesale and Department Store Union
SEDEPAC	Service, Development and Peace [Mexico]
SEIU	Service Employees International Union
SEWA	Self-Employed Women's Association [India]
SEWU	Self Employed Women's Union [South Africa]
SHARE	State Healthcare and Research Employees
SMWIA	Sheet Metal Workers' International Association
STIT	Textile Industry Workers Union [El Salvador]
STRM	Mexican Telephone Workers' Union
STWU	Swedish Transport Workers' Union
TANF	Temporary Aid to Needy Families
TVPA	Trafficking Victims Protection Act of 2000
TVPRA	Trafficking Victims Protection Reauthorization Act

TWSC	Tenants' and Workers' Support Committee
UA	United Association of Journeymen and Apprentices of the Plumbing, Pipefitting and Sprinkler Fitting Industry of the United States and Canada
UAW	United Auto Workers
UBCJ	United Brotherhood of Carpenters and Joiners of America
UDWA	United Domestic Workers of America
UE	United Electrical Workers
UFCW	United Food and Commercial Workers International Union
UFWA	United Farm Workers of America
ULU	United Labor Unions
UNI	Union Network International
UNITE	Union of Needletrades, Industrial and Textile Employees
UNITE HERE	Union of Needletrades, Industrial and Textile Employees–Hotel Employees and Restaurant Employees Union
USLEAP	U.S. Labor Education and Action Project
USWA	United Steelworkers of America
VISTA	Volunteers in Service to America
WEEL	Working for Equality and Economic Liberation
WEP	Work Experience Program [New York City]
WIEGO	Women in Informal Employment Globalizing and Organizing
WORC	Workers' Organizing Resource Centre [Canada]
WWP	Women Workers Project

THE SEX OF CLASS

INTRODUCTION

Dorothy Sue Cobble

A young female laundry worker is distraught when her boss tells her that she too will have to service him sexually if she wants to keep her job. And what a job it is: paltry wages, stifling heat, the dirty laundry relentlessly piling up around her, the huge unforgiving machines ready to scorch her hands along with the hot starched sheets. Her co-workers agree to confront the boss as a group. And with the help of a local worker organization, their fantasies of revenge take concrete form. They might have won, too, had not some of their husbands and boyfriends interfered; the women were needed at home, the men insisted; and besides, such aggressive public displays were unfeminine.

The story is hard to locate in time or place. It could be pre–World War I Chicago or Calcutta; it could be twenty-first-century Shanghai or San Francisco. As it turns out, it occurred recently in a New York City neighborhood I have walked through many times (Greenhouse 2004b). A rising economic tide lifted many boats in the United States in the 1990s, but class inequality also soared to levels not known since before the New Deal, producing extremes of ostentatious wealth and grinding poverty. New social and cultural distinc-

I thank the many contributors to this volume who offered helpful advice on this introduction. In particular, Heidi Hartmann gave me detailed and substantive comments that pulled me out of a number of intellectual swamps. My husband Michael Merrill helped formulate the ideas expressed here and smoothed the rough edges of the writing. I also thank the participants at the MIT Institute for Work and Employment Seminar for their thoughtful interventions when I presented a draft of this introduction in May of 2006.

tions, premised on material wealth and the unabashed display of it, have emerged as well. These coalescing class cultures sit uneasily in the midst of a society that still regards itself as middle class.

Such class matters have captured the attention of those in and out of the academy (New York Times and Keller 2005; Lardner and Smith 2005). Wealth disparities, blocked mobility, and the loss of good jobs are prime targets for social scientific investigation (Levy 1999; Appelbaum, Bernhardt, and Murnane 2003). Humanists dissect the psychological scars of poverty and the flourishing status-conscious world of the super-rich and the aspiring super-rich (for example, Bourdieu 1987). Governmental bodies, political pundits, and morning radio hosts debate globalization and its economic and social consequences at home and abroad.

This book too is about class.[1] It details the rise of class inequalities in the United States, and it offers portraits of the new labor movements that are arising in response. But it is also about the sex[2] of class. It is about the feminization of work and workers and the continued reluctance of those who study class and who rally on behalf of ameliorating class injustice to take sufficient notice of this fundamental revolution.

Much of the discussion of the new class inequality, for example, has focused on the declining incomes of working-class men—and certainly their downward mobility is cause for alarm. Yet class disparities among women have widened as well (McCall, chap. 1 in this volume), and the economic situation for many working-class women has been just as troubling. Women started at the bottom and they remain there today (Lovell, Hartmann, and Werschkul, chap. 2 in this volume). If class inequalities are to be remedied, researchers, policy analysts, and public leaders at all levels will need to understand why class disparities have increased among women, why women still predominate on the lower rungs of the occupational ladder, and why market and public policy solutions have had only limited success in addressing these problems.

The phrase *the sex of class*, as used here, has multiple meanings. On one level, it is simply about moving beyond the image of the working class as blue-collar men and thinking about the realities of class and of class difference as women experience them. In 2005, 46 percent of the nation's wage and salary

---

[1] I assume that class has cultural as well as economic dimensions, following the lead of E. P. Thompson (1963, 9) who notes that, just as there is no love without lovers, class exists not simply as a structure or a category but as a relationship created by and between people. This volume investigates both changing class structures and the shifting identities of groups and individuals.

[2] I use *sex* interchangeably with *gender* to refer to unstable and changing notions of sexual difference and of what it means to be a woman or man. As Joan Scott (1999) notes, feminists first used *gender* to signal that notions of sexual difference were socially, not biologically, constructed. But as biological sex has come to be understood as fluid and evolving, the original distinctions between gender and sex have collapsed.

workforce was female.³ But of those in working-class jobs—whether defined by low wages or lack of power or just all-around-dismal working conditions— arguably the majority were women.⁴ In short, a revolution has occurred: women have moved from the margins to the center of the working class. Yet our theories of class and our understanding of the jobs workers do, the problems they face, and the kind of social movements they are creating are decades behind these demographic realities.

The sex of work is changing along with the sex of the worker. Work is feminizing in the sense that more women are doing it. It is also feminizing in the sense that women's often substandard working conditions are becoming the norm, particularly for those without a college degree, still some three-quarters of the workforce. The casualization of work and the growth of low-wage, dead-end, contingent jobs are manifestations of this phenomenon. The proliferation of low-level white-collar and service occupations is another. Women have always held these jobs. What is different today is that men are now often in work arrangements and in occupations once reserved primarily for women (Cobble and Vosko 2000).

Paying more attention to women and to women's jobs, then, is essential if we are to understand the experience of the majority of workers. It is also a helpful place to begin for insight into the present and future of men's lives. The twentieth century witnessed a partial convergence of men's and women's lives as women moved out of the household economy into market work and gradually adopted the employment patterns of men: full-time, long-hour jobs; few career interruptions; and a work-first, family-second orientation (Moen and Roehling 2004). As the convergence continues and market work spreads across the globe, disrupting traditional agricultural and domestic production patterns and shifting dependencies to wage labor, women are now becoming the primary and even the sole breadwinners of many families (Ehrenreich and Hochschild 2002). In short, as the twenty-first century proceeds, working-class men are becoming more like women. They too hold secondary jobs or no jobs at all in the market, and they too feel the pinch of domestic and caretaking responsibilities when their partners spend time out of the home and put market work first.

But the sex of class refers to more than changing our image of who makes up the working class and whose experiences are taken to be the norm. It is about reinventing worker movements and the class politics they embrace. The

³ U.S. Department of Labor, Women's Bureau, "Women in the Labor Force in 2005," http://www.dol.gov/wb/factsheets/QF-laborforce-05.htm (accessed August 21, 2006).
⁴ Zweig (2000, tables 1–2) estimates that, in 1996, 60 percent of jobs were working class, using a definition in which power and control were central components. He calculates that 47.4 percent of those in working-class jobs were female. Women have increased their share of the labor force since then. They also predominate in the bottom half of the occupations he judged as working class.

labor movement has always had a sex. Most labor movements of the past arose in response to the needs and aspirations of a male-dominated blue-collar workforce. As that workforce changes and becomes more diverse, so too must the labor movements that represent it.

Integrating women into official positions of leadership in existing labor movements is part of what is necessary. Yet it is not simply a matter of inclusion or of inviting women to join movements that remain essentially unchanged. Many men's jobs may be assuming female characteristics and the lives of men and women may be converging as the breadwinner/homemaker divide continues to collapse, yet sex differences persist. Men and women continue to work in different sectors of the economy, doing different kinds of work. They are still held to different cultural and social expectations. Bodily differences matter as well. Fewer men than women, for example, must choose between keeping their job and bearing a child. Labor movements must be sensitive to the continuing realities of sex differences and how the sex of class matters in determining goals, choosing tactics, and devising institutional structures and policies.

Ending sex discrimination should be a priority for labor movements. As is generally acknowledged, sex-based employment barriers have lessened, with college-educated, white women making notable progress. But the progress made by some women should not blind us to the continuing sex-based disadvantages experienced by the majority. Sex discrimination persists and has very real consequences in the lives of working-class women. Full-time women workers earn about three-quarters the income of full-time male workers (McCall, chap. 1, table 1.1, in this volume), and women continue to be relegated to the lowest-paid, least-prestigious jobs. A whopping 90 percent of those earning less than $15,000 annually and over two-thirds of those making under $25,000 are women (Lovell, Hartmann, and Werschkul, chap. 2, tables 2.1–2.2, in this volume).

To make matters worse, although many men of all classes engage in caring labor at home and in their communities, the rise of female-headed families and the aging of the population has resulted in increased numbers of women caring for children and elderly relatives without the help of men, financially or emotionally (Reskin and Padavic 2002). The ability of labor movements to improve the lives of workers, men as well as women, is dependent on acknowledging these sex differences and crafting a new class politics premised on that recognition. Such a politics would find its strength through coalition-building *across* the sex divide rather than through adherence to a false solidarity that denies the salience of sex and of sex discrimination.

Perhaps as women approach majority status in labor movements across the globe, the sexual diversity of class experience will be more readily acknowledged. Women have been one-half of all unionists in Canada since 2002

(Morissette, Schellenberg, and Johnson 2005) and are moving toward the majority mark in the United Kingdom, Australia, and a host of other countries (Colgan and Ledwith 2002, table 16; Docherty 2004). In the United States, the feminization of organized labor picked up speed in the post–World War II decades with the expansion of service employment and the decision of many older married women to join the labor force. It has continued unbroken into the present day, with women constituting 43 percent of all union members in 2005 (Cobble and Michal 2002; Milkman, chap. 3 in this volume). Many of these women, both from the World War II generation as well as the Baby Boomer era, looked to unions to solve their problems, not just as workers but as *women* workers. They brought a different sensibility into the movement and pushed to transform its agenda and its practices. They raised issues of pay equity, of child care, of paid maternity leave, of shorter hours and greater job flexibility, and of an end to discrimination on the basis of sex, race, and ethnicity (Cobble 2004). In addition, women and female-majority unions were in the forefront of efforts to lessen discrimination based on sexual orientation (Hunt and Boris, chap. 4 in this volume). Still, as Milkman (chap. 3 in this volume) shows, despite the feminization of labor's ranks, the U.S. labor movement remains remarkably segregated by sex, with men concentrated in some unions and women in others. These "two worlds of unionism," to use Milkman's apt phrase, present a challenge to continuing progress for women because, in many ways, the two worlds remain distinct not only in their gender composition but also in their openness to reform.

The revival of interest in class and social justice movements among many gender scholars and activists could help improve conditions for working-class women and strengthen reform efforts within the house of labor. Younger women in particular view the problems of women through a class or race lens, joining movements to end sweatshops, pass living wage ordinances, or protect the labor rights of immigrants. Historically, working-class women made the greatest advances in transforming unions and raising their own status when they had the support of elite female allies and the backing of the larger women's movement (Cobble 2004).

But why should women, and men for that matter, turn to a labor movement that according to most commentators is in serious decline and disarray? First of all, as this book shows, although the traditional labor movement in the United States may be a mere shadow of what it was in its golden post–World War II incarnation, other labor movements are arising to take its place. The post–World War II labor movement drew its strength from industrial workers, largely those working in the mass production palaces of the day, churning out automobiles, steel, electrical equipment, and other basic goods. That work is now often done by machines and by millions of factory workers outside the United States. But as manufacturing spread beyond U.S. borders, so did unionism. One recent estimate is that, although official union membership has declined steeply in the majority of mature industrial economies since the 1970s, those losses have been more than offset by membership gains in the emerging industrial sectors of Latin America, Asia, and African (Docherty 2004). These new labor movements outside the United States, as chapters in this volume suggest, may in the long run end up enhancing worker power and labor standards in the United States.

Of equal importance, public- and service-sector unionism in the United States is far from moribund. Many of the older industrial unions from the 1930s have virtually disappeared, but public-sector unionism mushroomed in the 1960s and 1970s, drawing in teachers, clericals, health-care workers, and others. The movement peaked in the early 1980s with close to two-fifths of government workers organized (Cobble 2005). It remains undiminished today[5] as large public-sector unions such as the American Federation of State, County, Municipal Employees (AFSCME) and the American Federation of Teachers (AFT) continue to expand their ranks. Of equal importance, many unions such as the Service Employees Industrial Union (SEIU), rooted historically in nonfactory workplaces, have pioneered new organizing and representational practices among low-wage service workers, signing up thousands of janitors, home care, and day-care workers across the country (Cobble 1996; Boris and Klein, chap. 9 in this volume). In July 2005, a number of these unions broke from the official labor federation, the American Federation of Labor–Congress of Industrial Organizations (AFL-CIO), and set up their own rival labor center, dubbed the Change-to-Win (CTW) federation. Many of these organizing breakthroughs have involved women, particularly women of color (Bronfenbrenner 2005). Indeed, with close to 7 million women covered by union contracts, organized labor arguably is the largest working women's movement in the country.[6]

As white-collar unionism has flourished in Canada, Europe and elsewhere, U.S. levels have remained low, in part because U.S. labor law denies basic labor rights to millions of managerial and supervisory workers in the private sector (U.S. General Accounting Office 2002). Yet professional and technical associations are thriving, and if historical patterns hold, many of these associations will evolve into more unionlike entities. Both teachers and nurses, for example, organized initially into professional associations that focused on what they defined as professional concerns: status, control over workplace decisions affecting the worker-client relation, ability to set standards for competence, and the overall health of the sector. Gradually, these organizations in-

---

[5] U.S. Department of Labor, Women's Bureau, "Women in the Labor Force in 2005," http://www.dol.gov/wb/factsheets/QF-laborforce-05.htm (accessed August 21, 2006).

[6] Bureau of Labor Statistics, "Union Members in 2005," press release, January 20, 2006, table 1, http://www.bls.gov/pub/news.release/union2.txt (accessed June 4, 2006).

corporated more traditional union matters: salaries, benefits, seniority rights, and job protection. They also dropped their opposition to strikes and to collective bargaining. Today, union membership among teachers and nurses is commonplace.

The National Education Association (NEA), the nation's largest professional employee association with 2.7 million members, turned to collective bargaining in the 1960s, influenced by the example of its rival, the AFT, which had been pushing for teacher contracts and bargaining rights since the turn of the century (Murphy 1990). In addition to classroom teachers, the AFT organized classroom aides, school bus drivers, and other school personnel. In 1978, they also set up a health-care division, which represents nurses, therapists, technicians, pharmacists, doctors, and other health-care workers.[7] By 2005, two-fifths of organized women workers worked in education (Milkman, chap. 3 in this volume), an interesting parallel to a century ago when a comparable proportion of union women came from the garment industry.

Nurses embraced collective bargaining later than did teachers. The American Nurses Association (ANA) formally dropped its opposition to bargaining in the late 1940s, but few of its affiliated state nurse associations seriously pursued the union route. In the 1990s, however, the collective bargaining wing of the ANA grew by leaps and bounds, creating tensions within the association over how to represent the divergent interests of staff nurses and nurse managers. In 1995, the 60,000 member California Nurses Association left the ANA over the issue, eventually setting up a new independent national union for registered nurses in 2004. In 2000, the ANA also established its own national nurses union, the United American Nurses, which coordinates bargaining among ANA-affiliated state nurse associations. SEIU and other unions with health-care divisions are courting nurses as well. Currently, some 17 percent of nurses are affiliated with one of the many unions vying to represent them, making them among the more organized occupational groups in the United States (Gordon 2005).[8]

Yet many nurses and teachers remain wary of traditional unionism, finding it at odds with certain long-standing values within the profession. In response, some professional unions are moving toward a new unionism that melds the best traditions of professionalism and collective bargaining into a new amalgam (Kerchner 1999). Such a reconceived nurse unionism, for example, would concern itself with preserving the "ethic of care" and making it possible for nurses to provide quality care without abandoning the union em-

[7] For more information on teacher unionism, visit the NEA website, www.nea.org, and the AFT website, www.aft.org.

[8] For more information on nurse unionism, visit the websites maintained by the American Nurses Association, www.ana.org; the California Nurses Association, www.cna.org; the SEIU, www.seiu.org; and the AFT, www.aft.org.

phasis on "equity, collective rights, and improving the conditions of work and pay" (Armstrong 1993, 320). Nonprofessional service workers, such as the home care workers profiled by Boris and Klein (chap. 9 in this volume), also are struggling to combine these concerns and meet the needs of those giving the care as well as those receiving it.

New forms of worker representation and collective power are emerging in other female-dominated occupations and sectors as well. Immigrant women, many concentrated in domestic and household service, are banding together with the help of worker centers. As Fine (chap. 11 in this volume) details, new community-based worker centers now exist in more than one hundred cities across the country, and many have had a substantial impact on the lives of the millions of immigrant workers, documented and undocumented, who now populate the day-labor ranks of residential construction and household services, scrubbing the floors and pruning the bushes in suburbs and cities across the United States. Welfare and workfare recipients, historically excluded from a labor movement defining itself as limited to wage workers, have self-organized as well with the help of the Association of Community Organizations for Reform Now (ACORN) and other community-based groups. They continue to demand recognition as workers wherever their labor is performed, however it is compensated, mirroring the rise of labor movements among marginalized female workers globally (Tait, chap 10 in this volume).

This book argues that the growth of collective movements is necessary if the work and lives of the majority of working women are to improve. Certainly, education opens up job opportunities and raises pay (Lovell, Hartmann, and Werschkul, chap. 2 in this volume). And the labor movement should embrace educational access as a core worker right in the twenty-first century, just as it did in the nineteenth. Yet any solution premised solely on individual upward mobility and human capital investment is doomed to fail as long as employers set the terms of employment. Moreover, there will always be a need for nonprofessional workers, that majority sector of the workforce engaged in retail, clerical, goods production, construction, and support services.

Historically, protecting worker freedom of association and encouraging worker organization has increased the supply of good jobs both for those with more education, such as teachers, and those with less, such as laundry workers. It has also invigorated political citizenship; increased the likelihood of economic, social, and personal security during periods of ill health and dependency; and curbed the worst abuses in working conditions and work hours, thus ensuring that individuals have dignity and time for themselves, their families, their friends, and their communities. Government can take on many of these regulatory and welfare functions, but the most prosperous and democratic societies rely on a mix of private and public provision. Unions and worker associations are private voluntary organizations that regulate markets and attend to group welfare. They allow for participation from the bottom rather than rule from above. To the degree that they are local, democratic, and decentralized, they also can be conduits for creativity, innovation, and leadership development. Only very few individuals can bargain effectively in the face of organized capital; collective organization is necessary to equalize the relationship.

The Sex of Class is about growing unions and associations so that the needs of the majority can be met. It assumes that labor movements have a future and that women are helping to make that future a reality. It argues that women transformed labor organizations in the past and will continue to do so in the future.

The chapters in this book point to a number of specific changes that would strengthen the U.S. labor movement and improve the lives of working women. First, the boundaries of the labor movement need to be expanded. The traditional labor movement defines its membership too narrowly, often restricting membership to those workers capable of winning a labor contract from an employer. Not only is it virtually impossible for many workers to use the worksite-based election procedures currently available for securing a majority vote of their co-workers, only one-third of the workplaces where a majority vote is won ever succeed in convincing the employer to sign a contract (Cobble 1994; Compa 2004). Not surprisingly, as employer resistance to collective bargaining has grown and workers find it difficult to secure contracts, union membership has fallen.

But why should the labor movement be restricted to those covered by employer-signed contracts? Historically, the labor movement defined itself broadly. It was a big-tent movement, taking in a wide variety of worker organizations, many of which pursued goals other than contract coverage (Cobble 1997, 2001). As this book documents, workers today are organizing collectively and using that power to transform their working and living conditions. They are also using a variety of means to advance their interests. They rely on public opinion, political action, and community organizing to raise workplace standards and end discrimination (Nussbaum, chap. 8; Boris and Klein, chap. 9; Tait, chap. 10; Fine, chap. 11; Quan, chap. 13 in this volume); they seek better enforcement of existing domestic and international labor laws (Crain, chap. 5; Ontiveros, chap. 12; Fine, chap. 11); they are organizing across borders, relying on alliances with nongovernmental organizations (NGOs) and new labor and feminist transnational networks (Quan, chap. 13; Vosko, chap. 14). The official labor movement should reach out and expand, offering new mechanisms for group affiliation and embracing new strategies for worker advancement. It should move beyond contract unionism and become, once again, a more inclusive heterogeneous movement.

It is not just a fixation on labor contracts that limits the size of today's labor movement. Samuel Gompers, the first president of the AFL, insisted that organized labor limit its membership to wage workers. There was a certain progressive logic to this a century ago because many in the labor movement were still committed to ending the wage system, either by helping wage workers become small producers and businessmen, as was the principal strategy of the Knights of Labor, or by doing away with capital and hence wage labor, as was the dream of the Industrial Workers of the World.

One hundred years later, however, this foundational premise of the U.S. labor movement bears rethinking. As I have argued elsewhere (Cobble 1994, 1997), U.S. unions need to organize all workers and not restrict themselves to employees or to wage workers. For too long, the labor movement has let the narrow definition of employee in the National Labor Relations Act—a definition that by recent calculations excludes 22 percent of the private-sector workforce (U.S. General Accounting Office 2002)—determine who is and is not a worker. The movement needs once again to draw its own boundaries, which would include the growing numbers of managers, supervisors, and self-employed exempted under the law. It could also include the unemployed, the underemployed, and those on social wages or public assistance (Tait, chap. 10 in this volume).

Indeed, first-line supervisors, inside contractors, and the self-employed were once the backbone of the labor movement (Cobble and Vosko 2000). Today's workers look less and less like the traditional wage proletariat as they sell themselves, their products, and their labor power. Yet petty entrepreneurs, street vendors, and other informal economy workers have created one of the largest labor associations in India, the Self-Employed Women's Association (SEWA). SEWA is an important force in pushing for a fair distribution of India's new wealth and in expanding the boundaries of official unionism globally (Vosko, chap. 14 in this volume). The informal economy is not limited to the so-called developing countries, as is evident in the rise of self-employment in trucking, construction, household services, and other sectors of the U.S. economy. And North American unions, as Vosko discusses, have much to learn from the new unions such as SEWA that are emerging among informal economy workers worldwide.

The chapters that follow also speak to a second important theme: the need for labor to expand its message and address the diverse needs of workers. Female-majority unions were among the first to respond to the concerns of lesbian, gay, bisexual, and transgendered members, securing health benefits for unmarried partners and contract language forbidding discrimination against sexual minorities (Hunt and Boris, chap. 4 in this volume). Some of these same unions have helped move the issues of family leave and child care to the center of labor's agenda. In California, a broad coalition of unions came together under the leadership of the State Federation of Labor to lobby successfully for the first state law in the United States granting paid family and medical leave; in New York, union pressure resulted in a substantial expansion of the state child-care subsidy program (Firestein and Dones, chap. 7 in this volume). Yet not all unions embrace this new more diverse agenda, and, as Crain (chap. 5 in this volume) recounts, organized labor still lags in its commitment to end the "collective harms" of sexual harassment and sex segregation.

Still, a few unions stand out as models of how work-based organizations can respond to the complex and diverse identities of workers. Just as family leave is not for women only, as Firestein and Dones observe, the workplace redesign pioneered by the female-majority Harvard Union of Clerical and Technical Employees (HUCTW) may meet the needs of men as well as women. HUCTW is often cited as an example of women's ways of unionism, but that does not mean that only women find their model of representation appealing. The union's assumption (and that of its sister organization in health care) is eloquently articulated by the organizers interviewed by Lydia Savage (chap. 6 in this volume). They believe that men and women want a workplace and a union in which creativity and community are encouraged and in which labor-management institutions foster social and intellectual growth. Because in their experience few workers want a steady diet of confrontation, conflict, and anger, these organizers emphasize partnering with management. Yet they also have turned to more confrontational tactics when other approaches failed, as in their raucous strike over pay and benefit parity for part-timers.

The approach of these organizers underscores another theme of this volume: no one model of unionism is likely to fit all groups of workers. The labor movement is about self-representation, about groups of workers inventing the kind of workplace organization that best suits their own circumstances. A labor movement that tries to impose a single model of organization or a single message or a single strategy will only weaken and marginalize itself. The future of unionism lies in embracing diversity in union strategy, tactics, structure, and message.

A third and final set of articles (Ontiveros, chap. 12; Quan, chap. 13; Vosko, chap. 14 in this volume) links labor's future to its ability to forge ties with workers outside the United States and draws on the newly emerging strength of global labor standards and global worker movements. It should not be surprising that women are key figures in building these local-global connections. Labor women have always relied on allies outside the labor movement to advance their agenda, whether community groups, consumer organizations, women's groups, civil rights organizations, legal advocates, or government officials. The go-it-alone strategy was simply not feasible for most working women, given the nature of their jobs and their multiple responsibilities at work and home. In addition, responding in part to the rise of religious fundamentalism as well as to the precarious fate of women in the new global economy, a global women's movement emerged in the 1980s that has helped integrate gender into the policies of such diverse institutions as the World Bank, the International Confederation of Free Trade Unions, and the International Labour Organisation. These chapters, like others in the book, suggest that embracing difference, whether sexual, cultural, or political, is far from a weakness or a distraction. Rather, it is essential to the future of labor movements and of working women's equality.

On the cover of *The Sex of Class* is an image by Pulitzer Prize–winning photographer David Turnley of an immigrant woman from Mexico. Mostly she is hidden from us. Her face recedes into the darkness; only her brilliant yellow work gloves and the blue of her tank top are illuminated, suggesting perhaps that we know little of her except the hard work of her hands and heart. And indeed, as this book argues, the health of our economy, our families, and our communities rests upon the physical and emotional labor of millions of working-class women like her.

Yet this book also suggests that women like her are no longer willing to remain invisible. Her blue work shirt may not be the iconic one of old. Nor will the social movements she leads be the same either. As the essays in this volume make clear, the sex of class matters and those who wish to understand the future of work and of labor movements will need to pay attention to her pose, hand on hip, defiant and female.

PART I

WOMEN'S INEQUALITIES AND PUBLIC POLICY

Chapters 1 and 2 document the persistence of women's economic inequality and offer suggestions for public policy remedies. In the first chapter, Leslie McCall provides a portrait of the changing class and gender structures of U.S. society since the 1970s. She makes a case for greater attention to class-specific policies, given her findings of increasing class divergence among women as well as men and a singular lack of economic progress for those at the very bottom. The second chapter by Vicky Lovell, Heidi Hartmann, and Misha Werschkul makes an equally compelling case for the retention of gender-specific strategies in any package of reforms, given the disturbing consequences of gender discrimination for low-wage women workers.

Leslie McCall's careful charting of the changing economic status of women makes clear why it is so difficult to craft policies for women as a group: the kinds of inequality experienced by women at the top and at the bottom are quite different. Elite women have made impressive strides economically, moving into high-paying professions and seeing their salaries, status, and opportunities soar—what McCall labels "absolute progress." At the same time, because elite men have made considerable gains as well, the gender pay gap between men and women at the top remains firmly in place. This more limited "relative progress," as McCall notes, is cause for concern, particularly as it is likely rooted in the greater responsibilities of women for family and domestic labor. In contrast, women at the bottom, like men at the bottom, have made little absolute progress. And their moderate relative progress, as measured by the decline of the gender pay gap, is hardly a cause for celebration because much of it stems from the declining fortunes of the male members of their households. Remedying their situation, McCall argues, will require policy interventions that have more to do with class and that focus on lifting overall working-class income. Strategies targeted at women will need to be evaluated in light of class differences as well. Increasing women's human capital through education and skill training, for example, will always be important, but poor women will also need different kinds of educational opportunity. McCall recommends reviving apprenticeships, which do not require choosing between school and work, a choice many workers cannot afford to make.

Vicky Lovell, Heidi Hartmann, and Misha Werschkul approach the problems of low-wage women from a different angle. Focusing on the impact of current class-specific policies, they find much to be desired. Governmental wage floors have the potential to foster absolute progress for women. Yet current wage standards are abysmally low, and despite the flurry of new living wage ordinances, these policies only cover a tiny fraction of workers. Moreover, wage-floor regulation may encourage some employers to hire men and raise the salaries of higher-paid workers, leaving existing gender-based wage hierarchies unchanged. Gender-specific policies have their limitations as well. Efforts to integrate physically demanding blue-collar jobs have met resistance, and pay equity efforts have languished. Yet, as the authors note, without attention to changing deep-seated gender norms and practices that devalue women's work and restrict their job opportunities, women will continue to be disproportionately concentrated in low-wage jobs and receive less compensation than men for their labor and expertise.

Both chapters stress the need for new public policies attentive to gender and class inequities. And they rightly point to the benefits of enhanced educational opportunity, stronger government wage regulations, and more comprehensive antidiscrimination laws. As Lovell, Hartmann, and Werschkul note, such policies are needed to "ameliorate the worst effects of the unconstrained operation of free markets on women, minorities, and low-wage workers." By focusing on how workers are organizing collectively and increasing their economic and political clout, many of the chapters in the rest of this book show how these policies, as well as other reforms, can become reality.

1

INCREASING CLASS DISPARITIES AMONG WOMEN AND THE POLITICS OF GENDER EQUITY

Leslie McCall

Although many readers of and contributors to this volume come already interested in issues of gender and class inequality, the two are in fact rarely considered together. This chapter's primary objective is to make the case for why they should be. In particular, I focus on the need for contemporary gender inequality to be understood within the context of rising earnings and income inequality in the United States, or what I will refer to as rising class inequality because I consider earnings and income to be among the central components of one's class position (along with assets, education, and occupation, which I also discuss briefly).

Income and earnings inequalities among women, men, and families are greater now than they were three decades ago, and by some measures, more than they have been since the eve of World War II. As women's experiences in the paid labor force and in the families in which they live have become more divergent by class, so potentially has the nature of gendered economic inequality. Economic justice for women may therefore require more of an emphasis on class-specific strategies than now exists. This includes class-specific strategies that are tailored to reducing the high and rising levels of earnings and income inequality that the United States and many other countries around the world are experiencing.

To demonstrate the increasing importance of class inequality in under-

I am grateful to Dorothy Sue Cobble for helpful comments on an earlier version of this chapter.

standing recent shifts in gender inequality, this chapter provides an overview of trends in both forms of inequality over the past three decades. I begin by documenting trends in earnings and earnings inequality for men and women separately (i.e., class inequality). I then document trends in earnings inequality between men and women (i.e., gender inequality). Next, I consider trends in inequality among families because the economic well-being of individuals is affected by the income of the families in which they live. I follow this analysis with a simple model of the causes of shifts in gender inequality for individuals at the top versus those in the middle and bottom of the earnings distribution. The final section discusses the implications of my analysis for social policies and social movements aimed at reducing gender and class inequality.

Because this is a large agenda for a short chapter, my approach is to provide a brief review of existing research in each of these areas through the particular lens of class disparities among women. This lens is useful because it incorporates two additional themes alongside the more typical theme of women's changing economic status relative to men: (1) differences in the absolute progress of women in different class positions, and (2) differences in the pathways to achieving relative equality with men for women in different class positions.

By absolute progress, I am referring to women's achievement of significant increases in earnings, educational, and occupational attainment even if men have had similar increases. Such a scenario implies a decline in some forms of absolute discrimination—through, for example, wider opportunities for women to enter the professions—even as substantial relative discrimination appears to persist when comparisons are made to similarly situated men. A contrasting scenario is one in which absolute progress among women is more limited but relative progress is greater as a result of disproportionate losses among similarly situated men—through, for example, the decline in real earnings for men in the bottom half of the earnings distribution. Both scenarios have in fact occurred in the United States. I therefore give equal attention and weight to the achievement of women's absolute and relative progress and to the differences by class in the pathways to greater gender equity that these imply.

Earnings and Earnings Inequality by Class

The extent of absolute economic progress for men and women at the top, middle, and bottom of the earnings distribution is fundamental to assessing whether class inequality is increasing over time and whether the pathways to greater gender equity vary for individuals in different class positions. This section provides the basic building blocks for both by showing how real, inflation-adjusted earnings have diverged over the last thirty years for those at the top versus those in the middle and at the bottom, leading to increasing class disparities. This divergence in earnings has occurred for women as well as for men. It has resulted from a combination of increases in earnings at the top and either more modest increases, stagnation, or declines in earnings in the middle and at the bottom. Overall, earnings have increased more for women than for men, leading to a decline in the relative gender gap in earnings for all groups. However, as I argue, the predominant reason for the closing of the gap varies depending on one's class position and so, therefore, do the pathways to greater gender equity.

It is important to note that one's class position was not always so important in analyzing earnings trends. During the 1960s, for example, the earnings of the median (50th percentile) full-time male worker grew by about the same percentage every year as the earnings of the full-time male worker at the top (the 90th and 75th percentiles) and bottom (the 25th and 10th percentiles). Consequently, the average annual growth in earnings for the median male worker, which was roughly 3 percent, was an accurate reflection of trends in earnings for men throughout the earnings distribution. The same could be said of women's earnings during the 1960s, which rose at roughly 4 percent annually, as well as for family income during the longer postwar period between 1947 and 1973, which doubled for the middle three-fifths of families and increased slightly more for the bottom one-fifth and slightly less for the top one-fifth (Ellwood 2000, 12, 20; Mishel, Bernstein, and Boushey 2003, 57). David Ellwood has referred to this period as one of shared prosperity. In such an environment, the average or median does a good job of representing changes for the entire population because everyone gains to roughly the same degree.

In contrast, the post-1960s period is one in which the trend in earnings for the median worker is not the same as the trend for everyone else. Figures 1–4 illustrate the divergence in hourly wages from 1973 to 2003 for women and men at different points in the wage distribution (which includes wage and salary earnings). Among women, figure 1.1 shows that wages grew more than twice as much at the top (63 percent at the 95th percentile and 51 percent at the 90th percentile) than at the median (27 percent at the 50th percentile) and bottom (23 percent at the 10th percentile). The growth was relatively steady and steep throughout the 1980s and 1990s for women at the top and rather modest for women in the middle, except for the early 1980s and the late 1990s. Women at the bottom fared the worst (among women), with wages below their 1979 peak for the entire two decades between 1980 and 2000. However, the late 1990s were beneficial for raising wages among women at the bottom as well.

The consequence of these different trends in absolute earnings growth was

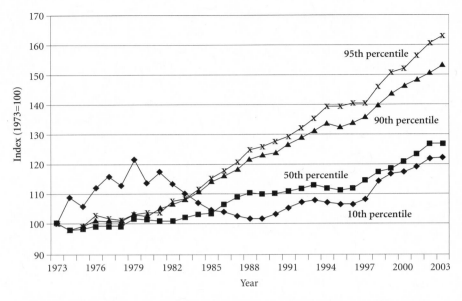

Figure 1.1 Changes in inflation adjusted hourly wages for women by wage percentile, 1973–2003.
The sample includes part-time and full-time, 18- to 64-year-old individuals with valid wage and salary earnings. The unincorporated self-employed are excluded. Earnings are adjusted for inflation using the CPI-U-RS deflator (see Mishel, Bernstein, and Allegretto 2005, app. B).
Source: Data from Mishel, Bernstein, and Allegretto (2005, table 2.8).

a rise in the level of wage inequality among women, as shown in figure 1.2. This figure charts two familiar measures of wage inequality—one for the top of the distribution (90th/50th) and one for the bottom (50th/10th)—in which a larger ratio indicates a greater degree of inequality. The hourly wages of women at the top were 1.8 times the hourly wages of women in the middle throughout the 1970s, but then the ratio rose steadily by over 22 percent to 2.2 times in the mid-1990s. The modest growth of wages at the median·and the uneven growth and decline of wages at the bottom meant that the 50th/10th ratio was about the same at the end of the three decades as it was at the beginning, with declines in the 1970s, increases in the 1980s, and little change in the 1990s. If we add the 90th/50th and the 50th/10th together, we see that the major growth in overall (90th/10th) inequality occurred in the 1980s.

This increase in wage inequality among women is a major part of the story of rising class inequality in the United States, and yet trends in men's earnings are the usual focus of discussions of the new inequality. Perhaps the key reason why there is more emphasis on inequality among men is illustrated in Figure 1.3, which shows an absolute decline in real hourly wages for men at the bottom and in the middle of the distribution between 1979 and 2003, although

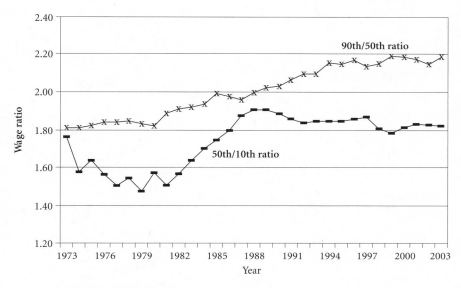

Figure 1.2 Changes in female hourly wage ratios, 1973–2003.
The sample includes part-time and full-time, 18- to 64-year-old individuals with valid wage and salary earnings. The unincorporated self-employed are excluded (see Mishel Bernstein, and Allegretto 2005, app. B).
Source: Data from Mishel, Bernstein, and Allegretto (2005, table 2.8).

growth was strong at the end of the 1990s for both groups. In contrast, at the top, hourly wages grew by 30 and 22 percent for men at the 95th and 90th percentiles. Thus, hourly wages declined or stagnated for at least half of all men, as opposed to 10 percent of women, and grew less than half as much at the top among men than among women.

These differences in wage growth rates between men and women—and the decline in the gender pay gap that they imply (as discussed in the next section)—give the mistaken impression that growing inequality is a reality only or primarily for men. In fact, levels and increases in inequality are comparable for men and women, especially in the top half of the distribution. The 90th/50th ratio grew from 1.8 to 2.2 between 1973 and 2000 for both men and women, as shown in figures 1.2 and 1.4. Not shown are comparable increases for men and women in levels of inequality between the 95th percentile and the median and between workers with a college education and those with a high school education. The college–high school wage premium, one of the most common measures of rising skills-based earnings inequality, is actually greater among women than among men (1.45 versus 1.40) (Mishel, Bernstein, and Boushey 2003, 153, 155). Although it is true that inequality in the bottom of the distribution is greater among men than among women (as shown in figs. 1.2 and 1.4), this component of inequality is now a smaller share of overall in-

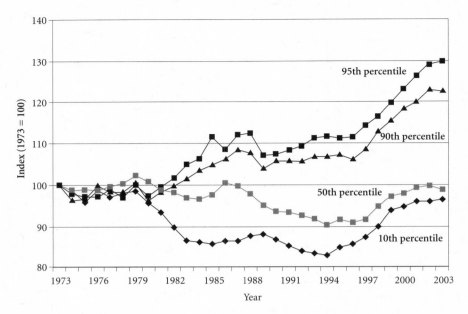

Figure 1.3 Changes in inflation adjusted hourly wages for men by wage percentile, 1973–2003.
The sample includes part-time and full-time, 18- to 64-year-old individuals with valid wage and salary earnings. The unincorporated self-employed are excluded. Earnings are adjusted for inflation using the CPI-U-RS deflator (see Mishel Bernstein, and Allegretto 2005, app. B).
Source: Data come from Mishel, Bernstein, and Allegretto (2005, table 2.7).

equality than the inequality at the top; that is, as of the late 1990s, the 90th/50th ratio is greater than the 50th/10th ratio for men, whereas this has always been the case for women. This is an important reversal and an indication of increasing similarity in the earnings and wage distributions of men and women.

The wage structure has changed in fundamental ways, then, for both men and women. This presents a different context for discussions of gender equality at work than would have been the case if wages had continued to grow steadily and evenly among male workers, as they had in the postwar period, during which antidiscrimination strategies were first crafted and implemented on a national scale (especially during the decade between the mid-1960s and mid-1970s). Theoretically, in such an environment, the male wage and occupational structure could be taken for granted as the implicit standard against which women's progress is measured, through, for example, occupational integration and comparable worth. We could even imagine comparable rates of absolute progress in the form of earnings growth and occupational integration among women at the top, middle, and bottom. Greater gender

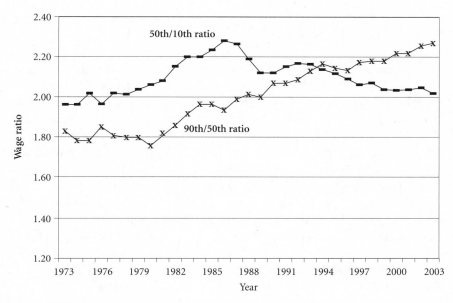

Figure 1.4 Changes in male hourly wage ratios, 1973–2003.
The sample includes part-time and full-time, 18- to 64-year-old individuals with valid wage and salary earnings. The unincorporated self-employed are excluded (see Mishel Bernstein, and Allegretto 2005, app. B).
Source: Data from Mishel, Bernstein, and Allegretto (2005, table 2.7).

equality would be less threatening because it would take place within the context of evenly distributed growth across class lines. In fact, for a brief period before deindustrialization intensified and after the passage of Title VII of the Civil Rights Act in 1965 outlawing gender and racial discrimination, this seems to have occurred (MacLean 2006).

But as this section makes clear, gender equality did not occur within the context of evenly distributed growth from the 1970s onward because of rising forms of class inequality. Instead, the male wage structure has itself become the object of much concern. This suggests that rising class inequality among men should not be ignored in crafting strategies for increasing women's economic security, particularly given growing similarities in the male and female wage structures. For example, because of the disproportionate allocation of earnings to the top, many forms of income redistribution will probably benefit both men and women in the bottom and middle, in absolute terms, regardless of whether the process of redistribution is gender-specific. There have always been those who see the wisdom of such a strategy; I am suggesting only that widening inequality has made this strategy more compelling. In the final section, I briefly discuss some specific strategies along these lines.

Earnings Inequality by Gender

The resurgence in class inequality and women's faster growth in earnings do not mean that gender inequality has been eliminated or reduced to trivial levels. Women's wages are still lower than men's, by approximately 20 percent at the median. This represents a 50 percent decline in the median gender gap since 1973. Unfortunately, there has been little attention to whether (and if so, why) the earnings gap between men and women differs for different classes (Blau and Kahn 1997, 2004; McCall 2001). The bulk of the evidence suggests that such differences in the gender gap are *less* now than they were several decades ago, so that the average gender gap is more similar to the gap at the top and bottom than it used to be. Much more research needs to be done to clarify these trends, however, and the increasing similarity in the gender gap across class lines is not the entire story. Something different is occurring at the extremes, among low-wage workers and workers with an advanced degree as well as among racial/ethnic groups. This redirects our attention once again away from an analysis of average trends and levels and toward an analysis of differences in the character of gender inequality by class as well as race. I first examine trends at the median, then at the bottom and among racial/ethnic groups, and finally at the top.

Except for a few notable exceptions, wage growth over the last three decades of the twentieth century was greater for women than for men throughout the entire distribution of workers, leading to a near universal decline in the gender gap between men and women and an increase in the ratio of female to male wages (the typical measure of gender inequality that is used here as well). As shown in figures 1.5 and 1.6, there is a remarkable degree of similarity in the female/male wage ratio for the upper 50 percent of the distribution and for all education groups but the top one (those with an advanced degree). For these groups, the ratio grew by at least fifteen percentage points—a sign that women's wages were becoming more similar to men's and thus inequality was declining—from a range of 0.61–0.63 in the early 1970s to a range of 0.77–0.81 in 2003. The ratio was relatively stable in the 1970s, increased substantially in the 1980s, and leveled off in the late 1990s. Because the spreading out of wages for women was similar to the spreading out of wages for men in the top half of the distribution, as shown in the previous section, there were similar proportionate increases in the ratio of women's to men's wages as well. At the median, this occurred through modest growth in women's wages and declines in men's wages, whereas, at the 90th percentile, it occurred through faster growth rates for women than for men.

We get a different picture if we look at low-wage workers, however. First of all, gender inequality is lower at the bottom that at the top or in the middle.

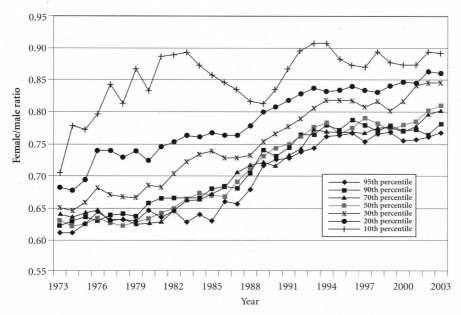

Figure 1.5 Changes in the ratio of female to male hourly wages by wage percentile, 1973–2003.
The sample includes part-time and full-time, 18- to 64-year-old individuals with valid wage and salary earnings. The unincorporated self-employed are excluded (see Mishel Bernstein, and Allegretto 2005, app. B).
Source: Data from Mishel, Bernstein, and Allegretto (2005, tables 2.7 and 2.8).

The female/male ratio is particularly distinctive at the 10th percentile. This ratio increased dramatically over the 1970s and early 1980s and then decreased precipitously over the rest of the 1980s. This roller-coaster pattern is explained by changes in the minimum wage, which greatly affects women's wages at the bottom (Dinardo, Fortin, and Lemieux 1996). The minimum wage was raised several times in the 1970s and then was not raised at all until 1990. The roller-coaster pattern is also explained by the steep declines in men's wages at the bottom, which were concentrated in the early 1980s. Wage equity for low-wage women, then, is highly sensitive to wage-setting policies and is somewhat illusory because low-wage men—the comparison group—have faired so poorly in the labor market.

This latter point also pertains to interpretations of gender equity within minority racial groups, in which minority male wages are relatively low as well. Because the gender gap tends to be lower among low-wage and minority groups, a more appropriate standard of comparison is needed for low-wage and minority women. For example, the median for white men rather than same-race/ethnicity men can be used to gauge the economic progress of mi-

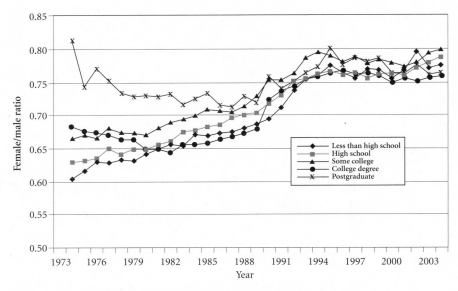

Figure 1.6 Changes in ratio of female to male hourly wages by education, 1973–2003.
The sample includes part-time and full-time, 18- to 64-year-old individuals with valid wage and salary earnings. The unincorporated self-employed are excluded (see Mishel Bernstein, and Allegretto 2005, app. B).
Source: Data from Mishel, Bernstein, and Allegretto (2005, tables 2.18 and 2.19).

nority racial and ethnic groups of women. Table 1.1 provides these comparisons.

For many groups, the ratio of women's to men's earnings is much higher within the same racial/ethnic group than it is across racial/ethnic groups, with white men as the cross-racial/ethnic comparison group. For example, the median earnings of Mexican American women are 84 percent of the earnings of Mexican American men but only 50 percent of the earnings of white men. We find differences of this kind that are at least twenty percentage points in magnitude for women who are African American, Hispanic, Southeast Asian, American Indian, and Pacific Islander. Although some of these ratios would increase if differences in human capital were accounted for, they would remain substantial nonetheless. For several Asian groups, however, earnings ratios within racial/ethnic groups are either comparable to or less than those with white men. Filipinas, for example, earn 65 and 81 percent of the earnings of Filipinos and white men, respectively, because Filipinos earn more than white men. Clearly, then, there is much variation in the economic standing of different racial/ethnic groups of women that a simple mean or median analysis between whites and nonwhites would miss.

One of the reasons why some Asian groups of women have earnings that are comparable to those of white men is that they have very high levels of edu-

TABLE 1.1
Median annual earnings for U.S. women and men by race and ethnicity, 1999[a]

Race/ethnicity	Women (dollars)	Men (dollars)	Women's earnings as percentage of	
			Men's of same race/ethnicity	White men's
White (only)	28,000	40,000	70	70
African American	25,000	30,000	83	63
Hispanic (any)	21,000	25,000	84	53
Mexican	20,000	23,900	84	50
Puerto Rican	25,000	30,000	83	63
Central American	18,000	22,500	80	45
South American	24,000	30,000	80	60
Cuban	26,000	31,000	84	65
Dominican	20,000	24,700	81	50
Asian (any)	30,000	40,000	75	75
Chinese	34,000	43,000	79	85
South Asian	30,300	35,000	87	76
Filipina	32,300	50,000	65	81
Southeast Asian	23,100	30,000	77	58
Korean	35,000	48,500	72	88
Japanese	27,700	38,000	73	69
American Indian	24,000	30,000	80	60
Pacific Islander	25,000	30,000	83	63

Source: Cotter, Hermsen, and Vanneman (2004).
[a] Earnings calculated for men and women ages 25–54, employed full-time/year-round.

cation. If we were to compare such groups with comparably educated groups of whites, it is not clear that they would fare as well. This is suggested by the seemingly atypical lack of improvement—let alone substantial improvement—in the hourly wage ratio between men and women with advanced degrees (refer again to fig. 1.6). In fact, the ratio fell from 0.81 in 1973 to 0.76 in 2003. At the beginning of the period, the ratio was nearly 20 percentage points higher than the median ratio, whereas at the end of the period it was lower. Thus, in relative terms—that is, if we think of gender equity as a relative achievement rather than an absolute one—the most educated women, whose average earnings are at the 90th percentile but include women across a wider range, have fared the worst of all in the past three decades. They have made strong absolute progress but virtually no relative progress.

What are we to make of these patterns, and, most important, what are the implications for gender wage justice today? One possible explanation for (or speculation about) the lack of progress toward relative gender equity among those with advanced degrees is disquieting. The argument begins with the observation that the working women who were most like working men in the earlier period and who are most like working men today are those with advanced degrees. Because of their substantial investment in education and strong earnings potential, their commitment to work has been relatively high and constant. A change in the female/male ratio for that group, then, is more likely to reflect changes in how they are compensated relative to men and less likely to reflect the impact of increasing education and experience, factors that are more consequential for other groups of women (Mulligan and Rubenstein 2004). It follows, then, that the stable level of gender inequality among those with an advanced degree reflects a stable level of relative discrimination. As Blau and Kahn (1997) put it in an analogous study of the wage distribution by percentile (rather than by education group), women in the top percentiles have been "swimming upstream" to keep up with a moving target (men in the top percentiles), one that is more and more distant from the middle or even upper-middle ranks in an increasingly unequal hierarchy.

In contrast, the closing of the gender pay gap in the rest of the distribution is more readily attributable to improvements in women's human capital in both absolute terms and relative to the human capital of similar men. Once these improvements have been made in the population of women workers as a whole, however, and more educated and experienced cohorts replace less educated and experienced cohorts, relative progress may stall. This is especially likely if the disadvantages faced by men at the bottom and in the middle reverse, as they did in the late 1990s, leaving the bulk of working women to swim upstream as their upper-class sisters did beginning in the 1980s. According to this explanation, then, the gender gap has narrowed because women's skills and orientation toward work have grown more similar to those of men and not because women are treated more equitably relative to men of the same caliber.

In sum, one of the key distinctions that is easier to appreciate today than a generation ago is the difference between relative and absolute progress for women. On the one hand, a remarkably similar level of relative gender inequality exists across education groups today. Yet those with the most education have made the least relative progress, and the relative progress that has been made appears to be slowing. From this perspective, there has been a consolidation of a particular regime of relative gender discrimination, especially for women in the higher-income brackets. What some are increasingly identifying as the lynchpin of this regime—the gender difference in family care, or family-based discrimination—is perhaps more visible today than in the past when other barriers were just as formidable. On the other hand, progress has been substantial for women at the top, in absolute terms and relative to all other groups (including most men).

In contrast, the greatest disparities for women at the bottom are not with men of their same standing but with women and men in more privileged class and racial/ethnic groups. Moreover, the gender pay gap at the very bottom, although smaller than for other groups, has not changed much since the early 1980s when men's wages bottomed out and increases in the minimum wage topped out. From this view, absolute progress and mobility for women at the bottom have been stymied by increasing class inequality in tandem with ongoing racial and gender discrimination. Consequently, the problems that women at the bottom face cannot be attributed solely to the workings of gender-based discrimination.

Income Inequality among Families

Because the economic needs of individuals are met by the earnings of the people they live with in addition to their own earnings, we need to consider whether rising inequality has permeated family life as much as it has work life. On the one hand, transformations in the family could have offset the growing level of inequality among individuals in U.S. society. Specifically, the increasing share of wives and mothers in the paid work force could have been concentrated in the families that were most exposed to the fall in men's earnings potential; in that case, income inequality among families may be less of an issue than the earnings inequality among individuals.[1] If so, the more salient issue may be a time squeeze between family and work. If widespread enough, the time squeeze—and the lack of family-friendly policies that would alleviate family-based discrimination against women—could serve as the basis for increasing similarities in the gender dynamics of families (Williams 2000).

On the other hand, some transformations in family life tend to reinforce rather than topple existing social conventions such as class distinctions. An important way this is accomplished is through homogamy (or assortative mating), the propensity to marry someone with like education, family background, race, or other characteristics (Sweeney and Cancian 2004). Increasing individual inequality can therefore serve as a source of increasing bifurcation in the residential, educational, and social environments of U.S. families (e.g., Lareau 2003). This growing inequality and segregation could in turn shape how families from different class backgrounds resolve the time bind between work and family. In particular, the affluent may be more likely to support the current system of private care because it provides high-quality services by costly but still relatively low-paid workers. Consequently, inequality—in the form of a low-wage, deregulated, private-care market, on the one hand, and a

---

[1] Roughly 40 percent of all mothers with children under 18 were in the paid work force in 1970; this increased to 70 percent in 2000 (U.S. Bureau of the Census 2006, table 579).

high-wage class of consumers of care work, on the other—could minimize the potential for commonalities among families in their orientation toward the time squeeze (Morgan 2005; Duffy 2005).

So which of these predictions is the more accurate one? Have increasing class inequalities among individuals been attenuated or accentuated by gendered and class shifts in the family? Overall, income inequality among families has in fact increased as a result of increasing inequality among individuals, especially husbands. The good news, however, is that this growth was attenuated by the equalizing effect of wives' increasing contribution to family income. Women in the top two-fifths of families log more hours of work per year (roughly 1,450) than women in the bottom two-fifths (between 800 and 1,200), but these disparities have been decreasing over time. Unquestionably, wives' earnings have contributed to absolute increases in real family income, countering declines in the earnings of husbands at the bottom and in the middle (Mishel, Bernstein, and Boushey 2003, 107, 110–111; Cancian, Danziger, and Gottschalk 1993).

Yet there are countervailing trends. A relative increase in single motherhood among low-income groups, an increase in assortative mating, and a relative increase in the rates of employment of wives with high-earning husbands can each spur further growth in inequality among families. All of these have occurred. First, single parenthood has increased most for women with low education and low income, due in part to the falling economic position of low-education men and thus their declining attractiveness as marriage partners (Ellwood and Jencks 2004). Second, there has been an increase in the correlation of both earnings and educational attainment among spouses over time.[2]

Finally, and perhaps most important, despite a net equalizing effect thus far of increasing employment among wives, the rate of increase in employment since the 1960s has been the greatest for wives with high-income husbands. This reverses the historical pattern in which the wives of low-income husbands were the most likely to work and the wives of high-income husbands were the least likely, a clear indication that when choices were limited married women worked out of necessity rather than choice.[3]

Although it is hard to predict, the labor force attachment of the high-skilled wives of high-income husbands is not likely to decline, except among the highest income families that can get by just fine without two earners (Goldin

[2] Research by Schwartz and Mare (2005) suggests that overall educational homogamy seems to have stabilized in the 1990s. This appears to be true as well for marital homogamy by income (McCall forthcoming).

[3] Cancian, Danziger, and Gottschalk (1993) show that these shifts are for whites only. The employment rate for wives of husbands in the 10th, 50th, and 90th percentiles of income were roughly 32, 30, and 15 percent in 1959, respectively; 43, 41, and 25 percent in 1969; and 58, 68, and 60 percent in 1989 (Juhn and Murphy 1997, 85).

2006). As we saw in the previous section, women with college and advanced degrees are more likely to work and to work longer hours than those with less education because their investment in education and earnings power is so high. Moreover, managerial and professional jobs are more rewarding and also demand more hours of work per week than most other jobs, setting in motion a time divide between overworked high-status workers and underworked low-status workers that results in an even greater income divide (Jacobs and Gerson 2004). The heroic increase in work by married mothers appears to be approaching a plateau in which these hours disparities may become locked in. For all income groups, the rate of growth in wives' hours declined in the 1990s, relative to the 1980s, by at least one-third. Overall, then, women's work behavior has tended to mitigate the class gap among families so far, but it may not do so in the future.

Explanations

In this section, I explore some of the reasons for recent changes in the contemporary class and gender structure of U.S. society. As shown in table 1.2, I present only two categories of explanations: gender-specific explanations that have been developed to explain gender inequality and class-specific explanations that have been developed to explain rising class inequality. Some factors have had cross-over effects into the other domain. Although both are important and their effects are difficult to empirically measure, I argue that gender-specific factors have been more important in advancing women's absolute progress at the top, whereas class-specific factors have been more important in advancing women's relative progress in the middle and at the bottom. Put another way, absolute progress has been greater than relative progress for women at the top, but the converse has been true for women at the bottom and in the middle. This suggests that, in the future, relative progress will be a more important goal for women at the top and absolute progress will be a more important goal for women in the middle and at the bottom.

At the top, absolute improvements dominate relative ones. Women with high education and earnings potential entered the labor force at a faster rate than other women despite the fact that the men they tended to marry had the highest earnings growth, especially over the 1970s and 1980s. Moreover, because of a greater increase in supply, such women ought to have had lower earnings growth than other women, but they did not, suggesting a strong demand for high-skilled women. These women also delayed childbearing more than women with middle and lower levels of education, an indication that the relative payoffs to pursuing work versus family shifted in favor of the former more for women at the top than for others.

TABLE 1.2
Explanations of improvements in absolute and relative gender equality

	Improvements in women's economic status	
Explanations	Absolute progress	Relative progress
Gender-specific (e.g., anti-discrimination law and affirmative action)	Declining discrimination in managerial and professional schools and occupations leads to occupational gender integration and earnings growth for women at the top.	
Class-specific (e.g., shifts in wage structure and wage-setting institutions)	Rising returns to and demand for high skills draws high-skill women into the paid labor force.	Globalization, deunionization, and postindustrial employment shifts disadvantage men and favor women in the middle.
		Minimum wage benefits women more than men at the bottom and tight labor markets benefit both men and women in the middle and bottom.

It is therefore likely that eroding discriminatory barriers in education and employment worked in tandem with expanding managerial and professional opportunities—including increasing returns to working in these occupations as a result of rising inequality—to spur greater labor force preparation and attachment among women who were best able to take advantage of this new environment (Black and Juhn 2000). Other evidence supports this conclusion as well, such as a greater decline in occupational segregation in middle-class occupations than in the working-class occupations that grew less rapidly (Cotter, Hermsen, and Vanneman 2004; Charles and Grusky 2005). Relative inequality persists, however, and by some accounts never declined, in part because men at the top have been advancing at a fast pace as well and because of persistent practices of exclusion in high-powered positions that demand extremely long hours of work.

In contrast, at the bottom and in the middle of the distribution, relative improvements dominate absolute ones, with gender-specific factors appearing to be less important than they are in explaining women's progress at the top. The most significant absolute increases in earnings for women in the middle (at the median) and at the bottom (at the 10th percentile) came during the tight labor markets of the late 1990s. For women at the bottom, increases in the minimum wage in the 1970s also meant absolute increases as well as reduced inequality with men at the bottom and with women at the median. Declines in the gender pay gap were also helped by declining real wages among men in the entire bottom half of the distribution in the 1980s. These declines were the result of industrial shifts, an increase in globalization, and a decline in unionization that all disproportionately hurt men relative to women in the lower half (Blau and Kahn 1997, 2004; Black and Brainerd 2004). The only period in which absolute improvements were greater than relative ones was in the late 1990s, when both women's and men's earnings improved at the bottom. The dynamic that characterizes the top throughout the entire period, in which women are swimming upstream to catch up to high-achieving men, becomes a possibility for women in the bottom half only in the late 1990s.

Thus, women's absolute progress in the bottom half occurred in fits and starts, but was modest compared to that of women at the top. Despite the early intent of antidiscrimination advocates to open up male-dominated blue-collar jobs to women, neither the absolute nor relative long-term progress of women in the bottom half appears to be linked in any strong way to an opening up of job opportunities because of a decline in gender discrimination. New job opportunities for working-class women were concentrated in sectors that were either already female-dominated, such as clerical and office work, or were becoming less remunerative as they became less male-dominated (Reskin and Roos 1991). For women outside the top rung, both absolute and relative progress is strongly affected by federal policies that are non-gender-specific and structural economic factors that are either detrimental to men or relatively constant, such as the declining earnings of low-income and minority men. Overall, then, a burning issue for women in the middle and at the bottom is absolute job quality, including, most significantly, absolute wage growth, concerns that they share with men in similar class positions.

Implications for the Politics of Gender Equity

In the era of rising class inequality and declining gender inequality, then, we have seen more absolute than relative progress for women at the top and more relative than absolute progress for women in the middle and at the bottom. In assessing the sources of ongoing relative gender inequality, the family wage gap or the mother tax (the wage penalty that mothers continue to endure relative to nonmothers who are the same in all other respects) has emerged as a leading culprit (Waldfogel 1997). As Joan Williams (2000) argues, with the majority of mothers in the paid labor force, it should be easier than in the past to forge common ground in challenging the male-based ideal-worker model in which full dedication to work at the expense of family is demanded, a model that women have been both unable and unwilling to achieve. Another key source of relative gender inequality that is given considerable attention is occupational sex segregation, or the wage penalty that women are saddled with for being employed in female-dominated occupations.

By comparison, there is little attention to the lack of strong absolute progress among women in the bottom half of the earnings distribution and to the increasing economic distance between these women and those at the top. Yet we live in a society that is increasingly stratified by earnings and wealth among both men and women, with little relief in sight. Moreover, women are increasingly involved in direct relations of inequality vis-à-vis one another as supervisors and supervisees, consumers and producers. Is it possible to address enduring gender disparities while improving the absolute economic progress of those at the bottom and in the middle?

I suggest that one way to do this is to prioritize policies that improve the absolute economic position of women in the bottom and middle. Unlike women at the top, these women face the triple burdens of low absolute pay, stagnation in pay among current and potential male partners, and nearly prohibitive costs for family care relative to total earnings. Unfortunately, the stagnation of male wages has never been of much concern to the feminist movement, and solving the high cost of family care is often given more attention than raising the wages of women at the bottom. Yet the three need not be mutually exclusive. As Dorothy Sue Cobble's history of postwar labor feminism reveals, "labor women saw higher hourly income as a core ingredient of a family-friendly workplace, [arguing] forcefully that raising hourly wages for both men and women was a way of reducing the double day [because it gave] them more choice about how to divide up market and family work" (Cobble 2003, 67). Without denying the great need for policies that support family care for all women and men, there continues to be an equally great need for policies that improve the pay and working conditions of low- and middle-income women and their family members.

Full employment and a higher minimum wage are extremely important for such groups. And, as many chapters of this volume will detail, trade unions and other forms of collective organizing among workers have considerable potential for helping reverse the tide of rising class inequality. But there are other non-gender-specific avenues of redress as well. An example of considerable current interest is organizational restructuring within corporations (Jacoby 2005; McCall 2004). This should be a feminist issue to the extent that it involves a restructuring of equity norms in a way that disproportionately benefits women and people of color in the middle and lower ranks of large corporations.

Additional non-gender-specific policies with the potential to benefit low- and middle-income women workers can evolve from thinking more expansively about how to reduce disparities in earnings and mobility prospects among women. This entails a shift away from the more typical—and still very important—emphasis on reducing disparities with men of the same class background, an emphasis that grew out of a period that predated rising class inequality and in which well-paying, blue-collar, male-dominated jobs were abundant.

To illustrate this shift in perspective, I close with a schematic proposal for reducing inequalities by increasing mobility into a female-dominated sector—the care sector, which is central to both women's work and family life. I define this sector broadly to include workers across the skill and pay spectrum, from full-fledged teachers and nurses to teaching, nursing, and other health-care assistants and child-care workers.

To begin with, a typical solution to the shortage of high-quality teachers and nurses is to raise their wages, improve their working conditions, and raise their status to lure the best and brightest women back to these professions. The best and brightest women, who used to become teachers and nurses, now go into medicine and law because the barriers to entering these higher-paying male-dominated professions have broken down. But it seems neither desirable nor feasible to attract them back if their interests lay elsewhere. Moreover, there is a relatively large group of women who would consider teaching and nursing to be excellent jobs, in terms of *current* pay, benefits, and even working conditions, relative to their existing jobs. Yet they may not be able to afford the college education that is required to enter these fields.

From this perspective, the problem with teaching and nursing is not that they are female-segregated ghettos offering low pay for high-skill caring labor, unable to attract high-skilled women from top public and private universities. Rather, the problem is a class-based one—a well-known bottleneck in the educational system that prevents aspiring but credit-poor women (as well as men) from getting the education that is required for the kinds of middle-class jobs that are widely available. A typical solution to training bottlenecks of this kind is an apprenticeship program. Thus, targeted and fully funded apprenticeship programs for those who can meet the basic prerequisites for entering a training program in nursing and education might be a promising solution. Of course, this would involve moving in the direction opposite to greater professionalization, the strategy most often advocated by nursing and teaching associations whose primary aim is to increase the status and therefore pay and working conditions of existing professionals.

Needed, then, are new *upward* mobility strategies for low-income women rather than *downward* mobility strategies for high-income women. This type of upward mobility approach is familiar to institutional economists and economic geographers and planners, perhaps less so to scholars and advocates in the fields of education and health care. It is also an approach that is more common among advocates of reducing class inequality than of reducing gender inequality. Advocates in each of these areas need to join together to implement high-road strategies for women to enter good-paying jobs in education and health care either from outside these sectors (e.g., retail) or from the bottom of the job ladders within these sectors (e.g., home health aides and teachers aides) (Fitzgerald 2006). A high-quality training system geared toward remedying skill shortages in large and vital sectors of the national economy—that also happen to be female-dominated—has the added virtue of improving services provided to U.S. consumers, which in turn can lay the foundation for broad public support. The politics of any upward mobility or redistributive strategy is, of course, a more complicated matter, but it seems no worse than usual in this case. Indeed, its potential may lie precisely in its simultaneous attention to multiple inequalities.

2

MORE THAN RAISING THE FLOOR

THE PERSISTENCE OF GENDER INEQUALITIES IN THE LOW-WAGE LABOR MARKET

Vicky Lovell, Heidi Hartmann, and Misha Werschkul

> The dream of a hopeful America is to say that if you work hard
> and dream big, no matter who you are, you can finish on top.
>
> *President George W. Bush, February 8, 2005*

Occupational mobility is one of the great myths of the U.S. culture. In a society popularly viewed as having no class distinctions or boundaries, the American dream promises that hard-working individuals, regardless of their background, face no limits to their career opportunities and monetary success. No demographic characteristic hampers achievement because the labor market offers equal employment opportunities to all, based strictly on merit.

Despite this idealized vision, U.S. workers' job experiences continue to be strongly shaped by race, ethnicity, socioeconomic background, and other personal characteristics. As a key element in our social, political, and economic hierarchies, gender remains a strong determinant of workers' education and training, work opportunities, jobs, and compensation. For instance, following individuals' work histories over a period of fifteen years (1983–1998), Rose and Hartmann (2004) find that one-half of all continuously employed men worked in majority-male jobs for their entire careers, while only 8 percent worked in majority-female jobs in all their working years. Women had slightly more varied work experience—two-fifths of those employed throughout the study period stayed in majority-female jobs through their work life and an-

TABLE 2.1
Distribution of women and men with strong labor force attachment, by
average annual earnings, 1983–1998[a]

Average annual earnings (dollars)[b]	Distribution (%)			Women (% of total)
	Women	Men	Total	
<15,000	17.4	1.3	8.3	90.1
15,000–24,999	27.1	9.5	17.2	68.7
25,000–49,999	45.9	45.1	45.4	43.9
50,000–75,000	8.3	29.7	20.4	17.7
>75,000	1.3	14.4	8.7	6.5
Total	100.0	100.0	100.0	36.7

Source: Rose and Hartmann (2004, table 5).
[a] Workers ages 26–59 with earnings in all fifteen years of the study period.
[b] All earnings are adjusted to 1999 dollars.

other two-fifths moved between male and female jobs, with the rest (20 percent) employed consistently in male jobs.

Even if pay and other outcomes were the same across jobs without regard to the sex of jobholders, the separation of women and men into different jobs might raise concerns about gender stereotyping and the lack of freedom of occupational choice. Compensation is, however, strongly influenced by the sex of a job's incumbents—jobs held predominantly by women pay less than those held mostly by men, even when skill requirements, work effort, level of responsibility, and working conditions are the same (Treiman and Hartmann 1981; Michael, Hartmann, and O'Farrell 1989; England 1992). Thus, occupational segregation affects women's material well-being and lifetime economic security and deserves serious policy attention.

One particularly harmful instance of the influence of sex on employment outcomes is women's disproportionate consignment to low-wage jobs. This is evident when looking at a cross section of workers (see table 2.3, later in the chapter), but the effect is more startling when we follow workers over time. Over 90 percent of prime-age workers (ages 26–59) with earnings in every year from 1983 to 1998 who average less than $15,000 per year are women (table 2.1). Only one in one hundred men averages less than $15,000 each year, compared to nearly one in every five women.

What are the best policies for moving women out of low-wage jobs? Some advocate gender-blind class-based solutions, while others favor direct changes in the gender hierarchy. This chapter explores those two paths. We begin with basic information about the low-wage labor market, including the demographics of workers in low- and higher-wage jobs. We next review class-based efforts to reduce poverty by increasing wage floors and gender-based strategies to increase earnings while reducing gender structures in employment. We then evaluate research on the effectiveness of these two approaches in improving women's economic security, reducing poverty, and increasing employment opportunity and pay equity. The chapter concludes with a discussion of additional policies to enhance women's employment outcomes.

What Is the Low-Wage Labor Market, and Who Works There?

Workers in low-wage jobs perform some of society's most essential functions, but often go unacknowledged. As table 2.2 shows, they teach our youngest students; care for home-bound, medically fragile people; prepare and serve food; keep offices clean; and ring up our purchases. Excluding waiters and waitresses (whose tip income may not be reflected in our data), median hourly wage rates are as low as $7.19 for these occupations; the overall median for all workers in low-wage occupations is $8.75.

Although most low-wage occupations have few skill, education, or training requirements, others demand specialized or continuing education. For example, preschool and kindergarten teachers must be trained and certified, hairdressers must complete cosmetology schooling and licensure, and a number of low-wage jobs are open only to workers with a high school diploma. Low-wage jobs held mainly by women are more likely to require some skills or education than are low-wage jobs that predominantly employ men. In fact, as table 2.2 shows, the low-wage occupations with the largest proportion of female workers (child-care workers; hairdressers, hairstylists, and cosmetologists; and preschool and kindergarten teachers) have the strictest licensing and education requirements.

Of the twenty-five low-wage jobs that employ the most workers, twelve are female-dominated occupations (in which 75 percent or more of jobholders are women). Many of these are office and administrative support occupations, and several are caring (or service) occupations. Two are professional occupations: preschool and kindergarten teachers, and teacher assistants. Of these twelve female-dominated low-wage occupations, all but two (file clerks and cashiers) have almost entirely female workforces. Only four of the twenty-five largest low-wage jobs are predominantly male: security guards, groundskeepers, agricultural workers, and laborers. Nine are relatively sex-integrated, employing both women and men, many in food preparation or serving.

Women's wages are lower than men's even at the bottom of the labor market. In the largest twenty-five low-wage occupations, men's average wage of $9.15 per hour is 8 percent higher than the average wage for women ($8.50).

African Americans and Hispanics are overrepresented in many low-wage

TABLE 2.2
Wages, training requirements, and worker characteristics of the twenty-five largest low-wage occupations[a]

| Occupation | Workers paid low wages (%) | Median hourly wage (dollars) | | | Training, education, and licensing requirements | Percentage of all low-wage workers | Percentage of all low-wage women workers | Percentage of workers who are: | | |
		All workers	Women	Men				Female	African American	Hispanic
Female-dominated[b]										
Cashiers	76.6	7.50	7.44	7.70	None	7.0	9.5	76.6	15.5	15.1
Nursing, psychiatric, and home health aides	48.2	9.50	9.38	10.00	None; employers receiving Medicare require tests for home health aides	2.7	4.2	89.8	34.4	12.3
Maids and housekeeping cleaners	63.5	8.22	8.22	9.24	None	2.5	4.0	89.1	16.8	39.3
Child-care workers	68.7	8.00	8.00	8.00	License and high school diploma	1.8	3.0	93.9	16.4	16.3
Receptionists and information clerks	35.9	10.27	10.30	10.27	High school diploma	1.5	2.5	93.1	9.6	13.2
Teacher assistants	42.7	10.01	10.00	10.27	Varies, high school diploma or some college; schools may require background checks	1.3	2.0	92.0	14.5	15.2
Personal and home-care aides	66.9	8.22	8.00	9.00	States may require formal training	1.1	1.7	87.7	20.6	16.2
Medical assistants and other health-care support occupations	37.3	10.27	10.53	9.50	High school diploma; states may require specific training	0.8	1.2	88.8	14.1	15.3
Preschool and kindergarten teachers	35.5	11.67	11.57	13.00	License; associate's or bachelor's degree or certification; continuing education	0.7	1.2	97.8	15.0	8.5
Hairdressers, hairstylists, and cosmetologists	47.0	9.65	9.60	12.32	Cosmetology school and license; continuing education	0.7	1.1	93.9	10.6	13.6

TABLE 2.2—cont.

Occupation	Workers paid low wages (%)	Median hourly wage (dollars)			Training, education, and licensing requirements	Percentage of all low-wage workers	Percentage of all low-wage women workers	Percentage of workers who are:		
		All workers	Women	Men				Female	African American	Hispanic
Tellers	41.1	10.00	10.00	10.00	High school diploma	0.5	0.8	88.3	9.9	11.6
File clerks	34.8	10.86	$0.93	10.78	High school diploma	0.4	0.6	81.1	12.6	11.8
Male-dominated[c]										
Laborers and freight, stock, and material movers, hand	43.5	10.00	9.24	10.25	None	2.4	0.8	16.8	15.6	18.9
Miscellaneous agricultural workers	73.8	7.70	7.19	7.96	None	1.5	0.5	18.8	2.7	46.8
Security guards and gaming surveillance officers	40.7	10.00	9.55	10.27	License; high school diploma for armed guards	1.0	0.5	22.7	27.9	13.0
Grounds-maintenance workers	51.9	9.24	8.25	9.24	None	1.6	0.2	6.3	7.2	43.2
Integrated[d]										
Waiters/ waitresses	83.6	6.00	5.90	6.67	None	4.8	6.4	73.9	6.9	12.9
Retail salespeople	51.3	9.24	8.22	11.28	None	4.8	5.2	51.2	10.8	10.8
Cooks	68.8	8.00	8.00	8.00	None	3.9	2.8	41.4	16.2	27.5
Janitors and building cleaners	49.4	9.40	8.22	10.00	None	3.0	2.1	32.0	16.1	26.9
Food-preparation workers	78.6	7.50	7.50	7.50	None	1.5	1.5	58.2	12.8	24.3
Stock clerks and order fillers	48.8	9.50	9.25	9.75	High school diploma may be required	2.1	1.3	37.6	13.7	16.1
First-line supervisors/ managers of food-preparation and serving workers	47.0	9.76	9.40	10.00	2- or 4-year degree often required	0.9	1.0	58.6	14.8	14.4

TABLE 2.2—cont.

Occupation	Workers paid low wages (%)	Median hourly wage (dollars)			Training, education, and licensing requirements	Percentage of all low-wage workers	Percentage of all low-wage women workers	Percentage of workers who are:		
		All workers	Women	Men				Female	African American	Hispanic
Packers and packagers, hand	59.5	8.50	8.25	8.99	None	0.8	0.9	60.7	13.1	42.5
Dining room and cafeteria attendants and bartender helpers	77.5	7.19	7.80	7.00	None	0.9	0.6	45.2	9.0	28.5
Total, 25 largest low-wage occupations[e]	56.6	8.75	8.50	9.15	—	50.3	55.7	60.9	14.8	19.4
Total, all low-wage occupations[e]	56.6	8.75	8.47	9.24	—	63.9	68.7	58.4	14.3	19.5
Total, all occupations[e]	25.9	13.69	12.32	15.06	—	—	—	48.2	11.0	13.3

Sources: Institute for Women's Policy Research analysis of the 2003 and 2004 Current Population Survey Outgoing Rotation Group files; Institute for Women's Policy Research summary of U.S. Department of Labor, Bureau of Labor Statistics, *Occupational Outlook Handbook, 2004–2005 ed.*, http://www.bls.gov/oco/ (accessed May 16, 2005).

[a] Wage data for 2003 are inflated to 2004 dollars using the Consumer Price Index Research Series Using Current Methods (CPI-U-RS). See http://www.bls.gov/cpi/cpiurstx.htm. An occupation is defined as low-wage if at least 33 percent of workers in that occupation earn an hourly wage rate below the poverty line for a family of four for full-time, year-round work ($9.28 in 2004). Low-wage occupations are shown here if they employ 1 percent or more of the total low-wage labor force. The sample excludes self-employed workers. There are 35,916,000 low-wage workers (represented by 104,231 observations in our data set) and 86,871,000 higher-wage workers (253,990 observations).

[b] In female-dominated occupations, 75 percent or more of workers are female.

[c] In male-dominated occupations, 75 percent or more of workers are male.

[d] At least 24 percent of workers in integrated occupations are female, and at least 24 percent are male.

[e] Includes higher-wage workers employed in occupations that we define as low-wage.

occupations, but, generally, not in the same ones (table 2.2). For example, 21 percent of personal and home care aides; 28 percent of security guards; and 34 percent of nursing, psychiatric, and home health aides are African American (compared with 11 percent of workers in all occupations). Forty percent or more of maids, miscellaneous agricultural workers, groundskeepers, and hand-packers are Hispanic, although Hispanics are only 13 percent of all job-holders. Food service workers are also disproportionately Hispanic. Whites are slightly overrepresented among some of the higher-paid occupations in the low-wage sector (preschool and kindergarten teachers, receptionists, and tellers), as well as among retail salespersons and waiters and waitresses.

One-quarter of the workforce earns low wages (table 2.3). The majority of these low-wage workers are female—nearly three of every five. African Americans (14 percent of low-wage workers) and, even more so, Hispanics are over-represented in the low-wage workforce (21 percent). Asian American and Hawaiian/Pacific Islander workers are present in the low-wage workforce roughly in proportion to their representation in the whole workforce (4 percent), as are American Indian/Alaska Natives (less than 1 percent) and non-Hispanics in other racial groups (1 percent).

Not surprisingly, workers with less education and younger workers more commonly hold low-wage jobs than workers with better educational credentials and prime-age workers. Over one-quarter have no education beyond high school, compared with only 7 percent of higher-wage workers. More than one in three low-wage workers has some college experience, but only 8 percent hold a college degree; in the higher-wage labor market, more than one-third of workers completed college and an additional 29 percent have some college experience.

But fully one-half of low-wage workers are in their prime working years (ages 25–54); among higher-wage workers, three-fourths are in this age group. Thus, while poorly paid jobs may offer young workers an entry-level work experience, they also employ a significant share of adult workers. As already noted, prime-age adults who average low earnings over many years are disproportionately female. Low-wage work is especially prevalent in the wholesale/retail trade and leisure and hospitality industries, in service and sales and related occupations, and among part-time workers.

Class-Based Strategies for Raising Women's Earnings

The main national-level U.S. policy to address low earnings is the gender-blind class-based minimum wage. Instituted through the Fair Labor Standards Act

TABLE 2.3
Characteristics of low-wage and higher-wage workers, 2003–2004[a]

	Low-Wage[b]	Higher-Wage[c]	Total
Number	31,713,417	90,654,167	122,367,584
Share of total (%)			
All	25.9	74.1	100.0
Men	21.2	78.8	100.0
Women	31.0	69.0	100.0
Median hourly wages (dollars)			
All	7.44	16.94	13.69
Men	7.50	18.00	15.06
Women	7.25	15.49	12.32
Gender (%)			
Male	42.4	55.1	51.8
Female	57.6	44.9	48.2
All	100.0	100.0	100.0
Race (%)			
White, non-Hispanic	60.0	73.2	69.8
African American, non-Hispanic	13.5	10.2	11.1
American Indian/Alaska Native, non-Hispanic	0.6	0.4	0.5
Asian or Hawaiian/Pacific Islander, non-Hispanic	3.8	4.6	4.4
Some other race or two or more races, non-Hispanic	1.3	1.0	1.1
Hispanic	20.7	10.7	13.3
All	100.0	100.0	100.0
Education (highest level) (%)			
Less than high school	28.1	6.5	12.1
High school	34.9	28.6	30.2
Some college, no bachelor's degree	28.7	29.1	29.0
Bachelor's degree or higher	8.3	35.8	28.7
All	100.0	100.0	100.0
Age (%)			
16–19	15.6	0.9	4.7
20–24	22.0	6.8	10.8
25–54	50.3	77.5	70.5
55–64	7.8	12.5	11.3
65 and older	4.2	2.3	2.8
All	100.0	100.0	100.0
Full-time/part-time status (%)			
Employed full-time	60.5	89.6	82.0
Employed part-time	39.5	10.5	18.0
All	100.0	100.0	100.0
Industry (%)			
Agriculture, forestry, fishing, and hunting	2.0	0.5	0.9
Mining	0.1	0.5	0.4
Construction	4.1	7.2	6.4
Manufacturing	8.5	14.6	13.0
Wholesale and retail trade	21.8	12.8	15.2
Transportation and utilities	3.0	6.0	5.2
Information	1.7	3.1	2.7
Financial activities	4.1	8.0	7.0

TABLE 2.3—cont.

	Low-Wage[b]	Higher-Wage[c]	Total
Professional and business services	7.3	9.6	9.0
Educational and health services	18.0	23.2	21.8
Leisure and hospitality	21.2	4.3	8.7
Other services	6.4	3.8	4.5
Public administration	2.1	6.2	5.1
All	100.0	100.0	100.0
Occupation (%)			
Management, business, and financial occupations	2.9	16.1	12.7
Professional and related occupations	8.1	25.2	20.8
Service occupations	35.5	10.1	16.7
Sales and related occupations	16.6	8.9	10.9
Office and administrative support occupations	14.1	15.8	15.4
Farming, fishing, and forestry occupations	1.8	0.3	0.7
Construction and extraction occupations	3.7	5.9	5.3
Installation, maintenance, and repair occupations	1.8	4.4	3.7
Production occupations	7.7	7.4	7.5
Transportation and material moving occupations	7.9	5.9	6.4
All	100.0	100.0	100.0
Job covered by a union or employee association (%)			
Yes	5.9	16.9	14.1
No	94.1	83.1	85.9
All	100.0	100.0	100.0

Source: Institute for Women's Policy Research analysis of the 2003 and 2004 Current Population Survey Outgoing Rotation Group files.
[a] Wage data for 2003 inflated to 2004 dollars using the CPI-U-RS. Sample includes all wage and salary workers ages 16 and over with positive earnings.
[b] Low-wage workers are those whose hourly wage rate produces less than the federal poverty line for a family of four with full-time, year-round work ($9.28 in 2004).
[c] Higher-wage workers are those earning $9.28 or more per hour.

in 1938, this wage floor is now set at $5.15 an hour and covers most jobs.[1] The federal minimum wage can be raised only by act of Congress and has not been changed since 1997, despite recent efforts to raise it to $7.25. The real value of the minimum wage has sunk to 74 percent of its 1979 purchasing power.[2] Full-time year-round work at the federal minimum wage yields only $10,712, well below the federal poverty threshold for a family of four ($19,307 in 2004).[3]

[1] The federal minimum wage law regulates the employment of more than 80 million workers (U.S. Department of Labor, "Coverage Under the Fair Labor Standards Act," n.d., http://www.dol.gov/compliance/laws/comp-flsa.htm [accessed August 30, 2006]), or roughly 56 percent of all employed Americans. Many higher-paid executive, administrative, and professional occupations are exempt (U.S. Department of Labor, "FairPay Fact Sheet by Exemption under the Fair Labor Standards Act [FLSA]," n.d., http://www.dol.gov/compliance/laws/comp-flsa.htm [accessed August 30, 2006]).
[2] Economic Policy Institute, *Minimum Wage Issue Guide*, 2006 (Washington, D.C.: Economic Policy Institute), http://www.epinet.org/content.cfm/issueguides_minwage (accessed August 30, 2006).
[3] U.S. Census Bureau, "Poverty Thresholds 2004," 2005, http://www.census.gov/hhes/www/poverty/threshld/thresh04.html (accessed September 19, 2005).

TABLE 2.4
Workers below current and proposed federal minimum wage, 2003–2004 (%)[a]

	Women	Men	Total
Current law			
< $5.15 per hour	2.6	1.2	1.9
≥ $5.15 per hour	97.4	98.8	98.1
Proposed increase—Fair Minimum Wage Act			
< $7.25 per hour	21.1	14.5	17.9
≥ $7.25 per hour	78.9	85.5	82.1
Indexed to federal poverty threshold (2004)			
< $9.28 per hour	43.5	32.6	38.2
≥ $9.28 per hour	56.5	67.4	61.8

Source: Institute for Women's Policy Research analysis of the 2003 and 2004 Current Population Survey Outgoing Rotation Group files.
[a] Wage data for 2003 inflated to 2004 dollars using the CPI-U-RS. Sample includes all wage and salary workers ages 16 and over with positive earnings.

The majority (61 percent) of workers earning the current federal minimum wage or lower are women.[4] In fact, almost three of every one hundred women workers earn $5.15 or less per hour, twice the proportion of men (table 2.4). If the federal minimum wage were raised to $7.25 per hour (as proposed by the Fair Minimum Wage Act, S. 1062, H.R. 2429, 109th Congress), women would disproportionately benefit because 21.1 percent of female workers earn $7.25 or less per hour, compared with 14.5 percent of male workers. If the minimum wage were indexed to the federal poverty level (for a family of four) of $9.28 in 2004, the wages of two-fifths of women workers and one-third of male workers would be raised.

Forty-five states have their own minimum wages regulating the few jobs not covered by the federal minimum wage (e.g., small firms not engaged in interstate commerce).[5] Superseding federal policymaking, nearly one-half the states have set a wage floor above $5.15. Some state minimum wages are indexed to inflation to maintain workers' purchasing power over time or automatically increase as the federal minimum wage is raised. In addition, a small number of municipalities have recently set their own minimum wages: Madison and three other cities in Wisconsin (these were all repealed when a new state minimum wage law was enacted in 2005); New Orleans, Louisiana (although this was struck down by the courts); San Francisco, California; Santa

[4] Eileen Appelbaum, Jared Bernstein, Janet Currie, Heidi Hartmann, Lawrence Katz, Ann Markusen, Edward Montgomery, Steven Raphael, and Cecilia Rouse, "The Minimum Wage and Working Women," 2004, http://www.cww.rutgers.edu/dataPages/minwagewomen6–18–04.pdf (accessed August 30, 2006).
[5] U.S. Employment Standards Administration, "Minimum Wage Laws in the States," http://www.dol.gov/esa/minwage/america.htm (accessed May 12, 2006).

Fe, New Mexico; and Washington, D.C. In recent years, several members of Congress have tried to evade the national standard set in the Fair Labor Standards Act by proposing that the minimum wage be adjusted on a state-by-state basis to reflect differences in the cost of living and other factors.[6]

Two related policies that seek even higher wage floors are living wages and self-sufficiency standards. Living wages explicitly link wage regulations with the notion that workers' earnings should provide an adequate income. They have been enacted in over 120 local governments.[7] Self-sufficiency standards are guidelines based on detailed computation of income needs for different family configurations in specific jurisdictions, although to date no legislation requires employers to pay wages that meet the self-sufficiency standard.

Living wage campaigns are often inspired by the privatization of government services, which entails the loss of higher-paid jobs, and tax breaks offered under economic development policies. Targeting employees of certain government contractors, they may cover only a specific set of workers in a given jurisdiction. For example, the San Francisco living wage policy applies to city service contractors, including nonprofit agencies, and leaseholders at San Francisco International Airport. New York City's living wage policy initially covered city contractors for security, temporary help, cleaning, and food services; it has since been expanded to cover more workers than any other city, including about 50,000 employees of city contractors, primarily working in health care, day care, disability services, and food services. Because of the generally narrow application of living wage laws, it is difficult to calculate the total number of workers affected by these wage standards; by one estimate, where such laws exist, on average less than 1 percent of all workers in the relevant geographic area are affected (Brocht 2001).

Living wage laws often stipulate different rates depending on whether workers receive health insurance through their jobs. The highest living wage currently in effect is $13.00 per hour ($14.75 for workers not provided with employment-based health insurance), enacted in 2002 in Fairfax, California. Even the current lowest living wage—in Jersey City, New Jersey, $7.50 per hour—is substantially higher than the federal minimum wage.

Self-sufficiency standards go much further, calculating specific wage floors that provide adequate income to cover the observed costs of basic needs such as rent, food, child care, health insurance, and transportation for families of different sizes and parent-child configurations in individual locations. Devel-

---

[6] See the Minimum Wage State Flexibility Act of 1999 (S. 1877 and H.R. 2928, 106th Congress); Minimum Wage State Flexibility Act of 2001 (H.R. 1441, 107th Congress).

[7] Mark D. Brenner and Stephanie Luce, 2005, *Living Wage Laws in Practice: The Boston, New Haven and Hartford Experiences* (Amherst: University of Massachusetts Political Economy Research Institute), http://www.umass.edu/peri (accessed August 30, 2006). See Living Wage Resource Center for an up-to-date list of enacted ordinances, http://www.livingwagecampaign.org.

oped by Wider Opportunities for Women[8] and other organizations, these wage guidelines may be more than double the federal minimum wage or the federal poverty threshold. For example, for Milwaukee County, Wisconsin, a single parent with one preschool child and another in school needs to earn $19.93 per hour (and work full-time) to cover the family's living expenses. To date, self-sufficiency standards have functioned primarily to establish a realistic assessment of workers' income needs in policymaking discussions (critiquing the federal poverty threshold as outdated) and in the design of education, job training, workforce development, and welfare-to-work programs; none has been enacted as a wage standard for employers.

Although these wage policies—minimum wage, living wage, and self-sufficiency wage standard—are technically gender-neutral, given the concentration of women at the bottom of the wage spectrum, wage standards that bring up the floor disproportionately apply to women[9] (Bernstein, Hartmann, and Schmitt 1999), increasing women's earnings and reducing women's poverty. They have less impact on women's wages relative to men's, overall, because they affect only the bottom of the labor market and because employers often raise the wages of workers in the next-higher wage category in order to preserve earnings differentials between groups—that is, an increase at the bottom may diffuse upward somewhat, toward jobs more often held by men, diluting the relative boost to women's earnings. Evaluating policy scenarios before the last federal minimum wage increase, Figart and Lapidus (1995) estimated that raising the wage standard from $4.25 to $4.75 would narrow the gender wage ratio by 1–2 percent. Stone and Kuperberg (2005) estimate that for their sample of municipal workers in the Northeast, if all city workers were paid a living wage of $10.88 per hour (in 2002 dollars), the gender wage ratio would not change at all (but, by definition, all poverty wages would be eliminated because the hourly wage chosen was set above the federal poverty standard).

Gender-Focused Approaches to Reducing Earnings Inequalities

Proposals to redress gender-based wage inequities are predicated on the view that occupational sex segregation is a key mechanism leading to unequal wages—women and men tend to do different work all along the wage hierar-

[8] This Washington, D.C.–based nonprofit advocates for improved employment opportunities for women, particularly in nontraditional fields for women, with a goal of improving their long-term economic security.

[9] David Fairris, David Runsten, Carolina Briones, and Jessica Goodheart, 2005, "Examining the Evidence: The Impact of the Los Angeles Living Wage Ordinance on Workers and Businesses," http://www.losangeleslivingwagestudy.com (accessed June 6, 2005).

chy, at the top and middle as well as at the bottom, and "society and employers appear to devalue women's work, at least in part because women do it" (Reskin 1993, 242). Remedies are thus focused both on improving woman's access to male-dominated jobs and on increasing wages in female-dominated jobs.

The separation of men and women into different occupations is a common and persistent characteristic of labor markets. It is typically associated with sex-based earnings differentials; due to poorly understood wage-setting processes, occupations held predominantly by women pay less than jobs held predominantly by men. The extent of segregation in an occupation becomes evident by comparing the number of jobholders who are women (or men) with the sex distribution of the whole workforce. At the aggregate level, it is generally measured by an Index of Segregation, which indicates what percentage of one group would have to change jobs in order for all occupations to be integrated.[10] The segregation index has decreased substantially over the past few decades—from 67 in 1970 to 52 in 2000—largely due to women's entrance into male-dominated occupations (Jacobs 2003). However, the influx of women into historically male-dominated occupations slowed, and may have stopped, during the 1990s. Nearly all the measured occupational integration in the 1990s was due to changes in the relative size of occupations rather than the integration of individual occupations because total employment in more integrated occupations grew faster than that in more sex-segregated occupations (Jacobs 2003).

Using a very detailed occupational classification scheme to calculate the Index of Segregation shows that the separation of women and men into sex-typed occupations is still pervasive and is nearly as prevalent in low-wage as in higher-wage occupations (table 2.5). In low-wage occupations, almost one-half of female workers (48.9 percent) would have to move into male-dominated occupations for low-wage occupations to employ equal shares of the female and male workforces. The comparable portion for the integration of the higher-wage labor market is only four percentage points higher, at 52.9.[11] Thus, efforts to achieve gender pay equity among low-wage workers face the same institutionalized differentiation of women's and men's jobs that is common in professional and other segments of the labor market.

Individual women's hard work, determination, family or social connec-

---

[10] The Index of Segregation, developed by Duncan and Duncan (1955), is defined as $\frac{1}{2}\Sigma \,|M_i - F_i|$, where M_i is the percentage of employed men and F_i is the percentage of employed women working in occupation i. The index equals 0 when the distribution of men and women across occupational categories is identical and 100 when occupations are entirely sex-segregated.

[11] There is a much finer level of occupational definition in higher-wage occupations than in the low-wage labor market, with an average of over 350,000 workers in each low-wage occupation and only 220,000 in higher-wage occupations (authors' analysis of the Outgoing Rotation Group files of the 2003 and 2004 Current Populations Surveys). If greater occupational differentiation were available for low-wage occupations, the Index of Segregation would likely be higher than is reported here.

TABLE 2.5
Index of sex segregation, by wage
level[a]

Low-wage occupations	48.9
Higher-wage occupations	52.9
All occupations	52.5

Source: Institute for Women's Policy
Research analysis of the 2003 and 2004
Current Population Survey Outgoing Rotation Group files.
  [a] An occupation is defined as low-
wage if 33 percent of the workers in that
occupation earn an hourly wage rate of
less than the poverty threshold for a family
of four for full-time, year-round work
($9.28 in 2004). There are 399 higher-
wage occupations and 102 low-wage occupations.

tions, and luck have allowed some to break into male-dominated work over the years. Historical factors such as wartime labor shortages have also provided at least temporary access to typically forbidden jobs (Milkman 1987). And perhaps most important, a series of federal actions in the 1960s and 1970s established a new legal framework outlawing gender-based employment practices in hiring and promotions: Title VII of the Civil Rights Act of 1964, making discrimination on the basis of sex (and race, color, religion, and national origin) illegal; the 1967 amendment of Executive Order 11246, establishing equity standards for federal contractors; and Title IX of the Education Amendments of 1972, mandating sex equity in education programs receiving federal funding (Conway, Ahern, and Steuernagel 1995).

Affirmative action has also helped women gain access to a broader range of work and to the higher pay that often rewards incumbents in previously closed occupations.[12] Women have dramatically increased their level of educational attainment, gaining the general and professional training necessary to move up. In 2004, 26 percent of women ages twenty-five and older had completed four or more years of college, compared with only 6 percent in 1960.[13] Today, about one-third of all lawyers and physicians are women (33.5 and 31.2 percent, respectively, in 2004; U.S. Bureau of Labor Statistics 2005).

Nonprofit organizations, women's advocacy groups, professional associations, and academic institutions have established outreach and training pro-

---

[12] Better access does not necessarily lead to equal pay; even in emerging occupations, women may be paid less than comparably situated men (Hoff 2004).

[13] U.S. Census Bureau, "Historical Educational Attainment Tables: Table A-1. Years of School Completed by People 25 Years and Over, by Age and Sex: Selected Years 1940 to 2004," 2004, http://www.census.gov/population/socdemo/education/tabA-1.pdf (accessed September 9, 2005).

grams to bring more women into fields that offer good compensation but remain largely male-dominated. One key target of these initiatives is blue-collar jobs such as construction and trucking. Many of these male-dominated jobs have well-established training, credentialing, apprenticeship, and hiring processes, which should help women obtain the needed credentials. They also pay well. Electricians, for example, average $719 per week, whereas average weekly earnings for all workers are just $638 (U.S. Bureau of Labor Statistics 2005). But so far, progress in integrating most of these occupations has been very slow. Firefighting, for instance, remains almost entirely a male pursuit—95 percent of incumbents are men.

There are significant cultural barriers to moving women workers into some higher-paying male occupations, particularly those historically associated with high levels of physical effort. But other jobs hold greater promise while offering good wages and benefits. For instance, women have very successfully integrated into the pharmacy profession (Phipps 1990), holding a share of these jobs that is slightly higher than women's total portion of the workforce and averaging weekly earnings of 85 percent of men's (U.S. Bureau of Labor Statistics 2005). In addition to professions in law and health care, opportunities are good in some computer-related occupations, financial analysis, and post-secondary education.

In the low-wage labor market, there are many more female-dominated than male-dominated occupations, and, comparing only those occupations with skill requirements, men's occupations such as laborers and security guards pay better than women's occupations such as child-care workers, cashiers, maids, and personal and home health-care aides (table 2.2). But pay is even higher for those low-wage jobs that require substantial skills, such as preschool and kindergarten teachers and several administrative support occupations, all of which are female-dominated.[14] Men's jobs that require similarly high skill levels are simply not low-wage occupations. Thus, improving wages in these higher-wage low-wage occupations may best be addressed by a comparable worth, or pay equity, approach that raises the wages of female-dominated jobs to the wages of male-dominated jobs with similar requirements.

For the millions of women employed in jobs held mainly by women, eradicating gender-based pay inequities that stem from occupational segregation requires changes in wage-setting practices. Comparable worth or pay equity campaigns seek to explicitly identify and redress wage disparities resulting from occupational segregation by sex (Stone and Kuperberg 2005). The 1963 Equal Pay Act took a major step toward equalizing wages by mandating equal wages for all workers in an establishment "for equal work on jobs the perfor-

[14] Men earn more than women in seventeen of the twenty-five largest low-wage occupations, including many of the female-dominated ones.

TABLE 2.6
Average hourly wages of continuously employed women and men[a] by career occupational groups, 1983–1998 (dollars)[a]

Tier[d]	Male sector[b]		Female sector[c]	
	Women	Men	Women	Men
Elite jobs	23	32	23	24
Good jobs	19	23	15	22
Less-skilled jobs	13	16	11	16

Source: Calculations based on earnings and work-hours data in Rose and Hartmann (2004, table 8), which uses the Panel Study of Income Dynamics.

[a] All earnings are adjusted to 1999 dollars. Analysis includes workers ages 26N59 with earnings in all 15 years of the study period. Because most men work full time, data for full-time women are compared to data for all men.

[b] Male-sector jobs are defined as those having a majority male workforce.

[c] Female-sector jobs are defined as those having a majority female workforce.

[d] Jobs are classified into tiers based on education and training requirements and pay. See Rose and Hartmann (2004, app. II) for a complete description of this classification system.

mance of which requires equal skill, effort, and responsibility, and which are performed under similar working conditions" (29 USC 206(d)). The scope of the Equal Pay Act has been limited by the courts to comparing the wages of women and men holding substantially the same job. Because, as we have seen, occupational segregation by sex is still common in the U.S. labor market, a remedy that compares wages across different types of jobs is needed. Comparable worth (or pay equity) policies compare the wages of those jobs held disproportionately by women with equivalent, but not identical, jobs done disproportionately by men. The comparable worth argument is that women's jobs that are equivalent to men's jobs are paid substantially less at least partly because of sex discrimination and that discrimination should be eliminated.

A recent study by Rose and Hartmann (2004) illustrates the relationship between wages and occupational sex-typing (table 2.6). When occupations are grouped into three categories based on training and education requirements (less-skilled, good, and elite jobs) and then also divided by the sex of the majority of jobholders, it becomes clear that in general men earn more when they work in the male sector than when they work in the female sector. Men also out-earn women in good and less-skilled jobs in both the male and female occupational sectors. (Perhaps when men work in women's jobs they are employed in different jobs within these tiers or earn more in the same jobs.) Although women who work in male occupations at both the less-skilled and good job levels earn less than men in those occupations, they nevertheless benefit substantially from working in the male sector rather than the female sector. Women gain 19 percent in less-skilled jobs and 21 percent in good jobs when they work in the male sector.

These wage differentials suggest that female-sector jobs may have a comparable worth problem (are paid less than male-sector jobs at similar skill levels). In the elite job tier, women earn approximately the same in both the male and female sectors, whereas men earn 24 percent less if they work in female-typed jobs, showing that men also can suffer wage loss from working in female-stereotyped jobs. (This also suggests that women still face barriers to entering the highest-paid male-dominated jobs or suffer severe wage discrimination when they work in these jobs, or both.)

In the textbook scenario, comparable worth analyses use a carefully designed point-factor system to analyze the essential tasks performed in a job and then to value these tasks by assigning points (Acker 1989). These points allow a direct comparison of the skills and knowledge required to hold a job, as well as the level of responsibility of duties performed by jobholders and the job's working conditions. Jobs with the same total point scores are held to be comparable so that, for example, librarians or nurses might be found to be comparable with engineers, or child-care workers with tree trimmers or dispatchers. The job evaluations also provide a basis for examining the relationship between job components and pay. When female-dominated jobs are found to pay less than comparable male-dominated jobs, the suggested remedy is to raise the pay of the undervalued female-dominated jobs. (Comparable worth is sometimes also referred to as equal pay for jobs of equal value.)

To reduce or erase sex discrimination, the job evaluation system must itself be purged of discriminatory valuations of work typically associated with one sex or the other—that is, it must give appropriate relative value to characteristics such as strength and emotional caregiving, neither assuming these skills are required for competent work performance where they are not (even if most current job incumbents have the attribute) nor overlooking the importance of skill achievements that are often ignored or considered innate for one sex or the other (e.g., the requirement that nurses provide emotional support to their patients; Treiman 1979).

Devising such a truly gender-neutral system of job analysis is "inordinately difficult" (Whitehouse, Zetlin, and Earnshaw 2001, 367) and, in application, deeply entangled in stakeholders' concerns about hierarchy and status (Acker 1989). To simplify the comparable worth job-comparison process, gender-based wage disparities could be addressed by raising the wages of workers in an employer's largest and lowest-paid female-dominated jobs, without undertaking a detailed analysis of tasks and responsibilities. One common method is to increase the reward for seniority in such female-dominated jobs as secretary because it is often found that incumbents in female-dominated jobs who have long tenure and have gained many firm-specific skills are paid little more than new hires (a phenomenon less common in male-dominated jobs.)

Pay equity campaigns usually target local or state government workers because salary scales for public workers are public information. These campaigns saw their greatest success changing wage systems for state civil service employees in the 1980s. Beginning with a pay equity process in Minnesota in 1983, twenty states implemented salary adjustment schemes that resulted in higher pay for female-dominated jobs (Hartmann and Aaronson 1994).

More recently, state legislatures have created a number of pay equity commissions or task forces to study sex-based wage disparities and recommend compensatory programs. In 2003, twenty-three state legislatures considered equal pay bills (Center for Policy Alternatives 2005). Some sought stronger enforcement provisions for existing equal pay laws, but many proposed new pay equity or comparable worth standards. Maine's Department of Labor issued regulations in 2001 to implement a groundbreaking law dating to 1966 that requires equal pay in comparable jobs for both the public and private sectors. The department has published compliance information on the law for both employers and employees.

Recent comparable worth studies have been completed for civil servants in Portland, Oregon; the County of Los Angeles, California; and the Clark County School District in Las Vegas, Nevada. In Los Angeles County, the study was followed by a significant wage hike for social workers. Pay equity wage increases have also resulted from the collective bargaining process between unions and individual companies. At the federal level, the Fair Pay Act, a proposal to require comparable worth in both the public and private sectors, is introduced in Congress regularly, as are bills to strengthen enforcement of the 1963 Equal Pay Act, such as the Paycheck Fairness Act.

Ridding an existing pay system of sex discrimination is a complicated political process. Workers unlikely to see their wages bumped up through the wage evaluation process have a stake in preserving their place in wage hierarchies. Unions and civil service personnel strive to maintain their roles in wage-setting. Administrators may seek to impose unrelated objectives once the process of reviewing job descriptions and pay is underway. Other technical aspects of the process, such as the selection of comparator jobs, affect the prospects for significantly changing women's relative wages. Also, as with living wage ordinances, raising the pay of women's jobs could reduce women's employment somewhat if employers hire men for the jobs or substitute other jobs for those whose cost has increased.

Looking at the labor market as a whole, theoretical analysis suggests, and empirical work confirms, that comparable worth policies can improve the gender wage ratio while reducing women's poverty and can do so with only small disemployment effects. Washington state's pay equity adjustment closed 30 percent of the gender wage gap in that state, and the Minnesota process added 0.08 points to the gender wage ratio there, increasing it from 0.74 to 0.82, without reducing women's employment significantly (Hartmann and

Aaronson 1994). Statistical simulations of the potential impact of pay equity adjustments conclude that, depending on the specific parameters of the envisioned policies, comparable worth can both substantially and disproportionately raise low-wage women's earnings (Figart and Lapidus 1995; Stone and Kuperberg 2005). In addition, Malveaux (1986) speculates, based on racial differences among women in occupations and employment sectors, that comparable worth may improve wages disproportionately for black women. Lapidus and Figart's (1998) analysis of wages by race/gender groups also concludes that eradicating racial bias in wage-setting by enacting comparable worth (comparing the wages of minority-dominated and white-dominated occupations) would disproportionately benefit African American and Hispanic women.

Because pay equity remedies have languished in the courts, new laws are sorely needed to make comparable worth a successful avenue for erasing pay inequities. To date, pay equity processes have been viable only in the public sector, where salary information is available. Without this knowledge, workers are unable to assess the fairness of their pay relative to their co-workers. The Fair Pay Act[15] requires employers to file salary data with the Equal Employment Opportunity Commission (EEOC), instructs the EEOC to make efforts to mitigate pay inequities, and allows class-action lawsuits. Measures such as these would significantly reduce barriers to women's pursuit of pay equity.

Gender-Based or Class-Based Remedies

As noted throughout this chapter, every approach to raising women's wages has strengths and weaknesses. By definition, those that target low-wage jobs will not do much for higher-wage women who also suffer from pay discrimination. Class-based strategies are limited in other ways as well.

Minimum wage laws are relatively universal, and few employers are excluded from their coverage. They help women disproportionately because more women work at minimum wage jobs than men do. Since most minimum wages are quite low, however, they do not prevent many full-time workers from being poor. A few states have set relatively high minimum wages and indexed them to inflation, but most states, and the federal government, have not. And, although minimum wage laws help women (and men) at the bottom, they do little to improve the overall male-female wage gap in the economy because sex-based pay inequities persist all along the wage hierarchy, from bottom to top.

[15] Fair Pay Act, S. 840, H.R. 1697, 109th Congress.

Living wage laws set a higher wage standard than that required by mini-mum wage laws and thus do more to reduce poverty among workers affected by them, but they have a more limited scope. They generally affect only city contractors in individual local jurisdictions. One estimate finds that even in geographic areas that have living wage laws, only 1 percent of local workers are affected on average. And, because so few workers are usually affected, liv-ing wage policies generally affect the gender wage ratios in their area labor markets only minimally.

Self-sufficiency standards, which indicate the wage levels that different families of different sizes and compositions need in different communities in order to achieve a decent standard of living, are higher yet, but they so far have not been required by law of any employers.

Often advocates who propose higher minimum and living wage standards hope that such standards will have spillover effects on other jobs. It has been found, for example, that about twice as many workers get pay raises when the federal minimum wage increases than there are minimum wage workers.[16] Liv-ing wage advocates hope that other private-sector employers, in addition to those with city contracts, will raise the wages of their low-wage workers. Al-though such indirect effects of these proposals would certainly be beneficial for workers, it should be noted that as these wage standards affect men and women at higher pay levels their effect on narrowing the gender pay gap diminishes.

Gender-based strategies have the potential to be implemented all along the wage hierarchy, from the lowest-paid to the highest-paid jobs. They address both the persistence of sex segregation in the labor market and women's lower pay wherever they work. The analysis of the low-wage labor market presented here shows that it too suffers from gender-based problems and would there-fore benefit from gender-based remedies. The low-wage labor market is nearly as sex segregated as the higher-wage market, and within the low-wage market, men earn higher wages than women, on average. Also, many of the female-dominated low-wage jobs require substantial credentials, whereas few male-dominated low-wage jobs do, suggesting that pay equity or comparable worth remedies are needed to raise the wages of high-qualification low-wage jobs dominated by women.

The 1963 Equal Pay Act, Title VII (1964), the 1967 federal executive order, and the 1972 Title IX have all made it easier for women to enter formerly male-dominated fields, such as bus driving, mining, protective services, police work, engineering, law, medicine, and journalism (some more successfully than others), and to be paid more fairly when they work in the same jobs as men do. Nevertheless, the research results presented here show that sex segre-

---

[16] Economic Policy Institute, *Minimum Wage Issue Guide*, 2006 (Washington, D.C.: Economic Pol-icy Institute), http://www.epinet.org/content.cfm/issueguides_minwage (accessed August 30, 2006).

gation and the wage gap still persist, suggesting that our present remedies are not sufficient.

Title VII, for example, applies to all workers who work for businesses with fifteen or more employees and thus covers about 80 percent of the work force. Enforcement efforts are relatively weak, however, and every year large class action suits are settled that bring women higher wages and better employment opportunities, indicating that violations are still common (Murphy and Graff 2005). Title VII has also generally not been held by the courts to require pay equity in jobs that are disproportionately held by women but that can be compared to male-dominated jobs that have equivalent requirements; thus, there is currently no federal law that requires comparable worth in the private sector. And, as noted earlier, some male-dominated jobs have been slow to integrate despite the fact that Title VII requires employers not to discriminate in hiring, job placement, and promotion.

The Equal Pay Act applies to at most the three-fifths of the female labor force that work in male-dominated or integrated occupations and may (or may not) hold jobs that are substantially equal to men's jobs at the same firm. (For example, some restaurants may hire mainly male wait staff at higher wages, whereas others hire mainly female wait staff at lower wages, so an integrated occupation is in fact sex segregated at the level of the employer.) And, because Equal Pay Act cases continue to be adjudicated in favor of plaintiffs every year, it is evident that women still do not always enjoy equal pay even when they work in the same jobs as men.

The executive order requiring large federal contractors not to discriminate and to undertake affirmative action to employ women in underrepresented job categories applies to a subset of large employers covering about 50 percent of the labor force. These too are underenforced—few federal contractors have ever been prevented from receiving federal contracts as a result of violations. Nevertheless, it is estimated that federal contract compliance improved the employment opportunities of women, especially African American women, and more so in the 1970s than in the 1980s when enforcement efforts were reduced (Badgett and Hartmann 1995).

Each remedy could be strengthened by more consistent enforcement and educational efforts and the allocation of greater public resources to these efforts. Improving the implementation of Title IX in our middle and high schools, for example, would expose more girls to nontraditional careers and ensure that they take more of the required coursework to pursue them. In some cases, laws could be stronger. Federal and state welfare-to-work and employment training programs could include expanded mandates to prepare women for nontraditional higher-wage employment. The Paycheck Fairness Act would improve provisions of the Equal Pay Act and Title VII. And where current law is largely missing, such as for comparable worth remedies, new law should be developed. In the interim, voluntary efforts could be encouraged, for instance by having a nationally reputable organization such as the National Academy of Sciences issue guidelines for employers to use in determining fair pay between female- and male-dominated occupations. Many voluntary activities by employers, such as increasing mentoring activities to enhance the retention of women in male-dominated jobs, could also improve employment outcomes for women.

As for class-based remedies, these have for the most part also failed to keep up with the need. The federal minimum wage would be vastly improved if it were indexed to 50 percent of the average wage and then automatically adjusted for average price or wage increases. Especially in the absence of federal action, more states should raise and index their state minimum wages. Cities should continue to explore and enact living wage laws, which set a higher-than-minimum standard. Such efforts, along with self-sufficiency standards, educate the public and policymakers on the wage levels that are needed for families to survive without public assistance.

All wage and labor market remedies may also be influenced by unanticipated factors or have unintended consequences. As we have seen, these are all political processes, dependent on laws and policies being established, on the one hand, and on the way human beings implement those directives on the ground, on the other. Enforcement efforts vary from place to place and across time. And efforts to achieve change can be stymied by those whose interests lie in maintaining the status quo. Comparable worth policies, for example, are often resisted by the higher-paid incumbents of occupations, who may not have particularly high skill levels and fear having their occupations downgraded. Yet many comparable worth efforts have occurred when unions are involved in collective bargaining and can ensure that workers' interests are addressed without undermining the goals of the policy (Acker 1989; Hartmann and Aaronson 1994). Living wage ordinances have also been found to vary in effectiveness depending on whether advocates monitor their implementation (Luce 2005).

When the wages of any occupation are raised above historical levels, employers may adjust to the new phenomenon by hiring different workers or hiring fewer workers. A common fear when minimum wages are raised is that unskilled workers, especially, will lose their jobs. In a study evaluating a living wage ordinance passed in Los Angeles in 1997, researchers found that about one-fifth of affected employers substituted more experienced workers with better English skills. Some researchers have argued that pay equity wage increases, too, may decrease the employment of women because higher wages can lead to reduced employer demand or to employment shifts from women to men.

Although all public policies have their downsides, the policies reviewed here are nevertheless needed, in our judgment, to ameliorate the worst effects of the unconstrained operation of free markets on women, minorities, and low-wage workers. When employers are allowed to discriminate without interference, some do so. When employers are allowed to pay low wages when there is no legal wage floor, many selling in competitive product markets will bid wages down. Women workers benefit from both class-based policies to bring up the bottom of the labor market and from gender-based policies that operate in all areas of the labor market. In our judgment, gender-based policies will always be needed to address women's pay. At a 77 percent wage ratio, women still have a long way to go to achieve equity with men in the labor market. Class-based policies to assist low-wage workers can accomplish part of the progressive and feminist agendas—increasing income security for poor women. But they do little to challenge the existing institutions that prescribe different roles for women and men in the labor market. Policies specifically targeting reducing occupational segregation and/or the wage disparities engendered by this phenomenon have a more radical objective: to challenge the stereotypes, norms, and practices that contribute to the devaluation of work done by women. Until these gender-based stereotypes, norms, and practices are eliminated, gender-based remedies will continue to be needed.

PART II

UNIONS AND SEXUAL POLITICS

In the decades following World War II, powerful new social movements arose in the United States demanding full citizenship and an end to discrimination on the basis of race, ethnicity, sex, and sexual orientation. African Americans, Mexican Americans, women, sexual minorities, and others asserted their group claims, often turning to organized labor as a vehicle for economic and social advancement.

Yet, as the chapters in this section vividly remind us, the relation between organized labor and the new social movements has not been an easy one. Nor has the experience of women and sexual minorities within organized labor been uniformly positive. But what lies ahead? How much has the labor movement been transformed by the new sexual diversity in its ranks? To what degree are the issues of discrimination on the basis of sex and sexual orientation incorporated into labor's agenda? Can a class-based movement respond adequately to the needs of a working class divided by sex and sexuality?

The authors of the three chapters that follow do not always agree on the answers to these questions. They offer differing assessments of labor's historical record toward women and sexual minorities, and they disagree on the potential of class-based movements to respond to the new sexual diversity of workers.

In chapter 3, Ruth Milkman analyzes the varied responses of unions to the feminization of work and the rise of the feminist movement. Women have flooded into organized labor, yet the impact of this sex change has been uneven. Milkman posits two houses of labor, standing uneasily next to each other. One is female-dominated and more influenced by the women's movement; the other remains more traditional in its gender composition and its sexual politics. In 2005, the American Federation of Labor–Congress of Industrial Organizations (AFL-CIO) split into two quarreling camps. But because the fracture was not along gender lines, each of the new federations is still characterized by sex segregation within its own ranks. Each has two wings: one female-dominated and one male-dominated. The fate of most organized women, then, for better or worse, is institutionally bound up with their unionized brothers. If history is any guide, union women will need allies outside the labor movement if they are to transform the sexual politics of the two national federations.

Gerald Hunt and Monica Boris's assessment of the response of organized labor to sexual minorities in chapter 4 reinforces Milkman's portrait of the bifurcated character of U.S. trade unionism. As was true with the civil rights struggle, the gay rights movement in the United States had economic as well as civil and political dimensions; and it too found some early allies within organized labor. But most of the gains for sexual minorities occurred in the 1980s and 1990s, after the civil rights and women's movements subsided. Overall, labor's response has been mixed, Hunt and Boris conclude, with female-majority unions pioneering gay rights and initiating far more substantive changes in their culture and institutional practices than male-majority unions. Still, by telling the story of how gay rights came to the fore in the United Auto Workers (UAW), an older male-dominated union that we might assume to be more closed to innovation, Hunt and Boris reveal the crucial impact that individuals can have both in top leadership and on the shop floor, as well as the way in which labor's traditional message of equal treatment and solidarity can be reworked to include new groups.

Yet, as Marion Crain argues in chapter 5, labor's power is shrinking and its ability to respond to the widespread economic disadvantages that women suffer due to sex segregation and sexual harassment is limited by its own ideology and the legal framework inherited from the New Deal. Unions raise women's wages and help them secure a range of benefits, including health care, pensions, and vacations, as well as family and medical leave, as noted in chapter 3. Moreover, since the 1940s, largely in response to the pressure of the rising numbers of women activists within its ranks, many unions have worked to close the gender pay gap and lessen women's double day of market and family work (Cobble 2004).

But labor's record on confronting sexual harassment and sex segregation, as Crain forcefully reminds us, is much less positive. These are emotionally fraught and economically charged issues that tap into deeply held beliefs about masculinity, femininity, and sexuality. Not surprisingly, union men have been more supportive of equal pay and family benefits than of efforts to change the hypermasculine, sexualized culture of many blue-collar trades. A new class politics, Crain suggests, cannot be created as long as unions give priority to the gender interests of men. Sexual harassment and occupational restrictions based on sex are group economic harms. And as Crain reveals, labor's tolerance of sex-based discrimination allows a "toxic workplace culture" to fester, ultimately threatening the economic and psychological well-being of all workers. Her chapter concludes with a compelling case for why ending these injuries should be a priority for trade unions and what concretely unions can do to appeal to the millions of sales and service workers outside its ranks.

3

TWO WORLDS OF UNIONISM

WOMEN AND THE NEW LABOR MOVEMENT

Ruth Milkman

Economic inequalities among women have grown in recent years (McCall, chap. 1 in this volume), even as women's earnings have become an increasingly important source of support for poor and working-class families. And although gender inequalities in the labor market have been diminished somewhat, the persistence of job segregation by sex and the concentration of women workers in low-wage jobs remain formidable problems (Lovell, Hartmann, and Werschkul, chap. 2 in this volume). Thus, the potential benefits of union membership for women workers in the United States today are more salient than ever before.

Yet the influence of organized labor in the United States has been radically diminished in precisely the same period in which female employment and its contribution to the welfare of working families has expanded so dramatically. Unionization rates have plummeted, employers have become increasingly adept at "union avoidance," and the legally protected right to organize is now honored more in the breach than in the observance. Only 12.5 percent of all U.S. wage and salary workers are unionized today, compared to a peak of about 35 percent in the mid-1950s. Moreover, in the private sector, the

I thank Galo Falchettore for assistance with the Current Population Survey (CPS) data that are the basis for the detailed analysis of unionization rates in the text and figures. The data set was created by merging the basic monthly CPS Outgoing Rotation Group files for January through December 2004. The sample includes civilian wage and salary workers age 16 or over. We used the sample definition and weighting procedures described in the introduction to Hirsch and Macpherson (2005).

unionization rate is now less than 8 percent.[1] The political influence of organized labor has also suffered substantial erosion, although less than the union membership figures by themselves would suggest (Dark 1999).

For the minority of workers who are unionized, however, organized labor remains a powerful source of economic empowerment. This is especially the case for women workers. Women who are union members earn considerably more than their nonunion counterparts. In 2004, female union members earned, on average, $19.18 per hour, which was 127 percent of the average earnings of nonunion female workers ($15.05 per hour). The wage premium for men was considerably smaller: male union members in 2004 earned, on average, $21.24 per hour, or 109 percent of the average earnings of nonunion male workers ($19.46). Nevertheless, the average for nonunion men was higher than the average for unionized women workers (Hirsch and Macpherson 2005, 21).

The "union premium" is not limited to wages. Both female and male union members are far more likely than their nonunion counterparts to have employer-paid fringe benefits, from health insurance to pensions to paid time off. Unionized workers are about 28 percent more likely to be covered by employer-provided health insurance than their nonunion counterparts, and the health insurance unionized workers receive covers a greater share of medical costs. The union advantage is even greater in regard to pensions: union members are 54 percent more likely to have pension coverage than their nonunion counterparts, and the types of pensions union members have are generally superior to those provided by nonunion employers. Similarly, union workers have more paid vacation and paid holidays than nonunion workers— about 14 percent more, on average (Mishel, Bernstein, and Allegretto 2005, 192–93).

Unions often secure improved conditions of employment not only for their own members but also for the workforce as a whole, mainly through their legislative efforts. One important example is minimum wage legislation, a long-standing labor movement priority at both the federal and state levels. Although almost all female union members earn more than the minimum wage, nonunion women have always been overrepresented among low-wage workers. Thus women workers are the main beneficiaries of increases in state and federal minimum wages, for which organized labor has long been the primary advocate.

Labor's legislative accomplishments also include pay equity, job protection for pregnant workers, and family leave—all of which benefit women workers

---

[1] These data, and all those presented in this chapter, unless otherwise indicated, are U.S. Current Population Survey data for 2004, the most recent available at this writing. For details, see Hirsch and Macpherson (2005, 27).

generally, not only the minority who are union members. The main proponents of the federal Family and Medical Leave Act, for example, were unions with large female memberships (Dark 1999, 166); a decade later, unions were also the prime movers behind the passage of California's paid family leave program (Firestein and Dones, chap. 7 in this volume).

Even in its weakened state, then, the U.S. labor movement today is a leading advocate for the interests of women workers. Unions directly represent over 6.5 million women workers and have indirectly improved the situation of millions more. Kate Bronfenbrenner (2005, 442) goes so far as to claim that "labor unions are the only major U.S. institution equipped to help women overcome [discriminatory] barriers in the workplace." Organized labor's role in this arena has expanded over recent decades as struggles for gender equality have gained support throughout the wider society.

Yet, like other organizations and institutions, unions inevitably reflect the wider social arrangements in which they are embedded. Just as gender inequality has been a persistent feature of U.S. society, so too it has been a problem within the house of labor. Throughout most of U.S. history, not only were women a minority of union members, but they were almost never able to gain positions of union leadership. Many male unionists believed that women were "unorganizable," a view that often became a self-fulfilling prophecy. Union leaders tended to see women's issues as divisive, and the majority of union agendas neglected to include such concerns as gender inequality in pay, discrimination based on marital status or pregnancy, flexible working hours, child care, and the like.

At the discursive level, too, until very recently, unions were overtly male-dominated institutions. Labor iconography was laden with images of traditional masculinity—from hard hats to bulging muscles to cigars. This not only mirrored the material reality of male domination within the organized labor movement, but also diminished the likelihood that women workers would turn to unionism as a potential vehicle for their own empowerment.

The cultural construction of unionism as quintessentially male was never entirely accurate—women have always worked (both inside and outside the household), and from the earliest period they organized themselves into unions even when male labor leaders were indifferent to their concerns, as the scholarly literature in women's labor history has taken great pains to document. Yet women remained at the margins of organized labor.

All this began to change starting in the World War II years, and even more so during the 1960s and 1970s, as women's presence in the U.S. workforce expanded and paid employment became increasingly central to their economic well-being. In recent decades, not only the workforce but also union membership has become increasingly feminized; and although women's unionization rate still lags behind men's, the gender gap has narrowed substantially. Unprecedented numbers of women have moved into union leadership, even if they remain underrepresented relative to the female share of union membership. More and more labor leaders have come to recognize that women workers, far from being unorganizable, are more receptive than men (on the average) to unionization efforts. Attention to women's issues has also increased within labor's ranks, both in collective bargaining and in the legislative arena (Milkman 1985, 1993; Cobble 2004).

Progress has been especially rapid in the last decade, since the leadership of the American Federation of Labor–Congress of Industrial Organizations (AFL-CIO) took a progressive turn with the ascent of John Sweeney to the federation's presidency in 1995. Sweeney established a Working Women's Department within the AFL-CIO for the first time, and reconfigured its Executive Council in a deliberate effort to increase the numbers of women (as well as people of color) in leadership. In 2005, when the Change to Win (CTW) Federation, a new 6 million–member national union federation, was established, a woman was elected as its top officer (Anna Burger of the Service Employees International Union, SEIU). Apart from these changes at the national level, the number of women leaders in individual unions has also grown over recent decades (Cobble and Michal 2002, 235–37).

A closer look, however, reveals that the pace of change has been markedly uneven, in part because the U.S. labor movement has a highly decentralized structure. Some of the nation's largest unions are affiliated with neither the AFL-CIO nor CTW, and even those that are affiliated tend to jealously guard their autonomy. Thus, the Sweeney administration's call more than a decade ago for improving women's status in the labor movement has had limited effectiveness, and in both federations there is wide variation among unions in regard to gender matters.

Just as job segregation by sex continues to bifurcate the labor market, so too, male and female workers have sharply differentiated relationships to the U.S. labor movement today. Many individual unions are still extremely male-dominated in both membership and leadership, maintaining their traditional stance toward women and gender issues. At the other end of the spectrum, among the unions that have a substantial female membership, some have begun to seriously promote gender equality. In that sense, it is somewhat misleading to even speak of women and *the* labor movement.

Several factors shape the variations among unions in relation to women and gender. One, as I have argued elsewhere (Milkman 1990), involves the legacy of the past and, especially, the historical period in which particular unions first took shape. In general, newer unions whose historical formation occurred when women were a more substantial part of the workforce, and when notions of gender equality were more widely accepted, tend to be more woman-friendly.

However, this perspective is incomplete. A wave of union mergers over the past few decades has disrupted the historical continuity that once made the period of formation of many individual unions such a strong predictor of their relationship to women. And whereas some unions have undergone serious membership erosion in recent years, others have achieved significant expansion—typically not only leading to growth in the numbers of female members in their ranks but also opening up greater opportunities for leadership than exist in unions that are stagnating or shrinking in size.

Perhaps the single most often cited factor shaping the distinct gender regimes of individual unions is the gender composition of the membership, which is itself highly variable. Occupational segregation by sex, despite some diminution over recent decades, persists as a key axis of division within the labor market (see Lovell, Hartmann, and Werschkul, chap. 2 in this volume).

Less widely appreciated is the fact that sex segregation in the labor market has a large impact on the gender composition of many unions, especially those that are occupation-based. Some such unions represent overwhelmingly male constituencies—notably the building trades, the pilots, and the firefighters—which have correspondingly limited interest in women's issues. Other occupational unions have largely female constituencies—for example, the teachers' and nurses' unions—and they tend to be far more engaged in issues of special interest to women and supportive of gender equality.

Unions that are organized along industrial or sectoral rather than occupational lines also vary in their relationship to gender questions. The cohort of industrial unions that took shape in the 1910s in the textile and garment industries had a largely female membership but a paternalistic male leadership. By contrast, those that emerged in the late 1930s and 1940s in industries such as auto and steel, even though they had a more male-dominated workforce, embraced an antidiscrimination ideology from the start—an ideology that was primarily focused on racial divisions but that union women often seized on to promote gender equality (see Milkman 1990; Cobble 2004). Both these cohorts of industrial unions have been dramatically reduced in size since the 1970s with deindustrialization and outsourcing, which has limited their ability to respond to changing gender arrangements in the wider society.

By contrast, public-sector unions, which are among the few labor organizations that have grown substantially in recent years, along with those representing health care and service workers, have vast female memberships. These unions have emerged as strong advocates of gender equality and other specific concerns of women workers. During the 1980s, for example, public-sector unions took the lead in the struggle for pay equity. And, because this is the main growth sector within organized labor, leadership positions open up relatively frequently, so these are the unions in which women have made the greatest gains in the top ranks of union leadership.

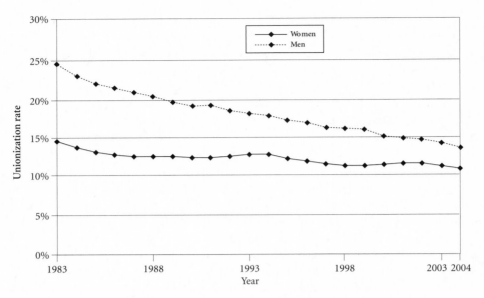

Figure 3.1 The declining gender gap in unionization rates, United States, 1983–2004.
Source: U.S. Department of Labor (2005, 81–82).

Union Membership Trends: Feminization and Segregation

With the dramatic influx of women into the workforce over recent decades, as well as changes in the distribution of unionization across occupations, industries, and economic sectors, the long-standing gender gap in union membership has narrowed substantially. As figure 3.1 shows, by 2004, 11.1 percent of all employed women were unionized, only slightly below the 13.8 percent figure for employed men.

Looking at the same data from another angle, the unmistakable trend is one of union feminization. As figure 3.2 shows, even as the nation's overall unionization rate has declined, the female share of union membership has expanded rapidly. In 2004, 43 percent of all the nation's union members were women—a record high, up from 34 percent only twenty years earlier, and just slightly below the 48 percent female share of the nation's wage and salary workforce.

Yet the feminization phenomenon masks another critical feature of the unionized workforce, namely that women union members are far more highly concentrated than their male counterparts in particular sectors, industries, and occupations. Thus in 2004, 60.8 percent of all unionized women were employed in the public sector (local, state, or federal government), com-

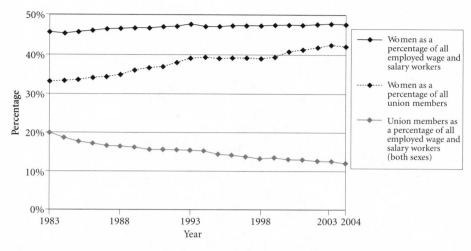

Figure 3.2 Feminization of the workforce and of union membership, and declining unionization, United States, 1983–2004.
Source: U.S. Department of Labor (2005, 81–82).

pared to only 36.7 percent of unionized men. Women are also more likely than men to be employed in the public sector (regardless of their union status): 19.1 percent of all female workers in the United States, compared with 13.5 percent of male workers, were employed in the public sector in 2004.

Only 5.4 percent of women employed in the private sector are unionized, compared to 10.1 percent of private-sector men; the disparity is similar in manufacturing—historically a union stronghold—where 8.3 percent of women are unionized, compared to 15.0 percent of men. By contrast, the gender gap in the public sector is much smaller (35.3 percent of women and 37.8 percent of men are unionized). Indeed, the growth of public-sector unionism is the key underlying trend driving the recent feminization of union membership.

Figure 3.3 shows the concentration of female union members across major industry groups in 2004. More than two-thirds of them (70.9 percent) are accounted for by only three industry groups—education, health care, and public administration.[2] By contrast, those three industry groups account for only 39.2 percent of the female wage and salary workforce (fig. 3.3). These are important and heavily female-employing industries, but as a comparison of the top and bottom pie charts in the figure 3.3 reveals, the importance of education and public administration in the world of female union membership is

[2] There is extensive overlap between female union membership in these three industry groups and in the public sector as a whole, in which (as previously noted) nearly two-thirds of unionized women are employed: 89.6 percent of female union members in education, 30.0 percent of those in health care, and 100 percent of those in public administration are public-sector employees.

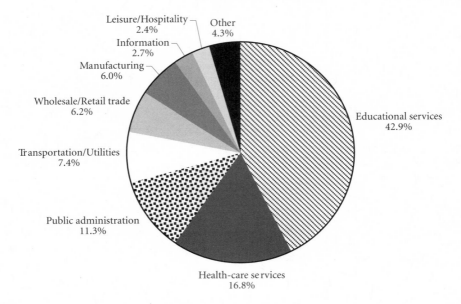

Female Union Members

Leisure/Hospitality
2.4%

Information
2.7%

Manufacturing
6.0%

Wholesale/Retail trade
6.2%

Transportation/Utilities
7.4%

Public administration
11.3%

Other
4.3%

Educational services
42.9%

Health-care services
16.8%

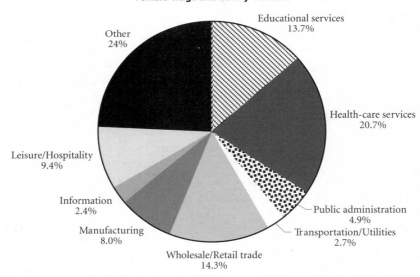

Female Wage and Salary Workers

Other
24%

Educational services
13.7%

Health-care services
20.7%

Leisure/Hospitality
9.4%

Information
2.4%

Manufacturing
8.0%

Wholesale/Retail trade
14.3%

Transportation/Utilities
2.7%

Public administration
4.9%

Figure 3.3 Female union members and female wage and salary workers, by major industry group, United States, 2004.

Source: Current Population Survey, Outgoing Rotation Group Earnings Files, 2004.

far greater than in the overall female workforce. (Health-care services, by contrast, actually account for a greater share of the female workforce than of female union members, as is also the case for other private-sector industries.)[3]

As figure 3.4 shows, the distribution of male union members across industry groups is far less concentrated, with 70.2 percent spread across five industry groups in 2004: manufacturing, transportation/utilities, public administration, construction, and education. These five industry groups accounted for only 30.9 percent of the male wage and salary workforce, again a far less concentrated distribution than that among female workers. Public administration actually accounted for a somewhat larger share of male than female union members (14.5 versus 11.3 percent). But whereas more than four out of every ten women union members were employed in education, that industry accounted for a relatively small share (12.4 percent) of male union members. By contrast, slightly over one-half (50.4 percent) of all male union members were in manufacturing, construction, and transportation/utilities—all predominantly private-sector industries that were the traditional strongholds of organized labor.[4]

Just as the world of work is highly sex-segregated, then, so too the world of unionism is sharply bifurcated into male and female segments. Today, the typical male union member is a private-sector blue-collar hardhat, whereas the typical female union member is a public-sector white-collar or professional worker employed in education, health care, or public administration. In some cases, male and female unionization overlap. Thus, as figure 3.3 shows, in 2004, transportation/utilities and manufacturing accounted for 7.4 and 6.0 percent of female union members, respectively (in contrast to construction, which accounted for less than 1 percent); similarly, as figure 3.4 shows, both public administration and education accounted for substantial shares of male union membership. But, on the whole, U.S. union membership is strongly gender-differentiated.

The industrial distribution of women union members also varies with race, ethnicity, and nativity, as figure 3.5 shows. In 2004, nearly one-half (49.2 percent) of white women union members were employed in education, a far higher proportion than for any nonwhite group. Although a relatively modest 25.7 percent of black women union members were found in education, an-

---

[3] The industry groups aggregated as "Other" in the bottom half of figure 3.3 are mainly poorly unionized but heavily female-employing fields such as financial services, which accounted for 8.7 percent of all female wage and salary workers in 2004; professional and business services, which accounted for another 8.5 percent; and "other services," which accounted for another 5.1 percent. "Other" also includes agriculture, mining, and construction, but these industry groups employed minuscule numbers of women.

[4] In the bottom half of figure 3.4, "Other" is primarily financial services, which accounted for 5.5 percent of male wage and salary workers in 2004; "other services," which accounted for another 4.0 percent; and the far smaller agriculture and mining industry groups.

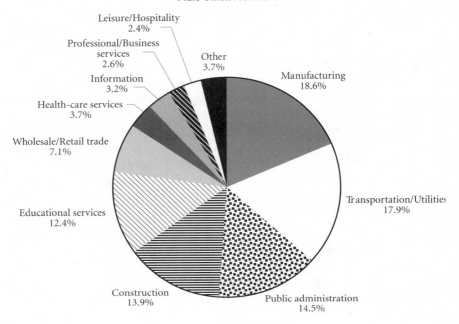

Male Union Members

- Leisure/Hospitality 2.4%
- Professional/Business services 2.6%
- Information 3.2%
- Health-care services 3.7%
- Wholesale/Retail trade 7.1%
- Educational services 12.4%
- Construction 13.9%
- Public administration 14.5%
- Transportation/Utilities 17.9%
- Manufacturing 18.6%
- Other 3.7%

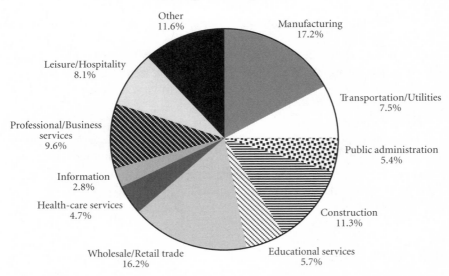

Male Wage and Salary Workers

- Other 11.6%
- Manufacturing 17.2%
- Transportation/Utilities 7.5%
- Public administration 5.4%
- Construction 11.3%
- Educational services 5.7%
- Wholesale/Retail trade 16.2%
- Health-care services 4.7%
- Information 2.8%
- Professional/Business services 9.6%
- Leisure/Hospitality 8.1%

Figure 3.4 Male union members and male wage and salary workers, by major industry group, United States, 2004.

Source: Current Population Survey, Outgoing Rotation Group Earnings Files, 2004.

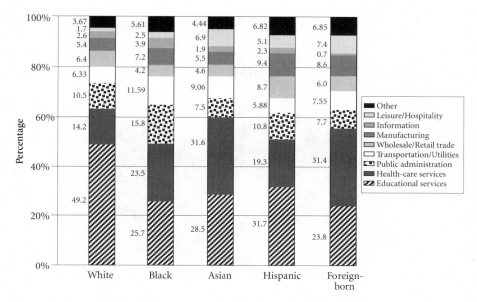

Figure 3.5 Women union members by race/ethnicity, nativity, and major industry group, United States, 2004.
Note: the categories White, Black, and Asian do not include Hispanics.
Source: Current Population Survey, Outgoing Rotation Group Earnings Files, 2004.

other 50.8 percent were in health care, public administration, and transportation/utilities; however, these three industry groups accounted for less than one-third of all unionized white women. Asian women union members also had a distinctive profile, with a relatively high concentration in health care, which accounted for nearly one-third (31.6 percent). Unionized Hispanic women were more evenly distributed across industries than the other groups shown; in their case, manufacturing accounted for a relatively large share of the total. Foreign-born women union members also had a distinctive profile.[5]

As we might expect, there are also differences in unionization rates for women of different races, ethnic groups, and between foreign- and native-born women, but these variations are relatively modest. In 2004, 10.9 percent of white women were unionized, compared to 13.6 percent of black women, 11.1 percent of Asian women, and 9.9 percent of Hispanic women; in that year, 9.7 percent of foreign-born women and 11.3 percent of native-born women were union members.

National data are not available on the distribution of women and men across individual unions, but such data do exist for California, the nation's most populous state, for 2001–2002. These are shown in figure 3.6. They once

[5] The industrial distribution of male union members also varies with race, ethnicity, and nativity, although those variations are not documented here.

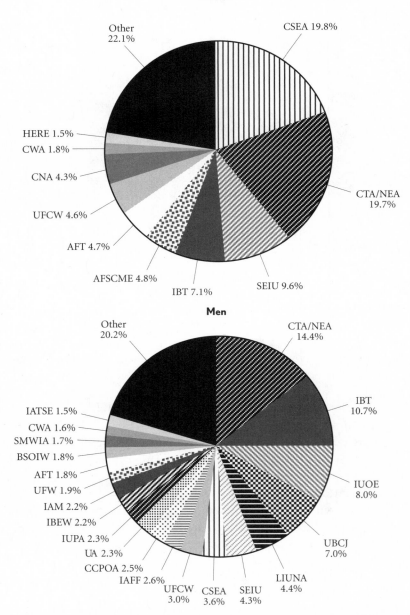

Women

Other 22.1%

CSEA 19.8%

CTA/NEA 19.7%

SEIU 9.6%

IBT 7.1%

AFSCME 4.8%

AFT 4.7%

UFCW 4.6%

CNA 4.3%

CWA 1.8%

HERE 1.5%

Men

Other 20.2%

CTA/NEA 14.4%

IBT 10.7%

IUOE 8.0%

UBCJ 7.0%

LIUNA 4.4%

SEIU 4.3%

CSEA 3.6%

UFCW 3.0%

IAFF 2.6%

CCPOA 2.5%

UA 2.3%

IUPA 2.3%

IBEW 2.2%

IAM 2.2%

UFW 1.9%

AFT 1.8%

BSOIW 1.8%

SMWIA 1.7%

CWA 1.6%

IATSE 1.5%

Figure 3.6 Union members, by gender and international union, California, 2001–2002.
Source: California Union Census (Milkman and Rooks 2003, 19).

again expose the high degree of gender differentiation among union members. Women are concentrated in a relatively small number of public-sector unions; the California School Employees Association (CSEA), the California Teachers Association/National Education Association (CTA/NEA), the American Federation of State, County and Municipal Employees (AFSCME), and the American Federation of Teachers (AFT) alone accounted for about one-half of all unionized women in the state, and this does not include the substantial public-sector membership of SEIU, the California Nurses Association (CNA), the Communications Workers of America (CWA), and others. Overall, 61.9 percent of the state's female union members were found in public-sector unions in 2001–2002, and another 13.8 percent were in mixed unions that included both public- and private-sector workers. By contrast, 36.5 percent of California's male union members were in public-sector unions and another 20.9 percent in mixed unions (Milkman and Rooks 2003, 18).

As figure 3.6 also shows, the unions now affiliated with CTW accounted for about one-fifth of California's female union members in 2001–2002,[6] and an even larger share (more than one-third) were in independent unions, which remain unaffiliated with either of the nation's large labor federations. CTW unions accounted at that time for nearly one-third of the state's male union members (fig. 3.6), of whom just under one-fifth were in independents. California's male members were dispersed over a far larger number of unions than were their female counterparts in 2001–2002. Some large unions—the CTA/NEA, SEIU, International Brotherhood of Teamsters (IBT), and United Food and Commercial Workers International Union (UFCW)—accounted for large shares of both male and female union members, but apart from that the distributions were highly gendered. It is striking that among the six unions that accounted for the largest share of the state's male union members, three are building trades unions (the International Union of Operating Engineers, IUOE; the United Brotherhood of Carpenters and Joiners of America, UBCJ; and the Laborers' International Union of North America, LIUNA), whereas a tiny proportion of the state's women union members were in those unions (1.1 percent, 0.6 percent, and 1.1 percent, respectively) in 2001–2002. Nearly one-third (30.1 percent) of all male union members in California at that time were in the building trades, compared to only 2.9 percent of women union members. And if we consider only the private sector, the building trades' share

---

[6] The CTW unions shown include SEIU, the United Needle Trades, Industrial and Textile Employees (UNITE), the Hotel and Restaurant Employees (HERE), the International Brotherhood of Teamsters (IBT), the United Brotherhood of Carpenters and Joiners (UBCJ), the Laborers International Union of North America (LIUNA), the United Food and Commercial Workers (UFCW), and the United Farm Workers (UFW). Since these data were collected, UNITE and HERE have merged into one union, called UNITE HERE.

of male union membership was nearly one-half (46.7 percent) of the state's male union members (Milkman and Rooks 2003, 18).

Gender and Organizability

Demographic variations in unionization rates are sometimes read as a gauge of the degree to which various categories of workers are interested in becoming part of the organized labor movement. However, this can be highly misleading. In the United States, where the workforce remains highly segmented by gender as well as race, ethnicity, and nativity, the main determinant of unionization rates for any given population group is the extent to which a given sector, industry, or occupation in which the group is concentrated has been successfully organized at some point in the past. As the disparities between the top and bottom portions of figures 3.3 and 3.4 suggest, the development of unionism has been extremely uneven. That unevenness is itself an artifact of the U.S. industrial relations system, which since 1935 has been based not on individual decisions about union affiliation but, instead, on a winner-take-all electoral process that leads to the unionization (or not) of entire workplaces. Given the limited amount of recent organizing, in most cases the main determinant of whether a given individual is a union member is where she or he happens to be employed and whether that workplace became (and remained) unionized at some previous time—regardless of that individual's pro- or anti-union sympathies.[7] Similarly, unionization rates by gender, race, nativity, and so on reveal little about the preferences of any particular category of workers.

Figure 3.7, which shows unionization rates and employment distribution separately for the highly unionized public sector and the largely nonunion private sector for a variety of demographic groups, suggests the underlying dynamic. The U.S. public sector is far more highly unionized than the private sector, not because public-sector workers are more pro-union (although they may be, because the experience of unionization itself tends to foster more positive attitudes toward unionism, all else being equal) but because there is generally less resistance to union activity when the employer is the federal, state, or local government than when it is a private-sector company.

As figure 3.7 shows, regardless of gender, race, ethnicity, or nativity, public-sector workers are far more extensively unionized than their private-sector counterparts. For example, although few Hispanic immigrants (of either sex)

---

[7] Of course, at the time of initial organization, the relative proclivities of particular groups toward unionism—along with many other factors—can and do matter.

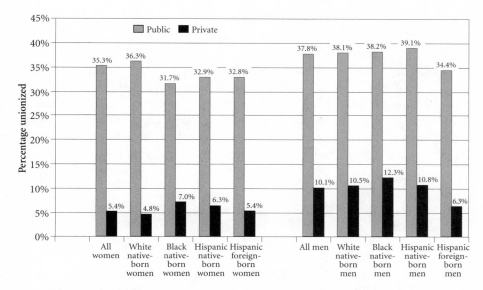

Figure 3.7 Unionization rates by sector for selected demographic groups, United States, 2004.
Source: Current Population Survey, Outgoing Rotation Group Earnings Files, 2004.

are employed in the public sector, among the few who are the unionization rate is similar to the public-sector rates of other demographic groups.

Male unionization rates are higher than those of women in both the public and private sector, as figure 3.7 shows, but that is not because men are more pro-union than women. Indeed, the available evidence (albeit fragmentary), suggests that precisely the opposite is true. Survey after survey finds that women have more positive attitudes toward unionism in particular, and toward collective approaches to workplace problem solving generally, than do men. Women also are more likely than men to state that they would vote for union representation in their own workplace, given the opportunity (see Freeman and Rogers 1999; Hart Research Associates 1998). The attitudinal data, in short, indicate that, at least in recent years (comparable data are not available for earlier decades), women are in fact more "organizable" than their male counterparts, contrary to the traditional stereotypes.

Further evidence regarding women's greater receptivity to unionism emerges from data on actual organizing campaigns. Women have accounted for the majority of new workers organized each year in the United States since at least the mid-1980s, as Kate Bronfenbrenner has shown. Her research also demonstrates that unions are significantly more likely to win representation elections in private-sector workplace units in which women make up the majority of the workforce than in gender-mixed or male-dominated units; the probability of winning is even higher in units in which women of color are the predominant group (Bronfenbrenner 2005; see also Milkman 1993). There are no systematic data of this kind available on public-sector organizing outcomes, but women make up the majority of workers in such recent high-profile organizing victories as those among home care and child-care workers. Yet the focus of most such recruitment drives today is not on gender issues as much as on low-wage work (and, in some cases, ethnic minority and/or immigration status); it is because of women's persistent concentration in low-wage work that they have disproportionately benefited from these recent successes.

Women and Union Leadership

One important factor that contributes to success in organizing women is having a female presence on union organizing staffs. Bronfenbrenner's research shows that the proportion of women among lead union organizers has increased over time, from about 12 percent of all sampled representation election campaigns in the late 1980s to 21 percent sampled at the end of the century. Significantly, in the more recent sample, among campaigns in which the workplaces involved had a predominantly female workforce, 42 percent were led by female organizers. As this research also shows, having women as lead organizers is associated with higher union win rates in representation elections (Bronfenbrenner 2005).

Organizers are on the front lines of labor's current efforts to survive and grow, but they are among the least powerful members of union staffs and elected leaderships. Men continue to dominate top union leadership posts throughout the labor movement, and in those unions whose memberships are overwhelmingly male, women leaders are few and far between. But in unions in which females make up the bulk of the membership, there has been considerable growth in the number of women among high-level union leaders.

Table 3.1 shows the relevant data for 1978 and 2000 for a selection of labor unions with the largest numbers of female members. In almost every case, the ratio of the female proportion of top leaders to the female proportion of members grew over this period—in several cases from a single-digit base or from zero! Although the individual unions vary greatly, and in no case does the female proportion of leaders equal the female proportion of union members, the representation of women among top leaders (union officers and executive board members) has increased dramatically over time in all these unions. Even in cases in which membership has declined, there is a steady advance in the representation of women at the top level of these unions, all of which have large female memberships. Although there is no systematic source

TABLE 3.1
Female membership and leadership in selected U.S. labor unions, 1978 and 2000

Labor union	Year	Female members		Female leaders	
		Number	Percentage	Top leaders (%)[a]	Number/percentage of female members (ratio)
AFSCME	1978	408,000	40	3	8
	2000	728,000	52	38	73
AFT	1978	300,000	60	25	42
	2000	600,000	60	39	65
SEIU	1978	312,000	50	15	30
	2000	650,000	50	32	64
NEA	1978	1,240,000	75	55	73
	2000	1,500,000	61	33	54
UNITE[b]	1978	610,000	72	11	15
	2000	330,000	66	30	45
HERE	1978	181,000	42	4	10
	2000	185,000	48	18	38
CWA	1978	259,000	51	0	0
	2000	320,000	51	12	24
UFCW	1978	480,000	39	3	8
	2000	700,000	50	11	22
IBT	1978	481,000	25	0	0
	2000	450,000	30	4	13

Source: Cobble and Michal (2002) and author's computations.

[a] Top leaders are union officers and executive board members.

[b] In 1978, UNITE was made up two separate entities: the International Ladies' Garment Workers Union (ILGWU) and the Amalgamated Clothing, Textile and Garment Workers Union (ACTWU). They merged in 1995 to form UNITE. The 1978 data entries merge and (in the rightmost three columns) are a weighted average of the figures for the ILGWU and ACTWU.

of data on this topic for the unions with predominantly male memberships, women are seldom found among the top leaders in those organizations. Thus, in leadership as in membership, the labor movement is bifurcated along gender lines, into two worlds of unionism.

Among the unions shown in table 3.1, only three remain affiliated with the AFL-CIO. The nation's largest union, with a majority female membership, the NEA, has long been an independent union, and in the summer of 2005 SEIU, UNITE HERE (the product of a merger between the Union of Needletrades, Industrial and Textile Employees, UNITE, and the Hotel Employees and Restaurant Employees Union, HERE, that took place in 2004), the UFCW and IBT disaffiliated and became part of the new CTW Federation (along with the

United Farm Workers of America, UFW, and the much more male-dominated carpenters' and laborers' unions). Some key heavily female public-sector unions—notably the AFSCME and AFT—however, remain within the AFL-CIO. As previously noted, CTW is now headed by Anna Burger, the first woman to lead a national labor federation in U.S. history.

• • •

Women's share of union membership and leadership has increased over the past few decades, and that trend is likely to continue. Women are dispropor-tionately employed in the public sector and in health care, which are among the few growth sectors for unionism. The fact that women seem to be some-what more positive than men in their view of organized labor, and more re-ceptive to unionization opportunities as well, only reinforces that prediction. Moreover, the language and iconography of labor is far less male-dominated than it once was, at least in the unions with substantial female membership. And women have a particularly visible presence in the few growing sectors of the organized labor movement. These changes are all the more impressive in the context of the broader challenges organized labor has faced in recent years as it struggles to survive in an extremely hostile political environment, facing employers who are intransigently opposed to unionism.

Yet organized labor in the United States continues to be made up of a highly segmented set of institutions. The long tradition of granting autonomy to individual unions, combined with the continuing reality of occupational segregation by sex in the labor market, has meant that the world of women's unionism is still largely institutionally separated from that of men. As labor struggles to reorient and remake itself in the twenty-first century, this is among the many challenges it will face.

4

THE LESBIAN, GAY, BISEXUAL, AND TRANSGENDER CHALLENGE TO AMERICAN LABOR

Gerald Hunt and Monica Bielski Boris

Pride at Work (PAW) is the official labor organization for lesbian, gay, bisexual, and transgendered (LGBT) Americans. It began in 1992, and was officially recognized as a constituency group of the American Federation of Labor–Congress of Industrial Organizations (AFL-CIO) in August 1997. By April 2005, there were sixteen chapters and nine other chapters in the process of being formed. The PAW website states that its mission is to "work within the labor movement to foster better understanding of the needs of LGBT union members."[1]

What do these developments speak to? Did the creation of a PAW constituency within the nation's foremost labor organization underscore broader developments and trends? Is the battle to fight discrimination based on sexual orientation now part of labor's mandate? In this chapter, we consider these questions using the inauguration of PAW in 1997 as the baseline for a chronological discussion. We examine labor's historical record on LGBT issues and assess recent developments, relying on a survey and interviews conducted with the thirteen largest U.S. unions between 1999 and 2004. We argue that U.S. labor's engagement with queer identities is a mixed message because there is much that is contradictory in the story we have to tell. We offer stories of surprisingly early acceptance by some unions, stories of unions that have fought just as hard for their LGBT constituents as for other oppressed groups,

---

[1] Pride at Work, http://www.prideatwork.org/story.html (accessed May 25, 2005).

and stories of unions that remain completely dissociated from issues of discrimination and harassment based on sexual orientation. We conclude that U.S. labor cannot claim to be a world leader on LGBT issues, even though some individual unions and locals are forceful advocates for sexual minorities.

Thunderstorms of Prejudice with the Odd Ray of Sunshine—Pre-1960

In their insightful book *Boots of Leather, Slippers of Gold*, Elizabeth Kennedy and Madeline Davis (1994) provide an account of the emergence of a working-class lesbian community in Buffalo from the mid-1930s to the 1960s. They offer a portrait of women who confronted incredible violence and hatred but who grew and prospered as a community in spite of it. Similarly, Marc Stein's (2000) tale of early gay and lesbian life in Philadelphia, Jonathan Katz's (1992) *Gay American History*, and John D'Emilio's (1998, 2002) accounts of early gay experiences also offer moving testament to the oppression and hostility endured by sexual minorities before the 1960s and the amazing resilience they showed. In all these histories, there are accounts of undercover surveillance and routine police busts of LGBT gathering places, jail sentences for homosexual acts (which were illegal in all states), beatings and bashings by the police and ruffians (mostly unreported), and a lack of legal recourse for blatant employment discrimination.

There is scant evidence to suggest that labor made any attempt to confront or question the violence, discrimination, and harassment experienced by sexual minorities in the workplace or elsewhere before the 1960s.[2] There are almost no accounts of unions offering a safe space for LGBT people or being prepared to fight on their behalf. Many unions were thought to be homophobic, and stories are told of bullying when a brother or sister dared challenge highly scripted gender or sexual identity norms (Kennedy and Davis 1994). For most LGBT workers, being a union member seemed to make no difference to their dignity or personal safety at work. In some cases, being unionized may have made the work experience even worse because unions helped to perpetuate a conspiracy of silence whereby member-on-member violence and harassment went unreported to management or the authorities and, even if reported, might be thought by authorities as the proper way to deal with fags and dykes.

The story of Harry Hay epitomizes the contradictions of the 1940s and 50s. Hay is held in high esteem as an early gay rights champion who started out as an employee and secret union organizer at Macy's in 1940s New York (Bain

---

[2] The arguments made in this section are derived from Adam, Duyvendak, and Krouwel (1999); Krupat (1999); Krupat and McCreery (2001); Osborne (1997).

1999).[3] Taken separately, either Hay's union activities or his homosexuality would have been grounds for Macy's to fire him. By the same token, his union might well have expelled him for being gay had it found out and would have been most unlikely to support him in a wrongful dismissal case against his employer. Equally contradictory, Macy's would have dismissed him if it had known he was a communist sympathizer, and the American Communist Party would have kicked him out if it had learned he was gay. Hay helped form one of the earliest gay rights organizations, called the Mattachine Society; all five founding members were communist sympathizers and union organizers, and all felt they could not be open in their union, their political party, or their workplace. Hay was ultimately marginalized by the Mattachine Society because his communist beliefs were thought too extreme and thus too great a liability once the terrorism of the McCarthy period took hold.

But history is seldom linear, and there are exceptional sidebars to the intersection of labor and the nascent gay rights movement of early to mid-twentieth-century America. One important story involves the Marine Cooks and Stewards Union (MCSU), which represented the men who cooked, cleaned, and served on the big passenger liners sailing the Pacific from the 1930s to the 1950s. Historian Allan Berubé has carefully pieced together the union's surprisingly early engagement with gay men (Berubé 1997; Bain 1999).[4] The MCSU was founded in 1901 by white men who were trying to prevent Chinese men from working on passenger ships; thus, its beginnings were overtly racist. These attitudes began to change in the 1930s when the union became more and more informed by its communist members, who supported and encouraged militant action such as the 1934 San Francisco General Strike. The union realized that employers would bust strikes by hiring disenfranchised minorities and that solidarity with racial minorities was a better and more likely-to-win option. This shift in perspective also helped to pry open the closet door for the large number of gay men who were members of the union, and from the mid-1930s the MCSU became noted for the presence of openly gay men in its ranks and leadership positions. This was probably a first for a labor organization anywhere in the world. Berubé notes that by the late 1930s the union was being dismissed by its critics as "red, black, and queer," but flew a big sign in its meeting hall that proclaimed "race-bating, red-bating, and queer-bating is anti-union" as visible evidence of its goal of solidarity through diversity. When ships were superseded by air travel in the 1950s, many of the men settled in San Francisco and opened the stores, bars, and restaurants that helped to establish that city as America's "gay capi-

---

[3] *Wisconsin Gay News*, http://www.instepnews.com/harryhaydead.html (accessed May 25, 2005).
[4] See also, Susan Styker, "Marine Cooks and Steward Union," 2005, PlanetOut, History, http://www.planetout.com/news/history/aahist/marine.html (accessed May 25, 2005).

tal" (Boyd 2003). This confluence of events also helped to position San Francisco as a critical center for some of the subsequent labor-gay alliances we discuss next.

The Seeds of Change Are Sown—the 1960s

As the 1960s unfolded, there was a lack of any kind of employment protection for gays and lesbians who were "out," and statutes criminalizing homosexual activity were widespread. The 1960s were the lead-in to a more liberal and progressive United States, however, and this had a profound impact on labor and on gay rights. Anti–Vietnam War sentiment and the decline of McCarthyism combined with the increasing number of women in the labor force, improved access to birth control, the expansion of alternative media outlets, the growing discontent of African Americans, and increased economic prosperity, all helped fertilize a resurgence in activism. A revitalized civil rights movement along with reenergized social movements based on feminism, gay rights, environmentalism, and peace, all began to expand and take aim at the political and social agendas of the country and its established institutions.

A rise in public- and service-sector unionism (teachers and health-care workers in particular) brought more women to labor's table during the 1960s. The Service Employees International Union (SEIU), for example, grew dramatically during this period. As Ruth Milkman (1985, 1993, 2005) notes, the shifts in labor's demographics that were taking root in the 1960s and that intensified during the 1970s helped to feminize the labor movement because the growth in unions occurred primarily in occupations dominated by women, and they acted as a catalyst to reformulate labor issues during a period of feminist resurgence.

The entry of more and more feminists into the labor movement brought to the foreground labor's lack of attention, first, to women's issues and, subsequently, to a larger set of diversity issues (Cobble 2004; Hunt and Rayside 2000). Women started to argue that many of the issues they cared about, such as maternity leave, child-care provisions, sexual harassment, and pay equity, were not being taken up by unions. Blacks and other racial minorities were also feeling a new sense of empowerment and became more vocal in their demands that unions represent their interests. At this time, employment-based discrimination was beginning to move toward the top of the gay rights agenda. Consequently, by the end of the 1960s, more than at any other time in their history, unions were being challenged by their own members to change.

Still, throughout this period, U.S. labor remained preoccupied by the concerns of men, whose interests were equated with class interests. Issues related to women and minorities, to the degree they were being articulated, tended to be seen as sectional concerns with the potential to create disunity and undermine the main goals. Thus, men with traditional views of labor and diversity continued to set the priorities and govern institutional procedures. But the seeds of change had been sown. More and more union members, especially women but also gay men and lesbians, felt they were not being adequately recognized, represented, or accommodated and were sufficiently emboldened to make their views known.[5] Bain (1999) tells the tale of union support in the mid-1960s for the right of a transgendered man at Macy's in San Francisco to wear lipstick after women had gained the right to wear pants. The union subsequently supported the man's right to wear dresses, but failed in its effort to have his sex-change operation covered by the union's health plan. However, such stories are told as exceptions; throughout the 1960s, labor remained generally indifferent to the strengthening gay and lesbian rights movement. But this was about to change.

The Dawning of Gay and Lesbian Labor Activism—the 1970s

The labor movement feminized more rapidly in the 1970s than in any other decade (Cobble and Michal 2002). The growth in public-sector unionism among female-majority occupations escalated, and many of these new entrants brought a tradition of feminist activism with them (Milkman 2005; Cobble 2005). Having more female members in unions also helped to create a membership base more open to issues of sexual diversity because women more frequently than men tended to support antidiscrimination initiatives for lesbians and gay men.

The repressive environment of the 1950s and the liberating environment of the 1960s cultivated a more activist gay and lesbian rights movement. By the 1970s, this activism was increasingly geared toward workplace discrimination. Early homophile groups such as the Mattachine Society, One Inc., and the Daughters of Bilitis had highlighted employment discrimination through their public demonstrations and publications, but with little recognition from society at large (D'Emilio 1998). As a measure of the severity of occupational discrimination, at the time of the New York Stonewall riots in 1969, gays and lesbians were specifically barred from employment in the civil service, most government agencies, the military, and teaching. There were no protections from employment discrimination in any U.S. jurisdiction, and employers could proscribe potential workers with impunity.

---

[5] For an elaboration of the points made in this section see Munroe (1999); McBride (2001); Cobble and Michal (2002).

Gay and lesbian teachers were among the first to push their unions to fight repressive employment norms because they were at great risk of being fired if they came out (Bielski 2005; Bain 1999; Frank 1999). The California Federation of Teachers passed a resolution in 1969 to end discrimination against gay and lesbian teachers, and in 1973, at its national convention, the American Federation of Teachers (AFT) passed a similar resolution to work for the repeal of state and local laws restricting the behavior of gay and lesbian teachers in their privates lives. That same year, the National Education Association (NEA) added sexual orientation to its union constitution's nondiscrimination clause. Building on these initiatives, gay and lesbian teachers' associations and groups sprung up in New York, Boston, San Francisco, and Los Angeles. In 1974, the United Federation of Teachers, the largest local of the AFT, located in New York, formed one of the first gay and lesbian labor caucuses, the Gay Teachers Alliance. Another group, the Bay Area Gay Liberation and Gay Teacher's Caucus formed in 1975, and it felt sufficiently empowered to picket the California Board of Education. Still, as a measure of the hostility teachers faced even within their unions, the Gay Teachers Association of New York had to lobby for three years before its members were allowed to place an advertisement announcing their group in the New York State United Teachers Association newsletter (Bain 1999).

One of the most influential and important alliances at this time involved the International Brotherhood of Teamsters (IBT) on the West Coast. In San Francisco, the Coors Brewing Company had been administering lie detector tests to potential workers, asking about their sexual orientation and their attitudes to unions. Harvey Milk, a prominent gay rights activist in the city, helped to organize a boycott of Coors beer in gay bars, and in return the IBT pledged to support a gay rights ordinance for San Francisco, as well as Milk's (successful) attempt to win a seat on the city's Board of Supervisors. The boycott proved to be quite effective. Coors's share of the California beer market dropped from 43 to 14 percent, and the boycott spread to other locations across the country (Bain 1999; Shilts 1982). Building on this success, Milk helped to pull together in 1978 a labor-queer alliance that included the AFT, the California State Federation of Labor, the IBT, and unions covering auto workers and steelworkers to fight the Briggs initiative, which was designed to expunge gay and lesbian teachers from the education system throughout California. Gay and lesbian teachers were fighting similar proposals in other cities such as Miami, but nowhere was labor support as strong as in California. Even though these sorts of initiatives were isolated, they did help to heighten awareness of workplace discrimination based on sexual orientation and the role that labor could play in defeating it. Harvey Milk was murdered in November 1978 by an anti-gay fellow supervisor who had become unhinged, in part, because of rising tolerance for homosexuals in his city. This event brought even further national attention and sympathy to the issues Milk had been championing (Shilts 1982).

In many ways, the pioneering role of teacher's unions in confronting gay and lesbian issues throughout the 1970s has not been sufficiently recognized. The level of attacks on teachers during this period, with initiatives such as Briggs, brought to the foreground the severity of discrimination facing teachers who dared to be "out" and highlighted the degree to which opponents were prepared to make use of false linkages, such as those between child abuse and gay men. The blatancy, falseness, and vitriolic nature of attacks on teachers helped to spur early organizing, and the fact that teacher's unions tended to be female majority, influenced by second-wave feminism, also contributed to their openness.

We're Here, We're Queer; We Belong to Unions; and We're Not Going Away!—the 1980s

Buoyed by the glimmers of success in the 1970s, increasing numbers of activists inside and outside the labor movement upped the volume on demands that labor oppose and fight sexual orientation discrimination within its own ranks and in society generally. The 1970s had been a decade of isolated but crucial victories, and by the 1980s activists had acquired more leverage and begun a decade of intensive organization and mobilization inside the labor movement. Activists challenged labor to confront its own biases and prejudices and to make good on its rhetoric of solidarity. The focus during this period was on self-organizing by gays and lesbians inside their own unions to build alliances and gain support. At the same time, gay and lesbian groups outside labor also began to exert pressure on unions to acknowledge and actively fight to end employment discrimination based on sexual orientation. During this period, a growing number of companies, public-sector organizations, and municipalities began to ban sexual orientation discrimination, putting even more pressure on labor to keep pace with progressive developments. Berkeley, Urbana, Austin, and Amherst were among the cities that had outlawed workplace discrimination by the early 1980s, and in 1982 Wisconsin became the first state to pass such a law. IBM and AT&T were the first major companies to add sexual orientation to nondiscrimination policies, and Lotus is noted as the first large private-sector company to include same-sex partners in its benefit packages in 1991. The emergence of AIDS also helped to expose discrimination and highlighted the necessity of obtaining health benefits from employers.

Inside unions, more and more people decided to come out and put a human face on the discrimination they experienced. Women had been the first to challenge union orthodoxy, and activists concerned with sexuality issues were able to benefit from the change in attitudes, policies, and structures that women had achieved. Sexual minority activists borrowed from the strategies that had been deployed by feminists, in particular by forming separate support groups. These caucuses became an organizing base where they could gain self-confidence, build political strength, and determine strategies, just as such forums had been for a previous generation of women activists. One of the earliest of these workers' groups, at the *Village Voice* in New York, negotiated in 1982 what might be the first same-sex spousal benefits package in a U.S. collective agreement (Frank 1999).

Miriam Frank (1999) and Christian Bain (1999) track the rise of caucuses in the 1980s. Frank notes that these caucuses often began as informal groups of friends, especially among women, who came together at conferences, both for social support and political strategizing. One of the earliest union-based caucuses to form was at the American Federation of State, County, and Municipal Employees union (AFSCME). This group celebrated a victory when in 1980 it became the first large nonteachers' union to amend its constitution to prohibit discrimination based on sexual orientation. Then, at the AFSCME convention in 1982, delegates passed a resolution to endorse the passage of legislation at all levels that would extend protection from employment discrimination to sexual minorities. At about the same time, a caucus was formed at another large union, the SEIU. This caucus was able to get sexual orientation into the union's definition of diversity in 1984. As well, during the 1980s, the SEIU passed two resolutions that professed the union's support for gay rights legislation and the extension of spousal benefits to same-sex partners and cohabiting, unmarried heterosexual couples. These developments, in turn, helped activists at the local level. In 1987, for example, an Oregon local of SEIU became one of the first unions to get sexual orientation protections into its contract language. Empowered by the successes at AFSCME and SEIU, activists began to pressure regional and national labor organizations to take a stand. In 1982, the Industrial Union Department (IUD) of the AFL-CIO, an amalgam of over thirty unions, including the auto and steelworkers, passed a resolution to protect gays and lesbians. And then, in 1983, the AFL-CIO itself adopted a resolution recommending that legislation be enacted at the federal level to protect sexual minorities in relation to housing, employment, accommodation, and government services. It also passed a motion urging the government to invest in AIDS research and treatment (Sweeney 1999).

By the end of the 1980s, self-organizing had intensified and gay and lesbian caucuses were becoming visible in more and more unions. Increasingly, these groups began to incorporate issues raised by bisexuals. Groups formed not only within individual unions and locals but across unions at the regional and state levels. By the decade's end, there was a major lesbian and gay labor alliance in San Francisco, an organization that had members from many different unions within the Bay Area. Regional gay/lesbian labor organizations had been established in centers such as Boston and New York (Roberts 1993). Boston's Gay and Lesbian Labor Activists' Network was founded by state and health-care workers and pushed its unions to fight for antidiscriminatory measures and benefit packages, and the Lesbian and Gay Issues Committee had formed at District Council 37 of AFSCME in the New York area (Frank 1999).

Frank (1999) argues that the spread of gay and lesbian union caucuses throughout the 1980s was a pivotal development and played a vital role in advancing gay and lesbian concerns within unions. Her analysis highlights the fact that these groups fought for sexual orientation nondiscrimination clauses in union constitutions and collective bargaining agreements, pushed for equality in benefit packages and leave provisions, and helped convince union leaders to mobilize against antigay political campaigns.

It was also during this period that the nomenclature *domestic partner benefits* became an important part of the strategic fight for equalizing benefits (Holcomb 1999). *Domestic partner* was the term activists coined to refer to the committed partner of a same *or* opposite sex employee, thus removing the requirement of marriage. Activists argued that, although a heterosexual couple could marry, the members should not be discriminated against if they choose not to marry, and in the process this argument made the fight for equal benefits relevant and attractive to a broader constituency.

Visible Progress—the 1990s

Throughout the 1990s, activists built on the momentum of the 1980s. They continued to push labor to be a visible and committed player in the gay, lesbian, and bisexual rights movement and increasingly included transgender issues in their demands. The dominant form of action continued to be grassroots pressure by seasoned veterans from caucuses that were now union-, city-, or state-based. And by the end of the decade, a nationally based forum was also securely in place. More than ever, during this decade, activists pushed their unions to take a more energetic role in the public arena in fighting the growing momentum of conservative, right-wing, often religious-based, antigay activists. In this way, a number of unions were convinced to support a boycott of the state of Colorado after it passed an amendment forbidding the enactment of laws against antigay discrimination in the early 1990s. Activists were able to rally union support for boycotts of Cracker Barrel Old Country Stores when the company began to search out and then discharge gays and lesbians. In 1990, activists successfully pressured the AFL-CIO president to make an official statement that union members with HIV/AIDS had the right to continue working. Moreover, increasing numbers of union locals were urged to seek protections and benefits for sexual minorities at the bargaining table. Pushed by its lesbian and gay committee, AFSCME District Council 37, for example, was instrumental in the 1992–1993 drive to achieve domestic partner benefits for New York City municipal workers. Noteworthy as well, after pressure by activists, the United Auto Workers (UAW) was persuaded to include sexual orientation in its nondiscrimination clause in 1993.

At the 1987 National Gay Pride March in Washington, D.C., the AFL-CIO had sponsored a reception at its headquarters for LGBT union activists. Activists came from cities throughout the United States, and this reception provided them with an opportunity to celebrate what had been achieved, meet one another, and learn about the work of others. Subsequently, LGBT labor activists began meeting throughout the Northeast to plan a strategy session scheduled for the day after the 1992 Gay Pride March. Word got out, and hundreds of activists and unionists from various cities and unions attended the meeting held at the SEIU headquarters in Washington. Those in attendance agreed there was a pressing need for a national gay labor organization (Osborne 1997; Bain 1999; Holcomb and Wohlforth 2001). Following this, in autumn 1992, activists interested in forming a national organization held a cross-union steering committee meeting for a group they called Pride at Work.[6] Then, in 1993, in conjunction with the twenty-fourth anniversary of the Stonewall Riots of 1969, a founding convention was held for the newly minted PAW organization. As a result of these developments, the biggest event of the decade, and certainly the most visible, occurred—the creation of a national queer-labor group. And by 1997, PAW had convinced the AFL-CIO to recognize it as an official constituency group (Holcomb and Wohlforth 2001).

The 1990s also witnessed a rise in transgender activism in general and in the workplace in particular. Individuals who challenged gender norms regarding dress, cosmetics, and behaviors, if anything, had been even more despised historically than homosexuals. Even within the gay, lesbian, and bisexual rights movement, people who confronted gender norms too severely tended to be marginalized. However, as more and more transgendered people started to assert their right to live and work openly with dignity and compassion as gender nonconformists, others, including union advocates, were forced to take note and see the linkages. In 2000, PAW officially expanded its mandate to encompass transgender concerns in areas such as sexual-reassignment surgical coverage in health benefit packages and workplace accommodations. In August 2004, a PAW transgender caucus was formed to provide additional support.

[6] Hareen Chernow (co-vice president of Pride at Work and Education and Training Director for the Massachusetts AFL-CIO), telephone interview with Monica Bielski, February 7, 2000; T. Santora (co-president of Pride at Work and CWA legislative representative), telephone interview with Monica Bielski, November 15, 2000.

The Post–Pride at Work Period—1997 Onward

The official recognition of the PAW group by the AFL-CIO represented an important milestone for LGBT labor activists. It spoke to a growing commitment within some of the largest unions in the country to confront and tackle sexual orientation discrimination. At the same time, it highlighted the fact that not all unions were on board. Nearly a decade has passed since the official inauguration of PAW. What has happened since then? Do more unions, especially those in the trades and construction, now support LGBT rights? Which unions have been responsive to LGBT issues and why?

To explore these questions, we rely on surveys and interviews conducted by Bielski (2005) between 1999 and 2004. First she surveyed thirteen of the largest U.S. unions to determine whether they had taken action on six key points:

- a nondiscrimination clause in the union's constitution that includes sexual orientation;
- an LGBT caucus at the national level;
- attempts to bargain for domestic partner benefits;
- provision of domestic partner benefits for union staff;
- sexual orientation diversity training; and
- lobbying for the Employment Nondiscrimination Act (ENDA), to outlaw employment discrimination based on sexual orientation.

She wanted to assess whether the response of these unions varied across sector and membership categories. Prior research (Hunt 1997, 1999; Humphrey 2002) suggested to her that union response to issues involving sexual orientation was higher in white-collar public-sector work settings where women were in a majority. As a result, she used information about the percentage of women members in each union and categorized them by sector and type of worker. To determine the distinction between blue- and white-collar workers, she collected information about the occupations or jobs of members within each union. Even though there has been a move away from having unions represent workers from only one occupational group or a single industry, she was able to classify these unions by sector as public, private, or mixed.

The results of the survey are shown in table 4.1. The data suggests that a growing number of the largest U.S. unions have now gone some distance toward the representation and protection of their sexual minority members. Sexual orientation nondiscrimination is now embedded in the constitutions of several of the largest unions. A number of these unions have an officially sanctioned gay and lesbian caucus, most have undertaken at least some collec-

TABLE 4.1
U.S. union response to sexual orientation diversity, 2002[a]

	Union	Membership	Collar	Sector	Women members (%)	Sexual orientation nondiscrimination clause in constitution	LGBT national caucus	Domestic partner attempts in collective bargaining	Domestic partner benefits for union staff	Sexual orientation diversity training	Lobbying for ENDA
Responsive	SEIU	1,800,000	Mixed	Mixed	50	Yes	Yes	Yes	Yes	Yes	Yes
	NEA	2,500,000	White	Public	61	Yes	Yes	Yes	Yes	Yes	Yes
	AFT	685,000	White	Public	60	Yes	Yes	Yes	Yes	Yes	Yes
	AFSCME	1,300,00	White	Public	52	Yes	Yes	Yes	Yes	Yes	Yes
	UAW	760,000	Blue	Private	20	Yes	No	Yes	Yes	Yes	Yes
	CWA	490,000	Mixed	Mixed	51	No	Yes	Yes	Yes	Yes	Yes
Less responsive	UFCW	1,400,000	Blue	Private	50	Yes	No	No	Yes	Yes	No
	IAM	740,000	Blue	Private	12	No	No	No	Yes	Yes	No
	IBT	1,500,000	Blue	Private	30	No	Yes	No	No	Yes	No
	USWA	635,000	Blue	Private	15	No	No	No	No	Yes	No
	IBEW	720,000	Blue	Private	10	No	No	No	No	Yes	No
Unresponsive	LIUNA	775,000	Blue	Private	5	No	No	No	No	No	No
	UBCJ	515,000	Blue	Private	3	No	No	No	No	No	No

Sources: For union membership numbers, U.S. Department of Labor, "Directory of U.S. Labor Organizations," 2002; for percentage of women members, Cobble and Michal (2002, 237).
[a] For details about the survey methodology consult Bielski (2005).

tive bargaining on same-sex benefits, and most offer sexual orientation diversity training. At the same time, based on this survey evidence, we must conclude that contemporary union response to sexual orientation discrimination continues to be mixed. Some unions have moved a considerable distance with policies and programs to protect and represent LGBT workers; others totally ignore issues related to sexual diversity.

As predicted, unions representing white-collar public-sector workers with a female majority are among the unions that have gone furthest in representing their sexual minority members. The teachers' unions, namely the NEA and the AFT, along with the largest public-sector union, AFSCME, have taken action on all of the initiatives measured. In addition, all the less responsive and unresponsive unions are private-sector unions representing a blue-collar, largely male work force, also confirming the initial hypothesis. These include the United Food and Commercial Workers (UFCW), International Association of Machinists (IAM), IBT, United Steelworkers of America (USWA), and International Brotherhood of Electrical Workers (IBEW). Two unions had absolutely no response to sexual diversity concerns: the Laborers International Union of North America (LIUNA) and the United Brotherhood of Carpenters and Joiners (UBCJ). These two totally inactive unions had the highest percentage of male members (over 95 percent). They are also known to have a strong tradition of fraternal, conservative masculinity, partly as a result of the apprentice model of training and mentoring used in the crafts and building trades.

One of the more interesting results is that among the leaders were unions that also represent many private-sector blue-collar employees. The SEIU, for example, continues to have one of the most progressive and proactive responses to sexual diversity issues of any union. It has not only taken steps internally and through union relations with employers to combat discrimination against LGBT workers, but it has also been at the forefront of political efforts to pass the ENDA and to defeat antigay referenda when they are on the ballot in state and local elections.

The leadership of SEIU is not surprising, however, given its progressive history. SEIU, like the teachers' unions, also provides a good example of the importance of female leadership and the influence of feminism in shaping the union's response to sexual orientation. Ruth Milkman (1993) categorizes SEIU as a new service-sector union and among a cohort rising in prominence during the 1970s. SEIU adheres to a belief in equality for all workers in terms of their treatment and compensation. It also embraces diversity in a manner that recognizes and celebrates differences between workers and the multiplicity of their identities (in contrast to some unions that believe in pursuing one unifying identity for all union members). As Milkman (1993) and Cobble (2004, 2005) point out, the second-wave feminist movement of the 1970s forged ties specifically with SEIU, and this helped to broaden SEIU's politics into a new class politics in which equality might be achieved through the acceptance and recognition of difference.

The United Auto Workers: A Complex Anomaly

The single most unlikely union to be in the responsive category relative to our initial prediction is the UAW.[7] To find out why this union is responsive, we undertook to trace in more detail its pattern of engagement with sexual orientation. The UAW began in 1935 entirely for industrial workers in the rapidly expanding automobile manufacturing sector and became noted for its "sit down" tactics as a way of pressuring industrialists into signing a first contract with the union. The union's most influential leader was Walter Reuther, who served as president from 1946 to 1970. Known as "the most dangerous man in Detroit," Reuther believed that all workers should share in the growing wealth of the nation and that unions should concurrently pursue social, political, and economic objectives (Lichtenstein 1995). Reuther's leadership and vision set a progressive and liberal tone for the union, one that remained in place long after his untimely death in an airplane accident in 1970. Of note, as well, was the large number of socialists, communists, and other leftists among the rank and file.

With the decline in domestic manufacturing in the 1980s, the UAW began to organize in what, for them, were nontraditional sectors. By the turn of the twenty-first century, it represented workers not only in manufacturing but in government, education, and the arts, as well as the nonprofit sector. In 1999, it organized 10,000 graduate student assistants at the University of California, and in 2000 it admitted workers at the Museum of Modern Art. The UAW has also acquired important and influential affiliates such as the National Writers' Guild. When combined with its various affiliates, it has 710,000 active members and 500,000 retired members, includes 950 locals, and has contracts with 3,200 employers based in the United States, Canada, and Puerto Rico.[8] Although the UAW is less powerful than it used to be, it remains a force to be reckoned with and, even though it is primarily a blue-collar male-dominated union operating in the manufacturing sector, it now has a more diverse membership base than its origins would predict.

Reuther's progressive legacy, in combination with the growth of women in the union during the war and their extraordinary record of feminist activism,

[7] This case study is based on Bielski (2005), with additional independent research undertaken by Gerald Hunt specifically for this chapter.
[8] Statistics taken from the United Auto Workers website, http://www.uaw.org/about/uawmember ship (accessed June 6, 2005).

both in the union and nationally, helps explain the UAW's responsiveness to issues of sexual orientation. As Kevin Boyle (1995), Cobble (2004), and Nancy Gabin (1990) point out, the UAW was involved in early battles for women's and civil rights, as well as fights to eradicate poverty, promote full employment, and shorten working hours. In her assessment of the union's response to gender, for example, Gabin (1990, 2005) indicates that by 2000 the UAW had acquired a respectable record of collective bargaining on issues important to women such as maternity leave and, among other things, had proven itself to be a strong supporter of legislation to eliminate employment discrimination based on sex. In 1944, the UAW held its first national women's conference, and in 1955 it established a Women's Department, the first of its kind in the United States. The UAW was also an early advocate for the elimination of racial discrimination. In 1946, it established a Fair Practices and Anti-Discrimination Department, once again, a first for a U.S. union. In 1961, it pledged to begin bargaining for antidiscrimination provisions in collective agreements, and in 1963 the UAW sent one of the largest contingents to the civil rights march on Washington. In 1970, it became the first union to endorse the Equal Rights Amendment. The union has been active on a broader set of social issues as well. In 1968, for example, it left the AFL-CIO because of that organization's support for the Vietnam War (rejoining in 1981).

Attention to sexual orientation discrimination was late in coming to the UAW and only started to emerge in the late 1990s; but developments occurred quickly. By 2005, the union had provisions in its constitution to prohibit internal discrimination on the basis of sexual orientation and had pursued language banning employment discrimination on the basis of sexual orientation in a number of collective agreements. It had also negotiated same-sex benefit coverage in many agreements, including those with the Big Three automobile makers. Moreover, the union had made commitments to support the concerns of LGBT individuals that extended beyond union policy and union contracts. It backed the Employment Non-Discrimination Act (proposed federal legislation to outlaw discrimination in the workplace on the basis of sexual orientation) and included sexual orientation issues in its diversity training programs.

The UAW's willingness to engage with sexual orientation discrimination, however, is not simply a product of its past or its progressive leadership. It is also a story of individual workers confronting the union with the fact that many of its work sites were homophobic and dangerous places for LGBT workers. Ron Woods and Martha Grevatt, two very brave and pioneering rank-and-file manufacturing workers at Chrysler, are two such workers whose actions made a difference. Woods and Grevatt first came out in their communities, then in their workplaces, and then to the entire union as activists working for equality for gay and lesbian workers. Their coming out in such a forceful way gave a public and personal face to issues of discrimination and harassment among auto workers. They spoke to the press, to union officials, and to other rank-and-file members at national union meetings about the extreme harassment and mistreatment they faced every day at work.[9]

The widespread publicity that Ron Woods and Martha Grevatt received helped to draw attention to the plight of auto workers. Woods was profiled in a long article in the *New Yorker* (J. Stewart 1997), and both of their stories were told in newspapers around the country. These articles told how Woods, a third-generation worker at Chrysler, had been physically attacked four times after co-workers saw a newspaper photo of him attending a rally protesting the antigay Cracker Barrel Restaurant chain. He took his complaints to the union steward, who did support him, but ultimately they decided on a transfer to another plant sixty miles away. Unfortunately, word followed and Woods once again was the subject of harassment. Woods persevered; over time support grew and eventually he was elected as a union delegate to the 1996 UAW bargaining convention, where he addressed other delegates, asking them to add sexual orientation to the union's antidiscrimination provisions. At first Chrysler refused to budge, but the issue was dropped when the company agreed to include sexual orientation in its Employee Standards of Conduct. When Woods continued to be harassed by co-workers, he sued Chrysler on the grounds of unsafe workspace, but settled out of court and left the automobile industry altogether.

But it was not just activists such as Ron Woods and Martha Grevatt who applied pressure on the UAW. Some top officers were sympathetic to gay rights, and after it merged with the UAW, the National Writers' Guild became one of the prime pushers to have the union address sexual orientation. At the same time, newly appointed AFL-CIO President John Sweeney was pronouncing his support of equal treatment for LGBT union members. Moreover, outside pressure from PAW and Parents and Friends of Lesbians and Gays (P-FLAG) helped draw attention to the seriousness of the issue. The leaders of PAW spoke directly with the UAW officials at the international who would be at the bargaining tables for the 1999 contracts with General Motors, Ford, and Chrysler. They organized letter-writing campaigns to UAW officials asking the union to push for contractual protection for gay and lesbian workers and for domestic partner benefits. The support of these and other organizations helped to emphasize that discrimination against auto workers was not just the concern of a few gay labor activists—it was a larger issue involving the rights of all gay people and the pursuit of social justice for all minority groups.

[9] Martha Grevatt, remarks presented at the National Gay and Lesbian Task Force Creating Change Workshop discussion, Athens, Georgia, November 10, 2000; telephone interviews with Monica Bielski, March 26, 2000, and February 25, 2003.

Labor Comes Out of the Closet—Sort of

The U.S. labor movement has demonstrated an increasing willingness to combat discrimination on the basis of sexual orientation. Larger unions representing teachers, public-sectors workers, and service workers have led the way. But even among some of the least proactive unions there are signs of change. In 2006, for example, a LGBT caucus was established in the IBT.

The readiness of U.S. labor to take up and pursue these issues owes much to an active lesbian and gay rights movement. Labor activism has taken off in part as a response to greater sexual minority visibility, which brought attention to issues of inequality in employee benefits and other discriminatory employer policies and revealed the heterosexual bias in union cultures and collective agreement provisions. The AIDS crisis also brought a focus on the significance of workplace issues because, in the early days of the epidemic, gay men were disproportionately affected by the disease and urgently required medical benefits for their partners.

These developments reflect years of hard work by activists and their allies within the trade union movement. Activists often worked tirelessly behind the scenes for years before progress was made. The early recognition of the need for support by SEIU, AFT, and AFSCME was also a significant factor in changing the landscape for queer unionists. The alliances that labor and sexual diversity activists formed helped to produce inclusive nondiscrimination policies, same-sex benefit coverage in collective agreements, and sexual orientation diversity training. Moreover, they have inched labor toward wider political involvement, such as lobbying the government on ENDA.

The attentiveness of U.S. labor to gays and lesbians has been part of a more general response to change within the labor movement itself. The overall decline in union density, threats posed by globalization and free trade agreements, and growing numbers of minorities and women in the workforce have all combined to increase union interest in retaining existing members and recruiting new ones.

The revitalized feminist resurgence in the 1960s and 1970s initiated a challenge to the status quo of many unions. Feminists raised postmaterialist concerns such as harassment and violence, and they legitimized the idea that traditional union cultures were part of the problem. Feminists not only raised labor's consciousness around discrimination, difference, and diversity, but pioneered the tactic of self-organizing into caucuses. Sexual minority activists were quick to model the idea of separate caucuses as a place to find support, formulate ideas, clarify demands, and strategize about how to confront conservative union leadership. Activists working within the labor movement have also been an important ingredient in convincing trade union leaders that brothers and sisters who happened to be gay, lesbian, bisexual or transgendered were a constituency worthy of fair and equal treatment.

The developments that have taken place over the past couple of decades in the United States have their parallels in at least some other developed countries. Labor movements in Canada, Australia, Britain, Germany, and the Netherlands, among others, have all made some effort to respond to the concerns raised by sexual minorities (Colgan and Ledwith 2002; Hunt 1999; Hunt and Rayside 2001). And in most settings, the response has been in a pattern resembling the one we have just recorded for the United States—white-collar public-sector unions and those with significant numbers of female members tending to lead the charge.

Overall, however, U.S. labor has been somewhat slower to join the struggle for LGBT equality than labor movements in other settings. The Canadian Labour Congress, for example, had by 1980 passed a resolution to end discrimination against sexual minorities, as had labor congresses in other countries, such as Australia. As well, by the mid-1980s, unions in other countries were already winning grievances and arbitrations in support of same-sex benefit coverage—developments that helped to establish precedent for legal challenges.

U.S. unions continue to face considerable opposition in their attempts to advance LGBT rights. The political strength of religious conservatives and other antigay groups found in the United States is unequalled in most developed countries (Hunt and Rayside 2001). This presents a formidable challenge to activists working for change within and beyond the labor movement. Still, by most measures, U.S. labor has come a long way out of the closet in the past twenty-five years. It has slowly shifted from being part of the problem to being part of the solution. LGBT issues have increasingly become important concerns for labor, and a growing number of unions have joined the struggle for equality. Not all unions are marching to this tune, but there is now sufficient momentum to have made a difference.

5

SEX DISCRIMINATION AS COLLECTIVE HARM

Marion Crain

Why is sex discrimination not seen as a key issue for organized labor? Why is the decline of labor unionism not a feminist issue? The answers to these questions lie in the artificial divide between workers' rights to economic justice and women's rights to workplace equality. This divide, created by the interaction of labor movement ideology and law, is neither desirable as a matter of union praxis nor inevitable at law.

The legal regime is characterized by a two-track system of rights. Workers' rights to organize and bargain collectively for economic justice are guaranteed by the National Labor Relations Act (NLRA), commonly referred to as the labor law, and enforced by the National Labor Relations Board (NLRB). Labor unions function as the watchdogs for these rights, which serve the interests of workers as a group. By contrast, workers' rights to be free from discrimination are guaranteed by Title VII of the Civil Rights Act of 1964, the core employment discrimination statute. Title VII prescribes remedies available through litigation to individuals or groups of individuals. The watchdogs for these rights are the employees themselves, aided by the Equal Employment Opportunity Commission (EEOC), civil rights, feminist or other nonlabor groups pressing for change, public interest law firms, or private attorneys.

Yet the lived experience of workers does not fit the two-track legal regime; the dichotomy between economic injustice and sex discrimination is illusory. Discrimination is often perpetrated through economic disadvantage, including unequal wages, job channeling into segregated occupations associated with differential rates of pay, and sexual harassment designed to police the gender boundary between occupations. At the same time, the impetus for union organizing and collective bargaining is about much more than economic rights. Workers organize to assert their humanity because they feel objectified and devalued (Fisk 2001, 93; Austin 1988, 30–31).

Labor's acceptance of the dichotomy between collective economic rights and individual rights to be free from discrimination at work has prevented it from taking on key issues that contribute to women's economic subordination, particularly occupational segregation by sex, associated pay inequities, and sexual harassment. Although some unions have endeavored to portray union challenges to sex discriminatory wage policies and practices that enforce occupational segregation as strategies that simultaneously advance workers' economic interests and promote class unity, the effort thus far has foundered on the shoals of the clash of gender interests within labor's ranks.

This gendered conflict is nowhere more evident than in the context of coworker sexual harassment, in which male and female members' interests are sharply antagonistic. Here, as elsewhere, unions seek to avoid entrenching the gender divide by adhering to the two-track system, eschewing a formal role in advancing antidiscrimination claims. In so doing, however, unions relinquish the moral high ground of the social justice agenda to nonlabor organizations such as civil rights groups, feminist groups, and other advocacy groups that seek vindication of statutory antidiscrimination rights at law. Ultimately, labor's absence from the quest for social justice undermines union strength and credibility in a world where the public, the courts, and workers embrace norms of sex and race equality but turn a deaf ear to complaints of class injustice.

I urge labor unions to challenge this false dichotomy by recasting sex discrimination claims as simultaneous demands for equality, dignity, and economic rights that resonate at a collective level rather than solely on an individual level. Labor unions could and should play frontline roles in strategic litigation and consciousness-raising around the economic disadvantages associated with occupational segregation by sex and sexual harassment, assisting workers with sex discrimination and sexual harassment claims both before the NLRB and in the courts. If labor unions fail to take up this charge, they not only risk perpetuating women's economic subordination, they solidify a superexploitable workforce whose vulnerability ultimately undercuts wage standards and working conditions for all workers.

Working Women and Unions: Adversaries or Allies?

Women workers and labor unions began as adversaries. The early history of exclusion and discrimination against women within U.S. unions has been well-documented (Milkman 1985, 1987; Kessler-Harris 1982). In the late 1800s and early 1900s, unionists viewed women workers as a competitive threat to the wages and job security enjoyed by male workers. At the same time, unions were committed to supporting the patriarchal family structure. This position was eventually translated into the family wage ideology, in which labor asserted the social right of the working class to "ideal" family and gender roles: female domesticity and male wage-earning responsibility. The family wage ideology connected class issues of subsistence and justice with gender roles. Although the origins of the ideology were in class unity, it ultimately set the stage for the ambivalence over women's right to occupy male jobs that followed (May 1985).

The labor market opportunities for women created by World War II, pressure by female trade unionists, and the influence of the burgeoning feminist movement during the 1960s and 1970s eventually altered unions' formal policies. As part of a new strategy to resist wage competition, unions embraced women as members and abolished openly discriminatory policies and contract provisions that had barred the hiring of married women (Cobble 2004; Milkman 1987; Gabin 1985). Several unions went even further in forging an alliance with women; the United Electrical Workers (UE) and the International Union of Electrical Workers (IUE), for instance, emerged as powerful voices against wage discrimination in the workplace, and both unions aggressively fought to eliminate wage inequalities at General Electric and Westinghouse using tactics such as grievances, pickets, and lawsuits to advance their cause (Cobble 2004, 101–3; Johnson 1993).

Beginning in the 1970s, union lawyers went further still, mounting challenges against wage inequities associated with occupational segregation by sex that struck at the very heart of employer control over the deployment of labor. Lawyers for the American Federation of State, County, and Municipal Employees (AFSCME) brought class action pay-equity suits under the Equal Pay Act and Title VII of the Civil Rights Act of 1964, coordinating litigation with publicity campaigns to raise public consciousness and to mobilize workers and other advocates, including academics, the judiciary, and other local and national organizational actors (McCann 1994, 62–64). The most potentially radical of these pay-equity theories, comparable worth, challenged employer job valuation and pay structures, asserting that male and female workers performing work that required comparable skill and education should receive equal pay. Similarly, in the 1980s the United Auto Workers (UAW) launched a class action suit against Johnson Controls, alleging that the company's "fetal protection" policy barring women from jobs involving lead exposure amounted to an unconscionable infringement on worker autonomy that constituted sex discrimination under Title VII.[1] Although the courts eventually closed the door to gender-based comparable worth claims in 1985,[2] the UAW's challenge to fetal protection policies was successful both in opening new work opportunities for women and in raising awareness of workplace toxins, encouraging the company to reduce lead exposure for all workers (Crain, Kim, and Selmi 2005, 575).

Union leadership in challenging discriminatory wage and job-channeling policies was critical to advancing the interests of women workers as a class. Attacking discriminatory pay structures and work rules enforcing occupational segregation offered an opportunity for unions to show how gender and economic class issues intersected in women's lives, operating to doubly disadvantage them. Comparable worth claims and challenges to fetal protection policies cast issues of sex-based wage discrimination and job channeling as dignitary harms that had both an economic and a gendered aspect. Most significantly, union involvement in these cases signaled that challenging sex discriminatory practices could redound to the advantage of all workers, reducing employer hegemony and enhancing workers' power as a class.

At the same time, however, union involvement in such cases highlighted the conflicts of interest that existed along gender lines within the unionized workforce. Union men saw comparable worth as a threat to their wage levels because, unless the employer increased the overall wage pool, higher wages for women came out of men's paychecks. Thus, pressing for wage parity was just as likely to result in leveling down as it was to increase wage levels for all workers (Brake 2004; Blum 1991). Moreover, if successful, comparable worth claims would produce job comparisons devaluing men's work in relative terms, eroding men's economic privilege in male-dominated occupations and undermining male gender dominance; ultimately, they threatened male gender identity. The unions' best efforts to frame these legal challenges as impacting "working person's" issues rather than women's issues were ultimately less effective in producing solidarity than proponents had hoped they would be (Blum 1991: 171–72).

---

[1] *UAW v. Johnson Controls, Inc.*, 499 U.S. 187 (1991).
[2] *AFSCME v. State of Washington*, 770 F.2d 1401 (9th Cir. 1985).

Toxic Air: Sexual Harassment as Collective Harm

The gender divide within labor's ranks soon surfaced starkly in the sexual harassment context. In 1986, the U.S. Supreme Court recognized sexual harassment as a form of sex discrimination under Title VII.[3] Union women were among the first to understand workplace sexual harassment as a group problem justifying a collective response. Women workers who complained to union stewards of workplace sexual harassment by male co-workers encountered resistance and hostility. Initially, stewards sought to protect their male members' job security by discouraging female members from filing formal sexual harassment complaints. When women persisted, unions took the position that sexual harassment was the employer's problem rather than the union's. Victims were referred to the EEOC or to private law firms rather than receiving union representation. The clear message was that the threats to male workers' job security posed by women's sexual harassment complaints raised collective economic interests that were the traditional province of unions, whereas the right to be free from sexual harassment on the job was a noneconomic personal interest unique to an individual woman.

Forced to confront the problem of sexual harassment in the arbitration context as defenders of accused harasser-members' job security, a number of unions representing workers in traditionally male occupations argued that women entering such occupations were required to tolerate hostile work environments and sexualized workplaces. Contending that male-dominated workplaces had always been characterized by coarse or rough-hewn conduct that could not be understood out of context, these unions asserted that women had assumed the risk of harassment by entering male-dominated work settings where it was well-known that sexualization was prevalent or that they had invited sexual harassment by joining in horseplay or laughing at sexual jokes (Crain 1995). Other women who raised harassment allegations found their personal credibility aggressively attacked by union leadership (Bingham and Gansler 2002; Crain 1995).

The frustrated women victims ultimately turned for redress to private lawyers, feminist organizations, or the EEOC, which filed antidiscrimination claims under Title VII against employers for failing to prevent sexual harassment in their workplaces (Crain 1995). The first cases involving unionized women workers reached the courts in the late 1980s and proliferated during the 1990s. These cases cast unions in cameo roles, either characterizing them as passive bystanders or joining them as defendants if the plaintiffs could esta-

---

[3] *Meritor Savings Bank, FSB v. Vinson*, 477 U.S. 57 (1986).

blish that the unions' conduct had exacerbated the hostile work environment (Brudney 1996, 1571). If the case against the employer was settled, the consent decree or settlement agreement typically contemplated no role for the union at all. Such decrees required employers to institute anti-sexual harassment policies drafted by the nonlabor groups representing the victims. Sometimes workplace task forces or committees were established to ensure future compliance, feminist advocacy groups served as watchdogs for workers' rights pursuant to the decree (even in unionized workplaces), or employers agreed to employ consultants to advise them on compliance (Crain and Matheny 1999, 1548; 2001, 1820–21).

Alternatively, the victims complained directly to their employers, who responded by taking disciplinary action against the harassers. The harassers then filed grievances with the union, challenging the discharge under the just cause provision of the collective bargaining agreement. The unions processed the grievances to arbitration, and the victims served as the key witnesses for the employer (Crain and Matheny 1999, 1552). Eventually, the courts developed an affirmative defense to Title VII liability for employers who had promulgated and enforced anti-sexual harassment policies.[4] Employers themselves took over drafting and implementation voluntarily (and often unilaterally) as a prophylactic measure.

Three high-profile sexual harassment cases arising in the union context during the 1980s and 1990s illustrate these patterns. In *Robinson v. Jacksonville Shipyards* (1991), *Jenson v. Eveleth Taconite Company* (1993), and *EEOC v. Mitsubishi Motor Manufacturing* (1998),[5] complaints by women union members about severe hostile work environment–style sexual harassment perpetrated by male co-workers and tolerated or encouraged by management went unredressed by their unions. Indeed, union stewards responded to the women's complaints in hostile fashion, sometimes with further harassment. In *Robinson*, the plaintiff complained to union officials about sexually explicit nude photographs hanging in the workplace, including a picture of a woman's pubic area with a meat spatula pressed on it, observed on a wall next to the sheet metal shop. The union not only refused the plaintiff's request to file a grievance, it undertook representation of the male membership as a class instead, announcing that it would grieve any rule prohibiting the display of pornography in the workplace as a violation of the male workers' First Amendment–protected freedom of expression. Following the women's complaint in *Jenson*, signs went up in the workplace stating, "Sexual harassment will not be reported—however, it will be graded." In addition, the union re-

[4] *Burlington Industries, Inc. v. Ellerth*, 524 U.S. 742 (1998).
[5] *Robinson v. Jacksonville Shipyards, Inc.*, 499 U.S. 187 (1991); *Jenson v. Eveleth Taconite Co.*, 824 F. Supp. 847 (D. Minn. 1993); *EEOC v. Mitsubishi Motor Manufacturing of America, Inc.*, 990 F. Supp. 1059 (C.D. Ill. 1998).

quired its members to uphold the union oath exhorting constituents to "defend on all occasions to the extent of your ability the members of the organization"; this type of mentality "virtually disabled the union from disciplining its own members." The women unionists named the union as a defendant in their complaint (Bingham and Gansler 2002, 41, 132, 177).

In *Mitsubishi*, the EEOC's investigation of the company disclosed that as many as 500 of the 893 women in the plant had suffered sexual harassment. The women autoworkers alleged misogynist conduct in the plant by both male autoworkers and supervisors, including physically abusing women (e.g., slapping women on the buttocks, touching their breasts and crotches); pinning sexually obscene signs to the backs of unknowing women; placing obscene graffiti on the fenders of cars coming down the assembly line and obscene pop–ups, which appeared unexpectedly, in the cars when women were assembling them; wrapping automotive parts in pornographic newspapers; assaulting women with factory equipment (e.g., placing hoses, wrenches, and air guns between women's legs); and playing pranks on women. Despite numerous complaints, however, the union refused to proceed with formal grievances. One complainant in *Mitsubishi* reported that the union steward told her that he would help her only if she first performed oral sex on him. Furthermore, when Mitsubishi organized a protest by its workers against the EEOC in the wake of the EEOC investigation, the local union remained "neutral," telling members that "they were free to attend the protest" at the EEOC offices (Crain and Matheny 1999, 1550).

In all of these cases, the unions prioritized male members' gender interest over women's economic interest. Sexual harassment was characterized as a personal individual harm directed at women's gender dignity rather than as a collective harm implicating their economic interests. At the same time, the unions saw the potential threat to male workers' autonomy and job security as collective economic harms justifying intervention. This response misconceives the nature of sexual harassment and the harm that it visits on victims. Unredressed harassment poses a serious risk of loss of employment for the target of the harassment; victims report a lowered sense of competence, feelings of demoralization, high absenteeism, and psychological and physical manifestations of emotional distress. The majority of victims either quit their jobs or seek a transfer to avoid the harassment. Alternatively, they are discharged or demoted for poor performance or absenteeism (Schultz 1998; Crain 1995, 22–29). Thus, the victims' economic interests are clearly impacted.

At a pragmatic level, union failure to take preventive measures against sex discrimination and member-on-member sexual harassment costs unions money that could be more profitably spent on organizing or bargaining. In recent years, unions that effectively collaborated in sexual harassment perpetrated by male members have found themselves spending significant amounts of dues monies to defend themselves against class action sex discrimination claims brought by their female members. For example, a federal district court recently approved a settlement agreement in a suit by female dockworkers against the International Longshoremen's Association (ILA). The women workers claimed that they were passed over for job assignments through the ILA hiring hall and were sexually harassed in the hiring hall and at the jobsite. The settlement agreement required the ILA to pay $1.65 million to the plaintiffs and their attorneys, to provide seniority enhancements to the plaintiffs, and to offer Equal Employment Opportunity (EEO) training for all union members (McGolrick 2005).

Union failure to actively oppose sexual harassment also places male job security at risk on both a collective and an individual level, exposing the harassers to discipline and discharge by the employer and simultaneously enhancing employer managerial authority. If the case is litigated and settled or otherwise resolved, the nonlabor group that provides representation to the victim(s) may end up drafting the anti-sexual harassment policy that will govern future workplace actions in sexual harassment charges, effectively usurping the union's advocacy and bargaining role (Crain and Matheny 1999). In *Robinson,* the proposed sexual harassment policy was drafted by the National Organization for Women's Legal Defense Fund, which represented plaintiff Lois Robinson in the action; in *Mitsubishi Motors,* the union was voluntarily joined in the consent decree, but was not represented at all on the panel that was charged with monitoring and reviewing Mitsubishi's compliance with the nonmonetary terms of the settlement, which included sexual harassment policies providing for prompt remediation (Crain 1995, 11).

Thus, union insistence that the employer bears the primary responsibility for preventing sexual harassment in the workplace cedes control over working conditions that go to the core of unionism—conditions that impact workers' dignity and job security. At the same time, union passivity undermines union power in the eyes of the workers, further centralizing power and control over the workplace in the employer (Crain and Matheny 1999, 1551). Lack of worker participation in constructing anti-sexual harassment policies at the bargaining table denies workers a voice in the construction of policies that affect the job security and working conditions of all. The employer who assumes responsibility for regulating workplace speech will implement prophylactic measures to block sexual harassment that invade all workers' speech and privacy interests on the job, blocking not only sexual expression but union-organizing speech as well (Austin 1988, 3). Thus, it is critically important that unions play an active role in the drafting of any restrictions on workplace speech.

More insidiously, union passivity deprives unions of an opportunity to protect all workers against supervisor or employer harassment (Austin 1988).

Employers advocate for legal responses to sexual harassment that minimize the risk that statutory protections against sexual harassment will "leach over" or morph into protection against nonsexual forms of harassment suffered by all workers (Vandervelde 2004, 497). After all, it is not gender alone that renders working women vulnerable to sexual harassment but the interplay between the gender hierarchy and the economic hierarchy in the workplace, which in turn is maintained by the coercive common law backdrop of the employer's power to discharge employees at will. Workplace harassment is thus toxic because it occurs in the shadow of "the latent threat of firing for no reason at all" (Vandervelde 2004, 501, 503).

Finally, sexual harassment creates a workplace culture that affects all workers in a workplace, men as well as women. There are no "bystanders"—all who witness it are simultaneously harmed and responsible (Resnik 2004, 248–49, 258). "Ambient" sexual harassment, "the indirect exposure to sexual harassment experienced by others in a victim's work group," has been correlated with negative job performance, the health and psychological responses strikingly similar to those suffered by direct victims (Roberts 2004, 366–67).

Workforce camaraderie and bonds between workers are also undermined by toxic environments linked to racial and sexual harassment. For example, in *Childress v. City of Richmond* (1998), white male police officers brought suit against the city under Title VII for creating and sustaining a hostile work environment for women and African American police officers. The plaintiffs argued that teamwork was essential to police work and that supervisors' discriminatory behavior drove a wedge between men and women and between blacks and whites. Because police officers' lives were at risk when they could not depend on their co-workers, the plaintiffs argued that the conditions of their employment were substantially impacted by workplace discrimination—even though they were not personally the targets. Similarly, in *Walker v. Mueller Industries* (2005),[6] a white male union steward complained to the employer of racial harassment among his co-workers, arguing that the harassment had poisoned his working atmosphere and injured him as a bystander. The employer retaliated against him. Both courts rejected the claims, essentially requiring a higher standard of proof of toxicity in the workplace for bystander complaints than is required for complaints filed by direct targets of sexual harassment.

Tolerance for sexual harassment and the toxic workplace culture that accompanies it are a subset of a larger problem that has garnered scholarly and legal attention in recent years: the effects on workers of psychological abuse, humiliation tactics, or workplace bullying (Fisk 2001; Yamada 2000). Three times more prevalent than sexual harassment, workplace harassment is de-

---

[6] *Walker v. Mueller Industries, Inc.*, 508 F.3d 328 (7th Cir. 2005).

fined as "repeated interpersonal mistreatment that is sufficiently severe as to harm a targeted person's health or economic status" (Namie and Namie 2004, 315, 326). Workplace harassment inflicts serious harm on its targets, including physical and psychological symptoms that undermine worker productivity and employer profit margins. High turnover, absenteeism, problems with customer service, and acts of sabotage and revenge impose additional costs. When such harassment goes unredressed by the employer, a cycle of abuse and retaliation ensues and the behaviors escalate. Canada (Quebec), France, Sweden, and the United Kingdom have enacted legislation addressing workplace psychological harassment or construed existing legislation to encompass and prohibit such conduct. Although not yet adopted in the United States, antibullying legislation has been introduced in California, Oklahoma, and Oregon (Yamada 2004). Because psychological harassment in the workplace produces a toxic environment rather than victimizing a single person, it is a logical target for union activism. Nevertheless, few unions have sought to address workplace harassment through collective action or collective bargaining.

Collateral harm to bystanders attributable to sexual harassment, however, is especially troubling because it undermines gender equality well beyond any individual workplace. Sexual harassment inflicts a collective injury affecting "the status of all women in the workplace where it occurs, in the labor market, and in society as a whole" (Roberts 2004, 365). Typically, sexual harassment at a jobsite is experienced by many women, not just the individual who complains (Roberts 2004, 366–68). In addition, witnessing sexual harassment puts all women on notice that they are transgressing gender boundaries by their presence in the workplace and deters them from seeking employment in or advancement to higher-paying traditionally male jobs, ultimately reinforcing sex-segregated employment (Schultz 1998). The prevalence of hostile work environment sexual harassment communicates a powerful message about women's role in society and their proper placement in workplace occupations that undermines the prospects for gender integration across traditional occupational lines (Schultz 1998; Crain 1995).

At a macro level, workforce diversity and integration are public goods—failure to fully integrate the workforce impoverishes the public dialog and the larger political democracy (Estlund 2003). Work plays a significant role in structuring citizens' cooperative interaction and socialization outside the family, forging bonds between workers and serving an educative function. The benefits of racial integration in the workplace are well-accepted and illustrative (Estlund 2003; Schultz 2000). The absence of women or their segregation in particular job categories deprives men of the opportunity to see women as peers and equals with whom they can discuss political and social matters. Ultimately, although it happens to individual women on a personal level, sexual harassment is a structural problem redressable only with structural (collective) remedies.

A Workforce Structured by Gender

The consequences for worker solidarity of conceptualizing sex discriminatory practices as individual harms rather than collective injuries are well illustrated by the labor movement's response to workplace sexual harassment. By casting sexual harassment as a private individual problem and eschewing responsibility for remedying it, many unions misconceived the nature of the harm, which was both economic and collective as well as dignitary and personal. In so doing, they missed an important opportunity to improve the working conditions of male workers as well as female workers, to bind workers together across gender lines, and to more effectively resist employer hegemony.

But the damage of construing discrimination as an individual injury that was not legitimate union terrain did not stop there. The prevalence of sexual harassment within the ranks of unionized workers reinforced occupational segregation by sex, cementing women's subordinate economic position. With the doors closed to them at high-wage, union-controlled trades and the boundaries of traditionally male-dominated high-wage manufacturing jobs policed by male coworkers through hostile work environment sexual harassment (Schultz 1998, 1804–5; Crain 1995, 18–22), women turned to retail sales, fast-food jobs, and cashier work. Such jobs typically feature part-time or temporary status, no job mobility, low wages, and no benefits. Women's overrepresentation in low-wage sex-typed retail and service occupations in which union density was low perpetuated the divide between labor's relatively highly paid core constituency and the unorganized female workforce, a divide from which many employers benefited significantly (Crain and Matheny 1999; Milkman 1987). Unsurprisingly, the same sectors were characterized by particularly intense managerial opposition to unions. The costs of organizing and servicing such bargaining units were relatively high (Crain 1991).

The long-term effects of the workplace divide along gender lines thus appear to be very serious for organized labor and, ultimately, for workers as a class. Despite heroic organizing efforts by the Service Employees International Union (SEIU), United Food and Commercial Workers International Union (UFCW), and other Change to Win unions, union density in the growing service sector remains low while at the same time labor's traditional manufacturing base is shrinking. Labor's initial reluctance to embrace and organize the female-dominated retail sales workforce paved the way for the evolution of an industry built on low labor costs in order to sustain low prices and typified by intense resistance to unionization.

Consider the structure of the jobs at Wal-Mart, dubbed by some the template for twenty-first-century capitalism and currently the largest private employer in the United States (Lichtenstein 2005; Head 2004). Employee turnover is estimated at 46 percent per year, and a twenty-eight-hour workweek is considered full-time employment (Lichtenstein 2005). It is no accident that a disproportionate number of women fill the lowest-wage jobs at Wal-Mart; the jobs were constructed for them on the assumptions that women were economically dependent on a wage earner who possessed a higher-paying job to which benefits were attached and that their job tenure would be short because women lack permanent attachment to the workforce. Ultimately, the prophecy became self-fulfilling. Studies show that a significant percentage of Wal-Mart workers in fact depend on spouses, parents or public assistance such as food stamps and Medicaid for basic necessities and health insurance (Featherstone 2004, 146–49; Head 2004). Indeed, some reports suggest that Wal-Mart actively encourages its workers to apply for public assistance and provides instruction to assist them in doing so (Featherstone 2004, 239–41). Wal-Mart's spending on health care is dramatically lower than that of other U.S. employers, and it is easy to see how the stores are able to operate at a competitive advantage (Greenhouse 2005b).

The persistent characterization of sex discrimination, sexual harassment, and women's struggle to balance work and family obligations as personal or individual creates an underclass that employers such as Wal-Mart are able to super-exploit. Not until Wal-Mart's market dominance threatened union leverage at the bargaining table in unionized grocery stores that must compete with Wal-Mart Super Centers did unions mount a large-scale organizing drive. Wal-Mart's adoption of hypercapitalistic strategies and its market ascendancy make this a daunting battle indeed (Rathke 2005).

Women workers have thus served as the labor movement's "canaries in the mines," their distress signaling to the labor movement that the "air" around them has become too toxic to breathe (Guinier and Torres 2002, 11). As a broader cross section of workers struggle for breath in a market characterized by the "Walmartization" of work, it is increasingly clear that women's economic subordination in the workplace threatens the well-being of all workers.

Opportunities to Forge Solidarity: Class Action
Sex Discrimination Claims

What opportunities exist for unions that wish to reframe sex discrimination as a collective harm and simultaneously forge solidarity across gender lines? I suggest that unions aggressively initiate and publicly support class action sex discrimination litigation against major employers whose low-wage, no-benefit jobs are predominantly occupied by women. This course of action has three advantages. First, union participation in high-profile discrimination litigation is cheap advertising for a labor movement that is striving to find its moral center, to recast itself as a social justice organization rather than a self-interested special-interest group and to appeal simultaneously to a demographically diverse workforce. Participation in litigation may also serve as a critical link in building bridges between the feminist movement and the labor movement, as it did during the pay equity litigation era (McCann 1994; Blum 1991; Milkman 1985).

Second, unions might play a valuable watchdog role in monitoring compliance with settlement of class action discrimination litigation. Despite their transformative potential, class action discrimination claims brought by nonlabor groups have so far produced little of lasting value because the initiating groups (government agencies, public interest law firms, or private attorneys) lack interest in fostering worker representation structures that will survive the immediate legal claim; instead, their interest in monitoring outcomes tends to decline after settlement (when attorneys' fees have been paid) (Selmi 2003). For example, in the 1994 class action sex discrimination case against Home Depot challenging job channeling and pay equity, the plaintiffs were represented by private attorneys who continued to serve as plaintiffs' representative in the postsettlement monitoring process. Although Home Depot agreed to take affirmative steps to improve female hiring into sales jobs likely to lead to management positions, Home Depot's progress toward its goal was effectively self-monitored; the postsettlement monitoring process was terminated a year and a half early (Selmi 2003, 1285–86). Similarly, in the class action discrimination case against Texaco asserting denials of pay increases and promotions based on race, Texaco settled the case by paying substantial damages and attorneys' fees and agreeing to improve hiring of women and racial minorities. A diversity task force established to implement the settlement's terms functioned primarily to repair the company's damaged public image, producing only a 0.8 percent increase in minority hiring and retention in Texaco's workforce during 1998 (Selmi 2003, 1280). Finally, the bulk of settlement monies paid in such cases typically goes to lawyers rather than to the workers. In the class action sex discrimination settlement against the ILA, for example, attorneys' fees and costs made up $1.5 million of a $1.65 million settlement.

In short, structural reform efforts initiated by union substitutes who are not stakeholders in that particular workplace are costly for employers and unions, may lead to ephemeral benefits for workers, and do nothing to build workers' class consciousness or feelings of solidarity. Even more worrisome, initial evidence suggests that the illusory promise of benefits obtained without personal investment undermines long-term union efforts to mobilize work-ers. For example, the Greengrocer Code of Conduct negotiated in 2002 be-tween the New York State Attorney General and greengrocers in New York City in settlement of wage and hour claims under the Fair Labor Standards Act conferred nothing more than workers were already entitled to at law and halted nascent union-organizing efforts rather than institutionalizing future representation structures (Hyde 2004). Leadership by an independent labor movement accountable to its membership is thus critical if the goal of struc-tural reform is worker empowerment.

If unions assume an active role as participants in class action discrimina-tion litigation, however, they could monitor the workplace for future compli-ance following settlement or judicial resolution of the claim. Placing unions in such a role would demonstrate to workers the union's potential efficacy as a defender of workers' rights and provide a foothold for future organizing ef-forts in that workplace. Indeed, unions might be successful in using the litiga-tion process itself as a vehicle for worker mobilization. Even ultimately unsuc-cessful litigation efforts may nonetheless legitimate a movement, publicize its issues, and spur subsequent political action (Lobel 1995; Lynd 1982). Justice is not a "stagnant snapshot," but a "turbulent, cascading river," and the use of litigation to obtain justice is a process of struggle over time—a dialectical rela-tionship exists between litigation and mobilization for change (Lobel 1995, 1333).

Third, using sex discrimination litigation to combat occupational segrega-tion by sex and raise wage levels at nonunion stores not only shores up the bargaining position of workers in shops in which unions are already present but also buttresses wage and benefit standards where they are being under-mined by nonunion competitors—for example, the threat posed to retail workers' wages and benefits by nonunion Wal-Mart stores. Such efforts track the traditional area standards rationale for the legal protection of what would otherwise be illegal secondary economic-pressure tactics by unions against an employer with which they do not have a labor dispute in order to raise the wage and benefit levels of a second employer. Thus, union members may law-fully picket a nonunion employer whose wages and benefits are lower than the standard set by union contracts in the area. In *International Hod Carriers, Local 41 (Calumet Contractors' Association)* (1961), the NLRB upheld such ac-tivity, noting that a "union may be legitimately concerned that a particular employer is undermining area standards of employment by maintaining lower standards," and reasoning that the union's pressure at the nonunion shop supports its legitimate bargaining objectives at unionized shops.[7] The area

---

[7] *International Hod Carriers, Local 41 (Calumet Contractors' Association)*, 133 NLRB 512, at 512 (1961).

standards rationale offers a way to align union advocacy on behalf of nonunion women workers with the interests of labor's existing constituency. Indeed, it is completely consistent with the logic of the marketwide sectoral organizing to which the SEIU (and more recently, the Change to Win federation) has committed itself: organizing the work rather than the individual workers or employers (Milkman 2006).

Consider *Dukes v. Wal-Mart Stores,* a high-profile class action claim challenging sex-based job channeling and associated sex-based wage disparities at Wal-Mart, currently pending in the federal courts in California. The case has the potential to be a landmark in civil rights law. Indeed, the judge who granted class certification to the 1.6 million-member class referenced the Supreme Court's watershed ruling in *Brown v. Board of Education,* commenting that Brown serves as "a reminder of the importance of the courts in addressing the denial of equal treatment under the law wherever and by whomever it occurs."[8] Although Wal-Mart has been notoriously hostile to unionism and is a frequent violator of labor law, and the UFCW is conducting an aggressive nationwide organizing campaign targeting Wal-Mart, neither the UFCW nor the American Federation of Labor–Congress of Industrial Organizations (AFL-CIO) has assumed a public role in the litigation. Not a single union filed a brief in support of class certification.[9] Yet obviously the low pay and inequitable wage structure at Wal-Mart are collective economic harms, and just as clearly they undermine the efforts of UFCW member unions to maintain and extend wages and benefits in labor contracts covering workers at the grocery stores that compete with Wal-Mart. Nevertheless, although union organizers played a key role in helping to connect women workers at Wal-Mart with plaintiffs' firms and nonprofit legal centers that ultimately filed claims on their behalf (Featherstone 2004), the unions eschewed the limelight in litigation.

With such compelling arguments in favor of union participation, why have unions kept to the shadows in cases such as *Dukes*? Two legal impediments to assuming a more public role come to mind. First, unions lack standing to file claims on behalf of workers that they do not represent. Although unions have often taken the initiative in legal challenges that ultimately benefited workers broadly—nonunion as well as unionized workers—they have typically done so in situations in which they already served as the majority representative for bargaining units in industries affected by the practice, such as in cases challenging unsafe working conditions under the Occupational Safety and Health Act, cases challenging fetal protection policies, and pay equity cases.[10] Clearly,

---

[8] *Dukes v. Wal-Mart Stores,* 222 F.R.D. 137, 142 (N.D. Cal. 2004).

[9] Brad Seligman, lead counsel for the plaintiffs in Dukes, e-mail to MacKenzie Fillow, April 2, 2005.

[10] *Industrial Union Department, AFL-CIO v. American Petroleum Inst.* 448 U.S. 607 (1980); *UAW v. Johnson Controls, Inc.* 499 U.S. 187 (1991); *AFSCME v. State of Washington* (1985).

then, unions could have participated as plaintiffs in the class action sexual harassment cases in which they already represented the female workers, such as *Mitsubishi* and *Jenson*.

But what role might unions play in advocating for workers that they do not represent? Standing issues do not block unions from funding legal representation for employees they do not currently represent as long as the union does not serve as the named party plaintiff. Nor is standing a barrier to filing an *amicus* brief. Unions also may provide assistance to employees that file unfair labor practice charges with the NLRB.

A second and more serious objection is that participation by a union in litigation that is still pending when a representation election is held would furnish grounds for the employer to have the election set aside under the NLRA if the union wins, on the basis that the union's provision of legal services to the workers amounts to vote-buying. Two Courts of Appeals have ruled that union sponsorship of class action lawsuits violates the NLRA by providing a significant benefit—the provision of free legal services to workers—that interferes with employee free choice in a subsequent election.[11] Because workers may perceive the benefit as the *quid pro quo* for a pro-union vote, it has coercive potential.

Although these cases present a significant hurdle, it is far from insurmountable. The vast majority of newly organized workers—approximately 80 percent, according to AFL-CIO estimates—obtain union representation rights outside the NLRB election process, through card-check authorization (Bureau of National Affairs 2004). The prohibition on vote-buying should not apply to card-check recognition. For example, the SEIU, which typically organizes workers outside of the formal NLRA process, recently filed a class action lawsuit on behalf of 2,000 janitors in California who were denied overtime wages. In addition to negotiating a $22.4 million settlement with the employers, the union used the lawsuit to publicize bad working conditions and to advance ongoing organizing efforts (Greenhouse 2005a).

Moreover, even a union that seeks representative status via election may avoid allegations of vote-buying if it takes the long view and either files the lawsuit well before filing a petition for a union election or waits until the litigation has concluded or settled before filing the election petition; unions are banned from conferring benefits that might impermissibly influence employee voting only during the critical period between the election request and

[11] *Freund Baking Company v. NLRB* 165 F.3d 928 (D. C. Cir. 1999) and *Nestle Ice Cream Co. v. NLRB* 46 F.3d 578 (6th Cir. 1995). Although the NLRB had ruled to the contrary in *52nd Street Associates (Novotel)*, 321 NLRB 624 (1996), the District of Columbia Circuit's more recent ruling in *Freund* makes it impossible for the Board to adhere to its view because the D.C. Circuit has jurisdiction to review all Board rulings. Nor is the present conservative Board likely to be inclined to overturn *Freund*.

the vote. Once the effects of the benefit have dissipated, the risk of impermissible coercion is slight (Carlin 2001).

Although unions have often eschewed long-term strategies for mobilizing workers in favor of more intense, short-term efforts that produce more immediate gains, there is considerable evidence that long-term organizing provides a stronger foundation that enables workers to withstand the employer's counterorganizing campaign and ultimately equips them to negotiate a better contract (Hurd 1993). When employer resistance is particularly intense—as, for example, in the case of Wal-Mart—long-term strategies may be the only effective route to organizing the workforce. A long-term union-organizing campaign conducted in combination with an aggressive public stance in class action discrimination litigation seems promising.

A New Charge for Labor? Challenging Sex Discrimination

Organized labor cannot afford to continue to maintain that combating discrimination is not the union's job. Class action sex discrimination claims now occupy center stage in litigation, and the judiciary seems more open to group action by workers in this form than ever before. *Dukes v. Wal-Mart Stores* is emblematic of the public interest in such claims and the moral outrage associated with them. A Google search by the case name pulled up more than seven hundred web pages; the story is in the newspapers, on the radio, and on television. The *Dukes* case has done more to raise public consciousness of job channeling and the continued prevalence of sex-based pay inequity than decades of collective bargaining and labor arbitration or individual Title VII claims in the courts. Union absence from *Dukes* and cases like it does not mean simply one less brief filed with the court; it means that an analysis that centers all workers' economic rights is missing from the development of litigation strategy and that any settlement will be negotiated without union involvement; workplace monitoring and new policies implemented in the aftermath of the settlement will occur under the aegis of nonprofit public interest law firms and feminist groups rather than unions. Thus, the union substitutes will receive the credit for asserting working women's rights, and working women will look to them rather than to unions for representation. No wonder the decline of labor unionism is not seen as a feminist issue!

Finally, the labor movement is progressively weakened as unions bow out of enforcing antidiscrimination norms and union terrain shrinks. Acceding to the two-track legal regime turns workers' rights into a zero-sum game in which the interests of labor's traditional white male constituency are pitted against those of women and minorities. And employers are strengthened by the ensuing conflict within the working class. Ultimately, all workers are held hostage to the terms of employment negotiated by the weakest, most vulnerable, individual women rather than by the group acting through a union at the collective bargaining table.

PART III

LABOR'S WORK AND FAMILY AGENDA

In the years leading up to World War I, 20,000 immigrant women in New York's garment district left their sewing machines idle and walked out en masse, leading to the renewal of garment unionism and boosting labor's ranks to a proportion comparable to the present day. Rose Schneiderman, a garment union leader and later influential friend and advisor to Eleanor and Franklin Roosevelt, memorably captured their dreams and those of generations to come. "The woman worker wants bread," she said in 1911, "but she wants roses too" (Orleck 1995, 7).

The search for bread and roses is being carried forward today by the labor men and women discussed in this section. Bread and roses unionism is about higher wages, economic security, and decent health care or what Kris Rondeau, a Massachusetts union organizer in education and health care, calls "standard-of-living issues." But it is also about roses: about making creativity, community, and learning possible at work and building stronger and more satisfying family and community relationships.

The union leaders interviewed by Lydia Savage in chapter 6 are energized by their belief in the capacities of the men and women they work with every day. Making work less rigid, monotonous, and demeaning is a daunting prospect, but victories, large and small, occur regularly in the workplaces represented by the Harvard Union of Clerical and Technical Workers (HUCTW) and State Healthcare and Research Employees (SHARE) unions. As workers gain confidence and skills, they solve their own problems, meeting with management to design more flexible work arrangements and improve their work, family, and community lives. There is no one secret to securing bread and roses in the view of these labor leaders and little expectation that the problems they encounter in the workplace will ever wholly disappear. Yet these unions practice what they preach, making it possible for union staff as well as union members to find participation in the activities of the union meaningful and even fun.

Chapter 7 offers two case studies of innovative union-led efforts to secure family-friendly public policies at the state level. As Netsy Firestein and Nicola Dones point out, the rising demands of employment are making it difficult for many workers to fulfill their caregiving and family responsibilities. Part of the problem is the growth of long-hour jobs and multiple jobholding among low-wage workers. The rigidity of low-wage work and the lack of family benefits for nonprofessional workers create additional barriers to meeting family needs for most workers. The Labor Project for Working Families, founded by Firestein, has a dual approach to solving these problems. It supports unions such as HUCTW and SHARE, which negotiate at individual worksites for better part-time jobs, better family benefits, and more scheduling flexibility. It also organizes politically, working with unions, community, and women's groups to improve government work-family policies. In this chapter, Firestein and Dones describe two recent significant political victories for the work-family movement: the passage in California of the first state law providing paid leave for family caregivers and the little-known but innovative efforts in New York to make state-supported child care available to all.

6

CHANGING WORK, CHANGING PEOPLE

A CONVERSATION WITH UNION ORGANIZERS AT HARVARD UNIVERSITY
AND THE UNIVERSITY OF MASSACHUSETTS MEMORIAL MEDICAL CENTER

Lydia Savage

In March 2005, I sat down with Kris Rondeau, Marie Manna, Jeanne Lafferty, Bill Jaeger, Elisabeth Szanto, and Janet Wilder to discuss their approach to representing workers in the Harvard Union of Clerical and Technical Workers (HUCTW) and the State Healthcare and Research Employees (SHARE) unions. HUCTW organized 3,700 clerical and technical workers at Harvard University in 1988 after a seventeen-year effort. HUCTW then moved on to organize 2,100 clerical and technical workers at the University of Massachusetts Memorial Medical Center (UMass Medical) through a sister local named SHARE, eventually winning by an overwhelming majority of the vote in 1997. All told, HUTCW and SHARE have organized and now represent nearly eight thousand workers.[1] Both unions have a predominantly fe-

I thank Dorothy Sue Cobble for putting together this volume and for inviting me to be a part of it. I also thank Pat Finn for transcribing the interview and Kirk Davis for editing assistance. I am especially grateful to all the organizers and members of SHARE and HUCTW who have spent time with me and shared their lives with me over the years. I deeply appreciate their energy, commitment to change, and good humor.

[1] HUCTW has about 4,800 members, all employed by Harvard University or one of its affiliated units, in 130 job classifications. SHARE represents about 2,400 workers (about 85 percent women) at UMass Memorial Medical Center in a private-sector health-care system with about one-half of their members in clerical or billing roles and the other half in patient care (e.g., nursing assistants) and technical positions (e.g., respiratory therapists). SHARE also represents workers at UMass Medical School, a public institution with 450 members (about 75 percent women) who are, for example, research technicians and library and clerical staff in a variety of settings, including public mental health units, adolescent units, and even an animal medicine department, which includes animal technicians. HUCTW

male membership in a broad range of occupations scattered across numerous geographical locations and individual worksites. The unions are affiliated with the American Federation of State, County, and Municipal Employees (AFSCME).

HUCTW, and to a lesser extent SHARE, have received much attention for their innovative one-on-one organizing strategies and their creative approaches to representing workers. John Hoerr's excellent book *We Can't Eat Prestige: The Women Who Organized Harvard* (1998) is a comprehensive history of HUCTW's beginnings. Other observers have written about the ways in which HUCTW and SHARE are models for a new more democratic and transformative unionism (Clawson 2003; Cobble 1996; Eaton 1996; Hurd 1993; Oppenheim 1991; Putnam and Feldstein 2003; Savage 1996, 1998, 2005).

The six organizers I interviewed reflect the variety of backgrounds of the union staff and the workers they represent.

Kris Rondeau began working as a technician in the medical school in 1976 and remembers that she was initially a "hard-to-organize worker." She eventually joined in the effort only to see the first election loss in 1977. She became a paid organizer in 1979 and is currently the team leader.

Marie Manna graduated from the University of Rhode Island in 1975 and became a Volunteers in Service to America (VISTA) volunteer before moving to New England to work as a community organizer. She wanted to bring those skills to the labor movement and began working at the Harvard School of Public Health in 1980. Within a few months, she became involved with the organizing effort. She joined the HUCTW staff in 1981.

Bill Jaeger graduated from Yale University and moved to Cambridge where he took a job at Harvard in 1984. He became involved as a union activist shortly thereafter and worked part-time without pay before eventually joining the paid staff full-time in 1985.

Jeanne Lafferty began working at the School of Public Health at Harvard in 1975. An antiwar activist, she quickly became involved with the

also represents about 120 social workers at Cambridge Health Alliance and a small unit of family liaison workers in Cambridge Public Schools. They have an organizing campaign underway at Tufts University for about one thousand people on its three campuses.

organizing effort. She is currently a union organizer, primarily for SHARE at UMass Medical School.

Elisabeth Szanto, another SHARE organizer, joined HUCTW as a student activist while an undergraduate at Harvard. After graduating, she joined the union staff in 1987 and helped with the 1988 Harvard election victory. Once the first contract was settled at Harvard, Jeanne and Elisabeth started driving to Worcester from Cambridge to meet with workers at UMass Medical Center and they have been "driving to Worcester ever since."

Janet Wilder graduated from Oberlin College and moved to Cambridge to work as an educator for the Office Technology Education Project. She taught health and safety to office workers and many other unions. She decided to work for HUCTW because it was innovative. She joined the SHARE staff in 1991.

The following is an edited transcript of our conversation.

LS: Everyone in this group comes to this conversation with a variety of experiences and concerns, but how would you describe the threads that link you together?

KR: We are very committed as a group of friends and colleagues to the idea that every one of our members matters and that the union should have a relationship with each member. That tradition of knowing every person is very hard, but we try hard, and we know thousands and thousands of individual members.

Our overall goal is to create community and to change work, and that is a really hard thing to do because there are many obstacles to change. The greatest dilemma for our organizations is trying to make sure that we build leadership and skills in our members while we also engage with the employer.

There are four things that link us in all these activities. First, we try to create as many opportunities for real participation by workers as possible. We regularly find ourselves in odd situations where the union wants to cultivate a collaborative relationship and the employer responds in an oppositional or fearful way. Often it's the other way around—the employer puts participation on the table and unions react negatively. But that's not our experience. In our locals, we seek as much participation as possible; that can be participation at work, work design, joint committees, joint learning—all kinds of activities around work and also in building community at work.

Second, we are all committed to learning and having workers have a consciousness of the importance of learning, so we promote this in every way we can.

Third, community-building. This is basically the idea that we—workers and unions—actually create the world we want to live in. We want to live by our values, and we want to create standards for the way people treat each other. How people talk to each other, civility, and these kinds of things are part of it, but we also include community and we always attach that to family as well. So it is not just building a community but also making sure that the employer understands when we say, "this worker is doing community-building work when she is taking time to raise her family." And that is important to everybody.

Fourth, we negotiate every day on standard-of-living issues—wages, reclassifications, benefits, health, time off—doing all the economic things that unions always do to build a middle class in the service sector. We do our part vigorously. So those are my threads.

LS: So how do you take those threads and weave them together in a structure that represents workers and recognizes that workers are looking for relationships, participation, and community in the workplace? How do you create union structures that simultaneously represent workers around the economic pieces traditionally addressed by unions that also bring in the quality of relationships with co-workers and supervisors?

ES: There is a huge mental shift required—a change in the culture as it currently exists needs to be made in individual relationships as well as larger projects. To give you one example, we had a patient care assistant (PCA) who was consistently late by fifteen minutes. Her manager kept writing her up. We wanted to find out why she was late all the time. The answer was she had to walk her kids across a busy street so that they could get to school safely. She had been paying a taxicab to drive them every day, but she couldn't do that any more. So she was getting them across the street, sending them on their way, and getting to work late every day.

We were lucky in having a good manager to work with and we ended up adjusting her schedule by fifteen minutes. We were looking for a simple answer to the simple question, "Why is she late?" In the end, the arrangement had time limits on it and eventually the kids got to be old enough that her shift could be changed back. That relatively simple shift-change presented different challenges than we'd anticipated, but after approaching the problem with a full sense of the story behind it, a solution presented itself.

Right now we are engaged in a large project of trying to improve the patient satisfaction levels in the hospital. This is an issue that our members care deeply about and the current leadership has made a top priority, but it has still been hard to get the project off the ground. For years there's been one way to do things: everyone comes in at 7:00 a.m. and leaves at 3:30—that's how it's done. There is a hierarchy in the hospital: higher-ups decide how to do things—that's how it's done.

But when you are trying to change the way patients experience their health care, you should ask the people who provide the care, and that is often the PCA. The nurses have to do more and more paperwork, and it's increasingly the people who get paid $10 an hour who actually provide the bedside care. If we're going to change the experience patients have, people who don't usually listen to people who make $10 an hour are going to have to listen to them and actually change how they do things. That's a huge mental shift.

Just a note about how this relates to economic progress. If the woman I was talking about before could afford to send her kids to school in a taxicab or owned a car, she wouldn't be late. We have members who get into trouble at work because they share one car for three adults in the family. If people had a basic standard of living where their neighborhoods were safe and they had public transportation or could afford private transportation, their lives would be a lot easier. And the workplace would be more stable. So, even in a story that is mostly about flexibility and respect, there is an important economic component.

BJ: I started working for the union when I was twenty-three years old and I was really surprised to learn that flexibility is not just one thing. Really, to make all the different parts of a life fit together, people need a lot of different things at different times. It would not be logistically or logically possible to negotiate an effective and specific flexibility policy in a collective bargaining agreement.

We have language in the Harvard-HUCTW agreement about flexibility and embracing the idea of alternative schedules. But I sometimes chuckle because when you meet a new Harvard manager, they will say, "Do you have flex-time?" Just the phrase always makes me chuckle. You can tell from the way it's framed that somebody thinks of four ten-hour days. My wife works for a city government with a flex-time program; there is one regular schedule and one alternative schedule. It's perversely silly given what people's real lives are like. We really only have one choice, which is to help our members negotiate—or, better yet, to teach them to negotiate—because we won't always know what they are going to need. And they don't always know what they are going to need. And what they need is going to change over time.

I didn't understand when I was twenty-three and I would hear parents—mothers in particular—say, "My child is turning eleven or twelve and starting middle school this year so I am going to need more time off." That made no sense to me. But now I have my own kid in middle school, so I am seeing that people actually need to change their schedules and have more free time in the afternoon when their kids age-out of elementary school after-school programs. It would be bizarre to say that we should have a program or a clause in our agreement that says, "People whose kids are getting out of elementary school are entitled to revise their schedules."

So we only have one choice, and that is to teach people to negotiate for themselves. That is a really simple, powerful idea. It can be a complex challenge, especially in a large, complex environment. But it's also a rewarding challenge; there's a long, long list of wonderful success stories in what people have been able to do. It happens every day that somebody is negotiating a change in their schedule or new flexibility or new understanding with the people they work with.

MM: We've had this idea from the beginning that people have complicated lives; the workplace doesn't want to let people have lives outside of work or complicated lives. It's a very old-fashioned idea. Basically the workplace isn't taking into account all the things that happened in American society in the past thirty years. Managers still operate as if there is one person going to work, earning the money, and somebody else is taking care of everything else. But it's just not true any more. When we first started organizing it wasn't true, and it's still not true.

To truly create a good modern workplace, employers must be more open to these kinds of changes. The ideal is to teach everyone to represent themselves in negotiation. But the overall culture has to support that. So we've got to work on both levels—the organization as well as the individual—to get these things going and to move them.

That is where these other structures come into play that we try to negotiate. Structures, not rules—that's the way I think of it. We negotiate for joint committees. At the outset it can be difficult to determine what a joint committee will be about. It might be concerned with anything under the sun, but you've got to have some premise so that people can be working together on whatever the issue is. It's a very fluid kind of thing, and I think that's how life is. Neither unions nor employers have responded to this well, but especially [not] employers.

KR: This antiquated idea of fairness meaning "sameness" hampers an institution's attempts to be more productive or to generate better quality.

JW: Developing flexibility for people's lives means changing the idea of what fairness is because *fairness* is often defined as doing the same thing for everybody. We often hear a manager say something like, "I can't do it for you because then someone else will want it, too." As a union, we don't buy that definition of fairness. In our view, fairness is trying to do the most important things for each person.

I had a case where a worker had a new baby. Her partner was a police officer who worked some day shifts and some night shifts but on a regular schedule. She worked the evening shift, but she wanted to work some day shifts in order to share child care with her partner. However, that manager's view was it just couldn't be done because you either worked days or evenings. "If I were to design an unusual schedule for you, I would have to do it for everybody." So she denied the worker's request.

So basically we said, "No, you don't have to do it for everybody. This is one person asking, so let's try to do it for her. If somebody else asks we will try to do it for them. If it doesn't work, then it doesn't work. There is no commitment in doing it for one person."

To solve this problem, our co-worker, Josh, talked to everyone and found somebody who wanted to switch a couple of days for a couple of evenings. Between the two workers, each working some days and some evenings, they would cover both shifts. To make the manager more comfortable, we included an agreement that, if one of them quit, the other woman knew that her schedule would go back to where it started. That way the manager wouldn't be locked into finding a new-hire who would accept a weird schedule.

It was such a lot of work to make the perfect schedule, to make it so that the manager could have no reason to say "no." If there hadn't been a union, the change would not have happened as it did; probably the new mom would have left to find better hours elsewhere.

This old idea of fairness as "the same for everyone" allows a manager to avoid the hard work of figuring out how to make schedules work for people with complicated lives. In health care, managers are so stretched. It's very difficult to do this incredibly labor-intensive thing. Managers don't have the energy even when they want to and know people well enough to make things work out.

ES: The union often plays that role of coordinator because we have a problem that needs addressing. We will do the work because we know people and they want answers. We can put their stories together. Although I'm glad there is a union to come up with a happy solution, I sometimes wish we didn't have to spend so much of our time doing that.

MM: We are trying to go in the direction of self-directed teams in work reorganization. If each of the employees managed the department on some level, then the group could coordinate and resolve scheduling issues more efficiently—we are trying to get to the point that employees are going to have more control over what goes on at work.

ES: In some cases, workers actually have the capacity to solve the problem, but they don't have the right to solve it.

MM: They haven't been given the right or the responsibility—that's a real shift. Early on as we worked with employees this way, some members would say, "I don't get paid as a supervisor. I shouldn't have to do that. That is their worry." And we are trying to shift that and say that workers can gain from this but they are going to have to take on more responsibility in order to do it. That's the big change that has to happen.

JW: So much of changing relationships between workers and supervisors is respect. Once you get people in a room talking about things they both care about, respect appears because everybody recognizes that patient care is always common ground. If you can find an excuse to put people together then that's the beginning of respectful relationships where people can break down hierarchy. It's that moment of realizing "You know so much about this question, let's figure this out together." The union has taken on the role of being the one who gets them into the same room and sets the ground rules for respectful conversation between people, with the hope that this dynamic becomes a part of the culture eventually.

BJ: We are completely sold on a set of ideas about new work systems that improve the working environment and the group organizational performance, whether you are talking about which employees will cover a given set of work hours or our members' happiness in their working environment. It absolutely works. It is worth working intensively in union-management partnerships to reexamine and redesign the work systems, to increase investment in training for workers, to increase self-direction and flatten supervisory hierarchies. And we have had success demonstrating to our members that the new work systems are worth it.

It's not always easy to convince our members—sometimes they've been invited in the past by management into participatory roles that proved to be empty. But the opportunity is available to management to make a significant improvement in the way the organization performs. The price for managers is the shift away from an old command-and-control way of thinking. For managers, that is a very hard choice. They really struggle with it.

Since we have been able to reorganize parts of Harvard and provide more opportunities for self-direction, more skills and strategies for planning coordinating roles, so far—without fail—our members have been interested in redesigning the scheduling. Unilateral workplace design doesn't work; there needs to be more flexibility to figure out the work schedule in a creative way. Our members are always interested in learning more, increasing skills, and improving organizational group performance. A supervisor in her office with her door closed can't figure out by herself how to make this schedule more flexible in a way that is going to respond to the needs and responsibilities that the workers have outside the workplace. But oftentimes the workers and their union can figure it out.

JW: I can't tell you the number of times that I've reached a point in a problem where I could see no way to bring the different viewpoints together, even after talking to every person involved. So I finally say, let's get everyone in the same room and have it out. It is remarkable to me how many times a problem solves itself as soon as you have everybody in the room. People stop demonizing each other. They stop stating their position so extremely. There's somebody in the room who makes sure everybody's on their good behavior and shapes the conversation around finding common ground. You walk out with an answer. At times I think, "How was that possible? I talked to everybody and I couldn't find an answer." But when they are all together they found one. That's one of the keys to the problem-solving model. The union doesn't hold keys to solutions, but we do coach and support members in the search to find those keys.

We don't have a traditional grievance procedure; we have a problem-solving process with mediation and arbitration as the final step. Problem-solving takes the adversarial nature out of the process and emphasizes union and management working together to solve the problem. The problem-solving process is not limited to issues spelled out in the contract. We coach the worker in everyday negotiation skills. It's remarkable what can get solved.

It actually changes the nature of work for the person who is involved in a very substantial way. Perhaps most important, by not taking the problem out of the worker's hands to be decided by others, as in a traditional grievance procedure, we can change the nature of work for the people involved. The next time, the worker may not need the union rep or HR [human resources], or may call the union rep just to strategize about it and then go solve the problem with their manager on their own. When people learn to represent themselves, the balance of power shifts.

ES: A huge number of problems are resolved at the first step in our problem-solving process. In the hospital union, we've had four arbitrations in seven years. To be frank, we had to do some to set a standard because some managers seemed to think that our more polite approach made us easier to push around. So we set some standards about what we wouldn't put up with. And the result is that now we do a joint investigation before any termination that we consider controversial. We don't have to go to mediation or arbitration very often; it's cheaper and we save a lot of time that way.

Very rarely is the problem-solving case something involving the contract; those mostly either don't happen or get quickly fixed. Usually it's a conflict between an employee and a supervisor. We resolve at least five or six hundred of those every year—sometimes through direct intervention but often by coaching the employee to represent him- or herself.

BJ: When a problem-solving process goes well, the other thing that happens is we educate and we provide the manager with a different way of resolving conflict. We were talking earlier about wanting to train all of our members to negotiate. Sometimes our members remind us that it only does so much good to have all these skills and strategies and all this enthusiasm if the managers are left out of the learning. We have to be working on the whole culture. The problem-solving process—if we are really dedicated and working really hard at it and invest in it—gives us the opportunity to build trust.

JW: It is an amazing union experience for the union reps to learn and do problem solving. Yet we constantly struggle—is it worth the time it takes to train someone new? It's relatively easy to give reps classes in problem solving, to provide ideas for what to expect and how to get through a tough meeting, and to talk about the role of organizing. But to really learn problem solving, we believe that organizers have to work one-on-one with each activist. We do problem solving in pairs for a while, then consult with everyone until they get really comfortable, and consult again as they take on tougher cases.

So much of problem solving is about relationships and trust, and you can't teach that in a class. We put a huge amount of work into the process, but the payoff is worth it. Repeatedly we are reminded how worthwhile it is to invest time in an activist. Each person who can solve increasingly complex problems and who can become a leader adds strength to the union and to the workplace.

LS: How are the unions approaching job redesign and learning?

BJ: In contract negotiations at Harvard, we have pressed repeatedly to increase the opportunities for learning in terms of formal education and training. We're just trying to remove barriers. We are trying to get cheaper or free on-site training opportunities and increased tuition assistance for formal education paths. We have good, negotiated policy language about using paid work-time for training, education, or professional development. Although time off is one of those things that the contract language treats well, we have to encourage our members to take advantage of it.

As an organization, we have to give more support and encouragement to our members to learn and be optimistic about learning. We need to interpret the contemporary American workplace for workers so they understand how important learning is. Much more often now I find myself saying to a member, "Do you know you have to do this? You have to take part in training programs." Or "You should finish that bachelor's degree. It might be a question of professional success or failure." We've seen that it's more urgent than it used to be and the stakes are higher.

I am working on a problem right now where a department head is giving up on retraining a couple of workers. The department changed its technology, so we are arguing about whether the department should invest and train these two women or lay them off and hire replacements. I went to a meeting with management about this, and they were talking about the worker's low skill levels. I thought part of this might be age bias; I had this vague feeling that I would look up their ages and discover they were in their fifties. They weren't—one worker is thirty-nine and the other is forty-one. So it's not only about age; it's about skills. I hope we are going to win, but it's one of those stories that makes it clear that, besides changing policies to lower barriers, we also have to encourage our members to jump higher, to climb higher.

KR: When workers connect with the union, each one can figure out how to become a learner. There are three levels of learning. One is internal learning through union programs; there's a wide array of these. The next level is job-related and career development-related. The third is what we will call "What about Shakespeare?" That is, learning for its own sake that may not be about the employee's career or directly connected to her capacity to be a union leader. However, we recognize that continuous adult learning is good for your pocketbook and your soul too.

JL: UMass Medical School has been notoriously—in the past—legal-minded. Problems were solved often by doing the minimum that would fly legally. There was no understanding of creative or cooperative problem solving. I think there are openings for us to work together now that we didn't have in the past. You can make small changes and fine things can happen that wouldn't have happened two years ago. Slowly this place has come to feel different to people, and that's a powerful thing. It is perceptible.

A key reason for that shift is that our union has always valued the idea of not becoming adversarial no matter how rough the going gets. A bad substitute for this would be to say, "All right, I guess we just can't do this." We try, rather, to look at another way of achieving a thing. It's a marvelous thing to work with good people at problem solving, negotiate a more creative contract, or put more learning into that contract.

MM: In a way, the workers at UMass Medical School are trying to create a workplace culture. That's not always easy to do; it's really been a collaborative effort to come up with a workplace personality and a culture that would hold people together.

We've always had this very basic idea that people should be able to represent themselves. That's what it's all about—people learning more about themselves and how to do things. The idea is that the more people can do for themselves, the more things are going to change. It might take longer that way, but it's actually going to change the institution.

We have taken the three most important things to our locals and created training opportunities for our members. Organizing, Connections, and Building Relationships is one of the workshops. The second one talks about everyday negotiation; what are the kinds of skills you need? How does the negotiator prepare? How do you think about negotiating with a supervisor?

The third is problem solving. These workshops have two purposes: showing people that this union has a very different approach to things and conveying the specific skills that we use. I feel like we need to put as much energy into that as we do into directly working with management. It will change the dynamic eventually.

BJ: As we build and reinforce the architecture of this idea, we want to add workshops on meeting skills and on customer service skills. This is interesting because, to some extent, it is in those areas where we are challenging orthodoxy because those are areas where there is a traditional, management-driven way of teaching people about how to do customer service and how to participate in meetings. Our workshops are going to say something different about that.

LS: And by customer you mean the people your union members are interacting with?

KR: Yes—students, faculty, visitors, and, of course, co-workers. Library workers have patrons and faculty assistants have students, and so on.

JW: *Customer* is not our word. It's a word that employers now call the people you deal with.

LS: It's interesting that HUCTW is working with employees on customer service and SHARE is working on patient satisfaction, when it seems like management should be focused on doing that work.

KR: That's exactly right. I began doing this work thinking that the places where we would have conflict with management would be how big the raises were.

JL: In fact, it is often more difficult to achieve change in the dynamics of employer-employee interactions than to negotiate for money.

JW: There are real things to be fixed that would make patients happier, that would make workers happier, that would make the place run better, that would make the hospital more productive, [and] that would probably get the hospital more money.

Unlike manufacturing, hospitals have not been profit-oriented organizations for very long; now they have to make money and they aren't set up for that. They are always scared about money and unable to figure out how to move forward because they are holding the roof together.

At a workshop recently, the facilitator told us the key to improvement is "First stabilize, and then innovate." That's the problem in the hospital, the stabilizing part. You can't get to innovate because there is so much going on in health care that you can't stabilize.

Our members say over and over, "I love my job; I hate the stuff around it." If we could remove the barriers that make our members' work needlessly difficult and give them the ability to do the work that they want to do, that would be best thing that we could do as a union.

We had a project in the CAT [computed axial tomography] scan department a while back. We put a huge amount of effort into it and involved everybody in the redesign of jobs: the prioritization of the patients, the standardizing of the protocol, and the reorganization of the workflow. We had it all figured out, but management wouldn't take the risk to endorse it and spend the little bit of money to start. No manager at the time was willing to take the risk if success couldn't be guaranteed.

Worker participation in work design is at the top of our priority list. We train members on organizing and problem solving. And we are doing a bunch of other things that don't need to come from the union, but we see a need to fill in gaps. We run pension workshops, for example. So we have got some worker-experts in those fields because we trained them. But it's not the kind of work we really want to be doing, which is figuring out how to redesign patient care to make it work better for the patients and employees.

MM: We are very persistent. There just isn't anything else to do. We are persistent about the quality of work as well as the quality of life. We can't just give up on that and go for the economic incentive. We figured out quickly, it's easier to get money than it is to get almost anything else. That's just such a soulless thing.

Maybe that's what work has always been. Maybe it's not a question of the way things are becoming. But is that what we want it to be? Is that how people want to spend their lives?

We just keep chipping away and trying to figure out what would make these different structures for participation effective. Even if an attempt doesn't work, everyone involved learns from the experience.

BJ: The hopeful note is, as a result of that persistence that Marie is describing, we're carrying out experimental projects in the Harvard setting—and we are documenting them. These projects focus on our union members being involved in the redesign of their work systems. There are encouraging results so far.

We have had real success in changing the way managers in those groups think. And those are some of the university's star managers at this point; people whose units are growing and who are being given more responsibility. There are instances that we can point to at Harvard that show us it's possible to realize some of these ideas, and we've had success in convincing Harvard to commit resources to support further experimentation.

Unions face the challenge of the lack of everyday democracy in the American workplace. There's a real opportunity to be thinking in terms of both structural approaches and also the fun, community-building approaches to workplace issues. I think it's an exciting and powerful democratizing effect when a union gives away chocolate in the lobby of a building, and especially when union members participate in redesigning their work system. The combination of those approaches is fun to think about.

ES: One of the things that I get out of a conversation like this is the reminder of the importance of persistence—basically we have to live our lives in a healthy way when our management partner is not ready to work with us and always be ready to accept them and to work in partnership with them when they are ready. If you are going to build something that almost no one else is building, you have to be patient. It's easier when we can work with the same managers over a few years, but there is a huge turnover in management, especially HR. We are constantly meeting new managers and going through a process that begins with them thinking, "Gee, they're really nice but I won't have to deal with them too much." And then pretty soon it's "Wait a minute—they're back."

There was one meeting Janet and I had with a new HR employee; he said, "I don't understand why we are talking about this. Haven't we answered this question before?" And his manager, who'd been there longer than him, just started laughing and said, "Yep. That's what SHARE does. They just keep asking the question until somebody gives them the answer they're looking for." It was a funny moment. It was good for the new guy, and it was good for my soul because we'd been working for a long time with the woman who said this. It made me happy that she noticed we persist.

One of the things SHARE wanted to talk about is equity for part-time employees. And that's a good example of persistence. HUCTW had a hard-fought battle over health insurance rates for part-time employees at Harvard. It was won many, many times. It certainly required bulldog persistence. It's important that we hold on to that. We have to keep thinking, "We may not get it this time, so we have to get it next time." We still have a lot of things we want to change about these workplaces, but if we had taken a short-term view of what's possible to change, we'd never have gotten as far as we have.

LS: Could you talk a little bit about the need for part-time equity? What it is and how did you get it?

BJ: Our experience is that voluntary, benefited, part-time work is incredibly important societal glue. For those reasons, and for the flexibility we were talking about before, people have to be able to work part-time for a period in their lives, or for most or all of their lives. The Harvard workforce is full of artists and writers and students, actors and moms and gardeners, ne'er-do-wells and scoundrels of various types. There are a lot of people—something like 15 percent—of HUCTW members who work less than full-time. Those people are doing great things, great community-building, community-serving things.

The big thing about equity for part-time workers is health care. When we talk with artists and musicians about why they work at Harvard, that's what they say. Part-time plus health care is the ticket for moms and dads, too. It's incredibly valuable and is way too rare. Tragically, I think many Americans are making decisions about things they love and care about based on the threat of losing health care.

ES: In the hospital, the percentage of our members who work less than full-time is enormous. It's partly because the hospital functions by having part-time employees who are eager for overtime or for extra straight-time hours and partly because every single person can be put into a weekend rotation.

A few years ago, when the hospitals merged, the resulting conglomeration tried to bring the benefits down to the lower level of whichever system had less. The old Memorial health insurance was structured so that you paid a much larger percentage if you were part-time and had family coverage. We altered that, based on the Harvard example.

JW: Another thing that we have done, based on the fact that people come in and out of the workplace, is we have worked hard to restore their time. For instance, if you left the hospital and came back, you got your previous time back for the purpose of calculating seniority lists and lay-offs and your vacation. Those things are based on total number of years you've worked there, not how long you've worked there recently.

It's interesting that some managers have the idea that the time an employee has been at a given workplace in one stretch is a measure of their loyalty. These managers believe that the decision is about an employee going to work for a competitor and then coming back because they've decided their first employer was really better. They believe the employee should have been loyal enough in the first place to never leave.

ES: Management sometimes also views an employee's children as competitors. If you are really loyal, you will figure out a way to stay at work and take care of your family. We have that a lot. For many of the incidents children have that call their parents away from work, the employer's response usually is something like, "Couldn't you get someone else to do that?" In response, his mother's saying, "He doesn't have a father." Or "Yes, but you wrote his father up for doing it last week." Or "Yeah, I could ask my mother, but she's working on another floor."

MM: In these cases, there's no recognition of the whole person. It sometimes seems as if all the other aspects of that employee vanish when she comes to work.

KR: On the other hand, I think that managers are suffering as much. In general, managers earn more and can outsource more of their domestic responsibility. But the modern paradigm has labor and management in pain. If there is any hope for the future, it might come out of this mutual misery.

I'd like to throw out two things that we might want to address. One is that we negotiate with employers for joint money so that we can go through processes of learning and discovery together or do projects together. And the other is work security.

There's a particularly amazing story that comes out of the SHARE local when the infamous Hunter Group came in to make drastic cuts there. We don't have bumping[2] because we don't believe in it. But we do have work security, which basically says that the institution and the union make a joint commitment to find somebody a job and there's money for training. We have all kinds of rules if somebody has to be laid off. Then we say your emphasis shouldn't be on who gets laid-off; it should be on finding that person a job. There's expansive work security, which means that the employer agrees to help find a job even if it's outside the bargaining unit so that union and nonunion jobs are up for grabs if there are vacancies.

We have had situations where management said they were going to lay off an employee and the workers got together to talk about it. One might have said, "I've been trying to cut my hours." Or another, "I would be happy to have Friday morning off." And together they figured out how to cut the hours rather than losing one person.

But the most successful piece [of the union's response to Hunter] was

[2] Bumping occurs when a worker with lower seniority is displaced so that a worker with more seniority can retain a position. Many unions provide work security through contract provisions that require seniority as an important factor governing lay-offs.

the volunteer system. If someone is under the threat of being laid off, we put out the alert to everyone in a similar job title: "If you would like to be laid off, please raise your hands and we will find out if it's a compatible swap." And then the person who was going to be laid off takes the other person's job and the person who wants to be laid off gets the lay-off benefits, including the training money.

JW: Many employees jumped at that combination of severance and money for schooling. Some workers said, "It was exactly what I was hoping for right now." One member wanted to retire in six months; with unemployment and severance money, she could move to Florida early and start building her house. She was ecstatic. Sometimes these arrangements allow a member to go and take care of somebody in their family.

I know one woman who has taken more of the training money than any one else. She swapped with somebody who was going to be laid off who had worked there twenty years. Now she's getting her bachelor's in psychology. She said, "I've never had this opportunity. I never had time to not earn a living and go to school. And I decided in the beginning that even though I initially didn't know what I wanted to do, I knew I would never be given this opportunity again." It's so exciting that she is going off finding a new life for herself.

The other guy whose life would have been drastically complicated by a lay-off is okay. He has a new position within the same hospital. His wife works there. They both have worked there forever. They commute together. Their whole lives are set up around working there. And he's really happy to learn a new thing in a different community with different people.

ES: What I loved about it, first of all, was that you had to have a relationship to make that job-swapping idea fly. Second, in a lot of these swaps there was an act of generosity, one member protecting another who couldn't afford a lay-off. People said, "She's a single mom. I'll find another job." I think it's another case in which the contract language is fairly exceptional. And then there was making it work on the ground, which is also exceptional. We trained dozens of employee reps to be with a person while they were hearing the news of their lay-off and to follow up with that person afterward.

JL: SHARE arranged for workers to be brought to a room after they heard the news of the lay-off. There they got more help in figuring out what some possible next-steps were. Then members had an individual rep assigned to them so that, when they went home and fully realized what had happened to them, they had a phone number to call.

JW: Their rep called them every day until they were okay. Then they called them again every few days until they were placed. So every single SHARE member who was laid off had someone to hold their hand from the moment they were laid off, from the moment of the horrible experience of hearing it. Afterward the rep was there to find out what resources were available. And the rep provided notes on paper for that member to take away with them, since it's hard to remember information when the words *lay off* are going off in their heads.

Every single person either decided to move on or found a job in the place. There were many people who did not want to work there again, but there was nobody who wanted to work at UMass Memorial who couldn't.

ES: And that's when we figured out what we were doing was really special. A manager who was laying off a nonunion person and who then laid off a SHARE person said to us, "I'm so glad you were here. I'm so glad that my person has you here with her because I feel so bad for these people." Of course we were here.

LS: What else do you have joint money with management for?

ES: We cared enough to foster a relationship to make sure there was joint money there to spend on facilitators and mediators and other things for direct projects. We have to really make them happen because otherwise you get to the point where management says, "Let's try this." And then there's the moment of realization: "Oh. Wait. Shoot. It's going to cost start-up money." So if we can remove that hurdle before we begin the conversation, it puts us that much closer to being able to do what we said.

KR: It may be some kind of heresy even among ourselves to say this, but I'm not sure that we believe in some broad culture change or that it's possible to decide to change an organization. Everything that we have ever done—let's say it's about accommodating schedules, more education, or career development or taking care of your mom or your children—every single one of those has been individually negotiated. As Janet said, it's a new definition of fairness, but it's also an idea that the problems that exist in the workplace are intractable and they require individual solutions. You can't do it cleanly in one fell swoop. So what you need to do—for work security, for problem solving, for flexibility, for learning and career development—is to grow deep roots in a community. It requires hundreds of people being involved figuring it out even in a single workplace. And you have to build deep skill in that community. If labor can do that, then labor has done something fabulous because it gives people the opportunity to figure out how to change work, which is a continuous challenge.

BJ: Skills make people powerful, and it's really cool to see our members figure this out, to see that the skills you have matter more than which box someone puts you in on an organizational chart. The people who are painted in the low boxes can have a huge amount of influence and can sometimes negotiate and maneuver in circles around the people who are in the higher boxes on the chart. I think that's really good for workers, [for] unions, and for the organizations employing our members.

Not everybody believes this. We have a lot to do to convince some of our members of that. I guess I'm saying skills not only trump position on the organizational chart but they trump contract language as well. Every day we see that happening. It's a big job we have to do helping all our members understand that. Some are deeply skeptical, but others really love the idea.

ES: We spent so many years agreeing to management's nervous requests that we sign something stipulating that a particular agreement would not be precedent-setting that they figured out we will agree that almost anything is non-precedent setting. Because we are quite confident that we could get that deal again if we need to.

But at the same time they're learning something about us, I'm learning something about the prevailing culture, which is that management believes that most unions wouldn't agree to change one lady's schedule by fifteen minutes so she can walk her kids across the busy street without demanding that everyone should have that right.

KR: People have a number of archaic beliefs. One of these archaic beliefs is [about] what a union is. Another one is that the rule of law is democracy—but it isn't; they are two separate things. A third is that a lot of people believe that a simple identity is better than a complex one. I don't think that's true. We have these archaic definitions, and they're holding us back from figuring out how to change work and fix some things that are really bad for us. I think for a supervisor it is much better to have a complex worker with a complex identity, even if she has to pick up her kids at four o'clock.

MM: That's what some managers can't get. They can't get that they're really gaining something by having that complex, intelligent, thoughtful person. Some people can't deal with that; they want the world to be very ordered.

BJ: What confounds me still about the everyday American workplace is the Grand Canyon–size gap between theory and practice in this regard. A lot of what we are talking about is the idea that American unions need to be reinvented. And it is clear that American management needs to be reinvented.

But you know what? Management reinvention has already been written. For thirty years, everything that has come out of the business school has said the same thing. It's been about management reinvention; it's just that the redesign of American business has not been implemented. I think the barriers are psychological, and they are about class and self-image. The reinvention of American management sometimes seems so much closer—so much more accessible—than the reinvention of American labor because it's been analyzed and scripted meticulously. It just hasn't been done yet.

ES: Recently one of our members, who is her department's union rep, called me to ask for her job description as a union rep. I said, "Sure, but why?" She said, "My supervisor is writing my performance evaluation, and she wants to say that I have learned new things and new skills and bring them to the department." I joyfully gave her the job description of a union rep.

Before our union election, this employee was anti-union, so I am especially happy that she is a rep. What's more, this supervisor had once physically escorted us out of the building from one of our informational meetings. The idea that these two people—the one that nervously walked us out of the building and the one who was always polite but thought the union was going to make the workplace too rigid—are sitting down and talking about how great it is that one of them has learned new problem-solving skills and brings those to her department, and the other one is giving her a better performance evaluation because of that seems to me to be symbolic of the possibility of change.

7

UNIONS FIGHT FOR WORK AND FAMILY POLICIES—NOT FOR WOMEN ONLY

Netsy Firestein and Nicola Dones

Imagine not being able to attend a school performance of your five-year-old or not being able to stay home with your daughter when she gets sick. Imagine that your mom falls and breaks her hip and you cannot get paid time off to care for her. Imagine trying to find child care during your 4 p.m. to midnight work shift or having to choose between getting fired or leaving your child home alone. Issues like these are faced by workers every day, yet they are often seen as personal problems rather than social issues in need of public solutions. And despite the growing number of workers taking care of elderly parents and other family members, the rise of single-headed families, and the increase of working mothers, we lack the basic social supports and social insurance that would help workers manage the growing demands of work and family.

For many workers today, a good job means a livable wage, family health insurance, a safe workplace, and retirement benefits. But increasingly it also means having workplace and policy supports that allow workers, both men and women, to care for their families. Such policies include quality, affordable child care and after-school care that correspond to work hours; flexible employment schedules that workers control; part-time work with benefits; paid

Parts of this article were adapted from Netsy Firestein and Lauren Asher, "Putting Families First: How California Won the Fight for Paid Family Leave," Labor Project for Working Families report, http://www.paidfamilyleave.org/pdf/paidleavewon.pdf (accessed June 6, 2006).

family leave; paid sick days for workers or a family member; and quality elder-care services that are affordable.

In this chapter, we look at how unions are helping to fight for the work and family policies that workers need. We describe two recent state campaigns: the campaign for paid family leave legislation in California and the New York state campaign to make child care more affordable for working families. In each case, the policies would not have been passed without the leadership of labor. They are examples of unions acting in accordance with the best and highest ideals of the labor movement. Rather than operating as a special-interest group or mobilizing simply to benefit current members, unions worked to create better jobs and an improved quality of life for all workers. The paid family leave law in California, the first of its kind in the nation, created a new benefit for working families that affects every private-sector worker (and some public-sector) in California. In New York, union-sponsored legislation greatly expanded the number of working parents who could receive state subsidies to help them pay for child care.

How the United States Compares

What many of us do not realize is how different the United States is for working women and families than are other countries. A report by the Project on Global Working Families (Heyman 2000) found that the United States lags behind other countries in many areas, including leave policies and services for children.[1] Consider the following:

- Worldwide, 163 countries offer guaranteed paid leave to women in connection with childbirth; the United States does not.
- At least seventy-six countries protect working women's right to breastfeed; the United States does not, in spite of the fact that breast-feeding has been shown to reduce infant mortality sevenfold.
- At least ninety-six countries around the world, in all geographic regions and at all economic levels, mandate paid annual leave (vacation); the United States does not.
- At least eighty-four countries have laws that fix the maximum length of the workweek; the United States does not have a maximum length of the workweek or a limit on mandatory overtime per week.
- The United States is thirty-ninth (and tied with Ecuador and Suri-

[1] Linda Giannerelli, Sarah Adelman, and Stefanie R. Schmidt, "Getting Help with Child Care Expenses," 2003, The Urban Institute, http://www.urban.org/url.cfm?ID=310615 (accessed June 6, 2006).

name) in enrollment in early childhood care and education for three-
to five-year-olds. Nearly all European countries perform better. A
wide range of developing countries have higher enrollment rates than
the United States, despite being poorer.
• In the United States, eligibility for child-care subsidies are set so low
that often even very low-income workers do not qualify. In the United
States, low-income families spend 14 percent of their earnings on
child care, whereas higher-earning families spend 7 percent.

For over a century, unions have fought at the bargaining table and in the
legislature to improve the work and family lives of U.S. workers. From the five-
day workweek to overtime compensation, from livable wages to retirement
pensions, unions have pushed for and won vital work family supports. In
2001, a resolution from the American Federation of Labor–Congress of Industrial Organizations (AFL-CIO) Convention pledged the continued support of
labor for working families, urging legislative action on a broad range of issues,
including paid family leave and universal preschool. These issues are now part
of the broader labor struggle that includes job outsourcing, loss of pensions,
and increased health-care costs. Recently, unions have pushed for laws to limit
mandatory overtime for health-care workers, provide unemployment insurance due to child-care responsibilities, expand the Family and Medical Leave
Act (FMLA), and use paid sick leave to care for family members.

Unions have always fought for change both through contract language and
through public policy; on the work-family front this is the case as well. At the
local level, unions have successfully negotiated family-friendly workplace provisions and innovative arrangements with employers such as flexible work
hours, elder-care benefits, and paid leave. Although there has been no research
documenting the extent of bargaining on these issues, the Labor Project for
Working Families (Labor Project) has tracked over three hundred contracts
with comprehensive family-friendly provisions. However, we believe that this
is just a small percentage of provisions that have been negotiated across the
country. Unions have negotiated paid family leave, flexible work arrangements, and other innovative benefits including a child- and elder-care plan for
hotel workers in San Francisco, a family-care plan for Oakland's transit workers, and a child-care fund for hospital workers in New York.[2]

Unions are also endorsing the Work and Family Bill of Rights, a document
originally created by the Labor Project in partnership with labor leaders and
updated by Take Care Net, a network of unions, advocates, and academics. It
recognizes that workers have certain fundamental rights related to work and

[2] Labor Project for Working Families, "A Job and a Life: Organizing and Bargaining for Work Family Issues," http://www.laborproject.org/bargaining/guide.pdf (accessed June 6, 2006).

family.[3] Although the corporate work-family agenda remains narrow in scope, labor's vision looks to encompass the larger economic picture and the right of all workers to care for themselves and their families with dignity.

Background

In 1993, the FMLA became law with the assistance of unions and other groups. It gives many working Americans the right to take up to twelve weeks of *unpaid* leave when a new child arrives, a family health crisis strikes, or they themselves are ill. The FMLA protects jobs and benefits, but it does not help pay the bills. Independent studies commissioned by the Department of Labor in 1995 and 2000 found that the primary reason people who need leave do not take it is that they simply cannot afford it. The research also found that nearly one in ten FMLA users is forced on to public assistance while on leave (Cantor et al. 2001).

As more people became aware of a right they could not necessarily afford to use, interest in paid family leave grew. Research and policy models looked at everything from unemployment insurance to social security to the commercial insurance market as possible vehicles for providing paid leave. In 1999, the National Partnership for Women & Families, which led the nine-year fight to pass the FMLA, launched the Campaign for Family Leave Benefits to fuel a growing movement to make family leave more affordable.

More and more, these issues are being addressed by unions at the state policy level to meet the needs of all workers. Five states (California, Rhode Island, New Jersey, New York, and Hawaii) already have a temporary disability insurance program that provides partial pay for a workers' own illness and to recover from pregnancy, usually referred to as pregnancy disability. Unions have helped to pass states laws allowing workers to use part or all of their paid sick time to care for a sick family member.[4]

Unions have also been involved in campaigns for universal preschool in many states. Georgia and Oklahoma provide preschool to all four-year-olds whose parents want to enroll them. New Jersey and New York have preschool programs that target low-income children and many of the teachers in those programs are unionized. Florida passed a ballot initiative for universal preschool, but it is not yet funded (Muenchow 2004). In California, advocates and unions are working on a state ballot initiative for universal preschool for the June 2006 election. Other states have efforts underway for similar pro-

[3] For more information, see the Take Care Net website, http://www.takecarenet.org.

[4] Labor Project for Working Families, "A Job and a Life: Organizing and Bargaining for Work Family Issues," http://www.laborproject.org/bargaining/guide.pdf (accessed June 6, 2006).

grams. Although many of these programs are still underfunded, the goal is to provide free, voluntary, universal preschool. Parents still need to find and pay for child care for the rest of the day, but this is a first step toward acknowledging the importance of care and education for young children.

California—Labor's Winning Fight for Paid Family Leave

On September 23, 2002, California became the first state in the nation to provide comprehensive paid family leave.[5] The new law, the California Family Rights Act (CFRA), gives most working Californians up to six weeks of partial pay to care for a new child or seriously ill family member (parent, child, spouse, or domestic partner). It is an extension of California's state disability insurance program, which has provided partial pay to workers taking time off for a nonwork-related serious medical condition since the 1940s.

At least three factors made California especially fertile ground for a paid family leave campaign. First, California already had a well-established system for delivering paid medical leave. Nearly all working Californians are covered by leave.

Second, a strong labor and advocacy base was in place. In 1999, with funding from the Rosenberg Foundation, the Labor Project formed the Work and Family Coalition. This coalition brought state and local labor (including the Bay Area labor councils), advocacy, and community groups (including childcare organizations and legal groups) together to support one another's efforts and improve California's work-family policies on a larger scale. Paid family leave was one of the main issues on the agenda.

The California Labor Federation (Labor Federation), which is the state-level AFL-CIO, also recognized the organizing potential of work-family benefits and was interested in issues that resonated with women and low-wage workers. A strong, progressive, and politically powerful organization, the Labor Federation saw improving state safety-net benefits, such as disability insurance, as the best way to help working Californians. The Labor Federation was a member of the Work and Family Coalition and had a successful track record on related legislation including pregnancy disability leave and family sick leave.

Third, California's favorable political climate made a difference. California's large and diverse population supports many groups representing the interests of women, children, seniors, parents, immigrants, disabled popula-

---

[5] Netsy Firestein and Lauren Asher, "Putting Families First: How California Won the Fight for Paid Family Leave," Labor Project for Working Families, 2004, http://www.paidfamilyleave.org/pdf/paid leavewon.pdf (accessed June 6, 2006).

tions, and others with a stake in family leave policy. It is also home to numerous employment law and civil rights organizations with expertise on complex issues relevant to paid leave. Many of these diverse organizations worked to pass the CFRA and FMLA, supported more recent family leave bills, and conducted outreach on family leave issues. For example, in the late 1990s the Legal Aid Society–Employment Law Center and the Asian Law Caucus began training unions and other groups and established a hotline for workers with family leave problems. They and many other organizations were interested in paid family leave and had long-standing relationships with one another and with the Labor Federation and Labor Project.

Democrats had controlled California's Assembly, Senate, and governor's office since 1998. Although business interests hold plenty of sway on both sides of the aisle, California's elected Democrats, including then-Governor Gray Davis, had very strong ties to labor and were generally responsive to progressive interests. The paid family leave bill was introduced at the start of an election year, with the state's incumbent governor running for a second term. Whether this timing would help or hurt the bill's prospects was unclear. Politicians needed votes from women, seniors, union members, and others likely to support paid family leave. The same politicians, however, also would be raising money from corporate donors and seeking support from fiscally conservative swing voters.

Building the Campaign

The story of how paid family leave became California law follows the broad outlines of any successful political campaign. Advocates invested in building awareness and relationships over time secured support from powerful partners, faced opposition and many unknowns, and succeeded through a combination of grassroots mobilization, political pressure, legislative maneuvering, media outreach, and compromise.

In late 1999, several important developments helped pave the way for a concerted paid leave campaign in California. First, labor achieved a major victory in its efforts to improve the state's social insurance safety net when Governor Davis signed a bill raising California's SDI benefit. The first benefit increase in many years, it cleared the path for labor leaders to consider expanding SDI to cover family leave. The same bill directed the Employment Development Department (EDD) to study the potential costs of providing paid family leave through SDI. EDD finished its study in summer 2000 and confirmed that paid family leave could be provided through SDI at a very modest cost.

In early 2001, the Labor Project secured a multiyear grant from the David and Lucile Packard Foundation. With these resources, a core group of labor and other advocates began building what it expected to be a two- to five-year campaign for paid family leave. The advocates organized a broad labor-community coalition, the Coalition for Paid Family Leave (the Coalition), which included seniors, women's, child-care, legal, and health organizations, as well as a diverse group of unions; drafted legislation; got technical assistance from the National Partnership for Women & Families; gathered personal stories that illustrated the need for paid leave; sought support from progressive business owners; built union awareness by holding workshops during the summer and fall of 2001; and worked with University of California academics to estimate the costs and benefits of paid leave, write op-eds, and provide testimony.

In his letter to the editor, "Paid Leave: $2 a Month; Happy Workers: Priceless" (*Santa Barbara News Press*, July 24, 2002), Paul Orfalea, the founder of Kinko's, Inc., stated, "Various things make people feel good about their work, not least of which is when they feel respected and valued by their employers. When one of my co-workers grieved, I grieved." He pointed out the common sense of offering such a benefit. "It seems that it would cost business more if it didn't provide this type of insurance, especially in these tough economic times." In her op-ed for the *San Jose Mercury News* (June 21, 2002), Kay Trimberger, a California sociologist, wrote about Jeff Norvet, a Hollywood cameraman, and his family, who were struggling to survive during his wife's battle with a serious medical condition: "SB1661 would clearly help families like the Norvets. . . . Passage of SB1661 would be a significant step forward in assuring that we can give care to our loved ones and get care when we need it." The testimony and op-eds made clear that workers were in desperate need of a way to take care of family situations without putting their families and their livelihood in jeopardy.

Although they did not expect the bill to go very far in its first year, the Coalition members wanted to build support for the campaign; they needed powerful political partners. One of the Coalition's founding members, the Labor Federation, became the bill's lead sponsor in August 2001. As the bill gained momentum, the Labor Federation followed through with testimony, lobbying, and grassroots mobilization, using its political clout at crucial points throughout the campaign.

State Senator Sheila Kuehl (Democrat, Los Angeles) agreed to be the lead author. A successful progressive legislator, Kuehl was respected by her peers across ideological lines and had a strong relationship with the governor. She introduced bill SB1661 in February 2002, and it soon became her top priority. When it was introduced, SB1661 provided twelve weeks of paid family leave, with the costs evenly split between employees and employers.

After the bill passed its first Assembly committee and as it worked its way through the state legislature, the Coalition increased its organizing and picked up more members and momentum. At the grassroots level, workers and union representatives handed out postcards at meetings. "I got postcards signed full time—at the labor council, the labor studies program as well as to employees we represent. I feel so proud of the work I have done to get this bill passed," said Dave Hurlburt, shop steward from the Communications Workers of America (CWA) Local 9410. The American Federation of State, County, and Municipal Employees (AFSCME), Service Employees International Union (SEIU), Amalgamated Transit Union (ATU), United Food and Commercial Workers International Union (UFCW), and CWA locals across California got postcards signed, along with Central Labor Councils, transit workers, nurses, and machinists. Coalition members staffed tables at conferences, and the American Civil Liberties Union (ACLU) of southern California set up a website letting supporters send faxes directly to their state legislators. On the media front, the Coalition launched a proactive press outreach effort. All this heightened activity and visibility kept feeding the momentum and led core Coalition members to devote even more time and energy to the campaign.

There was intense opposition from the business community, in particular the Chamber of Commerce, which argued that businesses, especially small ones, would be driven out of business or out of state if they had to pay their share of the benefit. They launched a countercampaign, sending legislators thousands of letters and faxes. In the end, the bill that passed in the legislature provided six weeks of paid family leave, all employee-funded. It took nearly a month for Governor Davis to sign the bill. He was also up for reelection in a surprisingly tight race, and he needed every vote he could get. The Coalition, which had grown from a small core to more than seven hundred unions, organizations, and individual members, pulled out all the stops. There was intense media coverage; pressure from women's organizations; and calls, postcards, e-mails, and letters from many unions, activists, national organizations, and the AFL-CIO. On September 23, 2002, the governor finally signed the bill.

The selling points for the California program were numerous. It would help a wide range of people, from low-income to upper-middle-class and from newborns to the frail elderly; it built on a program that already existed and worked; it did not cost the state or employers any money; and the cost to employees was very low. Research on paid family leave conducted in 2003 in California showed that public support for paid family leave was huge, with almost 90 percent of those surveyed favoring paid leave and the support extended to all segments of society. Over 40 percent of respondents had taken a family or medical leave at some point during the previous five years and almost two-thirds thought it was likely that they would need a leave in the next five years (Milkman and Appelbaum 2004).

Although California's paid family leave bill became law faster than even its most ambitious supporters expected, it did not come out of nowhere. Years of coalition work, labor leadership, and grassroots campaign and advocacy efforts stand behind this recent development. Still, it took a particular combination of raw political power, leadership, resources, organizing, consensus building, conflict, compromise, and a certain amount of luck to win. The Paid Leave Coalition is now actively engaged in an outreach campaign involving education and media to inform California workers about their rights to the new paid family leave benefit.

New York Unions—Expanding Child Care for Working Families

In 1994, with the realization that more and more working parents were struggling to find affordable, quality child care, the New York Union Child Care Coalition was started.[6] Originally made up of ten unions, including the 1199 SEIU, Office and Professional Employees International Union (OPEIU), and CWA District 1, the Coalition was committed to a comprehensive child-care, work, and family agenda. The main leaders initially were women within their own unions, such as Deborah King, executive director of the 1199 SEIU Employer Training and Upgrading Fund Job Security Program, and Donna Dolan, the Work/Family Director for CWA District 1. The Coalition grew to include twenty-five unions and won official recognition from the New York City Central Labor Council and New York state AFL-CIO, which identified access to affordable, quality child care as a top priority. The leadership also expanded to include male labor leaders such as Roger Toussaint, president of Transport Workers Union Local 100, and Ed Donnelly, legislative director of the state AFL-CIO.

The Coalition had a broad agenda. It sought to link union efforts to a broader statewide child-care agenda, to expand funding and services for quality child care, and to make the labor movement a leader in addressing work and family issues. It also hoped to use these initiatives to develop women's leadership in the labor movement.

Improving Child-Care Services

The Coalition has made significant strides in increasing union member access to child-care services. First, the Coalition worked to enrich Beacon School summer programs. The Beacon schools-based community centers are nonprofit organizations attached to or near local schools that offer services and activities for positive youth development in the local community. The Coalition worked collaboratively with community groups to provide curriculum

[6] Much of the information on this program was drawn from interviews with and e-mails from Sonte DuCote, organizer of the New York Union Child Care Coalition, and Deborah King, chair of the New York Union Child Care Coalition.

enrichment and to expand program hours. By also making contributions to the schools, such as sponsoring internships, paying summer teachers, and conducting informational outreach to unions and the surrounding community, the Coalition was instrumental in improving and expanding an important program for low-income and union families. Since 1995, over two thousand children between the ages of six and fourteen from union families have attended the programs free of charge.

Second, in 1998 the Coalition helped secure funding from New York City and the Department of Labor to expand the Satellite Child Care Program. The Satellite Child Care Program combined the best features of traditional family day care and center-based care. Originally restricted to the welfare-to-work population, new funding expanded the program to all working women. It linked family child-care providers, who provide child care in their homes, to a nonprofit agency. The women received training as licensed family child-care providers and became employees of the nonprofit agency through which they received comprehensive health, sick, and vacation benefits. They also became union members as employees of the Consortium for Worker Education (CWE).[7]

Taking on a Political Campaign

In 1998, the Coalition partnered with the Child Care That Works Campaign (CCTWC), a group of statewide child-care advocates, to launch a political action campaign to address the lack of quality, affordable, and accessible child care for working families. The goals of the CCTWC were to increase child-care subsidy funding and improve child-care quality, access, and affordability.

That year, the Coalition and CCTWC developed a mobilization strategy. Union members stepped up to tell their personal stories and start a frank discussion about why these issues were so important. Daneek Miller, bus driver and member of ATU Local 1056, was the first man to sit down and tell of his personal struggle trying to care for his family and drive a bus. "After my wife became seriously ill I struggled to find decent child care, but was unable to find anything consistent. My only solution was to get the children up at 5 a.m. and take them to work where they rode my bus from 6 a.m. until it was time for school. Luckily, the school was close to the bus route so I was able to drop them off at a stop two blocks away. Each morning they rode the bus for over two hours."

The mobilization strategy included sending 30,000 postcards from union members and advocacy groups to the New York Senate, Assembly, and governor about the need for expanded child care; having rank and file union mem-

---

[7] Funding from the New York state legislature was secured on a yearly basis. In 2005, the governor vetoed the funds and the program folded.

bers present testimony such as Miller's about their child-care problems at legislative hearings; and bringing busloads of union members, working families, and child-care advocates to several targeted lobbying days. Members from over twenty unions participated in these lobbying days and met with their district representatives about child-care issues. The CCTWC served as an initial grassroots organizing effort to communicate with state legislators while educating union members and their families about child-care issues. Over the next few years, the Coalition continued to sponsor several lobbying and advocacy days at which union members presented stories about their child-care challenges and met with state legislators.

As a result of increased activity, the Coalition had many successes. In 1999 the governor approved an appropriation of $162 million more in child-care subsidies (which served an additional 13,000 working families) and $15 million for child-care construction and renovation projects. In 2000–2001, the Coalition won an additional $120 million to provide 29,000 more working families with subsidized child care. It also won $40 million for recruitment and retention to support a wage supplement for child-care workers—an estimated 35,000 child-care workers, most of whom are women, benefited from this appropriation. The money also provided an incentive for child-care workers to earn additional credentials and stay in the child-care field.

Expanding Subsidized Child Care for Working Families

How were these victories possible? In 1999, the Coalition had organized members to sign up for state vouchers and subsidized child-care slots (government subsidies for low-income families). It learned that union members were reluctant to apply for child-care assistance through the social service system and that the system was not oriented to serve working people—the hours were not convenient, the locations were difficult, and the process was long and tedious.

As a result of this feedback, the Coalition discussed these problems during several open meetings in early 2000, with a high degree of participation, and it decided to focus on expanding subsidized child care for working families. This decision resulted in tremendous enthusiasm and buy-in. The policy agenda reflected a broad discussion among Coalition members as to policies to remedy the problems, consensus on what to work on, and engagement in the process at all levels—a good example of how a public policy process should work.

The Coalition developed the idea of a pilot project, called the Facilitated Enrollment Project, which would increase access to child-care subsidies/vouchers for working people. It would raise the income eligibility for child-care subsidies from 200 to 275 percent of the poverty level and put the labor movement front and center in the fight for quality, affordable child care. Under the current eligibility guidelines, in order to qualify for subsidies a family of four could not earn more than $37,700; under the proposed guide-lines, a family of four could qualify when making up to $51,840 (275 percent of the poverty level).

In 2000, the Coalition won support for the pilot project from child-care ad-vocacy partners in the CCTWC, as well as backing from key legislative leaders in both the state Senate and the Assembly. It began the campaign. During the next few months, more than five hundred union members went to Albany for a lobbying day, presentations were made to legislators by union members telling their child-care stories, and members directly lobbied their own legisla-tors. The unions kept close tabs on what was happening in key legislative com-mittees. Union leaders wrote and lobbied legislator leaders, especially the three most powerful leaders and the governor. The 1199 SEIU, AFSCME, United Federation of Teachers, Union of Needletrades, Industrial and Textile Employees–Hotel Employees and Restaurant Employees Union (UNITE HERE), and other major unions were engaged and involved. This had a signif-icant effect on the legislature.

That first year (2001), the legislature approved $5 million for pilot pro-grams in parts of New York City. The following year, the Coalition won $10 million and expanded the program within New York City. Eventually, the Coalition was successful in securing $33 million for five regions (New York City, Monroe County, the Capital region, Oneida County, and Westchester) to provide child-care and after-school subsidies to working families.

As of this writing, the program is still funded and going strong. Eligible workers can now apply for the child-care subsidies during evenings and week-ends at worksites, union halls, and community-based organizations, thereby making them more accessible to workers. Based on feedback from workers, the application form was shortened and simplified and can be mailed or faxed. Outreach for the program is conducted through unions, employers, and community-based organizations. Unions have organized child-care informa-tion fairs and offer parent education on the types of care and on choosing quality child care. Subsidies average $5,000–6,000 per year, depending on family income and size and can be used to pay for formal, informal, and after-school programs. This makes a substantial difference to working families pay-ing for child care. About 50 percent of the families receiving the child-care subsidies are union members.

Developing Leadership

In addition to the concrete economic gains the Coalition has garnered for working families, it has also helped rank and file members learn organiza-tional strategies related to politics and power. Most Coalition members had little understanding of the intricacies of the state legislative and budgetary process. In developing the campaign, Coalition members became educated about how public programs are won. For example, they have come to understand the need to have support from all parts of the state and the different approaches that need to be taken with the Assembly, the Senate, and the governor's office. Within the labor movement, they have learned that some unions are more influential with key legislators due to the concentration of the membership in various districts or because of particular histories or relationships. Coalition members are becoming quite sophisticated in strategizing about who should approach which legislator.

The Coalition emphasizes democratic and inclusive processes. Monthly meetings and subcommittee meetings are forums for analysis and sharing experiences and information. Relationships between union leaders and staff with power and influence in the labor movement are complex and delicate—the staff members depend on leaders for resources and advice, yet are aware that the leaders do not always fully share their agenda and are ambivalent about sharing power with women, perhaps even more so with women of color. The level of sophistication of many Coalition activists in dealing with this situation is growing each year. Coalition members are winning increased respect from male trade union leaders as they continue to work on these issues.

In order to provide more leadership opportunities for Coalition members, the Coalition established several subcommittees, including outreach, fundraising, and political action. The new committees are all led by women and address key areas of the Coalition's work, including service development and implementation, city strategy, and political action. Mentors with expertise in each area are assigned to work with the committees. For example, the political action director of the state AFL-CIO and the lobbyist for two of the large unions work closely with the political action committee. The Coalition recently received a grant of $20,000 from the CWE to provide leadership development for rank and file women union members on work-family issues. The first training had over sixty participants from unions such as the Retail, Wholesale and Department Store Union, AFSCME DC 37, and UNITE HERE. The goal was to build a network of labor women familiar with work-family issues who could return to their unions and carry the message forward by getting their unions to adopt a work-family agenda. An additional grant from the CWE paid for training for another thirty union women.

The Coalition is now working on leveraging city money for similar childcare projects and continues to do outreach for the Facilitated Enrollment Project. They are also working to expand the project into areas where there are large percentages of union members. Recently, the Coalition started to advocate for paid family leave policies in New York state. It remains committed to developing leadership among union women and to promoting work and family issues within the labor movement through both collective bargaining and political action.

Labor's Role in Work and Family Policies

Work and family issues such as child care and paid family leave are core union issues that affect most working families and union members—they are not for women only. Although many unions are bargaining for these kinds of policies and benefits, the impact is far greater when state and national laws are passed. In many cases, unions are in the forefront of these struggles for social supports and policies that allow workers to care for families while working to earn a living. There is huge potential in the labor movement to move public policy agendas. As we can see from the examples here, unions have the ability not only to lobby in state capitols but to mobilize their members to call, write, and visit their legislators and to turn out hundreds or even thousands of union members to events and rallies. By allying with progressive community forces, unions in many states are leading the way in labor-community coalitions for work and family policies.

The most significant and broadly applicable lessons that campaign participants drew from the California experience included having a broad base, having the support of California's labor unions as well as a strong legislative author, building a diverse coalition, having solid data to make the case, and having the resources to devote significant staff time to the campaign. The fact that the California Labor Federation was the lead sponsor cannot be underestimated. It put significant resources into the campaign and was effective in lobbying and pressuring the governor; it was able to generate thousands of postcards and messages to key legislators.

The New York Child Care Coalition also has become a strong voice in the state's public policy arena. It decided to focus on increasing access to state child-care subsidies by raising the eligibility levels, and it achieved remarkable success. The Coalition is now playing an instrumental role in getting labor and community groups mobilized around paid family leave legislation. In 2005, a bill for paid family leave passed the state Assembly, and the Coalition is working on passing it in the state Senate next.

These two case studies are not isolated examples. Union-led work and family coalitions are active elsewhere and are pursuing a range of issues. In 2006, legislation for some type of paid family leave had been proposed in nineteen states.[8] In addition, labor-community coalitions in eight states (Washington,

---

[8] For details, see the National Partnership website, http://www.nationalpartnership.org.

New Jersey, Maine, Massachusetts, Wisconsin, Georgia, New York, and California), working together as the Multi-State Working Families Consortium, are actively pushing legislation to address various worktime issues. These coalitions involve state labor federations, labor councils, and various unions working with community-based organizations to activate union members and community activists on behalf of family-friendly policies. Each state has a slightly different focus—from expanding the FMLA to requiring employers to provide a minimum number of paid sick days that can also be used to care for families to more comprehensive paid family leave laws.

In the 2005 legislative session, the Washington State coalition helped pass paid family leave legislation in the state Senate, but narrowly failed in the House. Massachusetts introduced legislation requiring employers to provide a minimum of seven paid sick days that can be used for a worker's own illness or to care for a sick family member, and in 2006, it introduced a paid family leave bill modeled on the California legislation. Wisconsin introduced a bill that would allow, under the Wisconsin Family and Medical Leave law, employees to use up to sixteen hours per year for school conferences and related activities. Maine passed a bill that allows workers to use a portion of their sick days to care for family members, and New Jersey has an active bill for paid family leave that builds on the state temporary disability program.[9]

Paid family leave and affordable child care are winning policy issues because they are important to everyone. Legislation was passed and funding was secured because a desperate need existed for such supports and unions made them a top priority. It is critical that we link work and family issues to the larger labor issues for all workers today. What do workers need? They need good wages, safe jobs, health insurance for themselves and their families, and retirement benefits—*and* they need affordable quality child care, paid sick days, paid family leave, flexible work schedules, and elder-care resources. These are not separate issues that we will win when we have won everything else; they are part of the fabric that is needed in today's workplaces, with today's workforce. No one is home baking chocolate chip cookies and taking grandma to the doctor. So we should stop acting like we all have full-time stay-at-home wives and force our workplaces to reflect the lives we now lead. Unions often set the standards for the workplace through collective bargaining; now unions are setting the standards for good public policies so that workers do not have to choose between their jobs and their families.

---

[9] In a number of other states, including Illinois, Oregon, Iowa, Washington, New York, New Jersey, California, Pennsylvania, Ohio, and Michigan, there are efforts to organize family child-care providers, and several states have enacted policies to allow these workers to unionize and collectively bargain with the state. As child-care workers become organized, unions will have more of a voice in public funding for child-care wages and, it is hoped, for broader funding of the child-care system.

PART IV

ORGANIZING WOMEN'S WORK

Part IV opens with Karen Nussbaum's engaging account of working women's movements from the 1970s to the present. Nussbaum describes the heady days of protest in the 1970s, when millions of women banded together in unions and associations to seek job opportunity, higher pay, and greater respect at work. Fed up with being treated like office wives or machines, clerical workers, for example, formed 9to5, a national working women's association. They filed lawsuits, picketed abusive employers, and orchestrated a host of media events, including turning National Secretaries Day into a contested ritual and collaborating on the hit movie *Nine to Five* with Lily Tomlin, Dolly Parton, and Jane Fonda. By the end of the 1980s, their actions resulted in dramatic changes in the perception and treatment of office workers.

But in the 1980s and 1990s, the working women's movement stalled, due in part to rising class differences. As Nussbaum observes, although white, college-educated women saw their careers boom, many working-class women and people of color experienced economic stagnation and loss. Collective mobilization also slowed in the face of employer and government hostility. Yet Nussbaum finds "hopeful signs" that may make a collective response viable once again for large numbers of women. She sees a new attention to diversity and institutional experimentation within the American Federation of Labor–Congress of Industrial Organizations (AFL-CIO) and a rising worker identity among women.

The next three chapters offer further evidence of the long history of women's collective action, and they too point to the likelihood of increased organizing among women in the future. In the 1990s, a majority of the significant unionizing victories occurred among women service workers, a disproportionate number of whom were women of color. In chapter 9, Eileen Boris and Jennifer Klein detail how the most prominent of these newly organized groups, home care workers, secured union contracts, adding over 100,000 new members to labor's rolls by the end of the 1990s. Their victory was decades in the making. Organized labor once viewed home care providers as unorganizable, but home care providers came to see themselves differently. They organized collectively and insisted that their labor be recognized and valued. Boris and Klein trace their group efforts over the last thirty-five years, beginning in the 1970s with the emergence of a national household worker rights movement; the local campaigns relying on community organizing, direct action, and lobbying; and the pioneering union drives led by public-sector, hospital, and service unions in New York City.

In chapter 10, Vanessa Tait turns our attention to another group of women whose status as real workers is suspect and who initially found their attempts to be part of the official labor movement rebuffed. Welfare women have a long record of community and political activism. In the late 1990s, as mandatory work programs for welfare recipients mushroomed, adding thousands of welfare recipients to public-sector workforces across the country, these no-wage workers organized for basic job rights, finding allies in ACORN (Association of Community Organizations for Reform Now) and other community groups. Forging a partnership with the established public-sector unions in New York and San Francisco proved more difficult, however, with some unionists seeing organized workfare workers as more of a threat than an opportunity. The boundaries of the women's movement have been more porous, with welfare women proclaimed an important constituency. Yet the Montana welfare women Tait describes, who lobbied and won state funds to allow them to care for their children, have yet to be fully integrated into the emerging work-family movement discussed in chapter 7.

Immigrant women are banding together to further their economic and political rights as well, often with the help of community-based worker centers. As Janice Fine documents in chapter 11, the number of worker centers exploded in the 1990s as immigrants poured into low-wage jobs in meatpacking, construction, and services. Immigrant organizing has attracted considerable scholarly attention, with astute case studies of how (mostly male) immigrants from Latin America are rebuilding unions in construction and janitorial services (e.g., Milkman and Wong 2001). In this chapter, however, Fine offers one of the fullest accounts of how (mostly women) household workers are organizing. She evaluates the various collective approaches they are using to improving their lives, from forming worker cooperatives to passing new labor-standard legislation to insisting that the wealthy New York City families who hire them treat them at least as well as did their former employers in Hong Kong.

All four chapters remind us that women workers have always relied on multiple routes to advancement. Clericals, teachers, nurses, home care aides, nannies, and welfare recipients—have all formed unions and won bargaining rights. But these same groups have also organized cross-class associations and community-based groups such as 9to5, the National Welfare Rights Organization, and New York's Domestic Workers Union who utilized alternative approaches. All of these institutions should be seen as part of an inclusive and heterogeneous labor movement dedicated to securing the rights, recognition, and respect women workers deserve.

8

WORKING WOMEN'S INSURGENT CONSCIOUSNESS

Karen Nussbaum

For more than three decades I have been organizing and representing working women with 9to5, National Association of Working Women, Service Employees International Union (SEIU) District 925, Women's Bureau of the U.S. Department of Labor, and the American Federation of Labor–Congress of Industrial Organizations (AFL-CIO). Over the years, I have seen changes in the status, opportunities, and consciousness of working women. In the early 1970s, when I was starting out as a clerical worker and then an organizer, an insurgent consciousness propelled a wide cross section of women to reconsider their role in life, be open to collective action, and challenge their employers. They believed change was possible.

A working women's movement emerged. Across the board, women came to think of themselves as providers and to rely on themselves. They pressed demands, often banding together in groups, associations, and unions. As a result, employers provided new opportunities for women, both as a legitimate response to women's demands and as a way to drive a wedge into the growing movement. A split in the workforce emerged between college-educated and non-college-educated women. Business created a safety valve to siphon off the growing demands of some women through new opportunities for careers as professionals and managers for college-educated women while holding the line on wages and reducing benefits for non-college-educated women and im-

Thanks to Carol Eickert for research assistance.

migrants. Under Republican administrations, government no longer acted as an advocate, working women came to believe that they could best solve workplace problems as individuals, and the impulse to organize stagnated. But the growing pressures of globalization and the strains on working families may be leading toward a new consensus for change.

In this chapter, I look at the attitudes of working women, especially office workers, based on my experience and the research of organizations with which I was associated—9to5 and SEIU in the 1970s and 1980s, the Women's Bureau in the 1990s, and the AFL-CIO in the last decade—in the changing economic and social context over that time.

"We type and file 9 to 5 . . ."

"9to5 Song," to the tune of "Charlie on the MTA"

Fran Cicchetti looked at the camera, explaining that, even though her job title at the insurance company was secretary, she was doing the work of an underwriter. She had asked for a promotion and was told to study a manual. A month later, she was denied the promotion and a man with less seniority was given the job. "That's when I started thinking that, as a woman, I had been lied to."

Fran was one of a dozen women office workers featured in a long-forgotten twenty-three-minute documentary shown on PBS in 1974 called *9 to 5*. The film captures the insurgent consciousness roiling among working women in the 1970s, from Charlene Gordon, who bristled at being called "my girl" by her boss who was many years her junior, to Donna Ricci, who complained that her low-level job still required that she wear stockings on very hot days. Karen Koenig was annoyed at the men who could be "practically sitting in the Xerox room and call me from the other end of the office and say 'could you make me one copy of this?' " Maggie LeBlanc wondered if the reason she could not get ahead after decades at her job was because she did not have enough formal education.

These women were the early leaders of 9to5, Boston's Organization for Women Office Workers, which began in 1973. 9to5 became a national organization and spawned a sister union in SEIU, District 925. 9to5 activists shared a new way of looking at their lives with millions of other working-class and middle-class women that would change opportunities for women and restructure the workplace.

The litany of complaints was surfacing wherever women worked, especially among the nation's 20 million women office workers in the early 1970s. They were passed over for promotion by less qualified men, called by demeaning names, asked to do petty tasks, and required to participate in the façade of being white-collar workers while earning less than blue-collar pay.

The 1970s: A Working Women's Movement Emerges

When I became an office worker in 1971, I was in good company. One out of three women worked as clerical workers, constituting the largest sector of the workforce. The stereotype of a typical worker may have been a man in a hard-hat, but women at keyboards outnumbered them and every other kind of worker.

Many of these women were relatively new to the workforce. Recruited from kitchens and nurseries, women fueled the growing service and information industries. And they did it on the cheap. They may have worn high heels and hose to work, but women office workers earned less than their blue-collar sisters. They were high school and college educated, working class, and middle and upper-middle class. Uprooted and exploited, they began to see themselves as economic agents that is, workers—and as social agents as they gathered around water coolers to share their gripes.

I was one of these women. My job as a clerk-typist at a university in Boston in the early 1970s paid the bills as I put my real attention to the compelling political work in the movements for women's rights and peace in Vietnam. But I began to understand the power in bringing the demand for women's equality into the workplace as I walked a picket line on behalf of a tiny union for waitresses during the winter of 1972. Eight waitresses at Cronin's Restaurant got fed up with lack of respect on the job; organized their own union, the Harvard Square Waitresses Organizing Committee; and went on strike for months. These women initially had no connection either to unions or the women's movement. Their daring and determination in a strike that could not win inspired me to find that same anger in other women workers and turn it into organized power.

The change in the lives of working women came at a time of economic, political, and social change. The year 1973—the year 9to5 was born—was a turning point in many ways. It was the year of the economic Great U-turn described by Harrison and Bluestone (1988), the year that the income gap between the rich and rest of society began to grow. *Business Week* (1974, 120) announced the shift in economic policy in 1974: "It will be a hard pill for many Americans to swallow—the idea of doing with less so that big business can have more. . . . Nothing that this nation, or any other nation, has done in modern economic history compares with the selling job that must be done to make people accept this reality."

Many African American women recognized the power of organization and movements through the struggle for civil rights; fewer white women came into the 1970s looking to organization as a way to solve problems on the job. But the women's movement was taking off with a fury, with hundreds of small groups popping up in cities around the country. I belonged to several myself: a free school for women offering classes in auto mechanics, silk screening for political posters, and street medicine; a group that created leaflets in the form of "Nancy" cartoons on women's liberation and antiwar issues, which we passed out on the street; and a women's karate class to which I brought a brick wrapped in rope every week—pounding our fists into the brick built up our punching power. A group of women concerned about health care met in the apartment below mine for months—they ultimately published *Our Bodies, Ourselves* (1969) the national best seller.

Consciousness-raising groups proliferated, with so many women seeking to join these small discussion groups in which they challenged themselves on their roles in their families and society that the alternative weekly newspapers ran listings with phone numbers for newcomers. Although these groups attracted primarily white middle-class women, women of color and working-class women also participated, and the sense in society that "if you have a problem then you join a group" took hold.

But few women turned to unions, and few union leaders thought working women were worth their attention. One union leader's comments were extreme, although his doubts about organizing women were not unusual. "You can't organize women," he explained to a 9to5 organizer, "because they think with their cunts not their brains."

In the context of this social ferment, scores of locally based, occupation-specific organizations of women workers sprang up around the country. 9to5 originated from a women's conference that had two purposes: to rally support for peace in Vietnam and to help women organize on the job. Women from the office workers' workshop became the core group for Boston 9to5. Over the next several years, women office workers formed organizations in a dozen cities; most ultimately joined together as a national organization in 9to5. Women coal miners, flight attendants, domestic workers, bank managers, sex workers, tradeswomen, and many others also started their own organizations.

When we started organizing 9to5 in Boston in the early 1970s, our first task was to convince women that the problems they faced on the job stemmed from an unfair system of employment rather than from their personal failings. The word *discrimination* was as foreign as *organizing* among these traditional women workers, and 9to5 staff and leaders did not use either word for some time for fear it would not be understood or believed.

Over time, women came to assume that discrimination was part of the job—from the grocery store clerk who told me, "I love my job, I love everything about my job. But I've been here 32 years and I know I'll never make manager because I'm a woman," to the office worker who said, "My head aches from bumping up against the glass ceiling," to the business executive who confided to me, "We participate in a conspiracy of silence."

As new entrants to the workforce, women were blindly hopeful. As their identity as workers grew stronger, they questioned their working conditions and opportunities. Their demands led to institutional changes, expanding laws and strengthening enforcement. And women broadened the debate to include new issues such as sexual harassment, the glass ceiling, and balancing work and family.

Beginning in 1973, the federal government set a new course on fighting discrimination. The Equal Employment Opportunity Commission (EEOC) signed a consent decree with AT&T, the nation's largest employer, for $45 million to address discrimination in recruiting, hiring, and promotion (1973); settled a discrimination suit against nine steel producers for $31 million (1974); and settled with General Electric for nearly $30 million (1978).[1]

The Office of Federal Contract Compliance Programs of the U.S. Department of Labor (OFCCP) was also invigorated in the 1970s. It looked at coal mining in 1973 when virtually no women worked in mining. By 1980, 8.7 percent of coal miners were women. OFCCP launched a special effort to reduce discrimination in the construction industry, setting guidelines in 1978 for women's representation on jobsites of 6.9 percent in three years, intended to keep increasing. As modest as these goals were, they were never met. Pressure from Cleveland Women Working, a 9to5 affiliate, resulted in OFCCP reviews at the five largest banks in Cleveland in 1978. Three years later, women officials and managers increased 50 percent (Citizens' Commission on Civil Rights 1984).

Pregnancy discrimination gained public notoriety when in 1976 the Supreme Court ruled that health insurance plans that did not cover pregnancy but did cover, say, hair transplants, was not discriminatory because the policy did not rest on "gender as such." Pregnancy is not related to sex? This was too much even for the U.S. Congress, which voted in 1978 to amend Title VII by passing the Pregnancy Discrimination Act.

Sexual harassment was named as an issue at the first public speakout in 1975 in New York City. That year, Lois Jensen began her job at Eveleth Mines, which would result in the landmark case that changed sexual harassment law twenty-five years later. In 1991, Anita Hill's sexual harassment charges against Supreme Court nominee Clarence Thomas riveted the country and provided a

---

[1] For more information, see documents on the EEOC website, "Milestones in the History of the US Equal Opportunity Employment Commission," http://www.eeoc.gov/abouteeoc/35th/milestones/ (accessed December 27, 2005).

nationwide tutorial on the subject. Sexual harassment claims to the EEOC increased steeply (Mankiller et al. 1998).

Calls to the 9to5 hotline also skyrocketed during the weeks surrounding Anita Hill's dramatic testimony. One caller, who was beginning to find her voice only decades after feeling the pain of discrimination on the job, told a story of persistent and egregious sexual harassment and wanted to know if it was too late to do something about it. "When did the harassment occur?" the counselor asked; she answered, "1945."

A younger woman, a night-shift janitor, told a story of being harassed by her supervisor. The counselor advised her and assumed that was the end of it. Three weeks later, the janitor called back with an update. "I told him if he ever bothered me again I would report him to a national women's organization. He hasn't touched me since." Like a growing number of women, she had the confidence that came from knowledge and the courage that came from feeling backed up.

Although 9to5 did not grow to be a large organization, we got a huge response from working women. 9to5 staff and leaders went on recruitment lunches with potential members every day of the week—sometimes three lunch meetings in a day. Hundreds of working women turned out for events. Thousands responded to surveys. Many more identified with 9to5 and cheered us on. The demands for "raises and roses, rights and respect" resonated among women throughout the workforce and emboldened women to take action on their own.

Women were also becoming more active in unions. Public-sector unionization surged during the 1960s and 1970s at the state and municipal levels, bringing in many women clerical workers and teachers. Public-sector unionism in big cities often grew out of the impulse of the civil rights movement and brought many African American women into the labor movement as members and leaders. At the same time, private-sector unionization, concentrated in male-dominated manufacturing industries, declined, changing the balance between men and women in the union movement.

The working women's movement also introduced a new generation of women organizers to unions, bringing enthusiasm and feminism. Young women went to work for SEIU, the American Federation of State, County, and Municipal Employees (AFSCME), United Auto Workers (UAW), District 65 of the Retail, Wholesale and Department Store Union (RWDSU), and International Brotherhood of Teamsters (IBT), among other unions. Led by an older generation, three thousand union women met in Chicago in 1974 to create the Coalition of Labor Union Women (CLUW).

The ferment of the 1970s was the basis of the success of Jane Fonda's movie *Nine to Five* (1980). Women were ready to reset the terms of the debate, and a farce turned out to be the perfect vehicle. *Nine to Five* reflected and propelled a change in consciousness. Fonda knew about 9to5, the organization, and wanted to support our work. For Fonda, that meant making a major motion picture.

She had to convince the studio there was a market for a movie about women office workers, who had been invisible in popular culture. (Ann Sothern's "Susie the Secretary" was the exception to the rule.) A briefing memo for studio executives made the case that there was an audience—20 million women office workers, one-third of the female workforce, starved for any reflection of themselves in the mass media.

The characters and anecdotes in the movie were derived from meetings that Fonda, the writers, and director had with 9to5 members. Capturing the frustrations of women office workers made *Nine to Five* the biggest box office hit of 1980. A comedy, the movie ridiculed the discrimination that was office business as usual—demeaning secretarial tasks, sexual harassment, and lack of promotions. The laughter of millions of people in theaters across the country ended the debate on discrimination. The question turned from being whether discrimination was a problem to what we should do about it.

9to5, the National Association of Working Women, used the momentum from the movie to organize. I went on a twenty-city tour called The Movement Behind the Movie, appearing on local TV talk shows in the morning and holding meetings and rallies after work. We chartered a dozen new chapters. A working women's movement was finding its voice in the workplace, government enforcement, the courts, unions, and popular culture.

1980s and Early 1990s: The Reagan/Bush Years

The working women's movement was derailed in the 1980s under the pressures of a changing workforce, the introduction of automation, employer opposition, and the ascendance of the right wing in government.

To contain the growing demands of working women, employers created opportunities for some women, opening up professional and managerial jobs for college graduates while resisting the demands for institutional changes that would improve jobs for all women. Women at both ends of the workforce continued to share common concerns of equal pay and work-family policies, but the intensity of the issues differed as the conditions of the two groups changed. Employers had created a safety valve. College-educated women who had been bank tellers were becoming branch managers; clericals in publishing companies were becoming editors. The percentage of women who were managers or professionals doubled between 1970 and 2004, from 19 to 38 percent (U.S. Bureau of the Census 1976; U.S. Bureau of Labor Statistics 2005). Fran Cicchetti, had she still been working in insurance, would have become an underwriter.

The automation of the office was having a profound effect on the work of women office workers. The office workforce was in turmoil in the early 1980s as tens of millions of workers made the transition to automated equipment and saw their jobs redesigned or eliminated altogether. New health and safety issues emerged, including stress from automated speed-up, carpal tunnel syndrome, and fears of radiation from cathode-ray tubes. At 9to5, we recognized a window of opportunity to raise fundamental questions about job design and how work is valued that we thought would last about five years—the time it would take for most workers to cycle out of their current jobs and into new automated jobs. A 9to5 report, "Race against Time: Automation of the Office," (1980, 10) rang an alarm about the negative impact of automation, predicting that most jobs would be "degraded, deskilled and devalued." We debated with computer industry leaders around the country. With SEIU, we introduced legislation regulating the introduction and safety of video display terminals (VDTs) in thirty-two states. The struggle over automation inspired songs such as "I've Got the VDT Blues." We had our own Deep Throat—an IBM insider who released secret documents to 9to5 revealing the company's own doubts about the safety of the machines. This agitation forced the computer industry to be more responsive to women's concerns and contributed to the organization of women office workers in the public sector and universities.

But private-sector clericals remained out of reach for organizing. Banks, insurance companies, and corporations were determined to resist unionization and union-busting firms made millions of dollars by fanning the flames of the threat of clerical organizing. "It's not the Teamsters [IBT] you need to look out for," one firm warned in its slide presentation at a union avoidance seminar, "It's 9to5," and the slide of two young women organizers flashed on the screen. A union staffer in the audience at this memorable Chicago seminar had "gone underground for six months to attend all the $10,000 union-busting sessions I could flim-flam my way into," often posing as a communication VP for a media company. "Unions for women spooked these business guys," she remembered. "Unions equaled Jane Fonda, communists, feminists, and, oh dear lord, lesbians. If you gave those frustrated angry women the right to form a union, you were done for."[2]

District 925 organized working women successfully in the public sector and in universities during these years, but our campaigns in private-sector companies were shattered. We organized the Syracuse office of Equitable Life Assurance with a 90 percent yes vote for the union. Yet we were not strong enough to organize the company nationwide nor could we prevent the company from closing its only unionized office in retaliation. Even small companies often turned out to have the resources of giant corporations behind them, such as

[2] Barbara Shailor, interview by Karen Nussbaum, Washington, D.C., November 16, 2005.

the radio station we organized in Boston that was owned by General Tire and hired the infamous union-busting attorney Alfred DeMaria from New York to represent the company at the National Labor Relations Board hearing.

These corporations were afraid of unionization among women workers. Fifteen years after the fact, the head of personnel of John Hancock told me that he barricaded himself in his office overnight before an announced 9to5 rally targeting his company, afraid that we would storm his office. And they were prepared to fight regardless of the cost.

Twelve years of conservative Reagan/Bush administrations put an end to government advocacy against discrimination and slowed down enforcement. The flurry of investigations into discrimination in banks came to an ignominious end in 1981, soon after Ronald Reagan took office. The staff at our Cleveland office got a breathless phone call from an investigator at OFCCP telling us that in a meeting of the new Republican leadership at the agency they had decided to end the investigation into National City Bank against the strong recommendation of the career staff.

The budget for enforcement agencies in the U.S. Department of Labor was cut by one-third to one-half in those years, and their mission had been redefined to encourage good behavior by employers rather than to enforce the law for workers. In addition, the appointment of conservative judges had cut off legal strategies as a way to expand the rights of working women. Unfavorable decisions by conservative judges in court cases on pay equity in the 1980s ended litigation as a strategy.

Although employers were keeping the lid on blue- and pink-collar workers to suppress organization and lower wages and benefits, pressure grew for equity and work-family balance especially in the higher ranks of the women's workforce. In 2004, 38 percent of women were managers and professionals and they held 17.5 percent of managerial jobs (U.S. Bureau of Labor Statistics 2005). But, although women were moving into managerial jobs, they were paid less than men and shut out of the top. As the 1994 report of the Glass Ceiling Commission, "Good for Business," points out, the U.S. workforce was growing increasingly diverse, yet 95–97 percent of senior managers were men and 97 percent of them were white (Glass Ceiling Commission 1994).

Women throughout the workforce experienced a steep increase in work hours. Between 1977 and 1997, men's total weekly work time increased 2.8 hours per week, but women's total work hours increased five hours per week, to forty-four hours, an extra six weeks of work a year (Bond, Galinsky, and Swanberg 1998).

The growing demands on working women led to currency for a new phrase, "work and family." In 1985, *Working Mother Magazine* began its yearly contest for the "100 Best Companies for Working Mothers." By the late 1980s, you could scarcely pick up a magazine that did not have an article about a major corporation catering to the needs of its women executives by providing job sharing, child care, or telecommuting.

Regardless of all the family-friendly talk, there were fewer social institutions to make up for the shift of women from the home into the workforce. Fewer people were covered by health insurance, school services were diminishing, and community programs were defunded. Parking lots were built to accommodate the cars of new workers, but subsidized child-care centers were not. Studies showed that family-friendly policies were primarily provided for professionals and managers at the headquarters office.

The pressures on women to be primary wage earners under increasingly difficult working conditions led a steady stream of women to unions. Women outpaced men as new members of unions every year starting in the mid-1970s. Although the majority of private-sector union organizing was done in workplaces dominated by men, the majority of *wins* were in workplaces dominated by women (Bronfenbrenner 2005). Public-sector victories also were more likely to be in female-dominated jobs.

Equity within the union movement remained a problem. Although some women were working their way up as leaders in local unions, there were few inroads into top-level leadership. In 1980, Joyce Miller, president of CLUW, became the first woman to join the AFL-CIO Executive Council. It was another thirteen years before two more women, Linda Chavez-Thompson and Gloria Johnson, were appointed. Fewer than five national unions, all of them small, had women as presidents.

Early 1990s to Today

The election of Bill Clinton as president promised a turn-around for working people. Famous for campaigning for people who "worked hard and played by the rules," Clinton signed the Family and Medical Leave Act (FMLA) into law as his first legislative action.

I joined the Clinton administration as director of the Women's Bureau of the U.S. Department of Labor, the highest seat in the federal government devoted to women's issues. With eighty staff members, a multimillion dollar budget, and the authority of the federal government, we had the ability to raise issues, support struggles, and influence the priorities of enforcement agencies.

We turned this dormant department with no enforcement authority into a fighting force pursuing our congressional mandate established in 1920 to "promote the well-being of wage-earning women." We convened conferences on sweatshop workers in New York City and the need for twenty-four-hour child care in Portland, Oregon. I held informal hearings on sexual harassment and health and safety concerns of casino workers in Las Vegas and walnut workers on strike in northern California. I met working women of every stripe to bring visibility to their struggles and incorporate their concerns into public policy: grocery store workers in Missouri, temp workers in Massachusetts, poultry workers in Mississippi, television writers in New York, and disabled workers in Chicago. President Clinton, First Lady Hillary Rodham Clinton and Vice-President Al Gore headlined more than a dozen working women's events around the country.

In 1994, we conducted the biggest survey of its kind in history—300,000 women of every race and age sent in the Working Women Count survey in six languages from every state and territory. The survey was distributed by 1,600 partner organizations, ranging from the Asian Immigrant Women's Association to Brigham Young University to the *New York Daily News*. The findings, confirmed by a national random-sample survey, were used to set an agenda for working women across the country. Women overwhelming said they liked working but were dissatisfied. As one woman put it, "How is it that I love my work but hate my job?" There was a surprising consensus across region, race, and income about what was wrong with their jobs: pay and benefits and the stresses of balancing work and family. We decided to mount national campaigns for equal pay and child care.

But the opportunity to make breakthroughs in public policy evaporated as the 1994 elections swept Republican majorities into the House and Senate and ended hope for progressive institutional change for workers under Clinton. Still, a new consciousness among women was taking shape—rejecting discrimination, objecting to the pressures on family, and identifying differences in class—and unions were ready for change.

The 1994 elections and the prolonged decline in union membership led to a revolt in the AFL-CIO. In 1995, John Sweeney won the first contested election to become president of the AFL-CIO. I left the Women's Bureau, where I had worked to leverage power on behalf of working women, to join the AFL-CIO, where it now seemed possible to once again build power through organizing. In the newly created Working Women's Department, we asked women about their priorities through bi-annual Ask A Working Woman national surveys; spearheaded campaigns on issues such as equal pay; convened women organizers; held national Working Women's Conferences including a gathering of five thousand women in Chicago in 2000; built consensus for a greater role for women leaders; and helped on organizing campaigns of women workers.

Women saw discrimination as a problem throughout these years. The AFL-CIO conducted seven research projects among working women (not just union women) from 1997 through 2004. Women consistently stated that strengthening laws to prevent discrimination ranked as a very high priority and voiced their support for affirmative action in particular. Nearly one-quarter of working women said they had been sexually harassed at work, nearly three-quarters said improvements on the job were needed to deal with a hostile work environment, three-quarters said a glass ceiling existed at their workplace, and one-half said that employers did a poor job in ensuring equal pay. And they were not imagining it. A 2005 study by the World Economic Forum found that the U.S. ranked fifteenth in terms of gender equality (Lopez-Claros and Zahidi 2005).

The 2000 AFL-CIO Ask A Working Woman survey cited the odd hours and difficult schedules women worked—28 percent regularly worked nights or weekends; nearly one-half worked different schedules than their spouse or partner. Control over work hours was an important issue as women struggled to meet the needs of their families. "[I need] more flexibility in work hours," one woman wrote, "so I can attend parent-teacher conferences and school events. We need my income to make ends meet, so my kids suffer." Meanwhile, basic work hours provisions—paid sick leave, paid vacation, and even the ability to retire—were declining.

These problems hit lower-income women hardest. Upper-income women responded to the pressures as well, sometimes by leaving the corporate world. The growth of women-owned businesses through the 1990s was attributed in large part to the lack of opportunity and flexibility in the workplace for career women. Lisa Belkin's 2003 *New York Times Magazine* article, "The Opt Out Revolution," was one among many that chronicled the decision of financially privileged women to leave the workplace for motherhood.

The difference in options based on income was real, and a growing sense of hardening class differences became an important part of public consciousness. The *Economist* cited "income inequality not seen since the first Gilded Age" (2004). Average real income of the bottom 90 percent of Americans fell by 7 percent between 1973 and 2000. Real wages fell for the average worker in 2005 for the first time since 1990, meaning that workers were effectively taking a pay cut during a time of remarkable corporate profits. The United States ranked the highest among highly developed countries in each of seven measures of *in*equality (Moyers 2005). The differential between the pay of the average worker and the pay of the average CEO rose from forty times greater in 1980 to three hundred times greater in 2003.[3]

Employer opposition to unions reached new heights. Twenty thousand workers a year were fired or discriminated against just for trying to organize a union. Employer opposition was so fierce that a 2005 study published by American Rights at Work found that union elections fail seven out of eight

[3] AFL-CIO website, "Executive Pay Watch," http://www.aflcio.org (accessed December 15, 2005).

basic standards for free and fair elections because of failures in the law and employer hostility.[4]

Barbara Ehrenreich's 2001 blockbuster book, *Nickel and Dimed: On (Not) Getting By in America*, captured the realization that the myth of the homogenized middle class was no longer true. A best seller for several years, Ehrenreich's book described real life for the 30 percent of the workforce who worked for less than $8 an hour, most of them women. The crisis for working families goes higher up the income ladder when we take into account the 45 million Americans without health insurance, a number growing by another million every year. Class differences grow even wider when measured by the gaps in quality education, public safety, access to the environment and culture, and leisure time.

By the late 1990s, working women were more sophisticated about the problems and more confident in their role as workers. In the AFL-CIO surveys, one-half to two-thirds reported they provided one-half or more of their household income. Seventy-nine percent of respondents to the 1994 Women's Bureau Working Women Count survey said that they liked or loved their jobs and expressed pride and satisfaction at being breadwinners for their families and a significant part of the workforce.

But there were differences between working-class women and people of color, on one hand, and white, college-educated professional women, on the other. In focus group research, non-college-educated women and women of color identified with the term *working woman* and shared common concerns. "I look at working women as women who need money. I look at myself," said one. They saw the need to work as a fact of life, not an option or a temporary status. "The woman has to work. It is not like it used to be," said another. Non-college-educated women were more likely to see men as different from them. They think men "get a better deal from employers" and a better deal at home. "[Men] don't have to worry about the kids," said a white woman, and a Latina woman agreed: "It seems like the women and the men, they both work at the same time. The man comes home, takes a shower, eats and goes to sleep and the woman is washing, cleaning, doing, doing and he is knocked out asleep."

But, although concerns were common, identity was solitary. "I depend on me, myself, and I," said one woman in 2003. Collective action was rarely even in the range of options. When asked, "Who do you turn to if you have a problem on the job?" women were far more likely to name their mothers or God than a union, a women's organization, or a government agency.

White, college-educated women had a strong sense of personal efficacy but did not identify with other women, did not see men as different, felt less in-

---

[4] See American Rights at Work website, http://www.americanrightsatwork.org/docUploads (accessed December 27, 2005).

tense about pressures on the job, and were even less likely to consider collective action. They reported they felt they had influence on the job.

"In stark contrast to the upscale women," an AFL-CIO research report from 2003 read, "they [working class women and women of color] feel their employers do not listen to them and that they have little power to make changes on their own. They feel they must rely on themselves—nobody else is helping. They push back at the idea of a union because they believe they can take care of their workplace problems on their own, and they think unions are mostly for men" (Lake Snell Perry and Associates 2003, 4).

The cultural icon of a working woman fighting for change morphed from *Norma Rae*, the heroine of the popular 1979 movie who organized a union at her textile plant in a hostile Southern town, into *Erin Brockovich* in 2000. Like Norma Rae, Erin Brockovich identified the corporations as the bad guys, but she was a lone ranger all the way, even dissing her female co-workers in the film.

If unorganized women felt unions were dominated by men, they were not the only ones. Frustrated by a lack of progress in improving diversity in unions, the AFL-CIO Executive Council Committee on Working Women undertook a comprehensive review of women in unions. Its findings were alarming. Women had outpaced men as new union members for twenty-five years and were approaching 50 percent of union membership.

Nevertheless, public opinion research among working women found that women's positive views toward unions had declined significantly since 1999. Between 1999 and 2003, women's view that unions are ineffective grew by nine points, from 44 to 53 percent, whereas men's attitudes moved in the reverse direction, dropping six points, from 54 percent ineffective in 1999 to 48 percent in 2003. Women's feelings toward unions overall remained stagnant between 1997 and 2003, whereas men's positive views increased twelve points.

The comments of women captured by focus group research reinforced the statistics. "[Unions are effective] only if the employer will go along with it," said one nonunion woman. "My feeling is that we have been getting a lot of promises and no action," said a union member. Old images of unions prevail. "I mean the ones you see in the newspaper always seems to be, you know, the Labor unions that's what you hear about, you don't hear very much about the Teachers Union," said one woman. "You know when I think of labor unions, I think of old men with grease under their nails," echoed another. White-collar nonunion women were surprised when told that one-half of union members were professional and white-collar workers. The opportunity to recruit large numbers of women into unions was being lost.

The AFL-CIO Committee on Working Women's Report (2004) identified deep dissatisfaction among women leaders. According to the report, the most important issues were the lack of commitment from unions to address the concerns of women, the lack of work and family programs, and the lack of effective structures and programs to support women in gaining leadership. The women leaders who were interviewed also raised complaints that women were often promoted to positions that held no real power. Decades of tokenism meant few women ran unions. In early 2005, only two out of sixty unions had a woman president and very few women were elected leaders at a high level in their unions, in a position to take on national leadership.

According to the report, "There is a clear road map for reaching working women. Women respond strongly to traditional women's economic issues—equal pay, work and family and control over work hours. . . . Tap into working women's sense of independence and self-reliance," and demonstrate that unions are for women by having visible women leaders (AFL-CIO Committee on Working Women's Report 2004, Executive Summary p. 1).

Hopeful Signs

Thirty years after the sweep of activity in the 1970s, working women have a clear identity as workers and have a strong streak of independence and self-reliance. In the last ten years, there has been a string of impressive organizing victories, primarily among women of color, hundreds of thousands of home health aides and tens of thousands of child-care providers (Boris and Klein, chap. 9 in this volume). White-collar workers are organizing, including 60,000 teaching assistants in universities.

The American Federation of Teachers (AFT), a majority-female white-collar union, has been adding close to 50,000 new members every year for the last ten years. The success of AFT can be attributed to its ongoing commitment to organizing, including in non–collective bargaining states; focus on its industry and reputation for working not just on wages, hours, and working conditions but on protecting and improving schools and the skills of its members; openness to new organizational forms, such as its successful associate-member organizing program in Texas; and the many women and people of color visible as leaders.[5]

White-collar women have also proven to be militant. Flight attendants have run an intermittent campaign of job actions they call Create Havoc Around Our System (CHAOS). One nurse union went on strike forty-nine times between 1999 and 2002 on the issue of mandatory overtime and staffing.[6] Working America, the new community affiliate of the AFL-CIO, is another break-

[5] Phil Kugler, AFT organizing director, conversation with Karen Nussbaum, 2005, Washington, D.C., May 19, 2005.

[6] Reported by the United American Nurses, one of a number of AFL-CIO unions that represent nurses.

through, sharing the innovative spirit of the experimental working women's organizations of the 1970s. Working America breaks from the U.S. labor movement's assumption that the only legitimate form of worker organization is collective bargaining. Like a 9to5 with men and resources, Working America has found an organizational form, message, and language that undeniably works—more than 1 million workers who do not have a union on the job joined in the first two years. Working America harnesses a new source of worker power to demand accountability from our politicians and corporations. Like an American Association for Retired Persons (AARP) or Move On.org[7] for workers, the astonishing success of Working America shows there is a hunger among working people to have a stronger voice on issues confronting working families. As Kedrin Bell, an administrative assistant in Kansas City, Missouri, explained, "I don't have the time between diapers and Little League to call all of Congress and voice my opinion, but as a member of Working America, I have a voice. Working America helps me to keep abreast of the issues that are important to me, and gives me the opportunity to have my voice heard. Through Working America, I become one voice among many."[8]

Finally, the concentrated work over the last few years of the AFL-CIO Working Women's Committee joining with the Civil Rights Committee resulted in changes to the AFL-CIO constitution passed at the 2005 convention. The resolution "A Diverse Movement Calls for Diverse Leadership" states:

> In too many cases, women and people of color still are underrepresented among union leadership. It is understandable that many women and people of color—the workers who are among those with the most to gain from union membership and who are most actively organizing today—do not feel welcome. . . . We will not allow women, people of color, gay or lesbian workers or brothers and sisters with disabilities to be denied the fruits of their labor in the workplace. We cannot be less vigilant and demanding of ourselves. (AFL-CIO Executive Council 2005, 9)

AFL-CIO constitutional amendments require delegations to future conventions to generally reflect the racial and gender diversity of its membership, an outstanding difference from current practice. In addition, at least fifteen positions on the Executive Council must be used to ensure diversity, roughly dou-

[7] MoveOn.org is a progressive organization that burst on to the scene in the late 1990s with a college-educated Internet-savvy activist base. It originally operated on the Internet, but moved into on-the-ground organizing as well. By 2005, it had 3 million members, leveraged public opinion, and had significant political influence.

[8] E-mail message from Kedrin Bell to Working America, May 2005.

bling the percentage of women and people of color. The resolution calls for a minimum mandatory standard for representation of women and people of color and requires plans to achieve higher levels of diversity at all levels of the AFL-CIO within four years. Last, affiliated unions and state and local labor councils are urged to adopt a set of diversity principles and to report on diversity within their organizations to promote accountability.

These dramatic changes came about at a low ebb of women's programs in the union movement. In 2002, the Working Women's Department was eliminated as a cost-cutting measure and some of its functions merged into the Civil and Human Rights Department. The national Working Women's Conferences were ended and the national campaigns on equal pay and work-family were phased out. "The elimination of the Working Women's Department was a wake-up call," remarked Patricia Friend, president of the Association of Flight Attendants/Communications Workers of America (AFA/CWA). In response, a small group of elected women leaders developed a set of diversity principles, which grew out of the 2004 AFL-CIO Committee on Working Women's Report, "Overcoming Barriers to Women in Organizing and Leadership." They met with members of the Executive Council one by one, made an alliance with the Civil Rights Committee, and promoted the principles at local and national union women's conferences and in a series of citywide meetings before the convention. This year-long organizing campaign paid off—no one opposed the proposals.

The election of Anna Burger as the chair of the break-away Change to Win Federation grows out of the focus on diversity promoted by this debate. Further change is awaited—none of the Change to Win unions is headed by a woman and only one union in the AFL-CIO has a woman president.

•   •   •

In 1974, the 9to5 women yearned for respect. "We are dignified and we want dignity," Charlene Gordon asserted. "The most crushing, crushing thing that can happen is that you are with a group of maybe students or teachers and somebody asks you what you do," Maria Millefoglie explained plaintively. The dismissive response when she told them she's a secretary "drops all enthusiasm for what you do in life." One big problem, she added, is "a lot of women refuse to admit they are exploited." When a group of waitresses sued Howard Johnson's for age discrimination in 1976, a reporter asked how they felt. "Hurt," they replied. Still, women in the 1970s were part of a wave of social movements operating in an environment that encouraged organizational solutions, with a responsive government.

Thirty years later, working women are tougher but more isolated. "There is a fierce streak of independence in these women," concluded pollster Celinda

Lake in 2003. "Just knowing what I do and where I am," said one woman, "I stand up for myself." When asked, "Who is on your side?" one typical response was, "Myself, just myself." Although they recognize their jobs are plagued with systemic discrimination, women often do not consider a collective response to be viable.

Today, the themes that move working women are different than thirty years ago—the need for good jobs undermined by the dynamics of a global economy and the desperate desire to balance work and family, as opposed to the "raises, rights, and respect" of the 1970s. And their feminism, although it may be unacknowledged, is built into their outlook, as opposed to being a new concept.

A woman who was a leader in an organizing campaign among hotel workers at the MGM Casino in Las Vegas told me that she exhorted her co-workers by saying, "The Lion is the symbol of MGM. *We* must be lionesses, and fight for our families."

She turned her consciousness into collective rebellion, but for others to do so will require more: an aggressive union movement that embraces diversity; a women's movement that understands that achieving women's rights depends on women realizing their rights as workers; a national campaign that succeeds in making labor rights a moral issue; and political leaders who side with workers over corporate interests and who commit to winning improvements for working families, so that, once again, change seems possible.

9

"WE WERE THE INVISIBLE WORKFORCE"

UNIONIZING HOME CARE

Eileen Boris and Jennifer Klein

"This is a caring job," declared a California In-Home Supportive Services (IHSS) personal attendant, who had nursed her elderly father so "he did not have one bed sore" (Delp and Quan 2002, 17). Although the "eyes, ears, feet and arms" for the disabled and frail, home care workers were "the poor helping the poor," who long had experienced "no recognition at all of our work" (Jones 1989). Before the stunning 1999 victory in Los Angeles County, when 74,000 entered Service Employees International Union (SEIU) Local 434B, "we were the invisible workforce," explained grassroots leader Esperanza De Anda (Delp and Quan 2002, 4). Afterward, the media celebrated these minimum-wage, predominantly Latina, black, and immigrant women for pulling off the largest increase of union membership since the 1930s (Greenhouse 1999b). The story of how providers of home services for individual low-income clients came to be recognized as workers illuminates the challenges of organizing the caregiver labor force, especially one in which the home is the workplace.

During the last half century, an expanded service sector generated low-wage insecure jobs. A racialized feminization of labor resulted, not only in the sense of women of color filling these new positions but also in terms of the

We thank research assistants Jill Jensen and Matthew Bloom for their labors, as well as Dorothy Sue Cobble for her comments. This research was funded in part by grants from the UC Labor and Education Research Fund, UCSB Faculty Senate, UCSB ISBER, and the Yale University Griswold and Morse Funds.

valuing of the work performed in them (Glenn 1992). Endemic to feminization were the conflation of the characteristics of the worker with the work itself, an association of service with ethnic or racial others, and a nonacknowledgment of skill or its obfuscation as a product of gender socialization rather than formal training. Carework particularly falls subject to this process. The nonwage labors of the wife or mother, performed out of love, obligation, and duty, morph into the low-wage tasks of the housekeeper, personal attendant, health aide, and child or elder minder. Before caregivers were even able to bargain for higher wages, benefits, and better working conditions, they had to see themselves as workers and fight for such recognition from the public, the state, and the very users of their services. They had to gain visibility and dignity, two key phrases in both self and the media representation of home care providers. They had to seek the right to organize in the first place.

This chapter traces the organizing of home care over the last thirty-five years in light of the nature of the work and in the context of social movements that together fought state efforts to resolve the crisis of long-term care on the backs of these frontline workers. First, we consider the labor of care. With the interaction between the provider and receiver of care central to the labor process, servicing people differs from making things. The structure of the job—on an interpersonal micro level as well as through macro-level state policies and health-care markets—generated the contours against which organizing occurred. Then we discuss how unionization depended on both making workers and defining employers. Home care unionism belonged to an effervescence of organizing among poor, black, and Latina women. It originated in social justice movements for domestic workers' rights, farm worker unionism, public-sector militancy bound up with political mobilization around state budgets, and the community organizing of groups such as the Association of Community Organizations for Reform Now (ACORN). These movements not only reached out to workers in casual or service sectors; they sought to invent new structures of representation and distinct notions of unionism that reflected, but were not limited to, the preponderance of women in this workforce.

Home care organizers began within the confines of New Deal labor law, signing up members workplace by workplace, with the aim of a positive National Labor Relations Board (NLRB) election. But they found themselves doubly stymied: by the industrial union model, premised on all employees laboring at the same worksite, and by the NLRB representation system, which assumed an unambiguous employer-employee relationship. They needed, instead, a form of unionism that could encompass the service provider–client relationship, as well as maneuver around the dispersed location of the labor. They required, as Dorothy Sue Cobble has argued, unions that offered "portable rights and benefits" and a means to "improve the image and standing of the occupation" (1996, 348, 345).

Like other service sectors, home care involves a "third party"—the client or consumer (Cobble 2001). But in this case, a fourth party, the state, perpetually created, shaped, and re-ordered the service relationship. Unions, then, could not succeed alone. State recognition and the funding necessary to improve conditions required a larger coalition with the consumers of care—organized seniors and disability rights activists. In contrast to the traditional contract focus of industrial unions, home care unionism had to plea for larger social goods, becoming advocates of better care in order to obtain better jobs for union members.

The Labor of Care

Cleaning bodies as well as rooms, home care workers engage in intimate labor, a kind of toil most essential but mostly stigmatized, as if the mere touching of dirt degrades the handler (Palmer 1989). Personal attendants, housekeepers, and health aides help the aged and disabled remain in their own homes by assisting with the activities of daily living. As one union activist explained, "it's a human service. Some people are without relatives and to make a cake or a pan of rolls for them means a lot." She viewed herself as "a little bit of everything—nurse, companion, psychiatrist, etc." (Parker 1980). In supporting dependent people, she also performed labor that theorists name "caregiving." Unlike other paid labor, caregiving requires "incomplete commodification" (Himmelweit 1999, 30–37). Exchanges are not interchangeable because each client has his or her own needs. Clients prefer to be called consumers, but actually they are not customers. Rather than being marked by an ability to pay, they are distinguished from shoppers of other goods and services by their inabilities, including meager finances and impaired capacities. They require being cared about in order to be cared for, necessitating that caregivers respond to the whole person.

Since the 1950s, states have delineated distinct categories of home care, creating job titles such as housekeeper, focusing on household chores; homemaker, providing custodial services, such as help with bathing and dressing; and home health aide or attendant, undertaking personal care, including assistance with mouth, skin, and hair. The continuous job retitling reflected the emergence of new funding streams, pressure from a nursing profession seeking protection from deskilling, and restructured welfare programs emphasizing job training. In practice, home health aides, attendants, and homemakers all performed household chores and custodial services (Trager 1973).

These workers labored in private homes, but the public sector either provided or paid for their services. Nursing home scandals and the deinstitutionalization movement justified government advocacy of home care as a cheaper, more efficient—as well as more humane—solution to long-term care. By the 1990s, Medicaid accounted for 43 percent of all long-term care expenditures. Although much of the spending supported institutional settings, over one-half of the expenditures on home care came from federal, state, and county funds, including old age and community health initiatives under Social Security. Social policies and reimbursement rates directly shaped the structure of the industry and the terms and conditions of labor (Burbridge 1993, 41, 44). So did assumptions that "women would always be willing to provide care and companionship for our loved ones" (Dawson and Surpin 2001, 7). Thus, the pay could be the minimum, the hours part-time, and the benefits absent. State contracting of services maximized the uncertainties of the labor, confused the employment status of workers, and, hence, jeopardized the service itself.

The invisibility of home care as caregiving further derives from conflicts between care as an act that overflows predefined boundaries and the Taylorized time-task schedules through which social workers, hospitals, and private agencies defined the job. The old managerial structures of the industrial era have served the labor of care as poorly as corresponding forms of industrial unionism. Public social workers and agency supervisors have measured the work by activities accomplished. They have reduced the job to household maintenance and bodily care, in contrast to intangibles, such as keeping someone company or chatting together about family and friends, which aides constantly remark as being essential to work well done. As policy analyst Deborah Stone notes, the rules of caring in the public sphere "promote disengagement, distance, and impartiality" while discounting the love, partiality, and attachment that many develop toward those cared for (2000, 93). Doing care requires negotiation and trust building, emotional labor absent from formal job classifications and bureaucratic regulation.

The caregiving relationship itself has generated obstacles to unionization. Caregivers could not imagine neglecting their charges or going on strike. "Sure, there are a lot of times I'd rather spend a little more time out shopping or whatever," confided one Contra Costa, California attendant. "But I always think . . . He can't do it by himself. Besides, I want to be here." This sense of devotion has kept nonrelative providers from quitting (Garofoli 1998). A 1998 report commissioned by SEIU concluded that many saw "their work more as service than as employment." Those attending family preferred better wages but downplayed compensation, such as an Armenian respondent who confessed: "We were doing it anyway. . . ." Latinas, tending nonrelatives, had more of a worker consciousness; so did African Americans who remained keenly aware of the association with domestic service—"we are cooks, we are chauffeurs, we are nursemaids, we are hazels. We are everything," one proclaimed in pride and disgust (Feldman Group, Inc. 1998, 2, 7, 8).

The ability to care also brought economic disadvantages as home caregivers engaged in self-exploitation, extending the hours of labor to meet the needs of their charges without overtime or higher wages. They accompanied people to doctors, for example, without reimbursement for travel or pay for the time. Relatives, who tend about half the caseload in California, had to leave other employment to be hired and then counties would pay them only for tasks beyond what social workers judged "normal household routine" (Ricker-Smith 1978, 85). Some elderly and disabled actually drew on social security checks to supplement caretaker wages, while their attendants turned to public assistance. Low wages, in turn, generated turnover, discouraged training, and increased the possibility that the care worker would be unreliable or unqualified.

Even though policymakers touted the occupation as an alternative to welfare, it failed to lift women out of poverty. This predominantly minority, low-income, middle-age female workforce faced, as SEIU organizers recognized, "all the issues of poverty in their neighborhood or public housing projects," as well as workplace conditions typical of service labor. Abuse, such as clients demanding that they wash outside windows, followed from imprecise job specifications. Workers suffered from the " 'client is always right' attitude" as well as from "the difficulty of putting together an 8 hour day with clients spread out all over the city" (Adams and Gallagher 1988, 1–3). Although a good proportion of home care workers were not looking for full-time work, SEIU organizers fought to make home care into a good job. Equating such a job with an eight-hour day, however, failed to address the difficulty of containing carework in such a framework.

Organizers, then, faced a continuing challenge to convince providers that they were employees. Karen Sherr, lead organizer for SEIU Local 250 in San Francisco during the mid-1990s, recalled, "when we had the first meeting, many people were amazed at how many others were there who were doing the same work as themselves. . . . They had absolutely no identity as workers" (Wick 2000, 26–27). The SEIU strategy would come to offer "an identity as a worker . . . part of a giant work-force, doing important work that merits recognition, respect, and decent standards" (Service Employees International Union [SEIU] 1992).

Making Workers and Defining Employers

In its composition and casualization, home care, then, has resembled other forms of low-wage service labor, but its workers faced additional disadvantages: located in the home, it was hidden from public view, with an ambiguous employment relationship. Just as some providers and receivers of care refused to acknowledge home care as work, legislators, governments, and welfare administrators repeatedly denied caregivers the status of employee and their own position as employer. Before unionization, new understandings of work and worker had to emerge that required changes in both law and consciousness.

Workers and their advocates confronted a hostile legal system. New Deal laws classified home companions as domestic servants, thus denying access to minimum wages, overtime, bargaining rights, or other workplace protections. This exclusion came from their association with the home and confusion with family but also from the racialized discrimination haunting household labor. Subsequently, only a few states extended any labor standards to domestics. The distinctions between personal attendants, home health aides, and domestics often blurred because the same people, over the course of their work lives, circulated from housecleaning to attendant work and back and often on and off public assistance as well. Unions themselves reflected this confusion; SEIU in New York referred to home attendants as household workers in the 1970s, and an early California group to concentrate on unionizing called itself the United Domestic Workers of America (UDWA).

Yet when domestics finally came under the Fair Labor Standards Act (FLSA) in 1974, personal attendants and other home care workers became classified as "companions," who, like casual babysitters, were exempt from minimum wage and overtime pay, even if employed by a third party such as the state or a private agency. Congress ignored occupational transformations in the health industry, so that, just as local and state governments in the 1970s encountered increased costs under Medicaid and related programs, labor-intensive care became possible on the cheap (Biklen 2003).

Public agencies constantly sought to obscure their responsibility as employers. Despite footing the bill and organizing the labor through state, city, or county departments of social welfare, even deciding who qualified for how many hours of care, governments designated workers as independent contractors. Who was the employer was hardly self-evident. In Washington, D.C., under federal oversight, home chore aides in one section of the Department of Human Services became employees while personal care aides, moved to another section in 1975, became independent contractors, even though they performed similar work (U.S. Congress 1979, 375–81). In California, between three-quarters and one-half of the funds for home care came from federal sources, with the state and counties perpetually jockeying over their percentage of the rest. The state cut the worker's check with funds from MediCal or general revenue. But there was no uniform mode of service delivery. Consumers/clients could hire, train, supervise, and terminate the attendant, who then was considered an independent provider. County welfare or health departments also could employ aides directly, or they could contract the entire service to for-profit or nonprofit vendors. New York and Illinois increasingly did just that and denied responsibility for collective bargaining, even though a combination of government monies funded these services. The different payment mechanisms, modes of service, and interpretations of FLSA created a continuously uncertain legal situation, with courts sometimes ruling that the consumer employed the caregiver, other times seeing her as a government worker or an employee of a private agency (Biklen 2003).

With lack of oversight, labor conditions and care quality deteriorated. No one knew how many hours an attendant worked, especially when the state issued the reimbursement check directly to the client; home attendants on call around the clock ended up making less than minimum wage because overtime compensation was not mandatory. Because many clients were incapable of managing finances, checks got lost or mislaid (U.S. Congress 1979, 378). Audits conducted in New York in the 1970s found "inordinate delays and errors in payment" from inefficient bureaucracies (Citizens' Committee on Aging 1977). California tried to balance its state budget in the early 1990s by delaying the checks of IHSS workers, made vulnerable by their employment status (Chang 2000, 141).

Even as Congress separated home companions from domestic servants, home aides became the major beneficiaries of the movement to extend labor rights to household workers. Led by the National Committee on Household Employment (NCHE), founded by the U.S. Women's Bureau, but revitalized by the black feminist lawyer Edith Sloan, and with support from the National Organization of Women and other mainstream feminists, the plight of domestic laborers turned into a highly visible civil rights issue (Cobble 2004, 198–200). As Eleanor Holmes Norton, chair of the New York City Commission on Human Rights, testified in 1975, "of all occupations that might make the point about the black women's stake in the movement for freedom, none seemed to me, could better dramatize the point than household workers" (New York State Assembly 1975c).

Organization among domestics hardly resembled traditional unionism. The Atlanta-based National Domestic Workers Union, founded by Dorothy Bolden in 1968, began as "a mutual aid group" providing solidarity for those engaged in individual negotiations (Tait 2005, 41–42). Under the auspices of the NCHE, Washington, D.C., home aides formed the Organization of Personal Care and Chore Services in 1979, both a lobbying and a bargaining group (Stevens 1979). They not only pressured the city council for inclusion under the district's minimum wage law, but requested Congress to instruct the district that they were "eligible to form a labor union." The local government refused to recognize them, despite assigning "where they work and the hours designated and the clients" (U.S. Congress 1979, 383). It took until 1994 for the personal care agents, aided by SEIU Local 722, to be reclassified as employees and thus qualify for health benefits, social security, and worker compensation (Service Employees International Union [SEIU] 1994).

The predominance of women of color and immigrants overlapped with the personnel in public or nonprofit service sectors, particularly hospitals, nursing homes, welfare agencies, and other city bureaucracies. Hence, the domestic workers' rights movement began to intersect with service sector unionism, which provided inspiration, tactics, and personnel to home care workers' organizing campaigns during the 1980s. An initial organizing force in the 1960s was the American Federation of State, County, and Municipal Workers (AFSCME). In New York City, with the largest home health caseload, homemakers first united as members of AFSCME Local 371, representing the New York City Department of Welfare. Along with social workers and case aides, homemakers were among the eight thousand strikers who shut down two-thirds of the city's welfare centers in 1965 (Perlmutter 1965).

Militant unionism at the Department of Welfare, however, involved more than simple contract negotiations between union and employer. Working conditions, caseloads, over-time compensation, promotional opportunities, and pay rates were tied to public budgets and social policy at the city and state levels. Consequently, unionists deployed traditional tactics for public-sector organizing: political action, public appeals, and legislative lobbying (*Public Employee* 1969; Slater 2004). To contain union militancy, after 1970 New York City reduced the workforce and reclassified homemakers as independent contractors. Although the workforce subsequently grew more than 200 percent without the benefit of any union (Citizens Committee on Aging 1977), the legacy from previous public-sector unionism was not lost—workers would win better wages and working conditions when they put pressure on state policymakers and made clear that standards of service depended on labor standards.

The question of employment rights for domestic workers became linked with service sector unionism in New York, where union activists and progressive legislators turned to the state for remedies. Starting in 1974, Bronx state Assemblyman Seymour Posner, a former social worker and AFSCME activist, pushed to pass a collective bargaining law for household workers. SEIU and civil rights groups, such as the A. Philip Randolph Institute, Urban League, National Association for the Advancement of Colored People (NAACP), American Jewish Congress, and NCHE, joined in support (New York State Assembly 1975a). SEIU viewed this legislation as an opportunity to extend organizing from building cleaners to household workers (New York State Assembly 1975b). Posner's bill passed in 1977, but, mirroring the federal level, amendments excluded "babysitters and companions to sick, convalescing, and elderly people" (Posner 1974a, 1974b). Law and policy continued to withhold formal acknowledgment of the labor of care as employment.

Nonetheless, with the backing of the civil rights community, SEIU's flagship and largest local, 32B-32J, led by its new president, John Sweeney, initiated a Household Workers Organizing Committee. Representing New York City's building supers, elevator operators, building maintenance crews, and office and store cleaners, including women who labored at night, 32B-32J had grown to almost 40,000 members by organizing small groups, building by building. Unlike most industrial unions, it understood that workers in nonindustrial settings were organizable. The institutional culture of this old American Federation of Labor (AFL) union facilitated seeking out the "invisible workforce" of home care.[1]

Vice-President Cecil Ward, the Trinidadian-born close colleague of Sweeney, took charge. By 1978, Ward had a staff of four women organizers working solely on the household-workers effort, a significant dedication of resources, according to Barbara Shulman, who became an assistant to Ward. Laura Hopkins and Josephine Bond, both African American former service workers, were among the lead organizers. Ward invoked the libratory metaphors of the civil rights struggle, telling home attendants, "we are on the march . . . to organize and to free you good people from slavery" (SEIU 32J-32B 1978b).[2] Because the new collective bargaining law did not apply to individuals hired directly by someone in the home, the Household Workers' Organizing Committee looked for firms and agencies that sent tens of thousands of workers into homes everyday. Although they did not initially set out to organize care workers, their attention was soon drawn to the so-called housekeeping programs of private charitable agencies. At the end of the year, 32B-32J filed its first NLRB petition to represent four hundred workers employed by the Housekeeping Program of the Federation of the Handicapped, who earned an average wage below the federal minimum (SEIU 1978; SEIU 32J-32B 1977, 1978a, 1978b).

Other unions in New York were paying attention to home care. SEIU Local 144, the second largest local in SEIU and predominantly representing nursing home workers, considered home care aides part of the same workforce that labored in nursing homes and hospitals. It initially sought to block employers from using the home for "off-site production" that could undermine the labor standards of those working in institutional settings (SEIU Local 144 1977). This aim took on greater urgency when the state froze Medicaid reimbursements to nursing homes in the mid-1970s. Local 144's home care drive also represented a response to New York's plan to close many of its nursing homes. Indeed, new nursing home construction essentially halted all together in the early 1980s. If, as health policy expert Barbara Caress put it, "home is where the patients are," Local 144 knew that was where the workers would be too, and it soon merged efforts with 32B-32J (Caress 1988, 6).

---

[1] Barbara Shulman, telephone interview by Jennifer Klein, Silver Spring, Md., April 8, 2005.
[2] Ibid.

Local 144 provided service sector experience to the all-woman staff who steadily built SEIU's home care union. By mid-1981, there were about 6,400 members, speaking eight different languages, and contracts with sixteen vendor agencies. A year later, the union claimed 14,000 home care members (SEIU 32B-32J 1981a, 1981b, 1982).[3] Yet, just as this drive was hitting its stride, a new president, Gus Bevona, took over 32B-32J and its fledgling home care local. Within a couple of years, Bevona succeeded in forcing out those who built this mostly women-of-color local. Suppressing internal democracy, organizing, and rank and file participation, the self-aggrandizing Bevona let the union coast (SEIU 32B-32J-144, 1983–1991; Bevona 1987; Greenhouse 1999a).

A third union, the National Union of Hospital and Health Care Employees Local 1199, eventually took the lead. Since 1958, when a group of left-wing pharmacists and drug clerks set out to organize the city's hospital workers, 1199 belonged to the civil rights struggle. In just over a decade, these overwhelmingly poor, female, and black and Latino/a workers swept through a sector once entirely ignored by the labor movement and excluded by the labor law. In organizing this new working class of hospital dietary, housekeeping, and maintenance staff; orderlies; aides; and clerks, 1199 cultivated a symbiotic relationship with black and Latino activists. From 1963 throughout the 1970s, it turned workplace organizing drives into political campaigns that won bargaining rights from the state. Whether organizing public or private employers, political pressure became essential to 1199's long-term success (Fink and Greenberg 1989).

After a failed attempt to merge with SEIU in 1982, 1199 became its chief rival. Organizing home care was a logical extension of its efforts since hospital aides and dietary workers often became home attendants or homemakers on weekends or at night. Like AFSCME before it, 1199 knew how to pressure politicians. But in key ways, 1199 was still very much an industrial union, used to organizing many workers in one place. Moreover, the leaders embraced the notion of reaching a different group than the white male constituency of industrial unionism, but they did not sufficiently acknowledge that the work itself also differed. 1199 paid little attention to consumers and rarely deployed a strategy based on the quality of care and service provided to patients. Perhaps because at the least sign of worker resistance management quickly exploited the humanitarian mission of hospitals, 1199 concentrated heavily on living wage demands. "Organizing," as leader Moe Foner said, "is key and everything else is peripheral" (Fink and Greenberg 1989, 202), but the lack of attention to the particular dimensions of care work reflected a narrow vision that initially impeded home care organizing.

---

[3] Sample ballot, from Barbara Shulman.

By 1985, 1199 represented 20,000 home care workers, and yet, after several years of collective bargaining, wages had risen only 80 cents above the minimum. Seniority differentials, vacation, and sick leave benefits remained miniscule; pensions and job security were nonexistent. Even union members providing twenty-four-hour care were paid for only twelve. When the union's 1987 contract ended, most earned less than $7,000 a year, well below the poverty level for a family of four (Caress 1988, 4, 9; Donovan, Kurzman, and Rotman 1993, 582).

It appeared that "collective bargaining with dozens of separate vendor agencies was proving futile" (Donovan, Kurzman, and Rotman 1993, 583). Contracts with the state and city government ultimately constrained agencies from negotiating real wage increases. If a hospital strike were a bitter pill to swallow, a home care workers' strike would be even more so. With around 48,000 separate, uncoordinated worksites and tens of thousands of frail and disabled clients dependent on attendants, workers could not easily walk out (Donovan, Kurzman, and Rotman 1993, 583). Moreover, in the 1980s, internal factionalism and racial polarization wracked 1199 itself.[4]

As New York City's various locals proceeded along lines laid down by the NLRB, the levels of union membership slowly but steadily crept upward. Yet the social movement that sought to revalue the gendered labor of care, empower women of color, and increase the quality of public benefits stalled. Community action techniques germinating elsewhere broke open the political and social potential of a care worker movement. In San Diego during the late 1970s, a group of black nationalists, inspired by Cesar Chavez, changed directions and established the UDWA.[5] After limited success at reaching domestic servants, they discovered a constituency in home care employees of companies with county contracts.

Civil rights unionism shaped UDWA from the start. With financial aid from the United Farm Workers of America (UFWA) and the Catholic Church, the new group sought to form "a poor people's union in an urban setting" for and by domestic laborers who fared even worse than those who toiled in the fields (Eldred 1980; Gross 1980; Reza 1989). It envisioned a membership that also would include private household, hotel maids, and nursing home workers. Reaching a scattered constituency proved daunting, even though organizers chatted with women waiting for early morning busses, crossing the border when necessary; set up house meetings; established neighborhood committees; and planned a service center to aid with housing and other problems (Eldred 1980). In April 1979, 150 delegates attended the first convention at a time

[4] Dan North, interview with Moe Foner, session #22, March 5, 2001, Columbia University, Oral History Research Office, http://www.columbia.edu/cu/lweb/indiv/oral/foner (accessed July 20, 2005).

[5] United Domestic Workers of America, "United Domestic Workers of America: Brief History and Background," http://www.udwa.org/history.htm (accessed May 15, 2005).

when San Diego County had about 15,000 domestics. But even then the union had targeted local government. IHSS was under persistent scrutiny for mismanagement and, with a constituency of the poor, elderly, ill, and disabled, it increasingly became caught in the vise of state budget negotiations and county attempts to pay as little as possible for the service. UDW founder Ken Seaton-Msemaji understood that organizing home care workers required political clout because "you really end up negotiating with the supervisors on the wages" (Parker 1980; Eldred 1980; Gross 1980; Seaton-Msemaji 1993).

Over the next eighteen months, the union's staff, grown to ten, put the house-meeting and community-oriented UFWA model into high gear, training eighty homemakers, who then organized their co-workers. Information from SEIU 250 led UDWA to focus on the county's home attendant contract up for renewal (Parker 1980). One breakthrough occurred in March, 1980 when organizers met Claudia Bowens, a fifty-ish black woman; Margaret Insko, a Chicana and domestic for over a decade; and Carol Leonard, a twenty-something white woman, who were leaving an employer-training session. Like other home care providers, these women suffered from underpayment and lack of sick days. Instead of the adversarial relationship emphasized by industrial unionism, they sought a movement that valued the care relationship, an exchange that could and should have multiple benefits for each side and could foster and reward employee-employer relations that were more collaborative than bureaucratic. They cared "about people and, in return, we think someone should care about us.... We are not just objects" (Parker 1980).

These women became central to the effort while the newly formed Domestic Workers Service Center mobilized local support for hearings before the Board of Supervisors (Eldred 1980). Through lobbying and testifying, the UDWA helped block the award of the contract to one company by getting the supervisors to throw out the original bids (Parker 1980). Members began to learn the lesson of unionization: "In unity we have *strength*," roared Bowens (Eldred 1980). Msemaji emphasized that "the biggest thing in their (union members) lives is that they've learned ... they don't have to settle for working conditions if they're not fair, that they can change things.... The contract is secondary to that" (Parker 1980).

In Chicago, ACORN also started community organizing among home care workers in the early 1980s. Its United Labor Unions (ULU) adhered to a philosophy similar to that of UFWA in seeking to enhance participation, mobilization, and militancy among low-wage workers. Key ACORN leaders and rank-and-filers came out of the welfare rights movement of the previous decade. Boston's ULU serendipitously discovered home care workers when petitioning to raise the minimum wage (Tait 2005, 107, 116–19). When home care locals in Boston and Chicago affiliated with SEIU in the early 1980s, they helped revitalize organizing within that service industry giant—unlike UDWA, whose short affiliation with SEIU from 1982 to 1984 degenerated into more than a decade-long jurisdictional war (SEIU 1984).

Chicago's ULU, renamed SEIU 880, combined direct action and political lobbying with agency-by-agency bargaining. As a community action group, 880 helped spearhead African American neighborhood campaigns for affordable housing, cheaper banking rates, and a citywide living wage ordinance. As a union, 880 stayed rooted in the ACORN culture. It consistently cultivated rank and file leaders from among female home attendant members, who were drawn in through tens of thousands of house visits. The women created a social world around the union, with regular meetings, parties, barbeques, recognition ceremonies, letter-writing campaigns, marches, and neighborhood alliances. They held "speak outs" and "honk-ins," stopping traffic. Demonstrations became public performances, complete with props such as a burial casket or giant penny. The union organized lobbying days, when members traveled to the state capital to pressure legislators and the Department of Rehabilitative Services (DORS) for pay increases and higher reimbursements for agencies, and they turned out huge numbers at public hearings in Chicago, Springfield, and Washington, D.C. Although 880 never gained a contract with DORS during these years, it won regular pay increases, a grievance procedure, biweekly pay, and a state agreement to deduct taxes from paychecks. The ACORN model enabled the union to address women's whole lives as workers, kin, caregivers, and community members (SEIU 880 1986–1995; Brooks 2005, 51–52). Most significantly, Local 880 innovated by organizing pressure at the source —the state budget.

Other unions began to take notice, especially in New York, where NLRB elections and three-year contract renewals were becoming dead ends. Local 1199 and another New York home care union, AFSCME 1707, saw that to achieve substantive gains they would have to step outside the NLRB bargaining structure and launch a political campaign. When 1199 and 1707 approached 32B-32J-144 to join them, Bevona refused (Caress 1988, 9). Here SEIU could not carry the movement forward, partly because it was not committed to union democracy and cultivating rank and file leadership but also because the leadership refused to recognize the essential elements that made unionizing different in home care: the service needs of clients, the community networks that linked these women, and the welfare state location of the labor.

1199 and AFSCME moved on without that once-pioneering union. Beginning with rallies outside city hall in 1987, they enlisted the support of Jesse Jackson, then running for president, and Cardinal John O'Connor (*Health/PAC Bulletin* 1987). They compelled Manhattan Borough President David Dinkins to hold a public hearing on the plight of the home care worker. Under the banner of the Campaign for Justice for Home Care Workers, they launched an educational drive to garner public support, with the slogan, "We Care for the Most Important People in Your Life." Finally, the unions led non-profit vendor agencies, themselves organized as the Home Care Council of New York, and nearly every liberal politician into their coalition. Together they pressured the governor and the mayor. After receiving no response the first time, they doubled their mobilizing efforts, brought in more politicians, religious leaders, and big-wigs and set off a full-scale press blitz. On March 31, 1988, after unprecedented negotiations between Governor Mario Cuomo's office and the unions, the state allocated the highest level of new funds for home care ever obtained. The agreement granted both unions a 53 percent wage increase, health insurance, guaranteed days off, and prescription drug coverage (Caress 1988, 4–14). Adopting the political philosophy of AFSCME, New York's home care unions from then on knew that enlarging the public budget was essential to enhancing the lives of workers.

Consumers Join the Coalition

Still missing from the organizing formula were the users of home care as active coalition partners rather than campaign props. In California, conflicting legal decisions in the late 1980s and early 1990s justified counties stonewalling collective bargaining. Thus, although the decade-long battle in Los Angeles saw all the hallmarks of the new social movement unionism—constant membership meetings, numerous demonstrations, and political education—improved conditions required legislative mandates and increased funding and, for that, workers had to join with consumers to lobby the state (Rivas 2005; Walsh 2001). SEIU strategists agreed that the union had to seek "concentrations of homecare workers employed by providers who are *state-funded*" (Adams and Gallagher 1988). Equally part of its strategy this time, SEIU argued for the "expansion of homecare as a progressive and compassionate health care delivery model" (SEIU 1988). It directed such arguments to consumers, promoting better care and deploying logos such as "There's No Place Like Home."

In 1987, when SEIU began its massive campaign, disability activists had spent nearly two decades fighting to choose, train, and control the attendants who made independent living possible. They particularly disliked the contracting of IHSS, finding in managed care an attack on consumer choice that reallocated limited funding away from services to supervision and company profits. Contracting not only interfered with self-control but risked the well-being of consumers by neglecting "certain authorized services under the *assumption* that family members and neighbors would do them" (Yeager 1993). Activists rejected "the concept that disabled people are 'cared' for," explained

Judy Heumann, co-director of the Berkeley-based World Institute on Disability, preferring to "refer to such programs as 'Attendant Services.'" These services, they insisted, were "a human and civil right" (Heumann 1987).

The consumer alliance with unions did not come easily. The coalition originated with lobbyists on the state level, who worked for both the California Foundation of Independent Living Centers and SEIU. It flourished through the efforts of dedicated organizers such as Janet Heinritz-Canterbury, formerly executive director of the Congress of California Seniors, who spent hours meeting in elder centers and with disability activists to build the trust necessary to carry forward the project (Heinritz-Canterbury 1993).[6] Disability rights activists asked, "Who will protect consumers?" (Russell 1993, 7–8). As Nancy Becker Kennedy fretted, "With a union fighting for 'terms and conditions' of their attendants and no one fighting for our basic right . . . to move, go to bed, have a shower, a bowel movement[,] a meal, it will be more of a David and Goliath situation than it already is" (Becker Kennedy 1993).

In contrast, seniors, represented by such groups as the Older Women's League and California Senior Legislature (CSL), worried more about reduced hours and competent aides than about their power relations with attendants (*Sacramento Union* 1993). Seniors groups too had been an active force in shifting state priorities from nursing homes to home care, but they rarely included workers' issues or voices. Starting in 1992, however, key activists from CSL agreed to work with SEIU on legislation, including standards that seniors wanted such as criminal background checks. Because of the Older Americans Act and its area agencies on aging, seniors were well organized at the county level; they in turn elected 120 delegates statewide, constituting the CSL, to represent them and intervene on legislative issues in Sacramento (Rivas 2005, 6–8). Thus, in joining the home care coalition, they could be mobilized at both levels: where services were provided and where legislation was shaped. Such county-level organization became even more important a decade later in Oregon, when SEIU and seniors lobbied state legislators district by district in 2001 to fund the voter-enacted Home Care Commission, which acted as the employer of home attendants (*Northwest Labor Press* 2001).

SEIU and the consumers, it turns out, had a common enemy: the state, with its desire to cap resources going to a program that allowed the elderly poor to remain in their own homes and younger disabled people to have a life apart from institutions and restrictive family settings. SEIU was ready to concede to the consumers what was needed to work together. Ed Roberts, a leader in the independent living movement, concluded in September 1993, "SEIU has gone a long way on this issue—no strikes, people with disabilities have the right to hire and fire—this is unusual" (Heinritz-Canterbury 1993).

---

[6] Janet Heinritz-Canterbury, interview by E. Boris, Los Angeles, Calif., April 13, 2005.

The concept of the public authority, a county commission that would serve as the bargaining unit for IHSS-independent providers, evolved from the desires of consumers and needs of the union. It came out of political action and lobbying by consumer allies. Laws in 1992 and 1993 funded counties to establish public authorities and central registries to locate the home care workforce. Authority boards were mandated to include current or past IHSS recipients. Whereas the San Francisco and Bay Area counties quickly created authorities and improved wages and benefits, Los Angeles—with half the state's IHSS caseload—dragged its feet until continual political pressure led the supervisors to cave in 1997. That disability activists were divided on features of the public authority, further slowing matters in Los Angeles, inadvertently shows the importance of strong coalitions for home care unionism (Russell 1996, 40, 50–51; Toy 1996, 41, 55). Two years later, the public authorities joined the unions and their coalition partners to win legislation compelling all counties to designate an employer by 2003 for collective bargaining purposes (Heinritz-Canterbury 2002, 12–13).

Visible Workers, Hidden Concerns

The process of struggle—as well as the progress to date—transformed the consciousness of careworkers, along with recognizing the value of the work (although monetary rewards remain inadequate). In shedding the status of independent contractor, homecare workers shook off their dependence on low-wage work that lacked the legal protection and social recognition normally accorded to employment in U.S. society. In turn, unions dropped some blinders that had prevented their seeing these workers at all. Home care workers were organizable but not by traditional methods. Even unions in the service sector—1199, AFSCME, and SEIU—had lessons to learn about care work, not only because of the three-way relationship among boss, worker, and consumer typical of service labor but also in the ways that home care differs from most commercial services. For those receiving government-subsidized care, the state determines what they purchase. The clients, then, are not exactly consumers, as we generally understand the term. Some people can afford to buy care freely on the market, but many hundreds of thousands are clients of the state. Public funding and government departments of aging, disability, and rehabilitative services shape the level and type of care they receive. Political mobilizing was as essential for clients as for workers. Community organizing movements such as ACORN helped show unions the way to mobilize both constituencies. Social movements among the disabled and the elderly also became crucial to home care unionizing; they not only had organized their own but had cultivated political strategies and relationships at the state level.

It took thirty years of experimenting, but by the mid-1990s SEIU—drawing on tactics developed by different unions in different locals—put together a winning formula. The California campaign built alliances, stepped outside the NLRB framework, organized 74,000 workers, and created new institutional state structures that enabled the union to function on a sectoral, rather than worksite, basis. The merged SEIU-1199 now has a major commitment to organizing home care attendants and aides. It is applying lessons learned in home care organizing to family day care, another arena of paid care in which the home is a workplace and love and labor become conflated. Coalitions of consumers and providers offer a new path for envisioning the home as a place with dignity for workers and families. But the question persists whether unionism can confront how care labor differs from even other forms of service work. Care involves multiple levels of inequalities: the diminished capacities of consumer/clients as well as the stigmatized status of workers. Collective bargaining and state regulation both have heretofore failed to address these inequalities or advance the quality of care as an interactive process between cared for and carer. Unions and advocates have focused more on proving that higher wages and benefits lessen turnover in trying to make home care a good job than they have advanced the practice of care, despite small projects such as San Francisco's Planning for Elders in the Central City.[7] Union activists promote medicalized skills training to upgrade the work while they remain skeptical of enhancement strategies incorporating psychological and emotional labor. At the same time, disability consumers worry that medicalization will reduce autonomy, transforming them into dependent patients.

The question of empowering care workers within their own organizations persists. All the reasons that bring women to home care in the first place, such as low-income, poverty, family responsibility, immigrant status, lack of training, and social instability, inhibit their ability to participate fully in unions. Given the large ethnic workforce, many still look at the job as family duty rather than as employment. Political unionism needs its members for campaigns, and the unions have brought their membership to city, county, and state halls. But to the extent that the home care unions become providers of services rather than educators and mobilizers, to the extent that they stop the effort to revalue caring labor, they can fall into a kind of bureaucratic unionism that reinforces the old racialized gender distinctions of care work and stymies the advancement of rank and file women.

[7] Karen Sherr, conversation with E. Boris, Berkeley, Calif., May 8, 2005.

10

EXPANDING LABOR'S VISION

THE CHALLENGES OF WORKFARE AND WELFARE ORGANIZING

Vanessa Tait

Bending to pick up litter scattered across New York City's Central Park, Edriss Anderson moved patiently, methodically, and with an air of weariness. Like most women on welfare, Anderson has worked hard all her life. A single mother of four children, she supported her family with low-wage service industry work, relying on friends and relatives for after-school care of her children. When she was laid off from her job as a janitor, she struggled to make ends meet on unemployment. When that ran out, she went on welfare and, like thousands of others, was promptly assigned to workfare—and was sent to work circulating through the park's winding pathways to pick up trash and empty garbage cans. Anderson called herself a "no-wage" worker because all she received in exchange for her twenty-two hours of labor per week was the continuation of her biweekly $176 welfare check and $55 in food stamps. That she is not considered a "real worker" is what motivated her to support a drive to organize the city's workfare workforce. "There's no other way to look at it but modern-day slavery," she said. "They're not paying you wages, they don't care if you get hurt, and they threaten to cut off your [welfare] benefits if you complain."[1]

Stories of workers who were once employed at union wages and benefits

My thanks to Craig Alderson, Dorothy Sue Cobble, Netsy Firestein, Dana Frank, and Taylor Hatcher for offering critical insights and important sources.
[1] Edriss Anderson, interview by Vanessa Tait, New York City, June 3, 1997.

but who later labored as workfare workers are also common. Hattie Hargrove, a custodial worker at the Long Island County Department of Social Services, was laid off from her union-wage job. Ending up on welfare, she was given a workfare assignment that landed her back at her old, formerly union job, performing exactly the same duties for her former supervisor and receiving only a welfare check and food stamps in return. Hargrove said she wanted union representation: "I would feel better because I'd be getting a paycheck and people wouldn't look down at me like I was crazy anymore" (Healy 1997).

Along with tens of thousands of other workfare workers, Edriss Anderson and Hattie Hargrove are part of a long tradition of poor workers' organizing that has grown out of community-based movements for economic, racial, and gender justice. As case studies in New York City, San Francisco, and Montana show, this tradition holds promise for broadening and strengthening the U.S. labor movement by bringing new participants, fresh ideas, and innovative organizing strategies to its work.

Welfare recipients across the nation were forced into workfare programs by the 1996 Personal Responsibility and Work Opportunity Reconciliation Act, which ended six decades of support guaranteed to the poor. The law transformed the federally administered grant entitlement program Aid to Families with Dependent Children (AFDC) into a state-run program of coerced labor called Temporary Aid to Needy Families (TANF), which requires that the majority of welfare recipients enter market work within two years and puts a five-year lifetime cap on benefits. Under TANF workfare requirements, participants receive only their welfare benefits for jobs that, until recently, cities, counties, and private corporations paid wages to their employees to perform. In this massive process of job restructuring, welfare recipients replace waged workers, who sometimes end up on the welfare rolls themselves.

Workfare programs have existed in limited form in some states since the 1940s. In recent U.S. history, as Nancy Rose (1995) argues, such policies have alternated between workfare (mandatory non-wage work programs targeted at the "undeserving poor"), and what she calls "fair work" (voluntary training or job creation programs such as the Depression-era Works Progress Administration, usually intended for those seen as "deserving" real wages). TANF falls into the former category, and its strict time limits on benefits and workfare requirements have resulted in dramatic reductions in the welfare rolls without improving the situation of the poor.[2] Between 1996 and 1999,

---

[2] There are wide differences of opinion on how welfare-to-work programs have affected the poor, from the rosy interpretation of the U.S. government's Ways and Means Committee, which calculated that poor single mothers were "economically better off" in 2001 compared with the early 1990s (*Green Book*, 2004 [Background material and data on programs within the jurisdiction of the Committee on Ways and Means, U.S. House of Representatives, WMCP: 108–6], http://waysandmeans.house.gov/Documents.asp?section=813, Appendix L, page 5 [accessed August 28, 2006]) to those who found that

AFDC/TANF enrollment declined by over 50 percent, and some 6 million recipients lost benefits (Delgado and Gordon 2002, 38). The number of single
mothers on cash welfare declined by 69 percent from 1993 to 2001.[3] Although
recent census data show a small drop in the overall poverty rate, poverty has
deepened for those who remain poor and increased among the working poor.[4]

Welfare is the unemployment insurance of last resort. It serves as the ultimate safety net for all working people but is used most by the lowest-wage
workers—most frequently women and people of color—who shuttle back and
forth from minimum-wage jobs, contingent work, or jobs in the informal
economy to welfare grants, food stamps, and housing vouchers. In addition,
welfare recipients often do the vital but unwaged and socially invisible work of
raising children and providing other types of care. Activists have long argued
that welfare grants are compensation for this essential labor and note that,
even if jobs at living wages were plentiful, an adequate welfare system would
still be necessary for those who cannot work because of family responsibilities.

Workfare is particularly difficult for women, whose work is dramatically
undervalued both in the labor market and in the home. Women still make
only 74 percent of men's wages, and nearly twice as many women as men
labor for poverty level wages; women of color face even sharper ratios due to
racial discrimination (Littman 1998, 71; Mishel, Bernstein, and Allegretto
2005, 128–33). Single parents (who are overwhelmingly female) face tremendous obstacles in participating fully in the labor market, from unavailable or
expensive child care to discrimination by employers who claim their parenting responsibilities will affect their attendance or performance. Poverty rates
are strikingly high among single-parent families; 52 percent live in poverty
compared to only 5 percent for families with two adults but no children (Albelda and Tilly 1997, 36–37). The median income of families headed by female single parents is 64 percent of that for male single-parent families
(Chadwick and Heaton 1999, 228). Due to the lack of state-provided or
-subsidized child care, combined with limited opportunities for living wage
jobs and society's relegation of parenting to mothers, it is women, more often
than men, who draw welfare benefits; not surprisingly, welfare recipients are

---

some welfare recipients' conditions declined while others improved (DeParle 2004; Shipler 2004) to
those who present evidence that welfare reform has dramatically worsened the situation of the poor,
who now face greater hardships than previously (Albelda and Withorn 2002; Heather Boushey and
Bethany Gundersen, 2001, *When Work Just Isn't Enough: Measuring Hardships Faced by Families after
Moving from Welfare to Work*, Washington, D.C.: Economic Policy Institute, http://www.epinet.org/
briefingpapers/hardshipsbp.pdf [accessed August 28, 2006]).

[3] *Green Book,* 2004, http://waysandmeans.house.gov/Documents.asp?section=813, Appendix L,
page 7 (accessed August 28, 2006).

[4] Wendell Primus and Robert Greenstein, *Analysis of 1999 Census Poverty and Income Data,* Center
on Budget and Policy Priorities, Washington, D.C., 2000, http://www.cbpp.org/9–26–00pov.htm (accessed August 28, 2006).

overwhelmingly female and disproportionately women of color (Burnham 2002, 50).

But across the nation, welfare rights activists are organizing as workers both outside and inside the home. Women are prominent in the movement's leadership, demanding safe jobs at living wages and fighting for policies that support their families. Using tactics borrowed from traditional unions, as well as strategies drawn from the women's and human rights movements, workfare activists have contested the conservative discourse around welfare reform and, at the same time, challenged notions of who is a worker and what sorts of work should receive monetary compensation. They have won practical benefits such as grievance rights, apprenticeships, and living wage jobs. In several states, poor women have brought the struggle full circle by organizing for legislation explicitly recognizing their work in the home as caregivers and allowing welfare payments to be used to support this work.

This activism is opening up new possibilities for organizing welfare recipients by making welfare rights a struggle framed in terms of workers' rights and women's rights. Workfare organizing offers the labor movement a unique opportunity to expand its boundaries and enlarge its notion of the working class in a very practical way by welcoming welfare recipients into its ranks as sisters and brothers. Similarly, it offers the women's movement insights into how class and race complicate gender equality. The movements for labor and women's rights have usually been separate from poor people's organizing. From the civil rights and welfare rights movements of the 1960s to today's working-class and gender justice movements, poor people have too often been seen as outsiders by more traditional employment-based unions or mainstream women's organizations. Both employers and trade unionists have long defined *workers* as those who are paid actual wages for labor outside the home for an employer, and that concept has been enshrined in federal and state labor laws. Today's organizing by welfare recipients—both as unwaged workfare workers and caregivers at home—presents a serious challenge to that notion.

Redefining Who's a Worker

Mandatory workfare programs exploded across the nation after the passage of TANF, creating a huge pool of superexploitable workers and presenting a challenge to both community and union organizers. Facing municipal budget cutbacks, the new welfare law handed politicians an opportunity to solve their financial woes by replacing higher-wage union workers with unwaged workfare workers. In addition to municipal and nonprofit employers, corporations were increasingly taking advantage of workfare as a plentiful source of cheap labor, along with generous tax subsidies provided by the federal government as an incentive for their participation (Wildavsky 1997).

Workfare organizing peaked during the late 1990s as workfare rolls swelled and unionization projects sprang up in several communities, from New York City and Milwaukee to Los Angeles and San Francisco. Forcing poor people into unsustainable and exploitative workfare jobs—without support for child care, transportation, or education—drove many off the welfare rolls and into the arms of private charities (Prashad 2003, 15). Others were cut off after they exhausted their limited period of assistance. Organizing among workfare workers has continued in the twenty-first century, although on a more modest scale given the shrinking size of the welfare population.

Compensation for workfare is mostly in the form of food stamps or rent vouchers, with the rest in cash welfare benefits—a combination that puts workfare workers, on average, far below the federal poverty line. Workfare rarely leads to permanent, living wage employment—for instance, less than one-third of New York City's workfare workers obtained full- or part-time jobs afterward. One study of over 100,000 welfare recipients revealed that those who did find work ended up shuttling between a string of low-wage jobs "at a dizzying pace, with only 17 percent employed by one company for more than three years" (Riccardi 2000, 1). Workfare is not beneficial for communities either—it displaces paid workers, depresses wages, and leads to lower labor standards (Krueger, Accles, and Wernick 1997). Workfare does benefit employers, who reap the benefits of cheap labor.

One of the largest and harshest workfare programs began in New York City in 1996, where Hattie Hargrove and Edriss Anderson worked. As attrition thinned the ranks of unionized city workers by some 20,000, Republican mayor Rudolph Giuliani filled their positions with about twice that number of part-time workers from the city's Work Experience Program (WEP). Rather than receiving actual wages, these workers were "paid" from the welfare benefits they already received—the equivalent of $5,000–12,000 per year (depending on size of family and rent costs). A unionized city worker made from two to eight times that amount—about $20,000 per year plus benefits for clerical and service workers or $40,000 per year for trades people such as painters and carpenters. An average workfare worker cost the city only $1.80 per hour for a twenty-hour workweek, based on a $577 monthly welfare check, of which one-quarter was paid by city and the rest by state and federal funds (Greenhouse 1998b; Fuentes 1996).

The sheer size of the WEP workforce meant a union of these workers could potentially be among the city's largest. With the city's welfare caseload at over 400,000, the number of workfare workers threatened to eventually outstrip public employees in the city, who numbered about 200,000 (Firestone 1996). Workfare workers accounted for about three-fourths of New York City's Parks

Department workers and one-third of the Sanitation Department. Until they began organizing, they had no right to grievance procedures, and those who contested their assignments or conditions could be sanctioned by welfare authorities and lose their benefits. Protective gear and proper safety training in handling hazardous wastes were also problems until WEP workers started organizing, as were access to drinking water and time for rest breaks. Workfare workers were required to wear special orange vests—"like a chain gang," as one WEP worker put it.[5]

Two community-based multiracial organizations began organizing workfare workers in New York City—first WEP Workers Together (a coalition of three neighborhood nonprofits) in 1996 and then the Association of Community Organizations for Reform Now (ACORN) in 1997.[6] Using direct actions such as pickets, sit-ins, work slowdowns, and public demonstrations, WEP workers in both organizations demanded better conditions, the right to a grievance process, and benefits such as day care and health insurance. For instance, WEP Workers Together staged a takeover of the parks commissioner's office after he refused to meet with WEP workers over the denial of warm clothing, gloves, rest breaks, and sanitary facilities in the parks. Echoing the welfare office occupations of the 1960s organized by the National Welfare Rights Organization, twenty-five workers marched into his office, followed by television news cameras, and won most of their demands. In another 1997 action, workers held a "baby-in," crowding into the welfare office along with their children to demand day care (Finder 1997; Tait 2005). WEP workers blocked trucks leaving sanitation garages, refusing to move until welfare officials met with them to address grievances. ACORN organized dozens of demonstrations across the city and filed several collective grievances—including one on behalf of nearly one thousand workfare workers—to build worker-to-worker solidarity and win concrete protections. These actions resulted in numerous improvements in working conditions and a formal grievance procedure for workfare workers but no actual wages.

ACORN began collecting signed cards authorizing it as the collective bargaining agent for the city's WEP workers, and by June 1997 it had the support of over 13,000—more than one-third of all workfare workers in the city and more than required for an election under labor law (Tait 2005). But because WEP participants' did not have legal status as workers, labor law did not apply. When the city refused to recognize the workers' wishes, the New York

---

[5] The similarities between workfare and prison labor are more than rhetorical; in one case, a Georgia recycling plant fired thirty-five trash sorters on a workfare program in order to replace them with prison contract laborers who made even less (R. Cook 1999).

[6] Workfare organizing in New York City and San Francisco is covered in depth in Tait (2005); on Los Angeles organizing campaigns, see Reese (2002); for an overview of labor's current relationship to welfare policy, see Simmons (2002).

chapter of the community/labor coalition Jobs with Justice facilitated a symbolic election in October 1997, setting up polling booths at over two hundred sites, including WEP workplaces, check-cashing centers, and other locations in low-income neighborhoods. Prominent politicians, clergy, and labor leaders, such as former-Mayor David Dinkins and Jack Sheinkman, Amalgamated Clothing and Textile Workers Union president, served as election observers. WEP workers voted 16,989 to 207 for ACORN (Ream 1997). Although the vote was nonbinding given the workers' legal status, the process publicly expressed their desire for union representation and put political pressure on the city to recognize their union.

Although New York City's workfare program provides the most dramatic example of exploitation and displacement, other cities instituted similar programs. For instance, in Los Angeles up to 26,000 workfare participants labored in area schools and hospitals (Reese 2002), and in Wisconsin tens of thousands of welfare recipients worked "for benefits," as Republican Governor Tommy Thompson attempted to end welfare altogether. Both locations had active ACORN workfare unions.

In San Francisco, thousands of workfare workers labored as cleaners on public transit and in parks. People Organized to Win Employment Rights (POWER), a community-based antipoverty organization, started collecting authorization cards for union representation in early 1997 and within five weeks gained majority support among the city's three thousand workfare workers. Because California's workfare workers, like those in New York, lacked formal collective bargaining rights under state law, POWER organizers believed direct action was essential to supplement more traditional union-organizing methods such as signature collection. Workplace actions won workfare workers breaks and equal access to restrooms and eating facilities (Tait 2005).

Following in the traditions of both community organizing and unionism, POWER started with small fights that could build a sense of confidence in workers so that larger battles could be won. By obtaining California Occupational Safety and Health Administration (Cal-OSHA) investigations at several work sites, POWER forced the city to comply with safety requirements, such as providing proper protective gear. After a raucous demonstration in late 1997 at San Francisco's bus and street-car terminal, management agreed to consult POWER before making any changes in working conditions, essentially recognizing the organization as a collective bargaining agent for workfare workers.[7] POWER officially declared itself an independent union in July 1998.

---

[7] Steve Williams, interview by Vanessa Tait, San Francisco, August 14, 1998.

Welfare Rights as Labor Rights

The traditional labor movement—the American Federation of Labor–Congress of Industrial Organizations (AFL-CIO) and its affiliated unions—began to take greater notice. The vast numbers of workfare workers being thrown into the labor market by new federal regulations meant they simply had no choice. "Instead of laying down a floor, beneath which wages will not fall," writes Bill Fletcher, AFL-CIO education director, "welfare repeal opens up a giant sinkhole, pulling into it the rest of the working class" (Fletcher 1997, 125). The spread of workfare was vastly enlarging capital's traditional "reserve army of labor," which had always served to undercut union wages and working conditions. "These workers, most of them poor mothers," as Frances Fox Piven notes, "are being hurled like hostages into the front lines of the campaign against workers. The plan is simple, bold, and big, and could be devastating to the affected unions" (1997, 114).

In New York City, some trade unions—notably Communications Workers of America (CWA) Local 1180, representing some seven thousand white-collar city workers, and several United Auto Workers (UAW) locals—denounced workfare and later actively supported the community groups organizing WEP workers. But the public-employee unions, which were most affected by workfare, and the AFL-CIO, on a policy-setting level, were slow to act. The reasons were complex, including a tendency on the part of many trade unions to service existing union members in preference to organizing new ones and trepidation about the transience of the workfare workforce. After much pressure from community groups and progressive unionists, the AFL-CIO announced in 1997 that it would support "aggressive organizing campaigns" for workfare workers "by integrating them into bargaining units [and] organizing new units" (American Federation of Labor–Congress of Industrial Organizations [AFL-CIO] 1997). But although there was ideological agreement on the dangers welfare repeal posed to living wage jobs, the practical relationships between community-based workfare unions and individual trade unions were, more often than not, troubled.

For instance, in New York City, the leadership of the city's biggest public-sector union and the one whose members had been most affected by workfare—American Federation of State, County, and Municipal Employees (AFSCME) District Council 37, with 120,000 members—largely sat out the battle, despite pleas from community groups to help with the organizing. Stanley Hill, District Council 37 executive director and a close political ally of New York's mayor, supported the city's workfare program for many years—that is, until April 1998, when nearly one thousand AFSCME-represented hospital workers were laid off and replaced by WEP workers (Greenhouse 1998a). The union later put itself at odds with existing community-based labor groups by collecting authorization cards of its own in an ultimately unsuccessful attempt to organize workfare workers. But the extended period of acquiescence by Hill—the union leader most able to pressure the mayor—allowed the city political room to vastly expand the workfare program.

Similarly, in San Francisco, the relationship between POWER and several Service Employees International Union (SEIU) locals, representing the majority of city workers, was problematic. Three SEIU locals tried to negotiate an apprenticeship clause for workfare workers in their contracts and form a joint city-union task force on workfare in 1997, all without consulting POWER. "We said 'Look, there have to be representatives of workfare workers on that committee,'" recalled POWER organizer Steve Williams, "'because the decisions will affect us.' The union's initial response was, 'Well, you're not members of the union, and this is a union contract, so you have no place in it.'" After POWER threatened to speak out against the contracts at a San Francisco Board of Supervisors hearing, the union agreed to accept workfare worker participation on the committee.[8]

Two years later, SEIU had changed its position and was in favor of the creation of a separate job title for workfare workers, experience in which they could use to qualify for regular civil service jobs (C. Cook 1999). But the support was largely rhetorical because SEIU did not commit any resources to the organizing campaign. POWER (which survived largely on foundation grants and solidarity memberships in the community) was eager for a joint organizing plan because it believed such a plan was more likely to succeed and it hoped that some workfare workers would end up in AFL-CIO-represented jobs in the future. SEIU, however, was not urgently concerned about workfare, in part because San Francisco had not experienced the widespread displacement of union workers as had occurred in New York City. Servicing members—rather than organizing new ones—was the local union's top priority. Of POWER, one SEIU representative told me, "They do their work well, but that's not the work that a trade union can do. We organize people who are salaried as employees."

This perception of a fundamental difference between regular workers and workfare workers is often a stumbling block for joint organizing attempts. It is not a new one. "To white working-class people, and even to many black workers," Richard Cloward and Frances Fox Piven write, "it appears that the welfare recipient is enjoying a free ride on their hard-earned tax dollars, meanwhile scorning the value of work and the self-esteem of workers" (1968, 558). Trade unions have often kept their distance from welfare recipients,

[8] Ibid.

viewing them less as unemployed or unpaid workers and more as a problematic underclass that threatens their own members' pocketbooks (as taxpayers) or their jobs (if hired as strike breakers). But the reality is different. Welfare recipients are overwhelmingly single mothers, who have experience working the double shift at home with their children and in the unstable low-wage labor market. Most suffer not from a missing work ethic but from an economy that provides neither the jobs nor the support systems, such as child care, that they need in order to work.

Against such attitudes, workfare activists insist they are legitimate workers, creating their own counterdiscourse by recasting welfare struggles in terms of social equality and civil rights. They have launched campaigns to transform public consciousness and change policy, using state and federal labor laws when possible to protect their rights. Community activists such as those of the Philadelphia-based Kensington Welfare Rights Union cite the guarantees of freedom from poverty and forced labor contained in the Universal Declaration of Human Rights, the United Nations Child Rights Convention, and the U.S. Constitution's Thirteenth Amendment, which states, "Neither slavery nor involuntary servitude . . . shall exist within the United States" (Cheski 1994). In Maryland, a community-labor coalition convinced the governor to issue an executive order prohibiting the use of tax credits to hire welfare recipients to cut payroll costs (Jeter 1997). A broad coalition of civil rights, women's, community, religious, and labor groups successfully pressured President Bill Clinton to protect workfare workers under federal employment laws such as the Fair Labor Standards Act and OSHA (Vobejda 1997). The federal government filed suit against New York City, charging it with not doing enough to protect female workfare workers from sexual and racial harassment by supervisors (Greenhouse 2001).

Union activists also fought against ingrained attitudes among their colleagues, not only about job displacement but also about the population of workfare workers, who sometimes differed from trade union members racially, culturally, and in terms of class. Elly Leary, vice president of UAW Local 2324 in Boston, was asked by the Massachusetts AFL-CIO to be its representative on a state welfare advisory board. She agreed on the condition that it help fund an independent welfare-labor coalition in which welfare rights activists would be on equal footing with unions. The state AFL-CIO, SEIU, AFSCME, and UAW were active in the coalition, Working Massachusetts, along with many community-based organizations (Leary 1998). Unions joined the coalition, Leary writes, because "they were afraid that 'those people were going to take our jobs unless we did something.'" To break down the us-versus-them attitude, coalition members visited central labor councils to facilitate conversations between welfare recipients and unionists. One exercise asked unionists to think of three stereotypes about welfare recipients and then three about unionists. The exercise almost always revealed both groups as "lazy, corrupt, [and] a drag on the economy," except for one crucial difference: "Welfare recipients are perceived to be black women, while labor is perceived to be white men" (Leary 1998). Activists working for change in their locals hope that discussions such as these will change how unions see welfare recipients—as working-class comrades rather than as enemies—thus laying the groundwork for cooperative organizing.

Every Mother Is a Working Mother

Like workfare workers, welfare mothers argue that their work should be socially respected and financially compensated, and they question why they are forced on to workfare programs outside of the home when they are already doing valuable work inside the home. They draw on a long history of both activism and legislative history. Early welfare programs were commonly known as "mothers' pensions," providing support to what Gwendolyn Mink calls "mother-workers" even while discriminating among them on the basis of race, ethnicity, class, and marital status. Although these state-run programs claimed "wide discretion to condition welfare benefits on moral worthiness as well as to decide whom they would make benefits available to and on what terms," they also implicitly recognized caregiving as productive work that should be supported by taxpayers' dollars (Mink 1998, 45–46). This ideal was included in AFDC, a prime component of welfare law since its passage in 1935 as part of the New Deal's Social Security Act. AFDC allowed widowed mothers to stay home with their kids. It was later amended to include single parents as well (Hardisty and Williams 2002, 54).

The welfare rights movement organized around respect for work during the time of its greatest expansion in the 1960s. From 1960 to 1972, welfare recipients' numbers expanded from 745,000 families to 3 million (Piven and Cloward 1977, 273–75). Spurred by this burgeoning population of recipients, local welfare rights groups sprang up across the country demanding higher benefit levels, the right to earn additional income without penalty, day care for working parents, and medical benefits. Activists from seventy-five welfare rights groups across the country founded the National Welfare Rights Organization (NWRO) in 1966. For the next several years, NWRO activists jammed into welfare offices and confronted authorities with demonstrations, picketing, and sit-ins, demanding a just welfare system and a guaranteed minimum national income.

NWRO's strategists thought benefits campaigns would bring greater numbers of recipients into a national network, leading to the passage of a guaranteed national income in Congress. Such a measure, if passed, would have amounted to a pay raise for NWRO's members, the majority of whom were single mothers working in the home. Although framed by the language of welfare rights, NWRO members made arguments that could have come straight out of the labor movement. Johnnie Tillmon, a mother of six from Watts, California, and the first chair of NWRO, spoke of the productive, socially important work welfare mothers performed. "If I were President," she said, "I would solve this so-called welfare crisis in a minute and go a long way toward liberating every woman. I'd just issue a proclamation that women's work is *real* work. . . . I'd start paying women a living wage for doing the work we are already doing—child raising and housekeeping. And the welfare crisis would be over. Just like that"(Tillmon 1971, 23).

In voicing these demands, Tillmon and other welfare mothers reframed the debate about welfare around the value of their unwaged work. NWRO was, in effect, their union, although their workplaces were scattered and they had no visible employer. By advocating for "motherwork," as Eileen Boris (1998, 35–36) has called it, NWRO activists "defied the devaluation of caregiving." In its organizing around this work, NWRO placed itself squarely within the tradition of feminist organizing, and as Premilla Nadasen argues, defined "welfare as a women's issue and the welfare rights movement as a part of the larger women's movement" (2005, 219).

Welfare rights activists today are building on this tradition by organizing for state legislation to support their parenting work. In Montana, Working for Equality and Economic Liberation (WEEL) convinced state and local legislators to establish a program that paid parents to stay home to care for their infants. The At-Home Infant Care Program allowed parents with incomes up to 150 percent of the poverty line to receive $384 per month for up to two years, an amount calculated to match 100 percent of what a child-care worker would make in the marketplace. The program was modeled on a 1997 Minnesota law allowing parents to receive a subsidy to care for their infants. Montana's program, however, was the first to come into being from grassroots pressure by welfare moms themselves.[9] "The phenomenal part of this policy is that it was created by low-income women to meet their own needs," said Mary Caferro, a WEEL activist who was subsequently elected to Montana's House of Representatives.[10]

Whereas the situation for any welfare recipient forced onto workfare is exploitative, for those with children it is doubly so. Parents on workfare are handed a list of child-care centers—most of them full or unaffordable—and

---

[9] Donci Bardash, Working for Equality and Economic Liberation, interview by Vanessa Tait, phone interview, March 19, 2005.

[10] Betty Holcomb, "Montana Women Score Victory on Valuing Caregiving," *Women's E-News*, September 1, 2002, http://www.womensenews.org/article.cfm/dyn/aid/1024/context/cover (accessed August 28, 2006).

told to report for assignments; if they do not show up, they can be sanctioned, or dropped from the welfare rolls. The financial burden laid on these women is staggering—nationally, of the 22 percent of working poor families headed by single mothers who paid for child care, 40 percent spent at least half of their cash income on child care and another 25 percent spent 40–50 percent (Wertheimer 2001, 3). In urban areas, the average annual cost of child care for a four-year-old is greater than the cost of public college tuition in all but one state, and in some places, child-care costs are double the cost of public college tuition (Schulman 2000, 1). Nonfinancial barriers are high as well; compared with mothers who had never received welfare, those who had been on AFDC are significantly more likely to be caring for at least one child with a chronic health condition (37 vs. 21 percent), and they are also far more likely to lack benefits that many middle-class parents take for granted, such as sick leave, vacation, and flexible work scheduling (Heymann and Earle 1999).

WEEL's members and advisory board—the majority of them women on public assistance with children—were personally familiar with these barriers. Political allies warned that paying welfare recipients to stay home with their kids could be controversial and encouraged WEEL to campaign for a living wage law instead. But WEEL's leadership was "adamant," said organizer Wendy Young, on winning public policy reforms that "value[d] the work of raising children."[11] After convincing state welfare officials to offer up $250,000 for a small pilot program to fund sixty families, WEEL spread the word about the program through radio ads and leafleting at child-care agencies. The program soon had a long waiting list, as well as bipartisan support for its continuation.

Under the program, participants are recognized as working through their caregiving in the home. Welfare rights activists point out that the job duties of parenting—child care, transportation, food preparation, education, and counseling—mirror those that are defined as paid work in the marketplace. Under the forced work provisions of the new welfare law, in fact, recipients are assigned the very same duties caring for other peoples' children. Child-care subsidies paid from welfare funding not only challenge deeply ingrained preconceptions about unpaid labor, women's work, and welfare; they make it clear that work in the home is as economically and socially valuable as work outside of it. Through their activism, poor women are organizing for a social wage for their motherwork, just as union activists are demanding that their members be provided with paid family leaves and subsidized child-care programs.

The At-Home Infant Care Program, begun in 2001, remains law in Montana, although in the wake of budget cuts no funding stream has been found to

[11] Ibid.

continue it. A similar program was instituted in Minnesota in 1997 and then reestablished again in 2004; New Mexico has a small pilot program in one county (National Partnership for Women and Families 2005). Activists in Arizona are organizing to establish a similar program.[12] In 2004–2005, federal legislation was introduced to fund at least five at-home infant-care demonstration programs (National Partnership for Women and Families 2005).

Similar pay-for-leave policies for employed people, funded from the taxes withheld from their paychecks, are high on the labor movement's agenda. The passage of the federal Family and Medical Leave Act in 1993 allowed millions of workers to take time off without pay for up to twelve weeks to provide care to children and other family members or to take care of their own medical issues. In 2002, after much lobbying by California's AFL-CIO labor federation, that state became the first in the nation to enact comprehensive paid family leave, and in the wake of the California victory, similar family-friendly paid leave laws, many backed by state and regional labor groups, are under consideration in a number of other states, including Florida, Massachusetts, New Jersey, New York, and Texas (Firestein and Dones, chap. 7 in this volume).

A New Social Vision for Labor

Over the last decade, welfare rights activists have successfully shaped a discourse about labor rights and gender equity that opposes the dominant conservative view. Much of the right's discourse about poverty is centered on the supposed irresponsibility of poor women of color and accompanied by a punitive and contradictory program of claimed family values along with forced no-wage or low-wage labor. Real family values support living wage jobs, parents' work in the home, and progressive policies such as family leave and child-care subsidies. Workfare activists are among the agents of change, working to transform the public policy discussion surrounding welfare away from racist and sexist notions about poor workers and to redefine welfare in terms of economic and social justice, as well as the continued fight for state support of caregiving work in the home.

This changing definition of work and workers has profound implications for the labor movement by infusing it with a deeper consciousness about the relationships of gender, class, and poverty. At the same time, the workfare and welfare organizing of poor women has the potential to transform the women's movement though a greater understanding of how class, race, and ethnicity shape and differentiate female lives. The issue of social wages for caregiving is

---

[12] National Child Care Information Center, "At-Home Infant Care Initiatives Sponsored by States," 2005, http://www.nccic.org/poptopics/stateathome.html (accessed May 15, 2006).

a crucial point of commonality for both labor and women's movements, and it opens up possibilities for collaboration and alliance building between poor and middle-class women. Welfare activists advocating compensation for at-home child care are engaged in essentially the same fight as union activists organizing for paid family leave. Both are demanding that caregiving be formally included in the social contract and that caregivers be compensated for the indispensable work they do.

The ideals embodied in workfare and welfare organizing—the right to a decent job at livable wages, support for children and families, and gender and racial equity—are crucial to the labor movement's revival and growth. They create possibilities for a compelling vision of social justice at a time when the labor movement most desperately needs to reframe its beliefs and goals, and they capture the high ground in the national debate about economic and social justice. For trade unions, organizing that takes into account workers' issues outside of purely employment-based concerns offers a way to join with other movements for social justice. For community-based groups working for welfare rights, women's rights, and racial/ethnic justice, putting their energies into labor organizing builds bridges with those unions whose work has centered on traditional employment-based organizing.

But ideals alone do not make a movement or produce the successful public policies that can result from grassroots activism. Actual organizing campaigns which take into account workers' needs for welfare support, paid family leave, labor protections, and living wage jobs have introduced new and fruitful directions for the labor movement as a whole. In San Francisco, POWER activists forced the city to create 850 living wage jobs for the city's workfare participants. They also won legal recognition of workfare workers from the state's Occupational Safety and Health Administration and got workfare workers included in the city's living wage ordinance. Direct action resulted in a formal grievance procedure, free public transportation for all workfare workers, and a 40 percent reduction in work hours with no reduction in welfare benefits. In Los Angeles and New York, workfare workers represented by ACORN have access to a grievance process when they are faced with unsafe working conditions, racial discrimination, or gender harassment (Nguyen 2001). New York unions and community groups worked together to win legislation that allowed for training and education, including college attendance, to satisfy welfare-reform work requirements instead of workfare. Perhaps most important, workfare unions act as de facto collective bargaining agents for their members, defending their rights primarily with direct action and worker solidarity. Although workfare workers are still not entitled to representational rights under labor law, workfare unions use legal remedies when possible under existing occupational safety and antidiscrimination laws.

Erasing the conceptual line between the poor and other workers has far-reaching implications for both workers' consciousness and movement practices. Such organizing often leads to deep personal change for those involved in it, bringing new understandings of class oppression and workers' rights to poor people who had previously seen themselves as outside the working class. Organizing for labor rights has changed the way welfare recipients see themselves and how their co-workers employed at "regular" jobs see them as well—as workers, joining together for equal pay for equal work and a safe working environment rather than as people begging for a handout. "We're workers just like anyone else," asserts Brenda Stewart, New York City workfare worker. "We want real job creation and all the benefits afforded to any other worker" (B. Stewart 1997).

By challenging established conceptions of what constitutes a worker, welfare and workfare organizing makes a unique contribution to the labor movement's sense of itself, demonstrating in a very real way how it might further expand to encompass all working people—including workers on unemployment and welfare and workers whose labor is transient, unwaged, or in the informal economy. Such concerns have a long lineage, from the Knights of Labor's commitment to organize all workers, no matter what their place in society, to some pre–New Deal AFL unions that, notes Dorothy Sue Cobble (2001, 85), opened hiring halls and employment bureaus, as well as facilitating portable benefits and union membership, in often successful efforts to organize contingent workers.

Today's trade unions have undergone a continuing shift in attitudes and actions toward workfare and welfare along these more open-minded lines. An AFSCME local in Kansas City pushed for a program to move four hundred welfare recipients into city jobs and give right of first refusal for entry-level jobs to workfare workers. Another AFSCME local in Indianapolis co-sponsored twenty-five workfare workers in full-time jobs in public agencies and offered them transportation and child-care support (Applied Research Center 1999). In some cases, trade unions and community organizations created joint structures for organizing. For instance, in New Jersey, CWA and ACORN launched an innovative joint campaign called People Organizing Workfare Workers in 1998 that attempted to organize the state's 10,000 workfare workers by collecting union authorization cards (Center for Community Change 1998). Workfare organizing has also strengthened relationships between some community-based workfare unions and AFL-CIO unions. For instance, in New York, workfare organizing led to strong relationships between ACORN and some progressive unions such as CWA Local 1180, which worked with ACORN to gain permanent ballot status for the state's Working Families Party. In San Francisco, POWER developed a close collaborative relationship with Hotel Employees and Restaurant Employees Union (HERE) Local 2 when some of HERE's members were laid off, ended up on welfare and workfare, and became active in POWER.

Community-based organizations and trade unions have significantly different institutional structures, constituencies, and organizing cultures. But they also have strong affinities for one-on-one organizing and principles of solidarity. Trade unions often excel on the political and legislative fronts and can bring a measure of institutional and financial stability to organizing campaigns. Community organizations have extensive experience in bottom-up organizing among disenfranchised and poor people, but have a difficult time maintaining stable funding or long-term organizing campaigns. Joint organizing projects hold the potential to transform the labor movement, building solidarity between waged and welfare workers while emphasizing mobilization and direct action. If successful, such organizing may also help unions transform their own internal cultures so that activist, bottom-up organizing becomes a greater priority.

Organizing against workfare and for welfare rights offers the labor movement an opportunity to look beyond the limits of its own institutions and join forces with community-based labor activists. Organizing alongside the grassroots organizations that have historically represented poor workers, with a broader notion of who workers are, will strengthen the labor movement in its fight against employer exploitation. Such collaborations help renew the labor movement's spirit and rebuild its strength by reconnecting employment-based unions with community-based movements for economic, racial, and gender justice. Expanding the traditional union goals of wages, benefits, and workplace protections into a broadly conceived movement for economic and social justice is essential to labor's survival and growth.

11

WORKER CENTERS AND IMMIGRANT WOMEN

Janice Fine

Poor women in the U.S. workforce have always faced multiple obstacles to collective action. They have been employed in industries that were historically excluded from labor and employment laws or in which these laws are difficult to enforce. Many work in caregiving occupations, which blur the lines between public and private. They are often assumed to be only temporarily in the paid labor force. They are more likely to earn low pay and face the double day of work and family responsibilities. Recent waves of immigrant women face these same challenges while also having to contend with transnational responsibilities, precarious immigration status in the United States, language barriers, and discrimination on the basis of ethnicity (see Boris and Klein, chap. 9; Tait, chap. 10; Ontiveros, chap. 12 in this volume).

As the skyrocketing service sector has given rise to increasing numbers of low wage jobs, the need to develop effective models for worker voice and power has become ever more urgent. In the past, for many U.S. workers, what an individual did at work was a sufficient constitutive category for organization. But now, for those who lack a strong occupational or industrial identity and move from job to job, it falls short of the mark. Often low-wage workers, especially immigrants, are more strongly influenced by the networks that operate inside that ethnic community than by previous job experiences or skill sets, moving not just from job to job but between industries. In the new community unionism, the ethnic, racial, gender, geographical, and even religious ties of low-wage workers stand in for or are an essential complement to craft and industrial identities (Fine 2005, 160)

One of the places in which domestic workers, child-care providers, waitresses, hotel housekeepers, garment workers, and home health aids are being brought together are worker centers. These grassroots groups join service provision, consciousness-raising, popular education, advocacy, and cultural expression to direct action campaigns for improvements in wages and working conditions. Although some of the first centers grew out of the civil rights movement and were founded by African Americans, the vast majority are now based in immigrant communities.

In this chapter, drawing on several years of research on worker centers throughout the United States, which includes data from forty surveys and nine in-depth case studies (Fine 2003, 2006), I offer first some general background on the rise of worker centers in the United States, their origins, goals, and strategies for action. Then I focus on women-centered projects and centers, examining first the national picture and then concentrating on two case studies of organizing domestic workers in New York. The chapter closes with an analysis of the relationship between worker centers and the established union movement.

Worker Centers: An Overview

Worker centers are community-based mediating institutions that provide support to communities of low-wage workers. Because work is the primary focus of life for many newly arriving immigrants, it is also the locus of many of the problems they experience. This is why, although they actually pursue a broad agenda that includes many aspects of immigrant life in the United States, most of the organizations call themselves worker centers. In many of these organizations, gender, along with race and ethnicity, is a central lens through which experiences in the global labor market are analyzed. Often women's work is targeted for organizing and women play leadership roles.

Worker centers have emerged in part in response to the decline of institutions that historically provided workers with a vehicle for collection action. Many of these institutions—civic groups, fraternal and mutual aid societies, local political party organizations, and especially unions—that once offered the opportunity for voice and action have either disappeared or declined dramatically. More and more, low-wage workers function within industries in which there are few or no unions or other organizational vehicles through which they can speak and act. Into this breach, new types of institutions such as worker centers have struggled to emerge over the past few decades. Most are relatively small in size and, measured in conventional terms, possess limited economic and political power. But, in the approaches and strategies they are pioneering and in the movements for justice they have been able to build at the local level, they have crucial lessons to impart.

Worker centers vary in terms of their organizational models, how they think about their mission, and how they carry out their work. Nevertheless, most have core features in common. Often workers come into a center because they live or work in the center's geographic area of focus, not because they work in a specific industry or occupation. Although they often target particular employers as well as industries within local labor markets, worker centers are not worksite-based. That is to say, unlike the traditional U.S. union, most do not focus on organizing for majority representation in individual worksites or on negotiating contracts for individual groups of workers.

All of them are hybrids that combine elements of different types of organizations, from fraternal organizations, settlement houses, immigrant civic organizations, and community-organizing and social-movement groups to unions, feminist consciousness-raising organizations, and producer coops. The majority of centers provide services, first and foremost legal assistance regarding employment-related issues, as well as English as a second language (ESL) classes, but they also play an important matchmaking role in introducing their members to services available through other agencies such as health clinics. Many function as clearinghouses on employment law, writing and distributing "know your rights" handbooks and conducting ongoing workshops. They conduct research and release exposés about conditions in low-wage industries, work with government agencies to improve monitoring and grievance processes, and bring suits against employers.

Because they are committed to going beyond advocacy to providing a means through which workers can take action on their own behalf for economic and political change, most centers place enormous emphasis on leadership development and democratic decision making, putting processes in place to involve workers on an ongoing basis and working to develop the skills of worker leaders so that they are able to participate meaningfully in guiding the organization. Many identify strongly with the philosophy and teaching methods of Paulo Freire and other popular educators and draw on literacy circles and other models that originated in the Central and South American liberation movements.

Although they may relate to a much larger number of workers, most centers have fewer than a thousand members and they view membership as a privilege that is not automatic but must be earned. They require workers to take courses and/or become involved in the organization in order to qualify.

At the same time, there is a lot of ambivalence about charging dues, and although about 40 percent of centers say they have a dues requirement, few have worked out systems to collect them regularly.

Centers have a social movement orientation and organize around both economic issues and immigrant rights. They pursue these goals by seeking to impact the labor market through direct economic action, on the one hand, and public policy reform activity, on the other. They have become enmeshed in the struggle for federal immigration reform and related issues such as access to drivers' licenses as well as housing, education, health care, and criminal justice issues. Many favor alliances with religious institutions and government agencies and seek to work closely with other worker centers, nonprofit agencies, community organizations, and activist groups by participating in many formal and informal coalitions.

Centers demonstrate a deep sense of solidarity with workers in other countries and an ongoing programmatic focus on the global impact of structural adjustment, trade, and labor policies. Some worker-center founders and leaders had extensive experience with organizing in their countries of origin and actively draw on those traditions in their current work. Some centers maintain ongoing ties with popular organizations in the countries from which workers have migrated, share strategies, publicize one another's work, and support one another as they are able.

The first worker centers were founded by black worker activists in North and South Carolina, by immigrant activists in New York City's Chinatown, along the Texas-Mexican border in El Paso, and in San Francisco. They arose during the late 1970s and early 1980s in response to changes in manufacturing that resulted in worsening conditions, factory closings, and the rise of lower-paying service-sector jobs. Disparities in the pay and treatment of African American and white workers and exploitation within ethnic economic enclaves and in the broader economy (including the informal sector) were also major catalysts for the creation of the first wave of centers.

The first worker center to focus on immigrant women in the borderlands, La Mujer Obrera (LMO), was started by feminist Central America solidarity and labor activists in El Paso in 1981 on the heels of a textile workers' strike by Mexican women workers at the Farah Clothing Factory. Over the next few years, thousands of women lost their jobs as major textile manufacturers shuttered their operations, giving way to small subcontractors and substandard working conditions. During the first five years after the passage of the North American Free Trade Agreement (NAFTA), 15,000 jobs left El Paso and LMO worked to join Mexican women workers to the global economic justice movement. Understanding their collective situation in the twin contexts of globalization and gender and linking this to members' individual narratives has always been the approach taken by LMO as well as by many other worker centers that organize among women.[1]

The second wave of centers emerged in the late 1980s and early to mid-1990s. They appeared as large new groups of Latino immigrants, some in flight from the Central American wars in El Salvador and Guatemala, came to live and work in urban metropolitan areas as well as the suburbs and growing numbers of Southeast Asians emigrated to the United States seeking work. Drawing on the first-wave centers for their organizational models, these centers were founded by a diverse set of institutions and individuals, including churches and other faith-based organizations, social service and legal aid agencies, immigrant nongovernmental organizations (NGOs), and unions.

From 2000 to the present, a new wave of centers emerged. Reacting to push factors of uneven economic development, hemispheric free-trade agreements, and the pull of plentiful U.S. jobs, many of the workers involved are from new chain-migration streams from communities in Mexico. Most of these continued to arise in U.S. cities. More centers are also being organized in suburban and rural areas and in southern states in response to the large concentrations of immigrants working in the service, poultry, meatpacking, and agricultural sectors. Yet more centers are emerging among recent Filipino, African, and South Asian immigrants, and more of these than in past waves are directly connected to faith-based organizations and unions. In 1992, there were but five worker centers in the entire country; by 2006, there were 140.

Women in Worker Centers

The ethnic makeup of centers varies from region to region and industry to industry (Fine 2006, 19). The majority of workers being organized through worker centers are from Mexico and Central and South America. Mexicans make up the largest number of immigrants in the United States, about 28 percent of all foreign-born people, legal or undocumented, and they are also the single largest presence in worker centers in the aggregate (Waldinger 2001, 37). However, worker centers are not an exclusively Latino phenomenon. The Caribbean and East Asian regions each account for 15 percent of worker-center participants, with West Africa and other African nations making up another 8 percent.

Of the forty centers I surveyed in 2003, 19 percent focused exclusively or

[1] La Mujer Obrera, "History of La Mujer Obrera and El Puente CDC: Building the Bridges for Mexican Immigrant Women," 2004, http://www.mujerobrera.org/index.php (accessed September 8, 2006).

primarily on women, compared with 24 percent, largely the day-laborer centers, that had a predominantly male membership base. Fifty-seven percent were of mixed gender. Some centers, such as Asian Immigrant Women's Advocates (AIWA) in San Francisco, the Garment Workers Center in Los Angeles, and the Domestic Workers Union (DWU), focus entirely on women in female-dominated industries such as sewing and housekeeping, and they have an explicit language about gender and gender oppression in their work. A number of general worker centers have projects that focus on female-dominated industries, especially child care, domestic work, and hotel housekeeping. Several centers, including Carolina Alliance for Fair Employment (C.A.F.E.) in South Carolina and the Tenants' and Workers' Support Committee (TWSC), had specific leadership development goals and programs that were explicitly geared toward women of color.

Many centers have had to contend with the reluctance of women to see their work as real work. As Hondagneu-Sotelo writes, "Paid domestic work is distinctive not in being the worst job of all but in being regarded as something other than employment. . . . many women who do this work remain reluctant to embrace it *as* work because of the stigma associated with it. This is especially true of women who previously held higher social status." Hondagneu-Sotelo writes about one Mexican woman who used to be a secretary in a Mexican embassy and who characterized her full-time job as a housekeeper and nanny as her hobby (Hondagneu-Sotelo 2001, 9). But for many women, the move to the United States can be freeing. Whereas men coming from Latin America to the United States are likely to take a loss in terms of social status and position in the labor market, most women do not experience that downward mobility—their histories and initial expectations are very different from many of the men. As a result of working and acquiring economic resources not available to them back home, their expectations of their own roles within the family shift. Their ability to work outside their own homes provides income and exposure to larger society, which helps them to achieve greater independence and status within the family (Jones-Correa 1998, 336–38).

Many of the women's committees and projects have strong consciousness-raising, political education, and confidence-building components because the centers believe that these issues have to be dealt with in order for the larger project of organizing women to improve their labor market positions to succeed. A closer look at organizing efforts mounted by two worker centers in New York to raise standards for domestic workers offers an opportunity to explore their approaches and strategies in greater depth.

Fuerza Laboral Feminina

The Workplace Project is a Long Island, New York-based worker center that was established in 1992 to try to meet the needs of the hundreds of thousands of Central and South American migrants who arrived during the 1980s. The group created a women's committee, Fuerza Laboral Feminina (FLF), after organizers observed that the women tended to keep quiet and defer to men in group meetings. FLF was created as a space where women could meet, discuss their lives and particular workplace issues they faced, build community, and plot strategy. Its first campaign targeted employment agencies that were charging usurious fees to women working as housekeepers (Fine 2003, 128–34)

Long Island's *domesticas* are in some important ways the female counterparts to day laborers. They all work under the table in the informal sector, where wages are paid in cash and no records are kept. Many are new arrivals who speak little English and have no acquaintance with U.S. labor laws. These women show up at the Workplace Project with terrible stories of unpaid wages, sudden dismissal, fourteen-hour days, and verbal and physical abuse by employers. Isolated in a workplace of one, with odd days off, during which they have to take care of basic personal business, the *domesticas* clearly needed support, but the Project members were not sure how to provide it.

Although the Fair Labor Standards Act (FLSA), which guarantees minimum wages and overtime, did not originally include domestic workers, Congress extended coverage to them in 1974. Despite being covered by the FLSA and the fact that, technically, employers are supposed to be paying taxes and contributing to social security, in reality the vast majority of domestic workers are part of the informal economy. This informality not only applies to modes of payment but also to the employment relationship in general. Most employers of domestic workers do not think of themselves as employers. Domestics are often fired without notice or severance pay. Women are sometimes fired because they are pregnant, and placement agencies routinely screen on the basis of ethnicity and race. But neither federal statutes such as Title VII of the Civil Rights Act nor state level antidiscrimination laws apply to workplaces with a single employee.

In looking over the cases of *domesticas* that had been brought to the attention of the Workplace Project, the women of FLF identified a common set of problems. In addition to the cases of verbal and physical abuse and unpaid wages, there were certain structural problems in the way the industry operated. Women who sought employment through agencies were charged a high fee and sometimes, when their initial placement did not pan out for one reason or another, they were forced to pay the fee again. Contracts specifying the terms and conditions of work between the women and their employers were rare or nonexistent. As a result, they had no set schedule of work, including the number of hours and days per week or a regular day off. Often they were not paid the minimum wage and did not know they were entitled to it. Despite their long hours and inability to leave the house, they were not provided with three meals a day by their employers or compensated for the cost of purchasing their own food.

Over a few months of trying to build a base among *domesticas*, FLF learned how hard they were to find and, when they did, how complicated their feelings were about their employers. Because *domesticas* were dealing with employers who were individual families, the employment relationship itself was completely privatized. Relationships were very personal. Some of the Workplace Project staff described it as "marriage-like"; the women viewed the families they worked for as their source of support. For live-ins, losing their jobs also meant losing their homes. Expressing grievances or negotiating terms such as wages or days off had to be done one-on-one with people who often viewed themselves as doing the women a favor in employing them or viewed the women as a part of their family (see Rollins 1985).

The group came to the conclusion that domestic workers were not able to be the enforcers in their existing work relationships. They decided that the recruitment message could not be a hard, confrontational one. Rather, a community-building approach was necessary. The idea was to find the domestic workers and build relationships among them to the point at which they would begin to see themselves as a group of workers with common problems that could be addressed through collective action. The recruitment rap to the women needed to be less about trashing the boss and more about respect, dignity, their feelings of isolation (including missing their own children), the idea that housework is hard work, and a basic presentation of their rights. The group decided to consciously stop using the term *trabajadoras domesticas* (domestic workers) because the women had a very strong negative reaction to it. It evoked for them a sense of being members of the lowest of the low, going back to how maids were perceived in their countries of origin. Instead, they decided to use only the term *mujeres que trabajan en casa* (women who work in the home).

The women had a very low consciousness of themselves as workers. When approached by an organizer, who asked something like, "*Trabajas?*" (Do you work?), the *domesticas* were likely to answer, "*No, trabajo en casa*" (No, I work in a house). They tended to think of their work-related problems as their own personal afflictions and not as issues they could work collectively to resolve. Typically, the *domesticas* who came to the Workplace Project showed up after things had become so unbearable that they had quit or had been fired and had heard the Project might be able to help them collect their unpaid wages.

The group designed an outreach strategy based on where these women were likely to go on their days off: Laundromats, supermarkets, and church. They created a survey the organizers could use to ask women questions and get them into a conversation. They also created a new four-week class specifically for this constituency, entitled Ingles Laboral Basico para Mujeres que Trabajan en Casa. Basic working English skills to be taught emphasized the words that these women really needed to know in their work, and the structure of the class was designed to maximize social time as a way to counteract their isolation. The idea was, through skits and discussions, to gradually introduce the women to the concept of collective action.

As the outreach proceeded, one issue that always resonated with the women was going after the placement agencies. They were often paying fees to the agencies that were far higher than the law stipulated. New York state labor law specifies that an agency placing women for domestic work can charge a worker no more than 10 percent of her first month's wages and must allow that fee to be paid over ten weeks. Instead, the agencies were charging double or triple what the law allowed and demanding that it be paid up front. In addition, they were knowingly placing women in jobs that paid much less than the minimum wage, sometimes as little as $2 per hour.

In July 1997, the organization kicked off a campaign to get Long Island agencies that referred immigrant women to domestic jobs to sign a basic Workplace Project Domestic Workers' Bill of Rights. In the statement, they agreed to charge fees in accordance with the law and to refer women only to jobs that complied with basic wage laws, including the minimum wage. The idea was that the Workplace Project would create a Good Agency List that would be distributed through the media, area churches, and synagogues to Long Island families, who would be encouraged to choose only agencies that were on the list. Agencies that refused to sign would be subjected to negative publicity, demonstrations, and letter-writing campaigns from homeowners letting them know that they would not use those agencies until they complied. Forty-two organizations were recruited to the cause and sent letters to each of the agencies urging them to sign and letting them know they would circulate the list.

The Workplace Project and FLF worked with the housekeepers they had been able to recruit, as well as other women's committee members and community allies, to conduct meetings with the employment agencies. Backed by rabbis, priests, and Workplace Project staff, the women told their stories. These included scouring an oven without protective gloves until their fingers bled, being attacked by employers attempting to rape them, and cleaning six houses in a single day without breaks for rest or food. They also included stories of being charged exorbitant fees by agencies and then being placed in homes with absolutely no idea what their rights were in terms of wages, hours, duties, or conditions of work.

By the end of the year, five out of the six agencies that specialized in domestic workers had signed the statement of principles and agreed to establish contracts between employers and employees to be used in job placement. What had they agreed to? Essentially, to comply with existing state labor law.

Although the domestic worker campaign on the agencies resulted in all of those targeted signing on, the victory turned out to be largely symbolic. FLF discovered that it had little or no impact in practice because there was no way to enforce the agreement or to effectively monitor the agencies' compliance. Frustrated with its inability to hold the employment agencies to their pledges, the Workplace Project and the women of the FLF launched a housecleaning cooperative called UNITY.

UNITY initially comprised twelve immigrant women who spent a year working with staff to develop the structure and marketing plan. Based on market research, outreach to potential clients through local churches, organizational allies within close proximity to the town of Hempstead, and early media coverage, ten families became UNITY's initial clients during January, February, and March 1999, providing employment for all twelve members of the cooperative. With this initial client base, UNITY placed ads in a local newspaper and received a strong response. Now it gets most of its customers through word of mouth.

UNITY sees its core mission not only as providing greater economic independence to housecleaners but also as engaging in consciousness-raising and leadership development. "The cooperative was founded . . . not just so women could have work, but also to give the women self-worth," said Lillian Araujo, co-op director, former vice president of the board of the Workplace Project, and former secretary of a coffee cooperative in her native El Salvador. "In each home, a woman suffers different kinds of problems. The first thing we did was attract members and look for work. Through that process we began to learn the problems that the women faced. We have various trainings about domestic violence, health in general, so that the women would be ready to deal with their problems," said Araujo (Fine 2006, 34).

There is a very strong emphasis on leadership development throughout the cooperative's activities: there are frequent in-house trainings, and members are also sent to specific leadership development workshops. Through biweekly meetings and other cooperative activities, there are multiple opportunities to develop skills, from how to set an agenda and run a meeting to public speaking.

The coop developed a system for distributing jobs to members that is based on the level of each member's participation in its activities. Members earn $20 per hour and contribute 10 percent of their wages earned to help cover operating expenses. In spring 2004, the cooperative had grown to eighty-one members. According to Araujo, some members are able to work full-time through the cooperative and others are able to get two or three days of work a week through it.

Several other worker centers are experimenting with cooperatives. Instituto de Educacion Popular del Sur de California (IDEPSCA) has a women's housecleaning and craft cooperative based out of its Pasadena, California, hiring hall. In January 2006, the Restaurant Opportunities Center opened a cooperatively owned restaurant in Manhattan and hopes to open more. Mujeres Unidas y Activas in San Francisco focuses on fighting domestic violence and fighting for immigrant rights; it operates the Caring Hands Workers Association, an economic development project that helps members get training and placement to work in home health care and therapeutic massage and then sets uniform rates and standards (Fine 2006, 33–37).

Let us now turn to consideration of a second case of domestic worker organizing.

Domestic Workers United

DWU, a New York City–wide coalition of domestic worker organizations, defines domestic workers as people who works directly for a private employer in a home; " as Ai Jen Poo, the lead organizer at DWU, put it:

> It's actually the people who are employed by the homeowner themselves—nannies, elder-caregiving, housekeeping, cooks. So it's a really broad industry and you have people who are working for middle-class and upper-middle-class families in Manhattan and the suburbs. Then you have people who are brought here by transnational business people working under work visas. You have people who are brought here by diplomats. You have people who work for other people of their same ethnicity in a higher class. It's a really diverse industry with lots of segments.[2]

A major part of the attraction for many women who join the organization is having a community of interest to feel a part of. "When I came to this country and started working as a baby sitter, I was exploited," said Jocelyn Campbell. "When I heard about DWU and I joined the organization, it lifted my spirits so much."[3] DWU has been steadily building a leadership core of nannies; according to Poo, as of June of 2005, it had a membership of eight hundred. It had an active base of about 250 and a loyal core of sixty to seventy. In addition, the organization is governed by eleven domestic workers.

In June 2003, DWU and its allied groups succeeded in getting the New York

---

[2] Ai Jen Poo, interviews with Janice Fine, 2004–2005, New York City.
[3] Jocelyn Campbell, interview by Janice Fine, June 2005, New York City.

City Council to adopt the Domestic Workers Bill of Rights, the first citywide legislation in the country that protects the rights of domestic workers. The organizing began in 2001, when Southeast Asian, Malay, and Filipino domestic workers, brought together by the Women Workers Project (WWP) of the Committee Against Anti-Asian Violence (CAAAV; a member organization of the DWU), worked together to develop a standard contract that was modeled on one in use in Hong Kong. They joined forces with Andolan, an organization largely of South Asian domestic workers from India, Bangladesh, Sri Lanka, and Pakistan.

According to Barbara Young, a long-time nanny and organizer with DWU, "There were a number of Filipino domestic workers who had been in Hong Kong and then came here as secondary migration. In Hong Kong, all domestic workers, no matter the ethnicity, no matter when they arrive, they all have a standard contract that women work under. So a lot of the women who were part of the WWP were really emphasizing the need for us to try to unite the industry as a whole and establish some kinds of standards."[4]

One of those Filipino women, Carolyn de Leo, arrived in New York in 1991 after working in Hong Kong under a standard contract. Working as a live-in for a wealthy Westchester couple, de Leo was promised health insurance and winter clothing but received neither. She worked twelve hours per day and was paid slightly more than $2 per hour. De Leon found her way to CAAAV, became a leader in the campaign, and is now one of the full-time organizers of the effort.

The groups developed a draft of a standard contract and a survey of domestic workers about their working conditions. When they hit the parks and playgrounds to talk to domestic workers, Caribbean and West Indian domestic workers, who had for generations been involved in domestic work in New York City, became involved as well. The groups started holding meetings all over Brooklyn. As organizer, Ai Jen Poo recalled, "The word of mouth was unbelievable, news of the contract spread like wildfire. At the first meeting there were twenty women and at the next one there were ninety. . . . They kept saying 'we need a union, we need a union' " (Fine 2006, 321).

Unlike FLF, which found it difficult to find domestic workers in suburban areas, DWU has more luck in parks and playgrounds in Brooklyn and especially Manhattan's Central Park, where a large number of nannies congregate with their charges. Women that the organizers meet during the course of their outreach are invited to monthly membership meetings held at a community center in Brooklyn. At the meetings, DWU leaders welcome the newcomers, update members about the status of current campaigns, and present workshops on topics ranging from federal immigration reform proposals to global-

---

[4] Barbara Young, interview with Janice Fine, June 2005, New York City.

ization. In addition, compared to FLF, the organization's rhetoric about domestic workers and their employers is much more confrontational.

It was through this outreach that Jocelyn Campbell, a leader of DWU who is originally from Barbados, became involved in the organization. In 2001, after nine years in the United States working as a nanny, she was working for a family in Tribecca when an organizer handed her a flier at a local playground. "I got excited about the whole thing, and becoming a member of DWU. The organization was offering an upcoming training for us, and I thought along with my nanny experience I needed to do this course because it entails child psychology, basic things that we do as a nanny.... I just felt the need to go back into training and have this certificate"[5] DWU offers a five-session nanny training course that covers child psychology and discipline, infant/child CPR, basic pediatric health and nutrition, work-related injury prevention, and best practices for negotiation and communication with domestic employers. Graduates receive a certificate of completion, résumé writing assistance, and a CPR certification card.

Although her employer liked the idea of the training and was initially supportive of Campbell's participation in DWU, as she became more deeply involved she was fired. Until that point, she had been taking care of the couple's ten-month-old baby since a few weeks after his birth and had always been told that she was doing an excellent job. "I left the job, but I didn't leave DWU; I continued with the organization because I think that what we're doing as an organization—our work—is very much needed in this industry. If we look at how this industry is, we have to keep organizing and building the organization as a whole because we represent low-wage workers who have no other recourse."[6]

DWU, Andolan, and CAAAV took their model contract to sympathetic city councilors, some of whom had worked as domestics or had members of their families who had, and the Immigrant Law Project at New York University helped them draft legislation based on it. Councilor Bill Perkins, in explaining to a *New York Times* reporter why he sponsored the bill, said, "Domestic workers are part of the most oppressed tradition of workers. My grandmother was a domestic worker, a housekeeper and nanny in Manhattan and I know all too well the low wages, unacceptable working conditions, lack of insurance— all of these prehistoric working conditions that so much of the city and this nation have moved away from" (Greenhouse 2002).

Brian Kavanaugh, chief of staff to City Councilor Gale Brewer, was the main sponsor of the legislation. Kavanaugh and Brewer concluded that the city did not have the authority to create broad new protections for domestic

[5] Jocelyn Campbell, interview by Janice Fine, June 2005, New York City.
[6] Ibid.

workers (as a contract establishing minimum standards would have done), but they felt the council could regulate the practices of domestic worker employment agencies through its power to grant and review their licenses. The proposed bill reflected this new emphasis.

Over the course of the campaign to pass the city council ordinance, DWU and the member groups held rallies, actions, and marches that were widely covered by newspapers throughout the city. Through its membership, the coalition had a stockpile of egregious cases of abuse and DWU worked with the women to tell their stories publicly. In July 2002, the organization organized an action at United Nations headquarters that called attention to the many cases of exploitation of domestic workers by diplomats, who are immune from prosecution. In October, hundreds of domestic workers marched through the streets of lower Manhattan. The women carried buckets and baby bottles and signs such as "I'm not your slave, I'm your employee." Over the winter and spring, the organization built support for the council bill, and it passed that June.

The bill requires employment agencies that place domestic workers to do two things. First, the agencies must make sure that the terms and conditions of employment are spelled out in writing when workers are placed in a job. Many domestic workers at the DWU described a bait-and-switch situation, in which they were told one thing by the agency when they were first given the assignment, only to discover a much different and usually more difficult arrangement when they arrived at the employer.

Second, the bill mandates that the agency get the employer who is hiring the domestic worker to sign a statement that lays out the state and federal rights that protect domestic workers and keep it on file and available for inspection. If an employer refuses to sign the statement, the agency is not supposed to place the worker with them.

Although the City Council was limited in what it could require, councilors passed a companion resolution to the legislation that called on the state and federal governments to enact and enforce broader protections. It also called on employers to agree to standard contractual terms proposed by the DWU.

In coalition with the Workplace Project, other worker centers and immigrant rights organizations, DWU is now working to pass sweeping legislation at the state level. The bill, which is supported by the state American Federation of Labor–Congress of Industrial Organizations (AFL-CIO) and 1199, calls on the state of New York to establish a living wage for domestic workers and require employers to pay it, along with providing health insurance, paid vacations and holidays, sick and personal days, and severance pay. The bill also calls for changes to existing state and federal laws that have excluded domestic workers, including the Family and Medical Leave Act and the National Labor Relations Act. Finally, it calls on the federal government to allow the employers of domestic workers to pay unemployment, disability, and workers compensation insurance on an annual, rather than quarterly, basis. Although the groups are realistic about the bill's chances of passage, they feel good about the fact that they have a legislative expression of what decent standards in the industry should look like.

DWU, Andolan, and CAAAV continue to build their bases among domestic workers—and especially nannies of color. DWU organizers visit Central Park playgrounds several times a week, where they are certain to find dozens of nannies caring for their young charges. They sit and chat, listen to the nannies' stories, and attempt to extract promises to attend the next general membership meeting. It is slow going but steady. The organization estimates that to reach a critical threshold of power, it needs to bring 10 percent of the industry's workers into the organization. DWU hopes to accomplish this through a combination of grassroots recruitment, highly visible demonstrations, and drawing public attention to compelling cases of nonpayment, discrimination, and abuse.

In late May of 2005, working with state attorney general Eliot Spitzer, DWU won consent decrees against eight employment agencies that had been screening candidates for domestic positions based on race. Posing as prospective employers or job applicants, members of the attorney general's staff found a pervasive pattern of discrimination—prospective employers were "routinely solicited for racial preferences." Based on that information, the agencies refused to refer domestics for particular jobs. According to the attorney general's office "some of the agencies openly noted 'no blacks,' 'no Islanders,' and 'prefers Europeans' in their internal records, which were then used to restrict eligibility for certain jobs" (Spitzer 2005).

In addition to targeting employment agencies, DWU is working to build a base of just employers by partnering with community groups to establish relationships with individual employers of domestic workers. The organization has created a partnership with Jews for Racial and Economic Justice (JFREJ), a progressive Jewish community organization in New York City. JFREJ and DWU have created Shalom Bayit, a project to reach out to employers of domestic workers through congregational organizing, and a series of community living room and individual meetings within Jewish communities of the upper west side and Brooklyn. In addition to turning out employers in support of DWU actions and the statewide legislative campaign, JFREJ is creating an employers' speakers bureau and a set of resources for employers on "everything from filing taxes to providing health insurance" (Jews for Racial and Economic Justice [JFREJ] 2005).

Multiple Models of Empowerment

As we have seen from these examples, worker centers are experimenting with a range of strategies for improving conditions for domestic workers, including direct action on individual employers and agencies, enacting minimum standards through public policy, and worker cooperatives. Due to the radically decentralized nature of the industry, organizations are developing strategies that enable them to impact more than one individual employer at a time. In this light, it is easy to understand why both the Workplace Project and DWU ended up targeting the placement agencies.

In general, worker centers have had to devise creative strategies to win improvements for low-wage workers in high-turnover industries and impermanent employment relationships, where subcontracting and independent contracting are the norm. The greatest accomplishment of these campaigns to date has been compelling individual employers to pay back wages to workers. Some centers find that simply contacting employers and requesting the money owed workers is often enough to get them to pay up, so surprised are they that someone is paying attention to the situation. When this proves insufficient, centers file wage complaints and stage protests outside businesses and private homes.

So far, organizations have been best able to win economic improvements for low-wage workers beyond individual cases by moving local and state government to require employers to comply with state and federal laws and to improve working conditions, as the DWU Domestic Workers' Bill of Rights sets out to do. But it is in the enforcement of these policy efforts that things fall apart. Government lacks the capacity to regularly patrol the hundreds of thousands of worksites and industries. The system depends on individuals coming forward to bring complaints, which is highly problematic for low-wage immigrant workers who are often unaware of their rights or afraid to exercise them.[7]

As a strategy for impacting conditions across the board in local domestic worker labor markets, co-ops, such as the one started by FLF, seem to have limited impact due to their modest scale. In areas such Long Island and New York City, where hundreds of thousands are employed as housekeepers, it is difficult to imagine worker co-ops altering labor market dynamics across the industry. Yet some have argued that the key to improving conditions lies in

---

[7] In 2002, the U.S. Department of Labor determined that the poultry industry was 100 percent and the garment industry more than 50 percent out of compliance with federal wage and hour laws. Low-wage immigrant workers are much more likely to bring cases when they are part of a group. Therefore, the FLSA should be amended to allow groups to bring cases. All lawsuits that can be brought by individual workers under the FLSA should also be allowed to be brought by representatives designated by those workers, which could be worker centers, unions, community organizations, or informal groups.

women achieving greater autonomy from their employers through a strategy of small business ownership and professionalization. For example, Mary Romero, sociologist, found that although Chicanas in Colorado turned to domestic work because they had limited options, through their efforts to eliminate employers from direct supervisory roles they were able to "restructure the occupation to resemble a more business-like arrangement." Once they had formed their own agencies and moved from being hourly employees to independent contractors, they experienced a greater sense of control, heightened dignity, and better pay (Romero 1992, 160–61).

Still, what DWU organizers first heard from the women was: "We need a union!" Traditional trade unions in industries such as domestic work, in which most workers are in one-on-one relationships with single small employers (individual families) have been notoriously difficult to organize and have largely failed. But, with the personal service industry skyrocketing, can we afford to give up on unionization as a strategy? Are unions simply off the table, or is it possible to imagine new models that are able to accommodate domestic workers and other low-wage immigrant workers? The evidence so far is quite mixed.

Worker Centers and Unions

When worker centers and unions are able to partner successfully, there are positive outcomes for workers in terms of improvements in wages and working conditions, union organizing, and passage of public policy, but these relationships are immensely complicated and challenging. Only 14 percent of worker centers in the 2003 survey I conducted had a direct connection to unions and union-organizing drives.

In terms of organizing, worker centers have related to unions in a variety of ways. When approached by a group of workers who were interested in joining a union, some centers have followed a practice of helping them find one that is interested, bringing the two parties together and then essentially handing the workers off to the union. Other centers have tried to maintain some level of involvement over the course of the organizing drive, although it is largely being run by the labor union. A smaller number of centers have participated in joint organizing campaigns with unions. In Omaha, Nebraska, Omaha Together One Community (OTOC) and the United Food and Commercial Workers International Union (UFCW) worked together and organized one thousand meatpackers. In New York City, Make the Road by Walking and the Retail, Wholesale and Department Store Union (RWDSU) jointly organized over one hundred workers at Footco, a small chain of ten sneaker stores. In many instances, however, especially in cases of smaller workplaces, worker centers have struggled to identify a union that is willing to organize the workers.

Yet political cooperation between worker centers and the traditional labor movement might pave the way for cooperative organizing campaigns. In 2001, the AFL-CIO, catalyzed by a strong push by the Hotel Employees and Restaurant Employees (HERE), made a historic decision to reverse its position on immigration. The AFL-CIO fundamentally altered its traditional stance of trying to block immigration and punish employers for hiring undocumented workers. Instead, it called for widespread amnesty, and in 2003 it worked with HERE to organize the historic Immigrant Workers Freedom Ride. In recent years, the AFL-CIO, as well as HERE and the Service Employees International Union (SEIU) (now members of Change to Win), have made immigration reform a major priority.

In January 2004, President George W. Bush, under pressure from the Mexican government as well as a growing number of U.S. employers dependent on immigrant labor, came out with a sweeping proposal for immigration reform. The centerpiece of the proposal was a new guest-worker program: employers, after alleging that they have tried to fill their available positions with U.S. nationals without success, would be empowered to hire temporary foreign workers. These workers would be issued three-year work permits that might be renewable for another three years. The program was not linked to the normal permanent residency and citizenship immigration tracks, and participants would have no greater advantage in applying for a green card. In 2005, Senators Edward Kennedy and John McCain set forth an alternative that established pathways to legal residency and citizenship but retained a guest-worker program.

Between March and April 2006, a powerful mass movement for immigrant's rights went public. More than 1 million low-wage immigrant workers, outraged by a bill passed by the House of Representatives that would have criminalized their presence in the United States, and all those who help them survive day to day emerged from the shadows and took to the streets. In major cities and minor suburbs from Los Angeles California to Long Island New York, remarkable scenes unfolded as undocumented workers took to the streets asserting, "*Somos trabajadores, no somos criminales*" (We are workers not criminals). On May Day 2006, the international workers' holiday seldom celebrated in the United States beyond the stalwarts of the left, close to 1 million immigrants engaged in the largest political strike since the movement for the eight-hour day in the late nineteenth century.

As the policy debate has heated up, the AFL-CIO has bucked the conventional political wisdom of its allies, including SEIU and HERE, that a new temporary worker program (albeit with strengthened labor protections and the possibility of applying for legal permanent residence) would be the price groups would have to pay for immigration reform. Arguing that "We must reverse the trend of allowing employers to turn permanent, full-time year-round jobs into temporary jobs and . . . long term labor shortages should be filled with workers with full rights," the AFL-CIO called on Congress to grant amnesty to the 12 million undocumented immigrants already in the country and significantly expand the permanent employment-based visas system (green cards) instead of establishing an expanded guest worker program to handle the future flow (American Federation of Labor–Congress of Industrial Organizations [AFL-CIO] 2006, 1). Deliberations over immigration reform continue in Congress, but the AFL-CIO's willingness to take a stand in favor of amnesty and in opposition to consigning immigrant workers to permanent second-class status is an opening for closer collaboration with worker centers and their national networks on federal policy.

Organizing the Future

Organized labor, in particular SEIU, has organized thousands of low-wage immigrant workers in recent years. Yet, most unions do not have mechanisms for affiliating individual workers who are members of worker centers, nor are there ways in which worker centers as organizations can join the AFL-CIO or international unions. During the several years that I have interviewed people at worker centers, I have heard many of them distinguish between "the labor movement," which they feel they are a part of, and "organized labor," which they do not. I think it is tragic that many worker centers view themselves as a movement that exists apart from organized labor.

In Britain, the Trade Union Council directly operates more than one hundred unemployed worker centers that help train and place unemployed workers. In the United States, the vast majority of worker centers are not branches of unions or central labor councils; they are foundation-funded and receive little financial support from organized labor. There ought to be ways that the worker centers as organizations can join up if they choose, without sacrificing the discrete identity and structural integrity of their groups. Models could be devised for worker centers as organizations to become affiliated, either through being chartered as locals by international unions or by becoming directly affiliated locals of the AFL-CIO or Change to Win. This is not a new idea. Dorothy Sue Cobble has documented that between its founding in 1886 and its merger with the CIO in 1955, the AFL directly affiliated 20,000 local unions. This allowed the AFL both to provide some form of representation to workers who were not a good fit with existing internationals and to experiment with a range of representational strategies (Cobble 1997).[8]

The first step to bridging the gap is for organized labor to stop looking at these organizations instrumentally—asking what is in it for organized labor in the short term. Organizations that are providing services to, advocating for, and organizing low-wage workers are carrying out functions that are essential to the twenty-first-century labor movement. They ought to be welcomed into the ranks of organized labor.

[8] In fact, in 2005, the Executive Council of the AFL-CIO voted to bring back direct affiliated local unions.

PART V

LOCAL–GLOBAL CONNECTIONS

These last three chapters put the challenge of lessening gender and class inequality in a global context. They remind us of the gendered face of globalization. In the twenty-first century, it is women as much as men who are crossing borders in search of employment and often it is women who are hired. They, not their husbands, brothers, or fathers, are more likely to be on the global assembly lines in Mexico, El Salvador, and Malaysia. The wages of women domestics, sex workers, casual laborers, and small vendors keep families, communities, and national economies afloat worldwide. How is the U.S. labor movement responding to globalization? What difference does it make that women are the new global proletariat? What can U.S. labor learn from the new unions, associations, and networks formed by poor women and their allies around the world?

These chapters point to the opportunities for worker mobilization and empowerment in a globalizing world. Multinational corporations are not invincible; nor can they fully escape the reach of the law, of public opinion, or of the fledgling but growing global working women's movement.

Maria Ontiveros opens this section with a blistering account of the lack of freedom and rights afforded female immigrants. Capital and labor both are on the move in the new global economy, but labor enjoys few of the economic or political hospitalities extended to capital when it crosses borders. In chapter 12, Ontiveros finds the unregulated free market an inadequate mechanism for ensuring fairness and economic progress for immigrant women, reinforcing a central tenet of this book. Yet she is less sanguine than other contributors about the potential of traditional collective bargaining and current antidiscrimination laws to take up the slack. Many of the jobs held by immigrant women fall outside the bounds of labor and employment law; undocumented immigrants (44 percent of whom are estimated to be women) often lack even the right to quit, the hallmark of free labor, as well as access to police protection, courts, and political citizenship. Unable to call on traditional legal remedies, immigrant women and their allies have relied on underused domestic statutes such as those barring coerced labor and human trafficking. In addition, they have fashioned innovative transnational strategies tied to regional and international trade agreements and labor statutes.

In chapter 13, Katie Quan also finds openings for worker mobilization in the seams of the new global economy. Women are "on the cutting edge of global labor organizing today," she asserts, and her path-breaking research, which pieces together the story of three successful cross-border campaigns involving workers in Latin America, Asia, Europe, and the United States lends her claim credibility.

Quan's three cases are instructive as well as inspiring, revealing the global networks now linking workers worldwide; the alliances emerging between community groups and unions; and the vulnerability of multinationals to cross-border solidarity, public shaming, and persistent strategic pressure. In her first case, nongovernmental organizations (NGOs), unions, and student groups in the United States are crucial in helping Mexican garment workers secure bargaining rights; in her second, NGOs and unions in Taiwan and Indonesia, joined by Cambodian workers who refuse to work overtime, contribute to reopening a shuttered factory in El Salvador. In her third case, the Service Employees International Union (SEIU) campaign to organize Securitas, the largest security contractor in the world, Chicago workers win a union contract after Swedish and other European Union workers pressure the Securitas corporate headquarters in Sweden. As Quan observes, here we see an often overlooked aspect of global solidarity. It is not just about "us" helping "them"; it is also about mutual aid and about "them" helping "us."

The Sex of Class closes with Leah Vosko's chapter on the new labor strategies arising among informal economy workers and their largely female advocates. She describes the significant organizing breakthroughs of new unions such as the 700,000-member Indian Self-Employed Women's Association (SEWA) and the innovative approaches to raising the living standards of impoverished women around the world adopted by feminist labor NGOs and transnational networks. Vosko argues that many of the strategies pioneered by these new female-led institutions, if adopted, could help North American unions reach out to the large numbers of precarious or nonstandard workers—by some estimates one-quarter of the work force—inside the United

States and Canada. Returning to many of the themes raised in the introduction and throughout the book, Vosko urges the official labor movement to expand its definition of who is a worker, embrace multiple approaches to worker empowerment, and forge new solidarities across sexual and cultural differences.

12

FEMALE IMMIGRANT WORKERS AND THE LAW

LIMITS AND OPPORTUNITIES

Maria L. Ontiveros

The U.S. workplace provides both tremendous opportunities and perils for female immigrant workers. Because the very nature of a market for human labor rests on the idea of people as commodities, the potential exists to treat people inhumanely in order to generate significant profits. The United States has implemented laws to protect workers in an attempt to mitigate these tendencies. These laws fail to protect female immigrant workers, however, for a variety of reasons. Because the traditional workplace laws do not adequately protect their interests, female immigrant workers have turned to a variety of less traditional legal approaches to remedy the exploitation they experience. Some of the most effective alternatives are located outside the traditional narrow approach of domestic law, which focuses on employee rights and protections of the employee as an employee. Instead, these alternatives tend to focus on the rights and protections of immigrant workers as human rights or women's rights issues or on a broader international understanding of workers' rights. This chapter begins by describing the various sources of workplace protection in the United States and then analyzes why these sources do not adequately protect female immigrant workers. It then discusses new approaches being taken by female immigrant workers to defend against workplace exploitation.

Sources of Workplace Rights

In the United States, two dominant legal philosophies define the contours of employment: freedom of contract and employment at will. Under these free market philosophies, the terms and conditions of the employment relationship are determined by a negotiation between the individual employee and the employer. In addition, under the doctrine of employment at will, the employer is free to terminate the employment "for good cause, for no cause, or even for a cause morally wrong" (Verkerke 1995). Within the free market framework, the employee's main protection comes from her market value and bargaining position. If the employer pays too little or treats employees too poorly, the employee will quit. In addition, a employer acting beneath market expectations in its pay practices or other treatment of employees will not be able to attract employees (Weiler 1990).

The basic free market approach has been modified by three different types of statutes: those regulating labor standards, those prohibiting discrimination based on protected characteristics, and those protecting the creation of unions and collective bargaining. Each of these statutes approaches the regulation of the workplace by focusing on the rights and protections given to employees as employees. When these rights are violated, the employee may bring a lawsuit alleging that her workplace rights have been violated. Most claims are filed first with an administrative agency, such as the Equal Employment Opportunity Commission (EEOC) or the U.S. Department of Labor (USDL). If the claim cannot be resolved at the administrative agency level, the employee may proceed to court. Most employees need to find an attorney to help them file a claim and guide them through the legal process.

Statutes regulating labor standards affect a variety of different terms and conditions of the employment relationship. The federal Fair Labor Standards Act (FLSA), passed in 1938, provides for a minimum hourly wage and for a premium to be paid for those hours worked over forty in a week. The Occupational Safety and Health Act (OSHA), passed in 1970, provides for minimum standards of health and safety in the workplace, including standards for ventilation, exposure to chemicals, and ergonomic setup. These statutes remove these terms of employment from the free contract model.

A second set of laws prohibit certain types of discrimination. These state and federal laws list specific protected classifications that may not be used as the basis for employment decisions. For instance, on the federal level, Title VII of the Civil Rights Act of 1964 prohibits discrimination on the basis of race, sex, color, religion, or national origin. The Age Discrimination in Employment Act, passed in 1967, prohibits discrimination on the basis of age against employees over the age of forty. The Americans with Disabilities Act, passed in 1991, prohibits discrimination against qualified individuals with a disability. Various state and local laws prohibit discrimination based on other categories, such as sexual orientation or marital status. Employers are free, however, to discriminate against any unprotected classification. For example, an employer may discriminate on the basis of zodiac sign or left-handedness. These laws limit the doctrine of employment at will to some extent because an employer may no longer fire an employee for any of these specific bad reasons. Employers also may not discriminate in other terms and conditions of employment (i.e., wages, promotions, and schedules), based on these protected classifications.

Many workers find protection in the workplace through union representation and collective bargaining. The National Labor Relations Act (NLRA), passed in 1935, protects most workers' rights to engage in concerted activity for mutual aid and protection, to join or assist a union, and to bargain collectively through that union over the terms and conditions of work. Under the terms of the statute, an employer may not penalize workers for engaging in these activities. Collective bargaining agreements (union contracts) generally protect employees from discharge without just cause, protect employees from arbitrary employment decisions in other terms and conditions of employment, provide for fair wages, provide for decent benefits, and provide an opportunity to participate in the workplace. Workplaces with union representation tend to be safer and evidence a higher rate of compliance with OSHA requirements as well. Instead of relying on an attorney to vindicate individual rights, an employee can exercise these rights on her own and exercises power as part of a collective with other workers.

Problems for Female Immigrant Workers

Although these four mechanisms (market forces, labor standards legislation, antidiscrimination laws, and collective bargaining) should provide comprehensive protection for workers in the United States, they fail to protect female immigrant workers. Although each woman is unique, these women as a group experience some similar problems. The women tend to work in a limited number of jobs: domestic work (including housecleaning and child care); agriculture; non-home-based janitorial and cleaning services; electronics; and apparel work (e.g., see Lovell, Hartmann, and Werschkul, chap. 2, table 2.2, in this volume). Employers often pay them less than the minimum wage, often do not pay overtime premiums, and sometimes refuse to pay at all. They labor in conditions that threaten their health and safety. The women suffer from sexual harassment and sexual abuse. They lack union representation, and they are treated in arbitrary and demeaning ways (Fine, chap. 11 in this volume).

TABLE 12.1
Problems for female immigrant workers and sources of workplace rights

	Source of workplace rights			
	Market transaction	Labor standards	Antidiscrimination Laws	Unionization and collective bargaining
Excluded from coverage		✓	✓	✓
Immigration issues	✓		✓	✓
Unrecognized type of injury	✓		✓	
Cultural limitations	✓	✓	✓	✓

Four major reasons explain why these laws do not adequately protect female immigrant workers: these workers are excluded from coverage of the statutes; immigration issues impair their effectiveness; the type of injury suffered by the workers is not recognized; and cultural limitations. Table 12.1 lists the impact of each of these problems on each source of workplace rights.

Exclusion from Statutory Protection

The current framework excludes these workers from statutory protection in several ways. Initially, many of the occupations in which the women work were specifically excluded from the statutes. The NLRA, for instance, does not protect domestic or agricultural workers who engage in collective action. By its very terms, an employer is free to fire or discipline union activists in these two industries without legal penalty. The major labor standards statutes also historically did not cover workers in domestic or agricultural work. Recently, the statutes have been changed to apply to these workers but with a different wage structure. For example, agricultural employers, as well as apparel and electronics employers, may base compensation for work on a piece rate. In these ways, the exclusion of occupations by these laws leads to exploitation.

The reasons for the exclusions provide insight into how the work of female immigrants is viewed, as well as how the workers themselves are devalued. Some suggest that the exclusion of domestic and agricultural workers reflects a racially motivated legacy of the chattel slavery system. Because most slaves performed either domestic or agricultural work, the South was unwilling to extend the same basic workplace protections to the freed slaves as was extended to other free labor. The legislative history of the FLSA supports this view (Linder 1987).

An alternate explanation looks to the nature of the work done in these industries. Domestic work is seen as part of the private familial sphere, as opposed to the public sphere. Society may feel that it is inappropriate to overregulate what goes on in a private home. In addition, as an extension of the type of unpaid work traditionally done by women, domestic work is sometimes not viewed as real work, deserving of the type of pay, benefits, and protection given to other workers. Finally, the nature of domestic work is often misunderstood. It is viewed as easy work done for benevolent employers, which does not need protection. In reality, domestic work is physically difficult, underpaid, and exposes workers to a variety of chemicals and other workplace hazards, including sexual harassment and abuse (Smith 2000).

For agricultural work, a different dynamic plays a role. Some argue for excluding farmworkers on the theory that small family farms form the basic structure of the industry and that requiring such farms to meet basic labor standards would drive them out of business, negatively impacting the nation's food supply (Luna 1998). Alternatively, the exclusion may result from the nature of agricultural industry, which has always been the most likely to view workers as simply another commodity or input. African slaves were clearly viewed as a commodity. On Hawaiian plantation, Filipinos were listed on supply lists in between fertilizer and fuel (Takaki 1983), and in California fields today, agricultural employers still think in terms of putting in for an "order of Mexicans" (Rothenberg 1998). The commodification of labor inherent in any labor market reaches its extreme in the field of agriculture (Ontiveros 2002; Luna 1998).

In addition to outright statutory exclusion, other forms of exclusion also affect female immigrant workers. Most of the statutes apply only to employers of a certain size. Title VII, for instance, covers only employers with fifteen or more employees. The NLRA and the FLSA also limit coverage by employer size. Because many female immigrant workers, especially in the domestic and apparel fields, work for small employers, they are disproportionately excluded by this limitation.

Female immigrant workers may also be excluded from the protection of the law through either the use of the independent contractor exclusion or the use of labor subcontractors. The statutory protections apply only to those considered by the law to be employees, and laws regulate only the actions of those considered to be employers. Unfortunately, many female immigrant workers do not fit this model because they are hired as independent contractors not employees. The law does not protect independent contractors because they are assumed to have equal bargaining power with employers (Linder 1999–2000). Classically, an independent contractor agrees on a set price to perform a completed task and then decides for herself how to do the job using her own tools. Unfortunately, this notion has been stretched beyond its classic formulation, so that many workers are now categorized as independent contractors even when they are not on equal footing with employers. Employers often mistakenly argue that home care workers and cleaners should be considered independent contractors.

In addition, the laws apply only to the relationship between the employee and her formal employer. In many industries, especially the agricultural and garment sectors, workers are formally employed by a labor contractor or sub-contractor, even though they are performing work for a third party. Labor contractors and subcontractors tend to be small immigrant entrepreneurs trying to earn a profit by providing or managing low-cost labor instead of engaging in physical labor themselves. In agriculture, the labor contractor contracts with the grower to provide a certain number of workers. The labor contractor, not the grower, is the formal employer. In the garment sector, the clothing manufacturer contracts with a subcontractor for a certain number of garments. The subcontractor, in turn, hires garment workers who actually sew the garments. The subcontractor, not the clothing manufacturer, is the formal employer. In both these scenarios, the larger entity, which is benefiting from the worker's labor, is insulated from responsibility while the contractor or subcontractor is often judgment-proof (Ontiveros 2002; Hayashi 1992).

Immigration Issues

A second category of problems for female immigrant workers involves immigration issues. Many immigrant workers live in the United States without the legal authorization to be or to work here. Currently, approximately 10.3 million unauthorized migrants live in the United States, and, in every year since 1995, the number of unauthorized immigrants has exceeded the number of authorized immigrants. About 44 percent of the adult unauthorized immigrants (3.9 million) are women, and over one-half of these women work. Approximately one out of every twenty-three workers in the United States (4.3 percent) is an unauthorized worker. Unauthorized workers are occupationally concentrated in farming, cleaning, construction, and food preparation. The industries in which they are most concentrated include private households, hotels, food manufacturing, agriculture, textiles, and construction.[1]

For these undocumented immigrant workers, an attempt to enforce their legal rights may result in the employer calling the Department of Homeland Security and in their own deportation. Deportation is a devastating experience. Transportation back home and the time spent in detention centers imperils the person's health. The worker may be separated from her family, including her children, if she chooses to hide their existence in the hope that they will be better off remaining in the United States without her. In many cases, she will try to reenter the United States again. Illegal border crossings are currently very difficult and often deadly. Approximately one person dies every day trying to cross the border from Mexico to the United States. In ad-

[1] Jeffrey S. Passel, "Unauthorized Migrants: Numbers and Characteristics," 2005, http://www.pew hispanic.org (accessed June 30, 2006).

dition, undocumented female immigrants face the real threat of rape and sexual abuse. Many reports confirm that both the men who smuggle women across the border and the agents of the Border Patrol routinely assault these women (Ontiveros 2002). Given the dire consequences of deportation, few immigrant women are willing to challenge workplace abuse. As a result, these women have very little bargaining power in relationship to their employers. The protection supposedly offered by the free market mechanism simply fails to apply to them.

For undocumented workers, the U.S. Supreme Court has also circumscribed statutory protection by limiting the remedies available to undocumented workers. In the case of *Hoffman Plastics, Inc. v. Nat'l Labor Relations Board*,[2] an employer illegally fired a worker for trying to form a union. Normally, such an employee would be entitled to reinstatement and back pay (an award of damages equal to the wages the employee would have earned had she not been illegally fired). But when the court discovered that the employee was undocumented, the employer refused to reinstate the worker and also refused to pay the back-pay award. The Supreme Court upheld this action, reasoning that to provide an award of back pay would trench on the immigration laws that prohibit the employment of undocumented workers. As a result of *Hoffman*, undocumented workers have limited remedies for violations of their rights under the NLRA. This same ruling has been extended to Title VII (Ontiveros 2004).

Several ill effects have resulted from *Hoffman*. First, undocumented workers may be dissuaded from seeking to vindicate their rights because they are left with little or no remedy. Second, employers have very little economic incentive to comply with labor and employment statutes in regard to undocumented workers because they are not financially penalized for violating their rights. Finally, employers and their attorneys have used this decision to investigate workers' immigration status because, they argue, it is relevant to the remedies available. Even though most courts have ruled against employers on this argument, the inquiries have created a chilling effect on immigrant workers who do not want their immigration status brought to light (Ontiveros 2004).

Fortunately, the *Hoffman* result does not apply to remedies under the FLSA. Courts distinguish these cases seeking unpaid or underpaid wages, including unpaid overtime, because the remedies serve to compensate employees for time already worked (Ontiveros 2004). Labor unions and community workers' rights groups often assist workers, including undocumented workers, in recovering the losses suffered from these labor violations (Greenhouse 2005a).

The free market system also fails to protect certain visa-authorized female

2 *Hoffman Plastic Compounds, Inc. v. Nat'l Labor Relations Board*, 535 U.S. 137 (2002).

immigrant workers because of the restriction on their ability to quit embedded in their visa authorization. Under the immigration visa program, many female immigrant workers enter the United States legally, with authorization to perform specific types of work. For example, the H-2A visa program allows agricultural workers to enter the United States and work under certain circumstances. Other unskilled, nonagricultural workers arrive under the H-2B visa program. The J-1 visa brings women to the United States to work as *au pairs*. The *au pair* visas circumvent the free market by setting pay and work conditions that are substantially below the market rate for other day-care providers (the pay rate is $139 per week).[3] In addition to shortchanging the female immigrant *au pair*, these provisions also drive down the wages for all child-care providers.

Each of these visas requires work for one particular employer. The visa is revoked if the worker quits or is fired, and the employee must then leave the United States. As a result, the employee's ability to quit an abusive work situation is substantially limited. These employees are also less likely to complain or agitate for better conditions for fear of being discharged and deported. Even if these visa employees wanted to complain, they would most likely be unable to find legal representation because Legal Services Corporation grantees, the federally funded attorneys who provide legal services for low-income people, are prohibited from providing legal assistance to most aliens. If they assist these workers, they will lose their federal funding.[4] Even when they are technically covered by the law, many immigrants—both documented and undocumented—are simply never able to secure their legal rights.

Type of Injury Not Recognized

Each source of workplace rights seeks to protect against a specific type of injury. In Title VII, for instance, the statute seeks to protect employees against discrimination on the basis of race, sex, religion, color, or national origin. For female immigrant workers, however, the type of injury they suffer may fall outside these categories—Title VII does not protect against discrimination based on alien or migration status. In the case of *Espinoza v. Farah*,[5] the Supreme Court specifically found that an employer may discriminate against noncitizen, legal residents on the basis of citizenship status without violating the prohibition against discrimination based on national origin. An employer may freely discriminate under federal law, then, on the basis of citizenship or

---

[3] U.S. Citizenship and Immigration Services, "Immigration Classifications and Visa Categories," 2005, http://uscis.gov/graphics/services/visas.htm (accessed June 30, 2006).

[4] D. Michael Dale, Maria Andrade, and Laura K. Abel, memorandum in support of petition for Mexican NAO Submission 2005–1 (H-2B Visa Workers). April 13, 2005, http://www.dol.gov.ilab/media/reports/nao/submissions/2005–01memo.htm (accessed June 30, 2006).

[5] *Espinoza v. Farah Mfg. Co.*, Inc., 414 U.S. 86 (1973).

migration status, leaving the female immigrant worker without protection because this type of injury is not seen as problematic under current antidiscrimination law.

In addition, Title VII does not consistently protect against discrimination based on multiple factors. For example, some employers discriminate against only particular types of women (i.e., African American women but not white women). When employment discrimination occurs at the intersection of more than one identity factor, courts have generally been willing to prohibit discrimination under Title VII based on two categories (i.e., race and sex) or based on a protected category plus a fundamental right (i.e., an employer may not discriminate against married women). For female immigrant workers, however, the type of discrimination they face may fall outside the protection of Title VII if only immigrant women, but not all women employees, are harassed, for example. As long as immigration and migration are not deemed to be fundamental rights or interpreted as being analytically equivalent to national origin, the nondiscrimination laws simply do not view the injury as one that should be recognized and compensated.

The free market system of workplace protection also does not recognize the type of injury suffered by female immigrant workers because of its reliance on the notion of choice. The free market model assumes that workers choose to accept only adequate workplace conditions. As long as an employee freely chooses to remain in a work situation, the argument goes, there can be no real injury. A variant on this argument, and one made by many in the general public, is that undocumented workers have no right to expect the legally protected minimum labor standards because they are involved in an illegal work contract. The assumption is that immigrant workers are simply not injured if treated in illegal ways because they are not entitled to expect the same minimum treatment as other workers. This approach is objectionable because it creates a caste of workers who labor below the otherwise established legal minimums (Ontiveros 2004).

Cultural Limitations

A variety of cultural issues affect the effectiveness of all labor standards, collective bargaining, and antidiscrimination laws. First, immigrant workers may not know what their rights are, especially if they come from a country with fewer or different workplace rights. Second, many may not feel able to speak up against an employer because of the power relationship between the employer and employee. The employer may also be in a gender- or race-privileged position relative to the female immigrant worker. Alternately, if the employer is someone with whom the employee has a kinship or community tie, the culture/community may discourage and dissuade the worker from objecting. Finally, the United States legal system may be ill-equipped to understand the worker's complaints. The problem begins on the most basic level, language, because many administrative agencies lack bilingual staff. On a deeper level, without bicultural training, many officials disbelieve workers when they make allegations or officials fail to grasp the significance of the treatment described by workers (Ontiveros 2002).

Frustration and Limited Success in the Current Model

Despite these limitations, female immigrant workers and their advocates have attempted to work within the existing framework to gain some protection. These efforts have met limited success or have led to a great deal of frustration. The case of *EEOC v. Tanimura & Antle* (hereafter *Alfara*),[6] begun in 1996 and settled in 1999, illustrates the limits of even a successful case. In *Alfara*, the EEOC investigated ongoing sexual harassment of Mexican female farmworkers and negotiated a $1.855 million consent decree (De Bare 1999). Three main factors account for the success of this case: the bravery and willingness of Blanca Alfara to come forward, the involvement of California Rural Legal Assistance (CRLA), and the presence of EEOC attorneys sensitive to immigrant issues. CRLA was able to overcome many of the cultural trust issues because of its long track record of helping the community. In this case, the EEOC broadened its focus from its traditional urban, black-white emphasis to one that included agriculture and the concerns of Latina/os and Asian Americans. Because the senior EEOC attorney on the case, William Tamayo, had a background representing immigrant workers, he realized that investigators had the potential to misanalyze crucial credibility determinations. He responded by lobbying for and getting training for EEOC attorneys and investigators on the cultural aspects of credibility determinations and on credibility determinations for victims of sexual assault (Tamayo 2000). Although *Alfara* had a successful outcome, it will be very difficult to duplicate without structural changes because of the unique personnel involved.

Structural changes, however, have been hard to effect. For example, few states have been willing to extend collective bargaining protection to agricultural or domestic workers or to address the problems associated with independent contractors and the subcontractor system. In 2002, the California legislature passed a bill that could have made inroads against this latter problem. The legislation, applicable to the agricultural, construction, garment, janitorial, and security-guard industries, would have required either filed writ-

[6] *EEOC v. Tanimura & Antle*, C99–20088, 867 Fair Employment Practice Cases (FNA) (N.D. Cal. 1999).

ten contracts or prohibited employers from entering into contracts in which the employer had knowledge that the contracted rate was so low that the contractor could not comply with all applicable laws and regulations. A liberal Democratic governor vetoed the legislation (Ontiveros 2002, 183).

Attempts to work inside or slightly reform the current system are unlikely to produce the desired results because of the paradigm or model on which they are based. The traditional U.S. legal model of workplace rights simply does not fit female immigrant workers or their problems. Thus, successful approaches have begun to develop outside the traditional model.

Alternative Domestic Approaches

Many successful extra-legal community- and union-organizing case examples exist (as other chapters in this volume attest); here I focus on the use and limits of the law. Within the domestic legal system, the beginnings of effective approaches have appeared in a model that focuses on the problems of immigrant women as a combination of human rights issues, women's rights issues, and workers' rights issues.

One innovative approach rests on the foundations of the Thirteenth Amendment to the U.S. Constitution, which prohibits slavery and involuntary servitude. In 1867, Congress passed the Anti-Peonage Statute pursuant to the Thirteenth Amendment. The Anti-Peonage Statute was recently amended by the Trafficking Victims Protection Act of 2000 (TVPA) and, in 2003, by the Trafficking Victims Protection Reauthorization Act (TVPRA).[7] The TVPA provides for criminal enforcement of trafficking and forced-labor laws by the government; the TVPRA allows individuals to bring their own civil lawsuits against those who have harmed them.

In the United States, a surprising number of people, including immigrants, are forced through the use of violence to work against their will, and the Thirteenth Amendment clearly encompasses criminal prosecutions against those who hold workers captive. The Coalition of Immokalee Workers (CIW), a workers' rights organization in southern Florida, has been instrumental in the successful prosecution of three such cases in 1997–2000 (Bowe 2003). The CIW discovered the existence of slave camps, in which workers picked crops for little or no pay and without the ability to leave. In schemes reminiscent of the debt bondage systems used to bind freed blacks in the years following the Civil War, the owners of these modern-day camps charged workers various

---

[7] Trafficking Victims Protection Act, Division A of the Victims of Trafficking and Violence Protection Act of 2000, Pub. L. No. 106–386, Division A, 114 Stat. 1464 (codified in scattered sections of 8, 18, and 22 U.S.C. 2000); Trafficking Victims Protection Reauthorization Act of 2003, Pub. L. No. 108–193, 117 Stat. 2875 (codified in scattered sections of 8, 18 and 22 U.S.C. 2003).

fees for job placement, transportation, housing, and so forth and refused to allow workers to leave until these debts were paid off. Those who tried to leave and those who offered transportation out of the camps were threatened, beaten, or killed (Bowe 2003). Because of their cultural knowledge and reservoir of trust built among the workers, the CIW was able to help some workers escape. They then pushed the Civil Rights Division of the Department of Justice to investigate and prosecute these claims.

Immigrant women were found to have been held in sexual slavery. After having been brought to the United States ostensibly to work in housekeeping or child care, the smugglers forced the women to work as prostitutes to pay off their debt for transportation. The women were never able to accumulate enough money to pay off their debt, and they were unable to leave because of threats of beatings and threats of reprisals against their families in Mexico. The clients for these women's sexual services were often agricultural workers. As a prosecutor for the Department of Justice described the situation, "You can't look at these as isolated labor violations or sex crimes. What you get with agriculture is a pattern of exploitation that can be understood only as a system of human rights abuses" (quoted in Bowe 2003).

The work of the CIW is especially important because it recognizes other avenues to improve the conditions of agricultural workers. In particular, it led a boycott aimed at Taco Bell, and its parent company Yum Brands, designed to force the company to demand that its suppliers of tomatoes operate without slave labor. In 2005, after four years of consumer boycotts and religious appeals, the CIW and Yum Brands agreed to a precedent-setting agreement that raised farmworker wages, developed an enforceable code of conduct for agricultural suppliers, and provided transparency in the record keeping of those farms supplying produce to Yum Brands.[8] Although the moral argument behind the agreement was a demand that Yum should be able to guarantee that its produce was not picked by slave labor, the outcome resulted in better working conditions for all agricultural workers, not just those held in slavery.

In California, the Human Trafficking Project of the Lawyers' Committee for Civil Rights of the San Francisco Bay Area has been focusing on civil litigation to help immigrant victims of exploitive labor arrangements. In October 2002, Kathleen Kim, former director of the Human Trafficking Project, began to address the civil needs of immigrants who are unable to leave exploitive relationships that they characterize as modern-day slavery. In conjunction with Daniel Werner of the Workers' Rights Law Center of New York, Inc., Kim co-authored "Civil Litigation on Behalf of Victims of Human Traf-

[8] Coalition of Immokalee Workers, "Victory at Taco Bell," 2005, http://www.ciw-online.org/agree mentanalysis.html (accessed June 30, 2006).

ficking," a manual that provides attorneys with information on logistics, procedures, and sample complaints to represent these workers. The manual identifies over twelve different legal causes of action that might be brought on behalf of these workers. Some focus on traditional employment statutes, such as the FLSA or Title VII, but many others conceive of the workers' problems or the employer actions in broader terms such as torts or racketeering.

The primary weapon in their arsenal, however, arises under the TVPRA and the civil remedies it provides for immigrants forced into exploitive work relationships. In a typical forced-labor case, an immigrant woman works excessive hours, is housed in substandard inhumane conditions, and is paid little or no money. She feels unable to leave the work relationship because of psychological or physical threats or threats of deportation. The law currently defines forced labor as labor procured through the use of "threats of serious harm to, or physical restraint against, that person or another person; by means of any scheme . . . intended to cause the person to believe that, if the person did not perform such labor or services, that person or another person would suffer serious harm or physical restraint; or . . . by means of the abuse or threatened abuse of law or the legal process."[9]

During its existence, the Human Trafficking Project helped many immigrant victims of trafficking and forced labor. Many of its cases involved helping immigrants who had been referred to the Project by the government after the government had undertaken criminal action against an employer. These cases tended to involve women trafficked into the United States to engage in prostitution. Most of its successful cases, however, involved female immigrants who had entered the United States as domestics, on visas, and had then been subjected to cruel and inhumane work relationships. In one case, the Project secured a settlement for a Kenyan woman who worked for a prominent African journalist. Although the worker had come to the United States expecting to provide child care and light housekeeping for reasonable pay, she ended up working sixteen-hour days with little or no pay, sleeping on the floor, and having no communication with her family or others without being monitored by her employer. She was also belittled and subjected to constant threats of harm to her and her family if she tried to protest her treatment. She eventually fled to a local domestic-violence shelter on a day when her employer was at work and the child whom she tended was at school. The settlement allowed the employee to begin a new life (Yeung 2004).

The Human Trafficking Project also worked on legislative changes. In 2005, it teamed with other groups to secure the passage of legislation in California that makes human trafficking a felony crime at the state level. The legislation,

---

[9] Trafficking Victims Protection Reauthorization Act of 2003, Pub. L. No. 108–193, 117 Stat. 2875 (codified in scattered sections of 8, 18 and 22 U.S.C. 2003).

known as the California Trafficking Victims Protection Act[10] and approved by the governor in September 2005, provides for a private civil cause of action and better access to federal benefits such as counseling, housing, and immigration assistance. The state bill also broadens the definition of force or coercion to recognize the more subtle forms of coercion often used to keep immigrant workers in exploitive relationships. Other states are now considering similar legislation, and Kim has testified at federal congressional briefings about human trafficking (Romney 2005; Smith 2005).

The approach taken by the Human Trafficking Project is significant because it seeks to define and name the harm done to a certain group of immigrant workers. The current law is inadequate and incomplete because it can only conceive of workplace harms in the traditional ways (violation of labor standards, discrimination, etc.). The harms experienced by immigrant workers in ongoing exploitive work relationships, however, involve issues of human rights and citizenship rights, as well as workplace rights. By using the language of modern-day slavery and human trafficking, the Project seeks to reconceptualize and expand labor and employment law to address the needs of these immigrant workers (Kim and Hreshchyshyn 2004).

Claudia Flores, an attorney, and others at the Women's Rights Project of the American Civil Liberties Union are also working to characterize the workplace harms of immigrant women in nontraditional ways. In 2004, on behalf of five Latina housekeepers who were hired by a New York City hotel and then subjected to sexual and wage exploitation, they filed a lawsuit that involved a claim for forced labor (*Trejo v. Broadway Plaza Hotel*, 2004). In a more recent lawsuit, they filed a claim on behalf of an Ethiopian domestic alleging that her treatment violates the Thirteenth Amendment and international law and treaties that prohibit enslavement and forced labor (*Chere v. Girmal*, 2004). In a third case, they filed a sexual harassment claim under a New York City statue that provides remedies for victims of gender-motivated violence (*Espinal v. Palacci*, 2004). They took this approach primarily because the employer was too small to be covered by typical discrimination laws, but it has drawn attention for its reconceptualization of the problem.

International Law Approaches

Legal advocates for female immigrant workers have also turned to international law to seek workplace protection. International law provides an appropriate avenue to address these issues because, in many other countries and within the international legal community, workplace protections are not de-

---

[10] California Trafficking Victims Protection Act (2005 California Statute A.B. 22).

fined as narrowly as they are in the United States—instead, workers' rights are viewed more broadly as basic human rights rather than as narrow statutory rights. This formulation of workplace rights extends protection to female immigrant workers, even if they do not fit the U.S. definition of the ideal worker. Treaties that could be used to establish rights of immigrant workers include International Labour Organization (ILO) Conventions 87 and 98; the Charter of the Organization of American States, agreed to in 1951; and the International Covenant on Civil and Political Rights, passed in 1976 (De la Vega and Lozano-Batista 2005). In 1999, the United Nations Commission on Human Rights appointed a special rapporteur to address the concerns of migrant workers. Following her investigations, the International Convention on the Protection of the Rights of All Migrant Workers and Members of Their Families (known as the Migrant Convention) entered into force on July 1, 2003. This convention should provide a powerful new tool to protect the rights of female immigrant workers (De la Vega and Lozano-Batista 2005).

Unions and others have used some of these treaties in an attempt to better protect immigrant workers. The American Federation of Labor–Congress of Industrial Organizations (AFL-CIO) and the Confederation of Mexican Workers brought a challenge to *Hoffman* under Convention 87 of the ILO. The ILO Committee on Freedom of Association condemned *Hoffman* and asked the United States to reconsider the legal rights of undocumented workers. In addition, in response to a request from the Mexican government, the Inter-American Court of Human Rights (IACHR) issued an advisory opinion that concluded that *Hoffman* violated the human rights of workers, which include certain labor rights and equal access to courts to protect these rights (Ontiveros 2004). The decision of the IACHR focused on the Charter of the Organization of American States and other customary international law in reaching its decision.

The North American Agreement on Labor Cooperation (NAALC), sometimes referred to as the labor side agreement to the North American Free Trade Agreement (NAFTA), has also emerged as a major tool for defining the rights of migrant workers in the United States. The NAALC requires that each signatory nation enforce its own laws as they relate to a variety of labor principles. Parties may file a submission with the National Administrative Office (now called the Office of Trade Agreement Implementation in the United States) of a member country to protest the lack of labor protection in a different country. The first group of submissions filed under the NAALC dealt with the rights of workers in Mexico.

Beginning in 1995, however, a number of submissions have been filed that address the rights of migrant workers in the United States. The first submission filed in Mexico regarding labor practices in the United States addressed the sudden closure by Sprint Corporation of its subsidiary La Connexion Familiar, the day before a union election was to be held. Although the submission focused on the effect of plant closures on the principle of freedom of association and the right to organize, most of the workers at La Connexion Familiar were female Mexican immigrants. The submission, filed in 1995, provided an opportunity for the Communications Workers of America (CWA), the Mexican Telephone Workers' Union (STRM), and the Canadian Communications, Energy and Paperworkers Union to work together and recognize the commonality of their problems. Sprint had closed a facility being organized by the CWA; Sprint was also set to begin a joint venture with the Mexican telephone company Telmex, where its policies could adversely affect the members of STRM (Kay 2006).

In 1998, two more submissions were filed that dealt with migrant workers in the United States—one regarding immigrants who picked apples in Washington state and the other dealing with poultry farm workers in Maine. Unlike the earlier Sprint case, these submissions directly addressed the rights and protections guaranteed to migrant workers. The Washington apple case, in particular, continued the development of transnational labor alliances. The International Brotherhood of Teamsters (IBT) worked closely with Frente Autentico del Trabajo (FAT), a confederation of Mexico's independent unions, on the submission. The collaboration allowed the unions to establish trust, which had been undermined by the negative aspects of the IBT cross-border trucking campaign. It also provided the IBT with the opportunity to understand the problems that apple pickers and other produce workers face in Mexico (Kay 2006).

These submissions have had a variety of positive results. The substantive outcome of the early submissions were modest: ministerial consultations between the U.S. Secretary of Labor and the Mexican Secretary of Labor; public outreach forums with migrant workers in Washington and Maine; and government-to-government meetings between the USDL and the Mexican Department of Labor to discuss the collective bargaining, discrimination, and health and safety concerns raised by migrants. One major result of the submission process has been the development of close relationships among unions in Mexico, Canada, and the United States (Kay 2005). In addition, the submission process has arguably begun the development of a set of North American labor rights available to any North American citizen (Kay 2006). These rights are significant because they address the full breadth of the work-related problems female immigrant workers face. They seek to create a set of rights that will be fully applicable to them, even if they are not the ideal worker.

In addition, there have been two substantive victories associated with the submission process, even though the outcomes did not directly result from the submissions. The first occurred in 1998, when the Yale Law School Workers'

Rights Project and other organizations challenged a 1992 agreement between the USDL and the Immigration and Naturalization Service (INS) whereby the USDL shared information, including immigration status, with the INS. This practice dissuaded undocumented immigrants from filing charges to protect their rights. As a result of the submission and a change in the USDL administration, the agreement was reversed and the USDL committed to no longer inspecting or reporting on immigration status (Wishnie 2002). Unions and others continue to use the submission process to challenge the ways in which United States law excludes immigrant workers. The most recent submission, filed by the Brennan Center for Justice at New York University School of Law and Michael Dale of the Northwest Workers' Justice Project in 2005, challenges the U.S. policy that prohibits Legal Service Corporation grantees from representing immigrants on H-2B and other visas. This submission is significant in that it is trying to establish the right to counsel as part of the rights granted under the NAALC (Dale, Andrade, and Abel 2005).

The second major victory associated with a NAALC submission occurred in North Carolina in 2004. The Farm Labor Organizing Committee (FLOC) of the AFL-CIO, has been working for years to improve the treatment of farmworkers in North Carolina and, for the last five years, has led a boycott against the Mount Olive Pickle Co., focusing on the plight of cucumber pickers. Many of the workers at these farms are guest workers on H-2A visas; others are undocumented workers. In 2003, the Farmworker Justice Fund, Inc., and Central Independiente de Obreros Agricolas y Campesinos (CIOAC) filed a submission in Mexico challenging the treatment of H-2A migrant workers in North Carolina. The Mexican government accepted the submission and began an investigation. In 2004, FLOC signed two historic labor agreements—one with the North Carolina Growers Association (representing over one thousand farms) and one with Mount Olive Pickle Co. (which buys much of its produce from the Growers Association).[11]

The agreements affect over eight thousand migrant workers in sectors including cucumbers, tobacco, and Christmas trees. The Growers Association agreement is the first union contract ever signed by farmers in North Carolina, and it is the first union contract explicitly covering guest workers (Greenhouse 2004a).[12] The Growers Contract provides for a nondiscrimination clause, a three-step grievance procedure, camp representatives to help ensure workers' rights, and a seniority system to end an alleged blacklist of workers who sought to protect their rights. The Mount Olive agreement raises the price the company pays to both its workers and the growers, and it pro-

[11] Farm Labor Organizing Committee Press Release, "Precedent Setting Agreement Reached, Mt. Olive Pickle Boycott Over," 2004, http://www.floc.com/html/presskit.html (accessed June 30, 2006).
[12] Ibid.

vides for ongoing discussions with various organizations on ways to improve farmworker housing and health care, as well as discussions with the Mexican government on the bribery and blackmail practiced by the recruiters of migrant workers in Mexico. These agreements appear to address the problems raised in the NAALC submission and provide immigrant workers with a true opportunity to participate in the protection of their legal rights. It also recognizes that immigrant workers are entitled to the same core labor rights as other workers.

Hope Lies in Innovation

The legal system in the United States can provide for some protection of workers. For the most part, however, female immigrant workers have fallen outside these protections. Our laws fail to protect them because their problems go beyond the scope of what the current law categorizes as labor and employment problems and because they are not seen as legitimate workers. Hope lies in innovative domestic and international legal approaches that address the problems of female immigrant workers through a framework based on a concern for human rights, civil rights, citizenship rights, and workers' rights. An alternative vision of workplace protection that encompasses this view will benefit all workers, not just female immigrant workers.

13

WOMEN CROSSING BORDERS TO ORGANIZE

Katie Quan

When President Bill Clinton signed the labor side agreements to the North American Free Trade Agreement (NAFTA) in 1993, he promised that it would create 1 million more jobs within five years and return the United States to prosperity.[1] But since that time, free trade and the new economic structures Clinton talked about have led to decidedly mixed results for the U.S. middle class. Although lowering tariffs and other trade barriers may have led to cheaper prices at the local Wal-Mart, this has happened at a tremendous economic and social cost. Over 1 million U.S. jobs have been displaced by NAFTA, and many workers who are lucky enough to keep their jobs find themselves under constant pressure from their employers to increase productivity by lowering wages and benefits.[2] Class disparities continue to widen as well (see McCall, chap. 1 in this volume).

Nor have Mexican workers benefited from NAFTA. Since free trade opened up between the United States and Mexico, the top 10 percent of Mexican households have increased their share of national income while the remaining 90 percent have either lost income share or not seen any change (Polaski 2004). This increase in poverty has led to bitter labor struggles in which

[1] William Jefferson Clinton, "Remarks by President Clinton in Signing the NAFTA Side Agreements," 2005, http://clinton6.nara.gov/1993/09/1993-09-14-remarks-by-clinton-and-former-presidents-on-nafta.html (accessed September 10, 2006).

[2] Robert E. Scott and David Ratner, "NAFTA's Cautionary Tale," July 20, 2005, Economic Policy Institute Issue Brief no. 214, http://www.epi.org/content.cfm/ib214 (accessed December 1, 2005).

worker activists face employer opposition and corrupt governments (Bacon 2005).

Before the 1990s, globalization was characterized primarily by textile, auto, steel, and other manufacturing industries moving product assembly offshore. However, in the past two decades, jobs in the service sector have also been outsourced in industries such as retail sales, data processing, and customer service. Not long ago, regionally based trade agreements such as NAFTA were the main trade strategies, but now the World Trade Organization has established a new era in which the whole world is being brought under a central free trade system. Increasingly, we live in an integrated global economy in which labor markets are global and workers are drawn more closely than ever into a common set of concerns (Quan 2004).

Traditionally, the counterweight to corporate greed has been the labor unions, but in the global economy the power of unions has diminished greatly. Heavily unionized industries are often the first to be slated for plant closure and outsourcing because union labor costs are higher. This, in turn, has a chilling effect on those nonunion workers who want to organize because the threat of plant closure intimidates workers who need steady incomes to feed their families and pay bills. Moreover, multinational corporations often actively seek to outsource to locations where unions are banned or weak. Countries such as Bangladesh expressly prohibit union formation in export processing zones, others such as Mexico encourage company unions that help employers control workers, and some such as China prohibit the formation of independent unions.

Unlike multinational corporations that maintain a central global headquarters with subsidiaries in various countries, unions are currently fragmented and unable to represent global labor markets. Existing union federations such as the International Confederation of Free Trade Unions (ICFTU) and sector-based global union federations bring national unions together in alliances, but they are loose federations and do not generally take on centralized organizing or collective bargaining.

In the absence of unions organizing globally, a number of nongovernmental organizations (NGOs) have stepped forward to promote labor rights. The most well known of these are the human rights groups that, along with unions, lead the antisweatshop campaigns. Their efforts mobilize consumers to force retailers and manufacturers such as Nike and Gap to adopt labor standards that apply to the factories of their suppliers, and they have spawned consumer campaigns for ethical purchasing among universities and local governments.[3] In

[3] For resources on the antisweatshop movement, see http://www.sweatshopwatch.org (accessed September 10, 2006); http://www.studentsagainstsweatshops.org (accessed September 10, 2006); http://www.sweatfree.org (accessed September 10, 2006).

the past decade and a half, this movement has succeeded in linking labor rights with human rights, and by most accounts it has prevented the worst forms of exploitation. However, it is not clear how many workers have actually formed unions as a result of these efforts.

Some unions have also experimented with campaign-based strategies that build cross-border solidarity around organizing efforts at particular companies. Not surprisingly, many of these campaigns involve women workers because the earliest foreign-investment programs concentrated on light manufacturing in sectors such as apparel, toy, and electronics, in which women workers were easily exploited. Women were paid very little, worked unbelievably long hours, and were subject to sexual harassment and physical abuse (Fuentes and Ehrenreich 1983). However, to the surprise of many, these women workers have been far from submissive, and in many countries they have braved tremendous obstacles to organize their co-workers and assert their rights. Not only have they organized in their own plants, but they have also engaged in complex multinational struggles that have brought powerful corporations to the bargaining table. Women workers are on the cutting edge of global labor organizing today.

In this chapter, I examine three campaigns involving women workers organizing across borders. I analyze why the workers decided to engage in cross-border organizing, what benefits they gained from this, and what role their supporters played. Then I compare the three organizing strategies to note the similarities and differences among them and draw observations about gender issues in organizing. Finally, I discuss the implications of these three case studies for future labor organizing.

The cases I analyze were selected from suggestions from over a dozen union-organizing leaders. They were chosen to show a range of actors, geographical locations, organizing strategies, and best practices. None of these campaigns has previously been comprehensively studied and documented.

The research for this study was carried out by semi-structured interviews with primary participants in the campaigns. Using information gained in these interviews and from studying public and nonpublic documents about the campaigns, I then approached other key players in an iterative process. Where rank and file workers might encounter employer or government reprisals as a result of being referenced here, I have changed the names of the workers; otherwise all names are real.

I disclose that I am acquainted with some of these informants from my previous work as a union leader in the Union of Needletrades Industrial and Textile Employees (UNITE) and from current volunteer work as a board director of Sweatshop Watch, the Workers Rights Consortium, and the International Labor Rights Fund.

The Sara Lee Campaign

Sara Lee is known to many in the United States as a food manufacturer, but it is much more. Gross sales total nearly $20 billion, and its holdings include textile and consumer products in addition to food products. It owns and operates apparel manufacturing facilities in *maquiladoras* (manufacturing zones that were established by the Mexican government for foreign investment). Working conditions in *maquiladoras* are notorious for being exploitative and repressive; workers struggle to earn $20–30 per week—not even half of a living wage—and regularly work ten to twelve hours per day. The majority of the workers are women, who often live with their families in *colonias* (shanty neighborhoods) that are unsanitary and unsafe. In order to prevent them from effectively voicing protest, employers often establish company unions that represent the employers rather than the workers.

Betty Robles, like millions of *maquiladora* workers in Mexico, had seen more than enough to make her angry. As a garment worker, Betty had seen a co-worker get her finger smashed on the job and not be allowed to get medical attention, observed many women getting sick from toxins in the plants, and personally dealt with sexual harassment. So in the early 1980s she helped to form the Coahuila chapter of Service, Development and Peace (SEDEPAC), a community-based workers organization that would give women working in *maquiladoras* the skills to speak for themselves and tools to organize for better working conditions.

SEDEPAC is a women's organization whose staff members are all former factory workers in the Mexican textile industry. It was originally established in 1983 to provide a venue for women to organize outside of unions, which are male-dominated and often do not respect women's leadership. Its efforts are focused on popular education for women in the *maquiladora* factories. The workers must commit to the organization and attend weekly Friday meetings. Training topics include labor and human rights, federal labor law, labor negotiations, conflict resolution, reproductive health, and health and safety in the workplace. A number of courses focus specifically on women's issues, such as workplace discrimination and sexual harassment, domestic violence, and self-esteem.[4]

In 2001, many of the participants in SEDEPAC's classes were employed by Confecciones de Monclova, a garment factory of 1,200 workers in Frontera, Coahuila, that was owned and operated by the Sara Lee Corporation and produced apparel for Disney, Champion, Hanes, and others (Worker Rights Consortium 2005). Conditions there were well known to be particularly harsh. For

---

[4] Jessica Ponce, e-mail correspondence with Katie Quan, February 16, 2005.

ten years the company had regularly violated government laws requiring double pay on holidays, refused to pay a legally mandated holiday bonus in December, and cheated workers out of their profit-sharing bonus by falsely claiming financial loss. Injuries on the job were common, yet workers were forced to say that they were not work-related.

Women made up 80 percent of the workforce at this plant, and they routinely faced sexual harassment and abuse. Management forced them to take pregnancy tests every three months.[5] In some cases women were required to show soiled sanitary napkins to prove they were having menstrual cycles.[6] Some workers who got pregnant were fired. Others who did not get fired were forced to work at the same pace as nonpregnant workers and were not given permission to see a doctor when they became ill. Many were eventually pressured to quit their jobs or were fired for being absent from work for maternity-related reasons.[7] It was not uncommon to see blood in the restrooms—the result of an abortion.[8]

There was a union in the plant that was affiliated with the Confederation of Mexican Workers, but that union regularly sided with management against the workers.[9] As a result of their training at SEDEPAC, however, the Sara Lee workers were ready to stand up for themselves. With help from Enlace,[10] an Oregon-based NGO, the workers and SEDEPAC began a campaign in 2000 to change the conditions of work at Monclova, including the unfair treatment of women workers. Their ultimate goal was to form an independent union that would be accountable to its membership.

Through a series of activities over the next two years, the workers steadily gained ground, but the company did not give in gracefully. It retaliated by firing a total of ten committee members and disciplining many more. To gain additional leverage, in June 2002 the Sara Lee workers, in collaboration with SEDEPAC and Enlace, decided to add an international dimension to their struggle by launching an international 10 for 10 Campaign, in which they demanded that Sara Lee pay $10 per day to workers in Coahuila, allow them to choose their own union, and commit to keeping the plant open—in exchange for a commitment by Sara Lee's consumers to pay 10 cents more for each garment purchased.

[5] Ibid.

[6] Veronica Carrizales, interview with Katie Quan, January 25, 2005, Berkeley, Calif.

[7] Jessica Ponce, e-mail correspondence, February 16, 2005.

[8] Betty Robles, telephone interview with Tomio Geron, February 2, 2005.

[9] Alan Howard, 2004, "The Women of Monclova," *Z Magazine Online*, 17(2), http://zmagsite.zmag .org/Feb2004/howard0204.html (accessed June 6, 2006).

[10] Enlace was formed in 1998 in Portland, Oregon, to build the capacity of immigrant and low-wage worker organizations to be more effective. Its main activities are leadership development and providing assistance to strategic campaigns. See the Enlace website, http://www.enlaceintl.org/wa/ enlace/ei/50/.

For the next two years, the Sara Lee workers reached out to unions, students, and community groups to tell their stories and gain support for their 10 for 10 Campaign. They asked supporters to join them in demonstrations at Sara Lee's Chicago headquarters, as well as at shareholders' meetings. Support committees were established in San Francisco, Boston, and New York, with organizations such as Jobs with Justice, the American Federation of Labor–Congress of Industrial Organizations (AFL-CIO), United Students Against Sweatshops, Neighbor-to-Neighbor, and dozens of other unions and community groups. Supporters also put pressure on university administrators and faculty who were on the Sara Lee Board of Directors. In a show of effective worldwide coordination, joint actions were held in numerous cities: Paris, Mumbai, London, Katmandu, Rome, Mexico City, Torreon, Frontera, Boston, Chicago, Tampa, New York, Los Angeles, Raleigh, and San Francisco. According to Peter Cervantes-Gautschi, Enlace executive director, it was the ability of a worldwide network of supporters to mess with Sara Lee that finally brought the company to the table.[11]

However, in April 2004 while Sara Lee was negotiating with the workers' new independent union CETRAUMP, the company announced the closure of the Monclova plant. The union had been negotiating with the assistance of the Workers Rights Consortium, an NGO charged with investigating labor standards violations in the production of U.S. university products made by Sara Lee. These talks had already produced a significant agreement allowing the workers to form a union of their choice—the first labor neutrality commitment by a transnational corporation in the *maquiladoras*. With the announcement of plant closure, however, negotiations shifted to demanding preferential rehire at other Sara Lee plants for all of the 250 Monclova workers. Largely because of the threat of losing university business, the company eventually agreed to this provision, and to date all of the ten worker leaders and over two hundred other workers have been rehired at a second Monclova plant. The remaining laid-off workers were given severance pay.

Other victories followed. In a letter dated September 22, 2004, Sara Lee's deputy general counsel, R. Henry Kleeman, stated in part, "employees at Monclova #2 may freely choose to belong, or not to belong, to a union of their choice and engage in lawful activities on behalf of that union without fear of retaliation."[12] Thus, after four long years of intense organizing, the Sara Lee workers had finally established the right to negotiate with their employer about wages, hours, and working conditions. The next challenge, according to SEDEPAC co-founder Betty Robles, "is to put a new system into place, one

---

[11] Peter Cervantes-Gautschi, telephone interview with Katie Quan, November 18, 2005.

[12] R. Henry Kleeman, letter to Scott Nova of Workers Rights Consortium dated September 22, 2004, copy on file at UC Berkeley Center for Labor Research and Education.

that respects the rights of the workers and assures Sara Lee shareholders and the public that the company is vigorously enforcing the highest global labor standards" (Robles 2003).

The Tainan Campaign

Tainan Enterprises is a $17.65 million Taiwanese firm with factories in China, Cambodia, Indonesia, and Taiwan that manufactures apparel for brands such as Gap, Land's End, and Ann Taylor. In May 2000, it opened a plant in San Bartolo, El Salvador's oldest free trade zone (FTZ), which, like Mexican *maquiladoras,* not only provides economic incentives to investors in the form of low wages and long working hours but also offers a nonunion environment. Of the 230 firms in El Salvador's FTZs, not one had won a union contract when this campaign took place (Worker Rights Consortium 2003).

On the wall of the Tainan workers' union hall in San Salvador, there is a conspicuous photo of an Asian man along with a letter of support that he wrote for them. The man is Chea Vichea, a prominent Cambodian labor leader who had forced Tainan Enterprises to negotiate with their union by organizing Cambodian Tainan workers to refuse overtime work when the Salvadorean plant was shut down.[13] Vichea was later murdered at a demonstration in Cambodia for reasons that are unclear.[14] Nevertheless the workers in El Salvador still think of him as one of them and believe that, given the political repression in Cambodia, he took great personal risks to stand up for them.

In spring 2002, the Salvadoran union, the Textile Industry Workers Union (STIT), which represented a majority of employees in one of the two Tainan production facilities called TS2, requested collective bargaining. Tainan responded by shutting down the factory and laying off all the workers. The company claimed that this was due to a lack of orders, but because supervisors had warned that the factory would close as a result of union activity, it was pretty clear that this had been done to break the union (Worker Rights Consortium 2003).

The closure of TS2 was hard on the workers, the majority of whom were women. "Many of the women in the Tainan factory and the FTZ in El Salvador are, if not the sole source of income, the most important source of income in the household," explained Teresa Casertano, an organizer with the AFL-CIO's American Center for International Solidarity (Solidarity Cen-

---

[13] Teresa Casertano, telephone interview with Tomio Geron, March 10, 2005.

[14] Vichea's union, the Free Trade Union of the Workers of the Kingdom of Cambodia (FTUWKC), was supported by an opposition political party led by Sam Rainsy. Thus, Vichea's death could have been the result of party politics or labor organizing.

ter).[15] Women also take primary responsibility for the basic needs of their children, including education. When the plant closed, many workers were forced to remove their children from a year of school because they could not afford the school costs.[16]

In addition, workers were blacklisted from other nearby factories, so they could not get factory jobs elsewhere (Worker Rights Consortium 2003). Ana Hernandez[17] had to support her three children. "It hasn't been easy. We all get by doing whatever work we can. I make tamales, two hundred every three days, which I carry in a basket on my head and sell around my neighborhood."[18]

In El Salvador and many other countries, when a plant closes due to union activity or other reasons, typically workers such as Ana collect their severance pay and try to get a job elsewhere. In this case, however, eighty of the Tainan workers made the remarkable decision to refuse severance pay and instead to force the factory to reopen. Their reasoning was based on Salvadoran law, which says that firms must settle all outstanding legal claims before moving machinery off the premises. To prevent the company from moving, the union advised the workers not to accept severance pay. It also filed nearly sixty complaints against the company on various issues that kept legal cases pending.

This unprecedented decision to sacrifice individual economic security for strategic collective goals required incredibly strong organization. The union's philosophy was: "Nobody eats alone. If only one has food and eats, we all eat one bite."[19] Their process of organizing emphasized collective decision-making and communication. "Every email we received was read out loud in the group, as were news reports, investigations, reactions, everything," said Gilberto Garcia, the coordinator of Labor Studies and Support Center (CEAL), a community organization that supported the workers. "We'd often meet every other day." Decisions were not delegated to one person; instead, the workers were all expected to participate and make decisions together.[20]

Significantly, the ability of the Tainan women workers to stay organized and strong also depended on the union addressing their family needs. Because caring for children was exclusively the responsibility of women, the workers brought their children with them whenever they were organizing—whether to meetings with the labor minister or on house visits to their co-workers. "It de-

[15] See the Solidarity Center website, http://www.solidaritycenter.org (accessed September 10, 2006).

[16] Teresa Casertano, telephone interview with Tomio Geron, March 10, 2005.

[17] The name has been changed to protect the worker from possible reprisals.

[18] Ana Hernandez, interview with Todd Jailor, June 12, 2003, San Salvador.

[19] Teresa Casertano, telephone interview, March 10, 2005.

[20] Gilberto Garcia, interview with Todd Jailor, June 13, 2003, San Salvador.

fined their union in a lot of ways. It's not unusual for [these] workers to have boatloads of kids around," recalled Teresa Casertano.[21]

Realizing that the workers needed leverage beyond their boycott of severance pay, CEAL helped the workers contact international supporters that could put pressure on Tainan. Through the Solidarity Center, contacts were made with supporters both in Taiwan (where Tainan had its corporate headquarters) and in Cambodia and Indonesia (where Tainan had other production facilities). This was a strategic decision to make Tainan Enterprises, an international supplier, the primary target of the campaign rather than retailers or manufacturers at the top of the supply chain. "These international suppliers are no longer simply Mom and Pop contractors," said Jeff Hermanson, a Solidarity Center campaign director, "today they are multimillion dollar companies that can play a critical role in influencing both the workers and the retailers in the global supply chain."[22]

To gain support in Tainan's home base in Taiwan, the Solidarity Center reached out to a small labor solidarity organization called Focus on Globalization (FOG), an all-volunteer NGO made up of labor activists and academics. FOG conducted intensive research about Tainan's business and produced a corporate profile of its officers, its shareholders, the locations of its other factories, and its political and social connections in Taiwan. This information helped organizers to identify pressure points and targets for the campaign.[23] Much of this research was done in Chinese, and many materials would have been difficult to access outside Taiwan.

After doing the corporate research, FOG began a series of support activities on behalf of the Tainan workers. First, they contacted business clients of Tainan and asked them to persuade Tainan to reopen its El Salvador factory. They also contacted ruling party Democratic Progressive Party (DPP), the politicians who support Tainan's business dealings. "We told them this company violates human rights abroad," said Hsing-Hsin Chen of FOG. "[The company's] in trouble, don't back them up, or it will hurt you."

In addition, FOG contacted the Taiwan Presbyterian Church about initiating a human rights investigation because the church has an official platform supporting human rights and because the CEO of Tainan, Tony Yang, was a prominent leader in the church. FOG also organized a major demonstration at Tainan's headquarters. This protest action, with local unions such as the Taiwanese Confederation of Trade Unions, students, and religious groups, featured street theater in which an NGO character pushed Yang into hell (rep-

---

[21] Teresa Casertano, telephone interview, March 10, 2005.
[22] Jeff Hermanson, interview with Katie Quan, October 6, 2005 in Washington, D.C.
[23] Hsing-Hsin Chen, telephone interview with Tomio Geron, March 1, 2005.

resented by paper flames). Yang was extremely upset by the skit, and later that day company executives contacted FOG saying they wanted to talk.[24]

FOG played a key role in the subsequent negotiations, both in Taiwan and in El Salvador. FOG's Hsing-Hsin Chen played a mediator role, helping the two sides: one an employer that knew very little about union protocols and the other the Salvadoran union that did not know about Taiwanese employers.

To gain support in Indonesia and Cambodia, the Solidarity Center and UNITE reached out to their networks of labor supporters. In Indonesia, Tainan workers were not unionized, so their ability to directly challenge Tainan was limited. But Solidarity Center organizers were able to get four Indonesian unions to write a joint letter to Tainan; they also organized leafleting and demonstrations outside the Tainan plant.[25]

The Solidarity Center and UNITE set up an Internet chat between the workers in El Salvador and Indonesia. This chat provided an opportunity for workers to talk directly to one another in real time and gave them a strong sense that they faced similar conditions. Teresa Casertano recalled, "They talked about what kind of work they do, what kind of products they make, conditions in their factories, wage comparisons. Then they came down to, 'do you want to try to do things together?' The answer from Indonesia was 'YES YES.' This was really amazing."[26]

Cambodia was considered Tainan's "jewel in the operation," producing 60 percent of Tainan's production worldwide.[27] Cambodian Tainan workers had noticed that they were doing much more overtime work and suspected that the closure of the El Salvador plant was the reason. These workers were unionized, so they did have some ability to challenge management on the conditions of their work. They combined their own demands about conditions in the Cambodian shop with the demand to stop the closure of the El Salvador plant. Led by Chea Vichea of the Free Trade Union of Workers of the Kingdom of Cambodia, they wrote a letter to Tainan, saying "We know you closed and locked out brothers. . . . We refuse to be scabs for your lockout." In a show of economic solidarity, they then refused to work overtime for Tainan.

Meanwhile, in the United States, supportive organizations were pushing on other pressure points up the supply chain. The U.S. Labor Education and Action Project (USLEAP) approached U.S. businesses that sold Tainan products such as the Gap, Van Heusen, Foot Locker, and Ann Taylor, demanding that

---

[24] Ibid.

[25] "International Solidarity against the Runaway Factory—On Labor's Tri-Continental Linkage in Tainan Enterprises Campaign," in *Asian Transnational Corporation Outlook 2004: Asian TNCs, Workers and the Movement of Capital*. 2005. Hong Kong: Asian Transnational Corporation Monitoring Network and Asia Monitor Resource Centre, 355–67.

[26] Ibid.

[27] Samantha Tate, telephone interview with Tomio Geron, February 1, 2005.

they send letters to Tainan to reopen the factory. USLEAP and other organizations also targeted the retail establishments of these stores for protests, which got some companies to agree to send letters to Tainan.[28] Coincidentally, the U.S. textile workers union, UNITE, already had a campaign going on against Gap, so it incorporated the Tainan workers' demands into its platform.

Tainan was getting pressure from all sides—Taiwan, El Salvador, the United States, and now Indonesia and Cambodia. "That was one of the reasons why I believe Tainan came literally crying to us, saying you can destroy our company everywhere in the world," said Teresa Casertano.[29] In July 2003, Tainan made a business decision to re-open a factory for the TS2 workers, signifying an unprecedented victory for Ana Hernandez and the other Tainan workers who, like her, had spent more than a year organizing with their children in tow and selling tamales to make ends meet. Now they were able to go back to the factory and negotiate for improved working conditions for themselves and their families.

The Securitas Campaign

Securitas is the largest security services business in the world, doing $7.4 billion in sales. It is based in Sweden and does business in over twenty countries, mostly in Europe and North America. Whereas building security used to be owned by local businesses, in the past fifteen years it has become a globalized industry dominated by a few large multinational corporations. Securitas bought up well-known U.S. security firms such as Pinkerton, Burns, and Wells Fargo. It has 250,000 employees worldwide, 120,000 of them in the United States. Yet, although the corporation makes huge profits, the U.S. workers who generate those profits through their services barely earn a living.

Five pairs of pants, four pairs of socks, and three layers of coats were not enough to keep Jolyn Vance warm. Vance, who was working outdoors for the Chicago Transit Authority in the bitter Chicago cold, caught pneumonia on the job in 2001, and got fired for missing work. Security workers who work for the Chicago Transit Authority are actually employed by Securitas, and in 2001 they were not provided with health insurance and were paid so little that they could not afford to purchase it. "If my child gets sick, I have to go to the free clinic and wait for hours to be seen," recalled Jolyn Vance, "We work hard, but we still can't get by."[30]

A high percentage of these workers are African American women. Security

[28] Stephen Coats, telephone interview with Katie Quan, January 27, 2005.
[29] Teresa Casertano, telephone interview with Tomio Geron, March 10, 2005.
[30] Jolyn Vance, telephone interview with Tomio Geron, March 4, 2005.

services have traditionally been a male-dominated workforce, but women of color are increasingly filling these positions. For these women, the hazards of a security job are often heightened. Vance recalled, "You have to remember that you have areas in Chicago not fit for a woman to be in. Some of them are pretty dangerous. We had no weapons, or radios to contact anyone if anything were to occur. We were more or less on our own."[31]

Not only do female security guards face harassment from the public on the job because they are women, they also struggle against gender discrimination. According to Chicago-based rank and file leader Denise Dawson, "Being a woman working in security is very hard. We have a lot of competition as far as men [are] concerned. Regarding management we have to be careful; we have to work harder to get the respect we deserve."[32]

In 2000, the Service Employees International Union (SEIU) started a nationwide campaign to organize security guards. The union saw that strategically it made sense because security guards work side by side with the union's members in its three key divisions: public sector, health care, and building services. The organizing program's first target company was Securitas because it was the industry's largest employer and would set the standard for other guard-contracting firms to follow in this fiercely competitive industry.[33]

But forming a union was not easy. First, the Securitas managers in the United States responded to SEIU in a hostile manner, sending threatening letters to their employees and telling the SEIU that they would not agree to voluntarily recognize it. Second, the union faced legal complications—the National Labor Relations Act (NLRA) does not allow security guards to vote to join a mixed union, such as SEIU, that has workers in it other than guards. In this context, a critical challenge for the union was to bypass the NLRA election rules and get Securitas voluntarily to recognize SEIU once the union could show that the majority of the workers supported it.[34]

To neutralize employer opposition, the union targeted up the service supply chain to the building owners and up the corporate ladder to the Securitas headquarters in Sweden. Organizers approached real estate and investment trusts and private-sector owners, warning that Securitas had adopted an anti-union position that might lead to a labor dispute. Neither the investment trusts or the private building owners wanted union problems with SEIU, given its well-known activism in the janitorial sector, so they agreed to be neutral.

To approach Securitas itself, SEIU reached out to the Swedish Transport Workers' Union (STWU), which represents the Securitas workers in the company's home country. STWU then contacted the European Transport Workers

---

[31] Ibid.

[32] Denise Dawson, telephone interview with Tomio Geron, March 15, 2005.

[33] Jono Schaffer, telephone interview with Katie Quan, February 24, 2005.

[34] Ibid.

Federation (ETWF), and the ETWF issued a strong public statement about the unfair treatment of U.S. Securitas workers, which was widely publicized in Europe and was deeply embarrassing to the company.[35]

In February 2003, STWU sent a delegation of leaders, including its international secretary Lars Lindgren, to Chicago to observe the conditions of the U.S. Securitas workers. SEIU activist Mona Ballenger recalls, "We showed them the security conditions we have to work in, with no weapons. When they saw the conditions that our members worked and lived in, they were almost crying. They were heartbroken."[36] Lindgren was most struck by the "lack of respect for working people. I was very sad when I realized that the U.S. is almost a 'Banana Republic' in terms of the rights of the working class."[37]

Lindgren returned to Sweden and demanded that Securitas negotiate fairly with its U.S. workers. With 80 percent labor market density in Sweden, STWU was not afraid of the company. Later that month, the CEO of Securitas, Thomas Berglund, met with the workers in Chicago. Jolyn Vance was one of those workers. "I let him know my kids were small. I'm raising them myself. My husband is deceased. I cannot make it on the money they pay us. I told him I don't think it's fair that I'm working for you and I can't get any benefits for my children or me." Berglund returned to Europe determined to settle this issue. He viewed unions as an asset and as institutions that promote good relations at the workplace. On March 13, 2003, Securitas agreed to a framework agreement that allowed the workers to form a union through card-check neutrality. Finally, Vance and her co-workers were able to negotiate a union contract that brought health insurance benefits to her and her family.

"It was a critical experience, something I'll never forget," recalled Joyce Grantham, SEIU organizer. "[The Swedes are] so passionate about what's going on in America. They [told] Securitas CEO Thomas Berglund that: in America if you mess with these people we're gonna make trouble for you at home."[38] This experience led SEIU staff and members alike to realize that solidarity is not just U.S. workers helping others; it is others coming to the aid of U.S. workers as well.

Based on the success of this campaign and others, SEIU is now stepping up global organizing. The union has hired a full-time staffer in the Geneva office of the Union Network International (UNI), the general union federation of service workers, who will coordinate international campaigns involving SEIU and European unions. According to Stephen Lerner, SEIU senior organizing director, "We're taking the union to a higher level now. Through UNI we are targeting two security companies and two cleaning companies." Lerner enu-

[35] Ibid.
[36] Mona Ballenger, telephone interview with Tomio Geron, February 24, 2005.
[37] Lars Lindgren, e-mail correspondence with Tomio Geron, March 10, 2005.
[38] Julia Grantham, telephone interview with Tomio Geron, March 8, 2005.

merated the goals: "to get majority membership in these companies; to identify places in Latin America, Africa, and Asia where we can get recognition; to negotiate global frameworks and local contracts, and to turn the property service section into a global union. We need to go way beyond solidarity."[39]

Why Go International?

From our case studies, it is clear that employer opposition was making local organizing impossible and that without the intervention of international supporters the workers would probably not have won. At Securitas, only when the Swedish unions put pressure on the Swedish corporate head office did the U.S. management change its anti-union practices. At Tainan, only when Indonesian workers, Cambodian unions, Taiwanese NGOs, and U.S. consumers jointly applied pressure did the company feel compelled to negotiate. At Sara Lee in Mexico, only when union and human rights supporters intervened did the company agree to rehire the fired workers.

These campaigns also went international because their multinational employers created globalized labor relations. Securitas made natural allies of SEIU and STWU because, as representatives of guards who work for Securitas, they had a common interest in helping one another. Similarly, the Tainan workers in El Salvador, Indonesia, and Cambodia all worked for the same employer, which meant that Cambodians refusing to work overtime had a real economic effect on the company that helped the Salvadorans.

Last, the workers built international campaigns because they had access to international networks. The Sara Lee and Tainan workers relied heavily on existing progressive union networks in the United States and anti-sweatshop networks internationally. The Securitas workers got to their Swedish employer through existing unions and federations. Without help from their unions or local NGOs, workers would have found it hard to tap into existing international labor support networks to carry out international campaigns.

The Role of International Supporters

Research assistance provided by international allies made a crucial difference. The Tainan workers got information about their employer from FOG. Similarly, research provided from the Securitas Workers Council and European unions proved to be so important that the SEIU hired a new staff person to

---

[39] Stephen Lerner, telephone interview with Katie Quan and Tomio Geron, February 3, 2005.

live in Europe and continue to do research and relationship-building for the union.

Workers in all cases relied on supporters for education and training as well as advice about various aspects of their organizing strategies. Sara Lee workers got advice about building a series of actions on the job from SEDEPAC and Enlace. Tainan workers got advice about ways to use severance law from CEAL and the Solidarity Center. And Securitas workers got advice about mobilizing European support from UNI and the STWU. Without advice of this kind, it would have been hard for inexperienced workers to chart complex strategy against multinational corporations.

In the Securitas and Tainan cases, supporters played another critical role in bridging a communication gap between the employer and employees, which enabled the disputes to be settled. In the Securitas case, the STWU helped SEIU bypass the anti-union U.S. Securitas management and go directly to the pro-union CEO in Sweden. In the Tainan case, FOG explained the concerns of the Latin American workers to its Taiwanese employer.

Perhaps the most important role that supporters played was to carry out solidarity actions in various countries. Enlace and its networks helped the Sara Lee workers carry out same-day actions in numerous countries. The Solidarity Center helped the Tainan worker surround their employer with economic and public pressure in El Salvador, Cambodia, Indonesia, the United States, and Taiwan. UNI helped the Securitas workers mobilize European unions to shame the CEO.

How the Strategies Differed

All these cases involved international campaigns, but they used different strategies to win. Confecciones de Monclova was owned and operated by the Sara Lee Corporation, so the workers chose Sara Lee as their target of organizing. Like most anti-sweatshop campaigns, the key legs of their strategy were media attention to exploited women workers and lots of grassroots e-mails and demonstrations calling for corporate accountability. Significantly, it was the Worker Rights Consortium report on university labor codes violations that finally led to direct negotiations with the company and brought about a final resolution.

In contrast, in the Securitas campaign, the SEIU chose not to make the primary target of its campaign the U.S. building owners or other companies who contracted security guard firms; instead, the union decided to target the international corporation that subcontracted security guards. It reached out to existing international bodies such as UNI, requesting assistance. Because the European unions were strong, their efforts succeeded relatively quickly and comparatively little other grassroots campaigning took place.

Finally, in the Tainan case, organizers again chose not to target up the supply chain to the retail brands, as has been done in most other anti-sweatshop cases, but instead to target the subcontractor level. To do this, the Solidarity Center reached out both to unions and NGOs to apply pressure worldwide.

Role of Women

In a globalized economy based on the exploitation of low-wage workers, it is not a coincidence that those most affected are women. Since the last century, women have been specifically recruited from impoverished rural areas to work in export-processing zones, where they are deemed easily exploitable and unlikely to stand up for their rights. As globalization expands, we can expect that this systematic recruitment of women workers to extend to other areas, especially the low-wage service sector.

The women workers in our case studies are examples of the harsh exploitation of women in the global economy. The Tainan women were treated so badly that they decided to organize a union, which prompted the employer to close their plant. Beyond typical low wages and long hours, the Sara Lee workers suffered the additional indignity of being required to show soiled sanitary napkins to prove that they were not pregnant or were fired when they did get pregnant, practices that are typical in many export processing plants in Latin America. The Securitas women guards stated that their jobs were more dangerous because they were women and that they needed to work twice as hard as men to gain respect, a common problem when women enter job fields that have been traditionally dominated by men.

Off the job, the women were still working, often shouldering all the responsibilities for their families. Many Securitas guards were single mothers, and Jolyn Vance grounded her pitch to CEO Thomas Berglund in her family. This reflected her priorities—what she was responsible for and what she cared about. Thousands of miles away in El Salvador, priorities were the same for the Tainan women, who often carried the burden of paying for their children's education even when they were laid off and their husbands still worked.

Gender differences arose in the context of organizing as well because organizing women is different from organizing men. The Tainan workers talked about bringing their kids to meetings, and the SEDEPAC trainings included a focus on sexual harassment, domestic violence, and esteem-building. SEDEPAC took gender organizing one step further by establishing itself as a women's organization, explicitly to give women an opportunity to share experiences, find a common voice, and develop leadership abilities free of the gendered power tensions that can arise in organizations of men and women.

Women's leadership was quite evident at the grassroots level. The case studies only hint at the incredible economic sacrifices of Ana Hernandez and her co-workers and their families at Tainan, the commitment and perseverance of union officers such as Jolyn Vance and Denise Dawson, and the visionary leadership of Betty Robles. NGO and union staffers such as Teresa Casertano of the Solidarity Center and Joyce Grantham of SEIU also played key roles in linking the grassroots efforts to the international campaigns. Less clear from the case studies is the role women played in developing the overall strategies for the international campaigns because the leaders of the NGOs and unions that were key advisors on international strategies were all men.

An issue in need of further study is the role of women's organizations in these kinds of cross-border labor struggles. The women's movement has typically stood against discrimination and inequality. Yet only one of the informants in these case studies mentioned support from women's groups other than the support that the Sara Lee workers got from SEDEPAC. Women's economic concerns, such as access to employment at Tainan, low wages at Sara Lee, and health-care insurance at Securitas, can effectively be addressed through negotiating good union contracts, and leadership development can be encouraged by local NGOs such as SEDEPAC. Yet the broader societal issues of social inequality affecting women workers, such as Salvadoran men not sharing in their children's educational responsibilities or U.S. men taking advantage of women security guards, will need the support of a larger women's movement that works to build respect for women of all classes if they are to be resolved.

Lessons for Global Organizing

If unions want to strengthen their position in the face of global corporations, they need to organize internationally. Some clues for how to do this effectively can be gleaned from these three case studies. International support networks, whether NGO networks or international union structures, were critical to the success of these campaigns. In the Sara Lee and Tainan cases, local NGOs linked with international NGOs. In the Securitas case, workers accessed international support through international union structures. Thus, strengthening the capacity of intermediary organizations such as NGOs to reach out to workers and making international union structures responsive to organizing campaigns should be a high priority.

New communication technology also proved crucial. The Sara Lee and

Tainan workers used e-mail Listservs to communicate with their supporters, and the Tainan workers used the Internet to chat with their counterparts in Indonesia and Cambodia. In global campaigns that take place over many time zones with different languages spoken, new technologies may help to bridge gaps in building worker unity, carrying out joint action, doing shared research, and other important functions of campaigns.

If unions are to successfully organize the new global workforce, they also need to pay attention to the specific concerns of women. They need to organize women as women. We have seen that SEDEPAC was established for women workers to have a space to build leadership insulated from the atmosphere in which organizing is dominated by men. This strategy made explicit use of the strong affinity that women workers have as a sex and created a safe space where they could share common concerns and develop the confidence to carry out organizing plans for the entire plant (including the men). Its success points to the need to develop gender-conscious models of organizing and to encourage such actions as framing union demands so that women's concerns are met, forming organizational structures that generate the increased participation of women, and establishing programs that strengthen women leaders. In addition, more can be done to tap women supporters who might not necessarily be focused on labor, such as women's human rights groups, educators, and researchers.

Finally, in terms of maximizing the gains made from international campaigns, the question arises as to how to replicate these successful cross-border organizing campaigns on a permanent basis. By definition, campaigns are temporal, and after they end the organizers move on, taking with them the valuable relationships and knowledge base. However, if unions and NGOs are to build an internal infrastructure that enables international organizing to take place on a more permanent basis, resources need to be allocated to accomplish this. From the Securitas case, we see that SEIU has made the first step by investing in staff and charting plans to organize on an international scale. But unions need to create new structures that facilitate cross-border cooperation and closer local and global ties to NGOs and other civic and community associations.

The lessons of international organizing campaigns can be applied to union activities other than organizing. If international campaigns made workers more powerful in organizing, then it makes sense that cross-border collective bargaining, education, research and political activity may also make unions stronger. A very few unions have attempted cross-border collective bargaining, but none has sustained these efforts. And the international education, research, and policy-level activity that takes place is currently small scale. For unions to influence global labor markets on a scale that can effectively counterweigh the increasing power of multinational corporations and international financial institutions, a greater consideration of multinational collective bargaining and other union activities is warranted. Otherwise, the current imbalance of power in global labor markets is only likely to grow.

On the whole, globalization has resulted in a greater consolidation of power for corporations and corporate institutions at the expense of workers. For Ana Hernandez, Betty Robles, Jolyn Vance, and their co-workers, the path to a better life has been to organize and fight for their rights, and in doing so they have built complex campaigns that point the way forward for all workers in the global economy. The role of strong, courageous women such as Jolyn Vance, Ana Hernandez, and Betty Robles cannot be underestimated or overstated. While fighting for their jobs and their families, they proved to be a formidable force against powerful multinational companies. Much more has to be done to bring their wisdom and leadership to the rest of us.

14

REPRESENTING INFORMAL ECONOMY WORKERS

EMERGING GLOBAL STRATEGIES AND THEIR LESSONS
FOR NORTH AMERICAN UNIONS

Leah F. Vosko

The size of the informal economy poses a monumental challenge to unions internationally. According to the International Labour Organisation ([ILO] 2002b, 6), the informal economy is particularly significant in industrializing countries in the geographic South, where it makes up one-half to three-quarters of nonagricultural employment. The informal economy encompasses workers including own account workers[1] engaged in survival activities, paid domestic workers, home workers (registered and unregistered), workers in sweatshops who are "disguised wage workers," and the self-employed in micro-enterprises operating on their own or with unpaid family workers (ILO 2002a, 2). The informal economy is deeply gendered; it links unpaid subsistence work or poorly paid work in the domestic sector and other spaces of social reproduction, performed mainly by women, and unregulated income generation (Prügl 1999; Prügl and Tinker 1996). Informal economy workers are not recognized. They lack protection under existing regulatory frameworks. They thereby stand outside the traditional trade union movement, and

The research for this chapter was made possible by a project on Workers and Social Cohesion funded by the Social Sciences and Humanities Research Council of Canada. I am grateful to the representatives of official trade unions, new unions, and feminist nongovernmental organizations that permitted me to engage in participant observation as well as to Dorothy Sue Cobble, Christina Gabriel, and V. Spike Peterson for their comments on earlier versions of this chapter.

[1] Own account workers are small-scale producers or service providers, found largely in industrializing contexts, who are part of the unregulated economy and not covered by existing labor laws and policies.

their frequent misclassification as either micro-entrepreneurs or subsistence producers exacerbates this exclusion and invisibility.

The working conditions of informal economy workers is a serious cause for concern for scholars and practitioners, including those tied to the traditional trade union movement who perceive the situation of these poorer workers as a threat to the living standards of workers in the geographic North. Such concerns, and the anxieties they provoke, contribute to a tendency to downplay the magnitude of the informal economy and overlook innovative global strategies for representation in discussions of how best to respond to the impasse in North American trade unionism. Yet contemporary organizing efforts of informal economy workers and workers' associations offer vital lessons for those concerned about strengthening labor organizations and expanding representation to include workers outside the ranks of traditional unions.

This chapter canvasses emerging strategies for organizing and representing informal economy workers in an attempt to draw insights for North American unions seeking to mitigate precarious employment and foster gender equity. I begin by conceptualizing the informal economy and describing its growth in the geographic South as well as the corresponding gendered rise of precarious employment in the United States and Canada. Next, I sketch three emergent organizational forms aimed at raising working and living standards for informal economy workers: new official trade unions, nongovernmental organizations (NGOs) focused on labor issues, and transnational feminist networks. I then offer an analysis of a debate at the International Labour Conference in June 2002 between representatives of these emergent organizational forms and the traditional trade union movement over how best to represent informal economy workers. The chapter concludes with a synthesis of what North America labor movements can learn from emergent global strategies centering on the informal economy, especially organizational forms seeking to fill the vacuum where models of trade union representation dominant since World War II are not viable.

Conceptualizing and Measuring the Informal Economy

The informal economy is a contested concept. Until the mid-1970s, the term *informal sector* dominated scholarly discourse, and it was used to denote income-generating activities of the working poor that are not recognized, recorded, or regulated by public authorities (Hart 1973). In the late 1980s, however, analysts began to view this term as a misleading moniker due to the heterogeneous set of the relationships it encompassed (Beneria 2001; Portes and Sassen 1987; Lim 2002). They also acknowledged a central and underrecognized issue—the process of informalization, marked by the increasing resort to subcontracting and eroding employment relationships, apparent in both industrializing and industrialized countries. This recognition gave rise to a consensus that the word *sector* cultivates a false dichotomy between formal and informal that led the concept informal economy to come into widespread use.[2]

The most reliable statistics on the informal economy, made available by the International Labour Organisation (ILO), cover a range of countries in Latin America, Africa, Asia, and Central and Eastern Europe (ILO 2002b, 11).[3] These statistics make it possible to sketch the main patterns and trends, as well as the principal features, of what is understood loosely as the informal economy. Countries in West and East Africa, South Asia, and the Andean region report the highest proportions of informal employment. Informal employment is also significant in Latin America, where it grew especially in the urban areas in the 1990s. In contrast, countries in Central and Eastern Europe report that it is growing but still less significant than in the geographic South. In about half of the countries for which data are available, the share of informal employment is higher for women than for men. But the fact that women often engage in multiple activities, many of which are either unpaid or traded for basic commodities, exacerbates their invisibility in official statistics, which assume a Western industrial single-occupation/worksite norm (ILO 2002a, 12).

The character of the informal economy in transition and industrialized countries is quite distinct from that in the geographic South; in these contexts, informal economy work centers less on subsistence activities and more on unregulated income generation. At the same time, global relations of inequality are also at play in the geographic North; for example, many migrant and undocumented workers engage in informal employment in southern Europe (ILO 2002a, 24). In the United States, too, employment characterized by unregulated and underregulated labor and unregulated or unlicensed enterprises exists in such sectors as garment and electronics, and in border regions as well as right-to-work states. As feminist scholars have long argued, these processes are tied to a reallocation of production whereby many women workers, (im)migrant workers, and workers of color labor under sweatshop conditions in the geographic North common to those in the informal employment in the

---

[2] Although I recognize the importance of these conceptual debates, I bracket them in this chapter for two reasons: to respect workers' self-definition and to focus attention on workers in situations which require protection because of the nature of the work in which they engage and the presence of large-scale unregulated income generated in the locations in which they labor. This second justification explains the chapter's focus on strategies emerging principally in the geographic South. My narrow aim is to sketch the strategies of groups of self-identified informal economy workers to improve their conditions as well as the representational challenges and opportunities these workers and their organizations pose for labor movements.

[3] These statistics apply the definition adopted by the Fifteenth International Conference of Labor Statisticians, which covers informal sector enterprises (or nonregistered units) and provides information on enterprises and workforces but offers limited insight into informalization.

South (Nash and Fernández-Kelly 1983; Ward 1990). Through global commodity and value chains, the phenomenon of informal employment in the geographic South and unprotected work in the North are linked in gendered ways (Mitter 1986).

The rise of precarious employment in the United States and Canada in the late twentieth century also corresponded to the persistence and, in some cases, the growth of the informal economy in the geographic South and transition economies in Europe. The precariously employed engage in forms of work characterized by limited access to labor and social protection, low pay, and high risks of ill health. They are distinct from informal economy workers in the geographic South who labor in the unregulated or shadow economy of income generation. However, they too often lack access to representation through unions (Vosko, Zukewich, and Cranford 2003; Barker and Christenson 1998). The gender of precariousness is also female in the United States and Canada. Women outnumber men in forms of employment, such as part-time temporary work, exhibiting the qualities of precariousness. Moreover, a gendering of jobs, whereby more precarious forms of work resemble so-called women's work in their conditions and quality, is affecting many women and some men, especially young men and men of color (Vosko 2000).

According to Standing (1997), seven securities characterized the era of labor market regulation in industrialized countries: labor market security, employment security, job security, work security, skill reproduction security, income security, and, most notably, representational security. In the post-1970 period, with the spread of precarious employment, these securities began to erode, ushering in an era of labor market deregulation, where precarious employment grew. One feature of this new era is deunionization, driven partly by the rise of contractualism and its constraining effects on union structures, policies, and strategies, including those defining who is part of the labor movement. In this context, North American unions are ill-equipped to respond to the new majority—that is, the many women, (im)migrants, and people of color working in precarious jobs that fall outside traditional union structures.

With the persistence of informal employment, many workers in the geographic South never benefited from the seven securities identified by Standing. In such contexts, struggles to secure better labor market regulation have cultivated representational forms responding to the needs of groups of informal economy workers, informed by gender-sensitive strategies. The approaches employed through such representational forms—from new official unions and labor NGOs to transnational feminist networks—are relevant to those concerned to strengthen labor organizations and expand representation to include workers currently outside the ranks of traditional trade unions in North America.

New Official Unions

New official unions of informal economy workers represent an emergent organizational form gaining prominence in industrializing countries and receiving considerable scholarly attention. These unions bring together "pragmatic persistence" and "aspiration for a cooperative economy" (Jhabvala 1995, 114). Operating both as welfare associations (drawing on cooperative economic strategies and social movement organizing to improve living standards for workers) and as trade unions (struggling for fair wages, decent working conditions, and protective laws), they weave together feminist visions of development and resistance.

The Self-Employed Women's Association (SEWA) of India is the most well-known example of a new union. SEWA originated out of the Textile Labor Association, a union of textile workers founded in 1920 by a woman inspired by Mahatma Gandhi, who supported creating organized collective strength and economic development through improving workers' consciousness. Certified as a registered trade union in 1972, and expanding rapidly since that time, it is devoted to a type of unionism attentive to all aspects of workers lives, from the workplace to the domestic sphere. Renana Jhabvala describes SEWA as an amalgam of the union movement, the cooperative movement, and the women's movement, while noting that "it was born in the labor movement with the idea that the self-employed [i.e., own account workers], like salaried employees have rights to fair wages, decent working conditions and protective laws. . . . and deserve recognition as a legitimate group of workers with status, dignity and the right to organize bodies to represent their interests publicly" (1995, 15). SEWA grew up in a decade in which women's rights became prominent on the international agenda, on the one hand, and in which own account work grew in India, especially among women, on the other hand.

In India today, over 90 percent of the workforce is in the informal economy (fully 94 percent of women workers) and own account work remains the dominant form of informal employment.[4] SEWA represents a large share of informal economy workers; its members, which number 700,000, fall into four groups cutting across various trades and services, including home-based workers, vendors, hawkers, laborers, and service providers, some of whom work in factories, and small producers.[5] SEWA presses for policy change at the state and municipal levels as well as the enforcement of laws to enable women workers to exercise their rights. The union also lobbies for laws on behalf of

[4] Namrata Bali, "We, the Self-Employed," 2005, *SEWA Newsletter* 1(1): 1, http://www.sewaacademy .org/maillist/images/logo.gif (accessed February 15, 2005).
[5] Ibid.

specific groups, such as street vendors seeking to access public space to sell their goods without harassment from municipal officials such as police. One of its primary victories in this arena is the passage in 2003 of a national policy on street vendors addressed to police, corporations, and town planners, enabling these own account workers to maintain their places in city bazaars and markets, although preserving vending spaces for women remains an ongoing struggle.[6] SEWA also works for the enforcement of laws such as those guaranteeing access to health care among groups such as *bidi* workers (or cigarette rollers), who are often confined to poorly ventilated workspaces, leading to high rates of tuberculosis, and of minimum wage laws, where they exist (Rose 1992, 124).

One of the unique features of the SEWA organizing approach is its view that cooperatives and unions may be combined in building a movement of informal economy workers. This commitment takes expression principally in its work with rural agricultural laborers, among milk sellers, and in the garment sector among quilt workers. In such cases, traditional tactics of trade unions, such as struggles for job security and decent wages, are combined with building producer and trade cooperatives, in which proceeds are invested in community social supports (such as improvements in housing and water supply) and in sustainable production practices and in which rates are set by producers collectively rather than by brokers or middlepersons, and with building social security cooperatives. SEWA leaders argue that cooperatives can contribute to improving wages or earnings by setting a standard among such groups as milksellers and embroiderers (Jhabvala 1995, 131). Correspondingly, in the *bidi* industry, union knowledge of the industry can help cooperatives organize more effectively (Rose 1992, 125). SEWA's organizing strategies in rural agriculture are also designed to build a movement by ensuring that every caste is represented in the union in a given area (Rose 1992, 149).

SEWA's strategies have implications for those concerned with development alternatives sensitive to women's needs. At the same time, as a union, its strategies have the potential to inspire new, and revive old, representational forms geared to workers falling outside of the norm of wage earning at a single workplace, once common among diverse groups ranging from truck drivers to artists and waitresses (Cobble and Vosko 2000). As one quilt-cover maker described the catch-22 situation in which she found herself, along with her colleagues, when SEWA first approached them to organize: "at first, we could not understand—are we workers or are we owners? Are we employees or contractors? Because this is the only world we knew" (Jhabvala 1995, 125).

---

[6] Leaders of Vendor Women's Union, SEWA, "Street Vendors: Still under Attack," 2005, *SEWA Newsletter* 1(1): 5–6, http://www.sewaacademy.org/maillist/images/logo.gif (accessed February 17, 2005).

Through consciousness-raising among workers such as these own account quilt-cover makers living in poverty with low levels of literacy and limited employment security, SEWA's strategies differ from the traditional union forms out of necessity. They are tailored to different forms of informal economy work and to distinct work arrangements, from home-based work to vending and contracting, always subscribing to the claim that "all workers are workers." SEWA's organizing strategies are also defined by the commitment of its leadership to pursuing a process of building union structures from the grass-roots level, which involves struggling against a range of actors, not only employers but contractors, traders, and public officials such as the police; against ineffective enforcement bureaucracy and legal systems; and against ineffective national laws and international policies. Now over thirty-years old, this new union has also inspired sister organizations elsewhere.

Feminist Labor Nongovernmental Organizations

NGOs are private and nonprofit organizations that claim to represent people "acting on their own volition" and that identify themselves as "self-governing," although the degree to which they incorporate democratic and representative structures varies (Tinker 1999, 89). They exist at the municipal, national, and international levels and include trade union federations, business think-tanks, lay religious councils, and social movement–oriented organizations.

NGOs are a heterogeneous group; there is no common organizational structure among them (Alvarez 2000; O'Brien et al. 2000, 16). Among those that are social movement–oriented, some NGOs focus on labor issues in alliance with trade unions and new unions, such as SEWA and the former Self Employed Women's Union (SEWU) of South Africa, whereas others focus on broader struggles related to gender equality (Meyer and Prügl 1999; Tinker 1999). Yet the dominant typologies of NGOs make scant mention of the labor NGO.

A labor NGO is any type of NGO that focuses on workers' issues; labor NGOs include organizations of marginalized workers unable to assert their rights collectively as workers through unions due to legal barriers or a dearth of organizing resources among unions. Many operate as proto-unions, although they often take the form of women's organizations, solidarity groups, or community organizations (Brecher, Costello, and Smith 2000; Gallin 2002). Distinctly feminist labor NGOs seek to expand the labor movement and to transform gender relations in this process. They are an important vehicle of collective organization, yet they are often dismissed by trade unions and neglected in the feminist scholarship on NGOs. They lie at the intersection between democratic membership-based trade unions, new unions, and labor NGOs. And they are a crucial site for advancing approaches to representation and organizing that embrace feminist practices of movement-building, involving the creation of solidarities that emerge from political movements (instead of being top-down) and that recognize (rather than elide) the diversity of work, workers' experiences, and workers' expressions of agency and their gendered character (Gordon 1999; Stall and Stoecker 1998; Ladd 1998; Mohanty 2003).

Feminist labor NGOs of informal economy workers include groups representing agricultural workers, domestic workers, street vendors, and home workers unable to defend their rights through new or official trade unions. Some are regionally based. A leading example is the Committee for Asian Women (CAW), an organization involving thirteen Asian countries aimed at improving the situation of women informal economy workers through popular education. Originating in 1981, CAW documents conditions of work in the informal economy and lobbies local and national governments and employers for better laws and improved enforcement (Committee for Asian Women [CAW] 2002).

Others operate as networks of regional and national organizations. A prominent example is HomeNet International, a labor NGO whose membership, like many other groups, has ebbed and flowed due to a heavy reliance on funding from international institutions. HomeNet has several regional branches, such as HomeNet South Asia, as well as national branches, such as HomeNet Thailand, the National Network of Homeworkers in the Philippines, and HomeNet UK. Founded in 1994, HomeNet is committed to "the promotion of democratic, membership-based organizations of homebased workers, most of whom are women . . . to give this huge, usually informal workforce a voice and collective strength to improve their own working and living conditions" (HomeNet South Asia 2002, 3). As a network, in the late 1990s and early 2000s it engaged in an extensive research project mapping home-based work globally in order to support organizing among home-based workers. National groups affiliated with HomeNet International, such as the Union of Embroiderers in Madeira, Portugal, also work to increase local prices and social security coverage among the groups that they serve.

Still other feminist labor NGOs are freestanding national organizations. For example, StreetNet, whose origins date to the late 1990s, is a voluntary organization of South African women committed to promoting the organization of street vendors. It is concerned, in particular, with limiting the harassment of street vendors by municipal authorities, evictions from selling sites, and confiscation of goods through the adoption of appropriate laws and policies regulating these activities (StreetNet Association 2002).

Although their activities vary, as a group feminist labor NGOs evolved partly in reaction to the inability of the labor movement to respond to de-unionization in the North and the persistence of the informal economy in the South. They are supported by many official trade unions, such as the Dutch-based Federatie Nederlandse Vakbeweging ([FNV] 1998). Three broad features characterize these organizations, and elements of each conflict with forms of trade unionism dominant in North America. First, similar to the new unions of informal economy workers, such as SEWA, feminist labor NGOs adopt an inclusive definition of the term *worker*. They argue that informal economy workers are workers in need of social protection rather than being entrepreneurs. According to Dan Gallin, former director of the International Union of Food, Agricultural, Hotel, Restaurant, Catering, Tobacco and Allied Workers' Associations (IUF), the organization that first brought SEWA into formal institutions of the international labor movement: "micro-enterprise development has been seen by some as a first step to launch own account homebased workers' careers as capitalist entrepreneurs. . . . We regard these views as inspired by neo-liberal doctrine without any relationship to what happens in the real world" (Gallin 2001). Flowing from this view is the contention that informal economy workers are part of the labor movement and that official trade unions must see them as a central and growing part of their constituency.

Second, feminist labor NGOs are typically committed to horizontal organizing (i.e., across sectors and industries) as well as vertical organizing (i.e., by sector and industry) among informal economy workers. Many trade unionists object vehemently to this approach to organizing, contending that horizontal organizing among informal economy workers accords too much emphasis to "less important relationships [such as cross-sector alliances between own account workers] while obscuring often more important relationships. . . . [They] favour a more vertical way of thinking that [recognizes] the organization of work in real economic sectors."[7]

Third, feminist labor NGOs typically support self-identification among informal economy workers—allowing individuals to define themselves as *workers* and to organize accordingly. Consistent with this process, rather than advocating containment (i.e., maintaining the informal economy as a self-contained universe), they support working with official trade unions to pursue formalization. Instead of disparaging workers in the informal economy, they support the naming of the informal economy and the granting of greater legitimacy to organizations of informal economy workers. Trade unionists typically object to expanding the labor movement to include organizations of informal economy workers unless they can demonstrate that they are demo-

---

[7] Christine Nathan, quoted in fieldnotes, June 6, 2002.

cratic, representative, membership-based organizations in the process of becoming unions. Some also view containment as a preferred strategy to formalization, although this issue is less divisive.

There are clearly tensions between leading feminist labor NGOs organizing with informal economy workers and official trade unions. However, there are also opportunities for advancing common goals, especially at the international level, where the question of how to improve the situation of workers in the informal economy made its way to the top of the ILO agenda in the early 2000s. Transnational feminist networks oriented to labor concerns represent one avenue for fusing this coalition.

Transnational Feminist Networks

Transnational feminist networks are loose groupings of actors lobbying internationally on a given theme (Keck and Sikkink 1998, 217). International feminist networks are long-standing—they have existed for over a century. However, *transnational* feminist networks are newer distinct entities that reflect a "conscious crossing of national boundaries . . . superseding nationalist orientations" (Moghadam 2000, 60–61).

Dating to the third wave of feminism, transnational feminist networks grew up in a context of constraints, such as economic restructuring, as well as opportunities, such as the emergence of a large population of educated mobile women willing to engage in cross-class and antiracist alliances around the world (witness the growth of world conferences on women). They are thus part of a family of global social movements and organizations (Moghadam 2000, 80; Desai 2002). Like NGOs, the structures of transnational feminist networks vary. Because they are often too ephemeral to reflect clear constituencies, transnational networks are not necessarily democratic or membership-based, prompting some to raise concerns about their potential role in the NGO-ization of the women's movement (Alvarez 2000; Lang 1997).[8] At the same time, these networks do not claim to be representative—they see themselves as playing a linking role between organizations globally.

Women in Informal Employment Globalizing and Organizing (WIEGO) resembles a transnational feminist network in many ways. Formed in 1997 by a group of feminists, it is a global research and policy-analysis network con-

[8] NGO-ization entails a shift away from experience-oriented movement politics to goal- and intervention-oriented strategies (Lang 1997). It turns on a set of paradoxical developments. On the one hand, it signals strong state (or intergovernmental organization) support for women's issues and, on the other hand, state (or intergovernmental organization) control over resource allocation. Desai (2002) argues that the process of NGO-ization cultivates the emergence of three types of women's NGOs: (1) fronts for government, (2) hybrid creatures that maintain links with movements and work inside and outside state or interstate systems, and (3) anti-expert movement-oriented organizations.

cerned with women living in poverty and working in the informal economy. WIEGO's mandate is to produce research, assisting organizations of informal economy workers in their efforts to promote policy changes of benefit to working women. WIEGO's activities pivot around five program areas: urban policies, global markets, social protection, organization and representation, and statistics. Its urban program pursues action research directed at such issues as the rights of street vendors. Its global markets program focuses on the impact of trade liberalization and globalization on women in the informal economy, especially home-based and own account workers. Its program on social protection pursues research on innovative approaches to providing social protection to informal economy workers. WIEGO's fourth program area on organization and representation is aimed at helping to strengthen the organizing capacity of women workers in the informal economy—in this area, its activities are led by feminist labor NGOs. WIEGO also works with global union federations and some national unions to put issues facing informal workers on the agendas of national governments and supranational institutions. In its fifth program area, WIEGO is involved in efforts to improve the collection of statistical data on informal employment worldwide in conjunction with various UN agencies (Women in Informal Employment Globalizing and Organizing [WIEGO] 2005).

WIEGO employs network forms of organization rather than bureaucratic forms typical of large traditional trade unions. In this way, it reflects the new organizational forms of the global women's movement, which involve supranational constituencies, objectives, and strategies. At the same time, WIEGO does not officially position itself as part of a women's movement. Rather, although many of its member groups take a decidedly feminist approach, the organization positions itself as an issue-based network of groups working around themes of concern to female informal economy workers. WIEGO is therefore willing to work in coalition with organizations ranging from new trade unions such as SEWA, to more traditional unions, labor NGOs, and international intergovernmental institutions. WIEGO's collaboration with intergovernmental agencies, such as the United Nations and various units of the ILO, distinguishes it from the prototypical transnational feminist network and makes it vulnerable to critiques that raise problems of accountability among such networks, especially when states or international institutions construct them as experts or surrogates of civil society (Alvarez 2000). Still, in its activities with feminist labor NGOs, new unions, and sympathetic trade unions, WIEGO has a linking role.

WIEGO has been particularly effective at the supranational level, where it has employed feminist praxes promoting dialog among labor NGOs, new unions, and trade unionists at international forums focusing on setting standards for home work and the issue of the informal economy. At this level, its success flows partly from the symbolic role of international labor standards. Yet it would be a mistake to downplay the activities of such networks, as well as of new unions and feminist labor NGOs, in this arena citing the overly simplistic claim that international labor standards have no teeth. Rather, as the general discussion on decent work in the informal economy hosted by the ILO in 2002 illustrates, debate at the supranational level has the potential to lay bare deep-seated tensions, as well as opportunities, that official unions representing workers at the national level rarely acknowledge due to the complexities of jurisdiction and the lack of resources for organizing and establishing new (or reviving old) forms of representation.

Decent Work in the Informal Economy: Supranational Dialog and Debate

In June 2002, the annual gathering of the ILO, called the International Labour Conference (ILC), addressed the meaning, persistence, and growth of the informal economy as well as strategies for raising standards for informal economy workers.[9] The annual ILC is a forum for debate about the substance and form of international labor standards, typically involving three sets of actors: national governments, organized business (known as the Employers), and organized labor (i.e., official unions recognized by the international trade union movement as representative, membership-based, and registered with the ILO; known as the Workers). Every session of this forum includes an Employers' Group and a Workers' Group that correspond with two of the ILO core constituencies, each with a designated spokesperson or vice-chair, alongside government representatives who speak for national governments and occasionally groupings of countries. However, NGOs were permitted to participate in a limited fashion in discussions of the informal economy on account of the lobbying efforts of new unions and feminist labor NGOs concerned to have the voices of women informal economy workers heard.

WIEGO took this opportunity to coordinate a coalition of groups, including representatives from trade unions with official status at the ILO, new official unions, feminist labor NGOs, and network-based organizations.[10] This coalition operated solely for the duration of the conference due to the diver-

[9] This section is based on participant observation at the ILC, 2002.

[10] Representatives from the following organizations participated in the coalition: Workers Educational Association; CAW; Textile, Clothing and Footwear Union of Australia; HomeNet UK; HomeNet South Asia; HomeNet Thailand; SEWA; SEWU; Zambia National Marketers Association; StreetNet International; Korean Women's Trade Union (KWUT); Southwest Center for Economic Integrity, representing the North American Alliance for Fair Employment (NAFFE); International Restructuring Education Network Europe (IRENE); Hong Kong Confederation of Trade Unions; Alliance on Contingent Employment, Toronto, Canada (ACE); National Network of Homeworkers, Philippines

sity of groups involved, some based in industrialized countries and some based in the geographic South, some focused on the informal economy and some concerned with forms of employment lacking protection more broadly. The coalition coalesced around the broad goal of improving the situation of workers in the informal economy. Its ability to adopt an authentic voice may be attributed to the feminist praxes of exchange, aimed at fostering active listening, that representatives of labor NGOs and new unions brought to the ILC and to the space that representatives of the trade unions with status at the ILO made for groups otherwise excluded, such as the invitation to all coalition members to join in the meetings of the official Workers' Group.

In official sessions as well as in behind-the-scenes meetings, the ILC in 2002 afforded the opportunity for dialog between representatives of official trade unions, feminist labor NGOs, and new unions of informal economy workers. It thereby offered a rare window into the tensions between the strategies new unions and feminist labor NGOs employ in representing informal economy workers and those typically adopted by recognized trade unions. The discussion revealed three underlying tensions over naming the problem, who is a worker, and appropriate modes of representation. At the same time, it opened space for the expression of common goals and for transcending differences.

Naming the Problem

The first point of tension centered on the concept of informal economy itself. On one side, the International Confederation of Free Trade Unions (ICFTU) and its affiliates took a position against naming the phenomenon in question *the informal economy* for fear that it would perpetuate dualism; on the other, coalition members, including feminist labor NGOs and the new unions, favored naming the problem precisely in this way. In open sessions, representatives of the new unions, in particular, advanced this view by objecting to the tendency, among some trade unionists, to disparage workers in the informal economy. For example, they criticized a first draft of the opening speech of the vice-chair of the Workers' Group, circulated to the coalition in advance, that noted: "[workers in the informal economy are] like weeds in a garden. In some gardens the weeds are growing because they are not considered weeds. *In others they are growing because it is believed that there is no need to weed a garden because they will go away on their own. In some gardens it's growing because everyone is waiting for someone else to weed the garden.*"[11] Coalition mem-

(PATAMABA); International Federation of Workers' Education Associations (IFWEA); IUF; Solidar, Belgium; HomeNet Chile; WIEGO; and Global Labor Institute (GLI).
[11] Nathan, quoted in fieldnotes, June 6, 2002 [emphasis added].

bers argued further that this "weeds in the garden" metaphor implied that the labor movement is limited to workers belonging to recognized trade unions rather than being open to all workers compelled to sell their capacity to labor and seeking representation through trade unions, where they exist, or the support of labor NGOs operating as proto-unions, where unionization is either impossible legally or not feasible.[12] In response to this criticism, the Workers' Group vice-chair dropped the metaphor, yet she continued to oppose the concept of informal economy because it could lead to different standards for different workers (Justice 2002; International Confederation of Free Trade Unions [ICFTU] 2002).

After lengthy exchanges with coalition members, the Workers' Group agreed to accept the concept of informal economy on the condition that they stress, in public discussions, "the *concept* behind the *term* 'informal economy.'" Through this emphasis, they meant to accentuate the Workers' Group concern with unprotected work (and workers) as opposed to the coalition's concern to identify a sector of the economy requiring a distinct set of international labor standards that would parallel existing standards.[13]

A deeper division lay below the surface of this debate over naming. Many representatives of recognized trade unions opposed the concept of informal economy because they feared that it would legitimize horizontal organizing. Although they preferred the term *informal economy* to *informal sector*, a large segment of representatives of official trade unions, especially those representing industrial workers, opposed any term of this nature because it "reflected a horizontal way of thinking." Consistent with the belief that informal economy workers represent an economic threat to the working and living conditions of unionized workers as well as to the precariously employed, especially in the North, this sizable and vocal group favored "a more vertical way of thinking that [recognizes] the organization of work in real economic sectors ... [which] makes it easier to address issues relating to the transformation of marginalized work into the economic mainstream."[14]

Conversely, coalition members largely supported horizontal organizing, which may involve grouping together workers in different sectors, occupations, and employment relationships, although they did not perceive it as implying tacit support for a dualistic approach to regulation because the formal

[12] Fieldnotes, June 7, 2002.

[13] Fieldnotes, June 5, 2002 [emphasis in quotation added]. Affirming this stance, a feminist trade unionist allied closely with feminist labor NGOs spoke elegantly about the constituency of women workers that the SEWA represents, noting that what unites them is their unprotected status; for her, the point was "to separate the term and the concept and make the concept be what we want it to be. That way, it could, for example, [mean that] ... workers need not be in an employer-employee situation" (Renana Jhabvala, quoted in fieldnotes, June 5, 2002).

[14] Christine Nathan, speech at ILC, June 7, 2002.

and informal economies are intimately linked in terms of production, distribution, and subcontracting.[15] Rather, they characterized the merits of recognizing the informal economy—and organizing horizontally in addition to vertically—as necessary steps toward extending protections to all workers.

Who Is a Worker?

The issue of who is a worker—who is part of labor's potential constituency—represented a second point of tension, especially between the representatives of industrial unions in North America and coalition members. In the tripartite discussions, the Employers' Group characterized the informal economy as a space of micro-enterprise. In sharp contrast, the Workers' Group argued that most people in the informal economy are workers in need of protection. Yet there was a lack of consensus over the categories of workers in need of protection both within and among the representatives of recognized trade unions, new unions, and feminist labor NGOs. Divisions were particularly sharp over whether *workers* in the informal economy included own account workers.

The status of the own account worker has long been contested. On one side are the trade unionists influenced by the industrial union model and a vocal minority of official trade unions representing craft workers. On the other side are the new unions and feminist labor NGOs. Each side holds different views on the proper domain(s) of union organizing as well (FNV 1998). At the ILC in 2002, the WIEGO coalition allied itself squarely with the Workers' Group, and one of its foremost goals was to convince the official trade unions that own account workers belong in the labor movement. Repeating the phrase "all workers are workers," coalition groups argued forcefully that labor standards should apply explicitly to own account workers.

Inside the Workers' Group, there were openings for dialog over who is a worker. Yet the representatives of official trade unions, especially those from the industrialized countries, were concerned primarily with workers in so-called disguised employment (or false self-employment) in the mainstream labor force. They had very little understanding of the situation of own account workers in the geographic South. Consequently, the representatives of feminist labor NGOs sought to educate their trade union allies on their definition of own account workers in the informal economy as well as on differences between these informal economy workers and self-employed workers in, for example, North American labor markets, who should have access to extensive labor rights and protections but are denied these rights by virtue of being labeled self-employed (e.g., truck drivers, artists, home care workers, and news-

[15] Fieldnotes, June 5, 2002.

paper carriers) (Cobble and Vosko 2000; Cranford 2005; Fudge, Tucker, and Vosko 2002; Tucker 2005; Vosko 2005).

Using testimonials, representatives of new unions and feminist labor NGOs argued that informal economy workers include small vendors, such as those associated with StreetNet in Zambia, and home-based workers, including those assisted by HomeNet Thailand. They contended that these workers are engaged in survival activities and confronting poverty even though they are labeled micro-entrepreneurs. They argued further that own account workers are organizing into proto-unions and that they are a veritable part of the labor movement that should be treated distinctly from entrepreneurs.[16]

Based on this extensive dialog, the Workers' Group ultimately took the position that informal economy workers include own account workers. The group refused to cede this terrain to employers, arguing that *"workers in the informal economy include both wage workers and own account workers*. Most own account workers are as insecure and vulnerable as wage workers in the informal economy and move from one situation to the other. Because they lack protection, rights and representation, these workers often remain trapped in poverty" (ILO 2002b, 41, par. 172 [emphasis added]). Feminist labor NGOs celebrated this expanded definition of who is a worker and some representatives of official trade unions also hailed it as a victory for the international labor movement, one that could help eliminate the formal/informal economy dichotomy. The relative safety of the international forum revealed tensions long obscured at the national and local levels and fostered productive debate over who is a worker.

Appropriate Modes of Representation

Disagreement over appropriate structures for representation was the chief fault line in the alliance between the official trade unions and the new unions and feminist labor NGOs comprising the coalition fused by WIEGO. Representatives of leading feminist labor NGOs, such as the CAW, as well as those of official unions, such as FNV, have a history of supporting labor NGOs as legitimate organizations representing workers in the informal economy. WIEGO was also on record for asserting that "informal sector workers are already organizing, partly in existing union structures originating in the formal sector, partly into new unions created by themselves, partly into associations which are sometimes described as NGOs but which are often in fact proto-unions" (WIEGO 2002, 7). Dan Gallin, former director general of the IUF, who helped bring the SEWA into this global union federation, and a WIEGO activist, argues similarly that unions are the "natural form of organization"

---

[16] Fieldnotes, June 11–13, 2002.

for workers (2001, 227) but that initially organization and representation frequently occurs in spaces "where unions and NGOs intersect" (Gallin 2002, 22). Several feminist labor NGOs took this position at the ILC in 2002 and called on the ILO to acknowledge the role of membership-based organizations of informal economy workers. Their perspective reflects the view expressed by Gallin that

> NGOs have developed in a social and political vacuum that *trade unions have allowed to grow since the end of World War II by withdrawing into their "core business."* . . . [this situation is] in contrast with the pre-war labor movement which had sought to bring about social change on a broad front and had created a variety of organizations including its own NGOs, as a basis of a counterculture and of an alternative society building itself within the shell of the old. (2002, 22, emphasis added)

This perspective also suggests that there are two dominant paths to collective organization. One path is organizing through a union or union federation willing to extend its field of activity to informal economy workers or self-organizing. The second route is creating labor NGOs or proto-unions of informal economy workers that will ultimately seek affiliation with a national union and/or a global union federation.

StreetNet, SEWA, and SEWU thus called for treating democratic-membership based organizations of informal economy workers similarly to official unions in international labor standards. In the context of the ILO, at a minimum, this meant extending supports for technical assistance to labor NGOs. But there was a stalemate on this matter. Representatives of official unions uniformly supported "the legitimate representation of workers [through] collective bargaining" (ILO 2002b, 39).[17] So, too, did many feminist labor NGOs, which called for the recognition of the new trade unions of informal economy workers but not of labor NGOs. In support of this position, they listed a number of successful unionization strategies such as those used in Ghana, with agricultural workers; in Benin and South Africa, with informal taxi drivers; in Colombia and the Netherlands, with home-based workers; and in India, with construction workers.[18] Their message was also that organization and representation through unions is the primary means of attaining and retaining voice for workers (ILO 2002b, 22).

Leading feminist labor NGOs, new unions, and many official unions concurred ultimately that many labor NGOs operate as proto-unions. This development empowered the representatives of groups such as CAW and HomeNet

[17] Fieldnotes, June 14, 2002.
[18] Fieldnotes, June 13, 2002.

Thailand, who used testimonials to describe their activities as proto-unions negotiating with labor brokers, subcontractors, and municipal officials and to affirm that their affinities lie with organized labor. The broader dialog also led to a consensus that new modes of organizing are necessary. But the official trade unions refused to go as far as recognizing organizations of workers in the informal economy on a par with unions.

Lessons for North American Unions

Global strategies aimed at raising the standards for informal economy workers, and the opportunities and challenges to which they give rise, offer important insights for North American unions seeking to improve the working and living conditions for the precariously employed and to foster gender equity. Enabling workers to define themselves as part of the labor movement, allowing multiple forms of representation to coexist, and embracing network forms of organization represent three strategies with the potential for improving representation among workers who have been served poorly by the forms of trade unionism dominant since World War II.

Many informal economy workers define themselves as part of the labor movement; for example, own account workers, such as the quilt-cover makers and *bidi* workers organizing with SEWA, identify as workers in need of protection and voice through trade unions. It took SEWA decades to gain legitimacy in the Indian labor movement and to participate in such forums as international labor conferences. Spaces are gradually opening up for these hitherto excluded actors, especially in the geographic South and at the international level through global union federations; the inclusion of own account workers within the definition of *informal economy workers* adopted by the ILO is a case in point.

Yet making greater space for self-identification is still pressing at the national level. There is no guarantee that the movement away from conceiving of own account workers as micro-entrepreneurs will filter down to the national level. Nor are there parallel mechanisms for extending the definition of *worker* in North America to include highly gendered forms of precarious self-employment, such as solo self-employment, much of which is also characterized by low income levels, lack of control over the labor process, and limited social protections and benefits. The willingness among unions to let such workers self-define is thus a critical precursor to such changes if the labor movement is to respond effectively to the new majority and press for political and legal change.

In North America, some self-employed workers have the capacity to organize. In the United States, independent owner-drivers of trucks have organized into unions, principally through the International Brotherhood of the Teamsters, and negotiated master agreements setting out the basic terms and conditions of work since the late nineteenth century (Cobble and Vosko 2000). So, too, have self-employed artists (Vosko 2005), fishers (Clement 1986), and construction workers in Canada (MacDonald 1998). In the 1990s and 2000s, unions such as the Canadian Union of Postal Workers, working closely with a national feminist labor NGO, have launched effective campaigns to organize and represent rural-route mail carriers, defined inappropriately as self-employed by political fiat (Fudge 2005). In urban centers such as Winnipeg, this union has also created a workers' center, the Workers' Organizing Resource Centre (WORC), to assist couriers and delivery drivers to exercise their rights and improve their working conditions (Bickerton and Stearns 2002). In Canada, there are a growing numbers of initiatives, including workers' centers, aimed at raising standards for the own account self-employed and other groups, similar to those based in the United States (Fine, chap. 11 in this volume). Some of these centers assist workers on a geographical basis (Bickerton and Stearns 2002), whereas others organize on the basis of form of employment or social location (Cranford et al. 2006). Most, however, adopt strategies typical of community unionism.

Drawing on a self-organizing model built around self-definition, these initiatives offer a few successful models to follow. Just as the case of SEWA illustrates that trade unions and cooperatives can be complementary vehicles for advancing workers' struggle and gender-sensitive development alternatives, established unions in North America could work more effectively with local feminist labor NGOs that are engaged with self-employed workers, temporary help agency workers, and others among the precariously employed. Building bridges between unions and pre-union forms, as well as between unions and service-based organizations such as the feminist labor NGOs, can only strengthen North America labor.

Although vital, encouraging self-identification is but one step toward limiting precarious employment and fostering gender equity through an expansion of the labor movement in North America. Another involves unions embracing multiple forms of representation, both sequentially and simultaneously. Global strategies for representing informal economy workers underscore the importance of this second step. Recall that new unions often arise out of established unions, splitting off and operating like feminist labor NGOs until they are recognized officially.

In the North American context, too, groups, such as artists, also organized first into associations before gaining legitimacy in the trade union movement and recognition in laws and policies. Some only attained the legal right to organize and bargain collectively in the early 2000s even though producers and employers had negotiated with them voluntarily for decades before the legislation enabling collective bargaining emerged. Some of these workers, such as those that produce products or perform work for producers, require forms of representation allowing for the negotiation of agreements of minimum terms. Scale agreements, common in the arts (Vosko 2005), offer one unique model for advancing an alternative form of representation. These agreements allow artists to negotiate contracts individually but prevent producers from paying any less than the scale (the minimum amount provided in a given agreement to an artist working in a sector in which an artists' association has been certified). They seek to minimize the precarious employment in the arts, and their virtue lies in their capacity to enable independent professional artists, who are neither employees nor dependent contractors, to attain minimum terms. Other groups require forms of representation borrowing from craft unionism as well as forms operating on the basis of geography (Cobble 1991; Middleton 1996). Still others, such as women and workers of color in home care, might be well served by combining new unionisms with features typically characterizing worker cooperatives (Cranford 2005).

The experiences of transitional or proto-unions, such as the feminist labor NGOs organizing with informal economy workers, offer key insights into fostering new, and reviving age-old, representational forms and ensuring that the strategies employed by unions address the interests of the new majority, especially women and workers of color engaged in precarious employment. They illustrate vividly that structures of representation must be in sync with the needs of workers and their communities in order to be sustainable. In some cases, being attentive to potential new constituencies of workers may call for network forms of organization, such as those forms employed by WIEGO, instead of or in addition to bureaucratic forms. For example, engaging in campaigns in coalition with feminist labor NGOs through national networks may enable North American unions to make substantive gains in a given sector, region, or group. Limiting precarious employment and fostering gender equity through efforts to expand the labor movement necessitate forms of horizontal as well as vertical organizing, drawing on a mixture of strategies, new and old, among wage workers and self-employed workers, among women and men, and among workers worldwide.

REFERENCES

9to5. 1980. "Race against Time: Automation of the Office." Self-published report.

Acker, Joan. 1989. *Doing Comparable Worth: Gender, Class, and Pay Equity*. Philadelphia: Temple University Press.

Adam, Barry, Jan Willem Duyvendak, and Andre Krouwel, eds. 1999. *The Global Emergence of Gay and Lesbian Politics: National Imprints of a Worldwide Movement*. Philadelphia: Temple University Press.

Adams, Kirk, and Mike Gallagher. 1988. Memorandum to Dave Snapp. "Targeting Homecare Organizing Projects." Copy for A. Stern, SEIU Organizing Department, 1 of 3, Folder "LA Home Health Care, 1988 Homecare," SEIU Papers, Reuther Library, Wayne State University, Detroit, Mich. November 16.

Albelda, Randy, and Chris Tilly. 1997. *Glass Ceilings and Bottomless Pits: Women's Work, Women's Poverty*. Boston: South End Press.

Albelda, Randy, and Ann Withorn, eds. 2002. *Lost Ground: Welfare Reform, Poverty and Beyond*. Boston: South End Press.

Alvarez, Sonia E. 2000. "Translating the Global: Effects of Transnational Organizing on Local Feminist Discourses and Practices in Latin America." *Meridians: Feminism, Race, Transnationalism* 1(1): 29–67.

American Federation of Labor–Congress of Industrial Organizations (AFL-CIO) Executive Council. 1997. "Welfare Reform and Union Representation." 17 February, Washington, D.C.

——. Committee on Working Women. 2004. "Overcoming Barriers to Women in Organizing and Leadership: Report to AFL-CIO Executive Council," March, Washington, D.C.

——. 2005. "A Diverse Movement Calls for Diverse Leadership." http://www.aflcio.org/aboutus/thisistheaflcio/convention/2005/upload/res_2.pdf (accessed June 7, 2006).

———. Executive Council. 2006. "Responsible Reform of Immigration Laws Must Protect Working Conditions for All Workers in the U.S." Statement adopted, San Diego, March 1.

Appelbaum, Eileen, Annette Bernhardt, and Richard J. Murnane, eds. 2003. *Low-Wage America: How Employers Are Reshaping Opportunity in the Workplace*. New York: Russell Sage Foundation.

Applied Research Center. 1999. *Workfare to Wages: A Bridge to Living Wage Jobs*. Oakland, Calif.: ARC.

Armstrong, Patricia. 1993. "Professions, Unions, or What?: Learning From Nurses." In *Women Challenging Unions: Feminism, Democracy, and Militancy*, edited by Linda Briskin and Patricia McDermott, 304–21. Toronto: University of Toronto Press.

Austin, Regina. 1988. "Employer Abuse, Worker Resistance, and the Tort of Intentional Infliction of Emotional Distress." *Stanford Law Review* 41: 1–59.

Bacon, David. 2005. *The Children of NAFTA: Labor Wars on the U.S./Mexico Border*. Berkeley: University of California Press.

Badgett, M. V. Lee, and Heidi I. Hartmann. 1995. "The Effectiveness of Equal Employment Opportunity Policies." In *Economic Perspectives on Affirmative Action*, edited by Margaret C. Simms, 55–91. Washington, D.C.: Joint Center for Political and Economic Studies; Lanham, Md.: University Press of America.

Bain, Christian. 1999. "A Short History of Lesbian and Gay Labor Activism in the United States." In *Laboring for Rights: Unions and Sexual Diversity Across Nations*, edited by Gerald Hunt. Philadelphia: Temple University Press.

Barker, Kathleen, and Kathleen Christensen, eds. 1998. *Contingent Work: American Employment Relations in Transition*. Ithaca: ILR Press.

Becker Kennedy, Nancy. 1993. Letter to Stan Greenberg. Box 7, Folder 36, Edward V. Roberts Papers, Bancroft Library, University of California, Berkeley, Calif. August 2.

Belkin, Lisa. 2003. "The Opt-Out Revolution." *New York Times Magazine*, October 26, LexisNexis (accessed December 15, 2005).

Beneria, Lourdes. 2001. "Shifting the Risk: New Employment Patterns, Informalization, and Women's Work." *International Journal of Politics, Culture, and Society* 15(1): 27–53.

Bernstein, Jared, Heidi I. Hartmann, and John Schmitt. 1999. *The Minimum Wage Increase: A Working Woman's Issue*. Issue Brief #133. Washington, D.C.: Economic Policy Institute.

Berubé, Allan. 1997. "The Marine Cooks and Stewards Union." Personal notes taken by Gerald Hunt during a lecture given at a Canadian Labour Congress conference on sexual orientation held in Ottawa, Canada.

Bevona, Gus. 1987. Letter to John L. Sweeney. SEIU President's Office, Box 217, Folder "Local 32B-32J-144, 1987," SEIU Papers, Reuther Library, Wayne State University, Detroit, Mich. January 6.

Bickerton, Geoff, and Catherine Stearns. 2002. "The Struggle Continues in Winnipeg: The Workers Organizing and Resource Centre." *Just Labor: A Canadian Journal of Work and Society* 1: 50–57.

Bielski, Monica Lynn. 2005. Identity at Work: U.S. Labor Union Efforts to Address Sexual Diversity Through Policy and Practice. PhD diss., Rutgers University.

Biklen, Molly. 2003. "Note: Healthcare in the Home: Reexamining the Companionship Services Exemption to the Fair Labor Standards Act." *Columbia Human Rights Law Review* 35: 113–50.

Bingham, Clara, and Laura Leedy Gansler. 2002. *Class Action: The Story of Lois Jenson and the Landmark Case That Changed Sexual Harassment Law*. New York: Doubleday.

Black, Sandra E., and Elizabeth Brainerd. 2004. "Importing Equality? The Impact of Glob-alization on Gender Discrimination." *Industrial and Labor Relations Review* 57(4): 540–59.

Black, Sandra, and Chinhui Juhn. 2000. "The Rise of Female Professionals: Are Women Re-sponding to Skill Demand?" *American Economic Review* 90(2): 450–55.

Blau, Francine D., and Lawrence Kahn. 1997. "Swimming Upstream: Trends in the Gender Wage Differential in the 1980s." *Journal of Labor Economics* 15(1): 1–42.

———. 2004. The US Gender Pay Gap in the 1990s: Slowing Convergence. Working paper no. 10853, National Bureau of Economic Research, Cambridge, Mass.

Blum, Linda M. 1991. *Between Feminism and Labor: The Significance of the Comparable Worth Movement*. Berkeley: University of California Press.

Bond, James T., Ellen Galinsky, and Jennifer E. Swanberg. 1998. *The 1997 National Study of the Changing Workforce*. New York: Families and Work Institute.

Boris, Eileen. 1998. "When Work Is Slavery." *Social Justice* 25(1): 25, 28–47.

Bourdieu. Pierre. 1987. *Distinction: A Social Critique of the Judgement of Taste*. Cambridge, Mass.: Harvard University Press.

Bowe, John. 2003. "Nobodies: Does Slavery Exist in America?" *New Yorker*, April 21–28, 106–33.

Boyd, Nan Alamilla. 2003. *Wide-Open Town: A History of Queer San Francisco to 1965*. Los Angeles: University of California Press.

Boyle, Kevin. 1995. *The UAW and the Heyday of American Liberalism, 1945–1968*. Ithaca: Cornell University Press.

Brake, Deborah L. 2004. "When Equality Leaves Everyone Worse Off: The Problem of Lev-eling Down in Equality Law." *William & Mary Law Review* 46: 513–618.

Brecher, Jeremy, Tim Costello, and Brendan Smith, eds. 2000. *Globalization from Below: The Power of Solidarity*. Cambridge, Mass.: South End Press.

Brocht, Chauna. 2001. "Pay Laws Making a Difference across U.S." *Lexington Herald-Leader,* September 2, H1.

Bronfenbrenner, Kate. 2005. "Organizing Women: The Nature and Process of Union-Organizing Efforts among U.S. Women Workers since the mid-1990s." *Work and Occu-pations* 32(November): 441–63.

Brooks, Fred P. 2005. "New Turf for Organizing: Family Child Care Providers." *Labor Studies Journal* 29(4): 45–63.

Brudney, James J. 1996. "Reflections on Group Action and the Law of the Workplace." *Texas Law Review* 74: 1563–99.

Burbridge, Lyn C. 1993. "The Labor Market for Home Care Workers: Demand, Supply, and Institutional Barriers." *The Gerontologist* 33: 41–46.

Bureau of National Affairs. 2004. Daily Labor Report no. 190, Oct. 1. Bureau of National Affairs, Washington, D.C.

Burnham, Linda. 2002. "Welfare Reform, Family Hardship and Women of Color." In *Los-ing Ground: Welfare Reform, Poverty and Beyond*, edited by Randy Albelda and Ann Withorn, 43–56. Boston: South End Press.

Business Week. 1974. Editorial. *Business Week*, October 12, 120.

Cancian, Maria, Sheldon Danziger, and Peter Gottschalk. 1993. "Working Wives and Fam-ily Income Inequality among Married Couples." In *Uneven Tides: Rising Inequality in America*, edited by Sheldon Danziger and Peter Gottschalk, 195–222. New York: Russell Sage Foundation.

Cantor, David, Jane Waldfogel, Jeffrey Kerwin, Mareena McKinley Wright, Kerry Levin, John Rauch, Tracy Hagerty, and Martha Stapleton Kudela. 2001. *Balancing the Needs of*

Families and Employers: The Family and Medical Leave Surveys, 2000 Update. Report prepared at the request of the U.S. Department of Labor, Washington, D.C.

Caress, Barbara. 1988. "Home Is Where the Patients Are: New York's Home Care Workers' Contract Victory." *Health/PAC Bulletin* 18(fall): 4–14.

Carlin, Michael. 2001. "Are Union-Financed Legal Services Provided Prior to a Representation Election an Impermissible Grant of Benefit? An Analysis of *Nestle, Novatel,* and *Freund.*" *North Carolina Law Review* 79: 551–75.

Center for Community Change. 1998. "ACORN and CWA: Combining Self-Interest around Welfare Reform." *Organizing* (June–July).

Center for Policy Alternatives. 2005. *2003 Equal Pay Legislation.* http://www.stateaction.org (accessed May 3, 2005).

Chadwick, Bruce A., and Tim B. Heaton, eds. 1999. *Statistical Handbook on the American Family.* 2nd ed. Phoenix: Oryx Press.

Chang, Grace. 2000. *Disposable Domestics: Immigrant Women Workers in the Global Economy.* Boston: South End Press.

Charles, Maria, and David Grusky. 2005. *Occupational Ghettos: The Worldwide Segregation of Women and Men.* Stanford: Stanford University Press.

Cheski, Cynthia. 1994. "Reforming Welfare." *Human Rights* 21(4): 10–11, 42.

Citizens' Commission on Civil Rights. 1984. *Affirmative Action to Open the Doors of Job Opportunity.* June, Washington, D.C.

Citizens' Committee on Aging. 1977. *Systems Analysis of the Home Attendant Program.* New York: Community Council of Great New York, NYHRA.

Clawson, Dan. 2003. *The Next Upsurge: Labor and the New Social Movement.* Ithaca: Cornell University Press.

Clement, Wallace. 1986. *The Struggle to Organize: Resistance in Canada's Fishery.* Toronto: McClelland and Stewart.

Cloward, Richard A., and Frances Fox Piven. 1968. "Workers and Welfare: The Poor against Themselves." *The Nation,* November 25, 558–62.

Cobble, Dorothy Sue. 1991. "Organizing the Post-Industrial Work Force: Lessons from the History of Waitress Unionism" *Industrial and Labor Relations Review* 44(3):419–36.

———. 1994. "Making Post-Industrial Unionism Possible." In *Restoring the Promise of American Labor Law,* edited by Sheldon Friedman, Richard W. Hurd, Rudolph A. Oswald, and Ronald L. Seeber, 285–302. New York: Cornell University Press/ILR Imprint.

———. 1996. "The Prospects for Unionism in a Service Society." In *Working in the Service Society,* edited by Cameron L. Macdonald and Carmen Sirianni, 333–58. Philadelphia: Temple University Press.

———. 1997. "Lost Ways of Organizing: Reviving the AFL's Direct Affiliate Strategy." *Industrial Relations* 36(3): 278–301.

———. 2001. "Lost Ways of Unionism: Historical Perspectives on Reinventing the Labor Movement." In *Rekindling the Movement: Labor's Quest for Relevance in the Twenty-First Century,* edited by Lowell Turner, Harry C. Katz, and Richard W. Hurd, 82–96. Ithaca: ILR Press.

———. 2003. "Halving the Double Day." *New Labor Forum* 12(3): 63–72.

———. 2004. *The Other Women's Movement: Workplace Justice and Social Rights in Modern America.* Princeton: Princeton University Press.

———. 2005. "A 'Tiger by the Toenail': The 1970s Origins of the New Working-Class Majority." *Labor: Studies in Working-Class History of the Americas* 2(3): 103–14.

Cobble, Dorothy Sue, and Monica Bielski Michal. 2002. "On the Edge of Equality? Working Women and the U.S. Labor Movement." In *Gender, Diversity, and Trade Unions: In-*

ternational Perspectives, edited by Fiona Colgan and Sue Ledwith, 232–56. New York: Routledge.

Cobble, Dorothy Sue, and Leah F. Vosko. 2000. "Historical Perspectives on Representing Nonstandard Workers." In *Nonstandard Work: The Nature and Challenges of Changing Employment Arrangements*, edited by Francoise Carré, Marianne A. Ferber, Lonnie Golden, and S. A. Herzenberg, 219–312. Champaign: Industrial Relations Research Association.

Colgan, Fiona, and Sue Ledwith, eds. 2002. *Gender, Diversity, and Trade Unions*. Routledge: London and New York.

Committee for Asian Women (CAW). 2002. "Women Workers in the Informal Economy: Lobbying for Change." *Asian Women Workers' News Letter* 21(April): 2.

Compa, Lance. 2004. *Unfair Advantage: Workers' Freedom of Association in the United States under International Human Rights Standards*. Ithaca: Cornell University Press.

Conway, M. Margaret, David W. Ahern, and Gertrude A. Steuernagel. 1995. *Women and Public Policy: A Revolution in Progress*. Washington, D.C.: CQ Press.

Cook, Christopher D. 1999. "Turning Welfare Workers into City Employees." *Christian Science Monitor*, February 11, 3.

Cook, Rhonda. 1999. "Prisoners 'Hired,' So Ex-Welfare Clients Fired." *Atlanta Journal and Constitution*, June 18, 1A.

Cotter, David A., Joan M. Hermsen, and Reeve Vanneman. 2004. *Gender Inequality at Work*. New York and Washington, D.C.: Russell Sage Foundation and Population Reference Bureau.

Crain, Marion. 1991. "Feminizing Unions: Challenging the Gendered Structure of Wage Labor." *Michigan Law Review* 89: 1155–221.

———. 1995. "Women, Labor Unions, and Hostile Work Environment Sexual Harassment: The Untold Story." *Texas Journal of Women and the Law* 4: 9–81.

Crain, Marion, Pauline Kim, and Michael Selmi. 2005. *Worklaw: Cases and Materials*. Newark: LexisNexis.

Crain, Marion, and Ken Matheny. 1999. "'Labor's Divided Ranks': Privilege and the United Front Ideology." *Cornell Law Review* 84: 1542–626.

———. 2001. "Labor's Identity Crisis." *California Law Review* 89: 1767–846.

Cranford, Cynthia J. 2005. "From Precarious Workers to Unionized Employees and Back Again?: The Challenges of Organizing Personal-Care Workers in Ontario." In *Self-Employed Workers Organize: Law, Policy, and Unions*, edited by Cynthia Cranford, Judy Fudge, Eric Tucker, and Leah F. Vosko, 96–135. Montreal: McGill-Queen's University Press.

Cranford, Cynthia J., Tania Das Gupta, Deena Ladd, and Leah F. Vosko. 2006. "Conceptualizing Community Unionism: Organizing for Fair Employment in Toronto." In *Precarious Employment: Understanding Labour Market Insecurity in Canada*, edited by Leah F. Vosko, 353–77. Montreal: McGill-Queen's University Press.

Dark, Taylor E. 1999. *The Unions and the Democrats: An Enduring Alliance*. Ithaca: Cornell University Press.

Dawson, Steven, and Rick Surpin. 2001. *Direct Care Health Workers: The Unnecessary Crisis in Long-Term Care*. New York: Paraprofessional Health Care Institute for the Aspen Institute.

De Bare, Illana. 1999. "Record Settlement in Farm Workers' Suit; Lettuce Grower Will Pay 1.85 Million in Harassment Case." *San Francisco Chronicle*, February 24, B1.

De la Vega, Connie, and Conchita Lozano-Batista. 2005. "Advocates Should Use Applicable International Standards to Address Violations of Undocumented Migrant Workers'

Rights in the United States." In *Human Rights and Refugees, Internally Displaced Persons and Migrant Workers: Essays in Memory of Joan Fitzpatrick and Arthur Helton*, edited by Anne Bayefsky, 517–50. Boston: Martin Nijhoff Publishers.

Delgado, Gary, and Rebecca Gordon. 2002. "From Social Contract to Social Control: Welfare Policy and Race." In *From Poverty to Punishment: How Welfare Reform Punishes the Poor*, edited by Gary Delgado, 25–52. Oakland: Applied Research Center.

Delp, Linda, and Katie Quan. 2002. "Homecare Worker Organizing in California: An Analysis of a Successful Strategy." *Labor Studies Journal* 27(1): 1–23.

D'Emilio, John. 1998. *Sexual Politics, Sexual Communities: The Making of a Homosexual Minority in the United States, 1940–1970.* 2nd ed. Chicago: University of Chicago Press.

———. 2002. *The World Turned: Essays on Gay History, Politics, and Culture.* Durham: Duke University Press.

DeParle, Jason. 2004. *American Dream: Three Women, Ten Kids and a Nation's Drive to End Welfare.* New York: Viking.

Desai, Manesha. 2002. "Transnational Solidarity: Women's Agency, Structural Adjustment and Globalization." In *Women's Activism and Globalization: Linking Local Struggles and Transnational Politics*, edited by Nancy Naples and Manesha Desai, 15–33. New York: Routledge.

DiNardo, John, Nicole Fortin, and Thomas Lemieux. 1996. "Labor Market Institutions and the Distribution of Wages, 1973–1992: A Semiparameteric Approach." *Econometrica* 64(5): 1001–44.

Docherty, James C. 2004. *Historical Dictionary of Organized Labor.* 2nd ed. Lanham, Md.: Scarecrow Press.

Donovan, Rebecca, Paul A. Kurzman, and Carol Rotman. 1993. "Improving the Lives of Home Care Workers: A Partnership of Social Work and Labor." *Social Work* 38: 579–85.

Duffy, Mignon. 2005. "Reproducing Labor Inequalities: Challenges for Feminists Conceptualizing Care at the Intersections of Gender, Race, and Class." *Gender & Society* 19(1): 66–82.

Duncan, Otis Dudley, and Beverly Duncan. 1955. "A Methodological Analysis of Segregation Indexes." *American Sociological Review* 20(2): 210–17.

Eaton, Susan C. 1996. " 'The Customer Is Always Interesting': Unionized Harvard Clericals Renegotiate Work Relationships." In *Working in the Service Society*, edited by Cameron L. Macdonald and Carmen J. Sirianni, 291–332. Philadelphia: Temple University Press.

Economist. 2004. "Ever Higher Society, Ever Harder to Ascend." *Economist*, December 29, Special Report: Meritocracy in America. http://www.economist.com/world/na/display Story.cfm?story_id=3518560 (accessed December 15, 2005).

Ehrenreich, Barbara, and Arlie Hochschild. 2002. *Global Woman: Nannies, Maids, and Sex Workers in the New Economy.* New York: Henry Holt & Company.

Eldred, Lynn. 1980. "United Domestic Worker: Power and Pride." *San Diego Newsline*, November 26–December 3, n.p.

Ellwood, David T. 2000. "Winners and Losers in America: Taking the Measure of the New Economic Realities." In *A Working Nation: Workers, Work, and Government in the New Economy*, edited by David Ellwood, Rebecca M. Blank, Joseph Blasi, Douglas Kruse, William Niskanen, and Karen Lynn-Dyson, 1–41. New York: Russell Sage Foundation.

Ellwood, David T., and Christopher Jencks. 2004. "The Uneven Spread of Single-Parent Families: What Do We Know? Where Do We Look for Answers?" In *Social Inequality*, edited by Kathryn M. Neckerman, 3–78. New York: Russell Sage Foundation.

England, Paula. 1992. *Comparable Worth: Theories and Evidence.* New York: Aldine de Gruyter.

Estlund, Cynthia L. 2003. *Working Together: How Workplace Bonds Strengthen a Diverse Democracy*. New York: Oxford University Press.

Featherstone, Liza. 2004. *Selling Women Short: The Landmark Battle for Workers' Rights at Wal-Mart*. Basic Books: New York.

Federatie Nederlandse Vakbeweging (FNV). 1998. *Organizing in the Informal Economy: the Role of Trade Unions*. Amsterdam: FNV Mondial.

Feldman Group, Inc. 1998. Focus Group Memo Homecare Workers. Prepared for the Homecare Workers Union, Heinritz-Canterbury Papers, undeposited. April.

Figart, Deborah M., and June Lapidus. 1995. "A Gender Analysis of U.S. Labor Market Policies for the Working Poor." *Feminist Economics* 1(3): 60–81.

Finder, Alan. 1997. "Marchers Call on Giuliani to Support Workfare Union." *New York Times*, December 11, B24.

Fine, Janice. 2003. Community Unionism in Baltimore and Long Island: Beyond the Politics of Particularism. PhD diss., Massachusetts Institute of Technology.

———. 2005. "Community Unions and the Revival of the American Labor Movement." *Politics and Society* 33(1): 153–99.

———. 2006. *Worker Centers: Organizing Communities at the Edge of the Dream*. New York: Cornell University Press/ILR Press.

Fink, Leon, and Brian Greenberg. 1989. *Upheaval in the Quiet Zone: A History of Hospital Workers' Union Local 1199*. Urbana: University of Illinois Press.

Firestone, David. 1996. "New York Girding for Surge in Workfare Effort." *New York Times*, August 13, B2.

Fisk, Catherine L. 2001. "Humiliation at Work." *William & Mary Journal of Women and the Law* 8: 73–95.

Fitzgerald, Joan. 2006. *Moving Up in the New Economy: Career Ladders for U.S. Workers*. Ithaca: Cornell University Press.

Fletcher, Bill Jr. 1997. "Seizing the Time Because the Time Is Now: Welfare Repeal and Labor Reconstruction." In *Audacious Democracy: Labor, Intellectuals, and the Social Reconstruction of America*, edited by Steve Fraser and Joshua B. Freeman, 119–31. Boston: Houghton Mifflin.

Frank, Miriam. 1999. "Lesbian and Gay Caucuses in the U.S. Labor Movement." In *Laboring for Rights: Unions and Sexual Diversity Across Nations*, edited by Gerald Hunt, 87–102. Philadelphia: Temple University Press.

Freeman, Richard B., and Joel Rogers. 1999. *What Workers Want*. Ithaca: Cornell University Press.

Fudge, Judy. 2005. "Deemed to be Entrepreneurs: Rural Route Mail Couriers and Canada Post." In *Self-Employed Workers Organize: Law, Policy, and Unions*, edited by Cynthia Cranford, Judy Fudge, Eric Tucker, and Leah F. Vosko, 56–93. Montreal: McGill-Queen's University Press.

Fudge, Judy, Eric Tucker, and Leah F. Vosko. 2002. *The Legal Concept of Employment: Marginalizing Workers*. Ottawa: Law Commission of Canada.

Fuentes, Annette. 1996. "Slaves of New York." *In These Times*, December 23, 14–17.

Fuentes, Annette, and Barbara Ehrenreich. 1983. *Women in the Global Factory*. New York: Institute for New Communications.

Gabin, Nancy. 1985. "Women and the United Automobile Workers' Union in the 1950s." In *Women, Work, and Protest*, edited by Ruth Milkman, 259–79. Boston: Routledge & Kegan Paul.

———. 1990. *Feminism in the Labor Movement: Women and the United Auto Workers, 1935–1975*. Ithaca: Cornell University Press.

———. 2005. "Labor Unions: United Auto Workers." In *Readers Companion to U.S. Women's History*. New York: Houghton Mifflin. Online edition: http://college.hmco.com/history/ readers com/women (accessed June 10, 2005).

Gallin, Dan. 2001. "Propositions on Trade Unions and Informal Employment in Times of Globalization." In *Place, Space and the New Labor Internationalisms*, edited by Peter Waterman and Jane Wills, 227–45. Oxford: Blackwell Publishers.

———. 2002. "Organizing in the Informal Economy." In special issue on *Unprotected Labor: What Role for Unions in the Informal Economy? Labor Education* 2(127): 21–26.

Garofoli, Joe. 1998. "Recognizing Caregivers' Hard Work." *Contra Costa Times*, September 4, A03.

Glass Ceiling Commission. 1994. "Good for Business: Making Full Use of the Nation's Human Capital." Washington, D.C.: Federal Glass Ceiling Commission.

Glenn, Evelyn Nakano. 1992. "From Servitude to Service Work: Historical Continuities in the Racial Division of Paid Reproductive Labor." *Signs* 18(1): 1–43.

Goldin, Claudia. 2006. The Quiet Revolution That Transformed Women's Employment, Education, and Family. Working paper no. 11953. National Bureau of Economic Research, Cambridge, Mass.

Gordon, Colin. 1999. "The Lost City of Solidarity: Metropolitan Unionism in Historical Perspective." *Politics and Society* 27(4): 561–80.

Gordon, Suzanne. 2005. *Nursing against the Odds: How Health Care Cost Cutting, Media Stereotypes, and Medical Hubris Undermine Nurses and Patient Care*. Ithaca: Cornell University Press.

Greenhouse, Steven. 1998a. "Layoffs Rupture Tie between Giuliani and Labor Leader." *New York Times*, April 25, B1.

———. 1998b. "Many Participants in Workfare Take the Place of City Workers." *New York Times*, April 13, A1.

———. 1999a. "Chief of Building Workers' Union Leaves with $1.5 Million," *New York Times*, February 3, B1.

———. 1999b. "In Biggest Drive since 1937, Union Gains a Victory," *New York Times*, February 26, A1, A15.

———. 2001. "Federal Suit Accuses City of Not Acting on Harassment Complaints in Workfare Jobs." *New York Times*, July 5, sec. 1, p. 27.

———. 2002. "Wage Bill Would Protect Housekeepers and Nannies." *New York Times*, March 25, B1.

———. 2004a. "Growers Group Signs the First Union Contract for Guest Workers." *New York Times*, September 17, A16.

———. 2004b. "Rewards of a 90–Hour Week: Poverty and Dirty Laundry." *New York Times*, May 31, B1.

———. 2005a. "Among Janitors, Labor Violations Go with the Job." *New York Times*, July 13, A1.

———. 2005b. "Can't a Retail Behemoth Pay More?" *New York Times*, May 4, C1.

Gross, Greg. 1980. "Homemakers Union to Sign Its 1st Pact." *San Diego Union*, November 20, 1.

Guinier, Lani, and Gerald Torres. 2002. *The Miner's Canary: Enlisting Race, Resisting Power, Transforming Democracy*. Cambridge, Mass.: Harvard University Press.

Hardisty, Jean, and Lucy A. Williams. 2002. "The Right's Campaign against Welfare." In *From Poverty to Punishment: How Welfare Reform Punishes the Poor*, edited by Gary Delgado, 53–72. Oakland, Calif.: Applied Research Center.

Harrison, Bennett, and Bluestone, Barry. 1988. *The Great U-turn: Corporate Restructuring and the Polarizing of America*. New York: Basic Books.

Hart, Keith. 1973. "Informal Income Opportunities and Urban Employment in Ghana." *Journal of Modern African Studies* 11, 61–89.

Hart Research Associates, Peter D. 1998. "Working Women's View of the Economy, Unions, and Public Policy." In *Not Your Father's Labor Movement: Inside the AFL-CIO*, edited by Jo-Ann Mort, 69–85. New York: Verso.

Hartmann, Heidi I., and Stephanie Aaronson. 1994. "Pay Equity and Women's Wage Increases: Success in the States, a Model for the Nation." *Duke Journal of Gender Law and Policy* 1: 69–87.

Hayashi, Dennis. 1992. "Preventing Human Rights Abuses in the U.S. Garment Industry: A Proposed Amendment to the Fair Labor Standards Act." *Yale Journal of International Law* 17: 195.

Head, Simon. 2004. "Inside the Leviathan." *New York Review of Books*, December 16, 80–89.

Health/PAC Bulletin. 1987. "Home Health Workers Seek Gains." summer, 29.

Healy, Melissa. 1997. "N.Y. 'Workfare' Not So Fair after All, Some Say." *Los Angeles Times*, July 5, 1.

Heinritz-Canterbury, Janet. 1993. Letter to Ed Roberts Box 7, Folder 36, Edward V. Roberts Papers, Bancroft Library, University of California, Berkeley, Calif. September 20.

——. 2002. *Collaborating to Improve In-Home Supportive Services: Stakeholder Perspectives on California's Public Authorities*. New York: Paraprofessional Healthcare Institute.

——. Unpublished papers. 1990–1999. Undeposited.

Heumann, Judy. 1987. Letter to Phyllis Zlotnick. Box 21, Folder 6, World Institute on Disability Papers, Bancroft Library, University of California, Berkeley, Berkeley, Calif. January 5.

Heymann, Jody. 2000. *The Work, Family and Equity Index: Where Does the United States Stand Globally?* Boston: Project on Global Working Families.

Heymann, Jody, and Alison Earle. 1999. "The Impact of Welfare Reform on Parents' Ability to Care for Their Children's Health." *American Journal of Public Health* 89: 502–5.

Himmelweit, Susan. 1999. "Caring Labor." The *ANNALS* 561: 27–37.

Hirsch, Barry T., and David A. Macpherson. 2005. *Union Membership and Earnings Data Book: Compilations from the Current Population Survey*. Washington, D.C.: Bureau of National Affairs.

Hoerr, John. 1998. *We Can't Eat Prestige: The Women Who Organized Harvard*. Philadelphia: Temple University Press.

Hoff, Timothy J. 2004. "Doing the Same and Earning Less: Male and Female Physicians in a New Medical Specialty." *Inquiry—Excellus Health Plan* 41(3): 301–15.

Holcomb, Desma. 1999. "Domestic Partner Health Benefits: The Corporate Model vs. the Union Model." In *Laboring for Rights: Unions and Sexual Diversity across Nations*, edited by Gerald Hunt, 103–20. Philadelphia: Temple University Press.

Holcomb, Desma, and Nancy Wohlforth. 2001. "The Fruits of Labor: Pride at Work." *New Labor Forum* 8(spring/summer): 9–20.

HomeNet South Asia. 2002. *Newsletter of the South Asian Network for Homebased Workers*, April 2.

Hondagneu-Sotelo, Pierette. 2001. *Doméstica: Immigrant Workers Cleaning and Caring in the Shadows of Affluence*. Berkeley: University of California Press.

Humphrey, Jill. 2002. *Towards a Politics of the Rainbow: Self-Organising in the Trade Union Movement*. Aldershot, UK: Ashgate.

Hunt, Gerald. 1997. "Sexual Orientation and the Canadian Labour Movement," *Relations Industrielle/Industrial Relations* 53(4): 731–53.

Hunt, Gerald, ed. 1999. *Laboring for Rights: Unions and Sexual Diversity across Nations.* Philadelphia: Temple University Press.

Hunt, Gerald, and David Rayside. 2000. "Labor Union Response to Diversity in Canada and the United States." *Industrial Relations* 39(3): 401–44.

———. 2001. "The Geo-Politics of Sexual Diversity: Measuring Progress in the U.S., Canada and the Netherlands." *New Labor Forum* 8(spring/summer): 37–48.

Hurd, Richard W. 1993. "Organizing and Representing Clerical Workers: The Harvard Model." In *Women and Unions: Forging a Partnership,* edited by Dorothy Sue Cobble, 316–36. Ithaca: Cornell University Press.

Hyde, Alan. 2004. "Who Speaks for the Working Poor? A Preliminary Look at the Emerging Tetralogy of Representation of Low-Wage Service Workers." *Cornell Journal of Law & Public Policy* 13: 599–614.

Indonesian Tainan Workers. 2002. Letter from Indonesia workers to El Salvador workers. July 10, Jakarta.

International Confederation of Free Trade Unions (ICFTU). 2002. General Discussion on the Informal Economy (unpublished platform). On file with author.

International Labour Organisation (ILO). 2002a. *Decent Work in the Informal Economy: Report VI.* International Labor Conference, 90th Session, Geneva.

———. 2002b. *Report of the Committee on the Informal Economy. Sixth Item of the Agenda: the Informal Economy (general discussion).* Provisional record, ILO.

Jacobs, Jerry A. 2003. "Detours on the Road to Equality: Women, Work, and Higher Education." *Contexts* 2(winter): 32–40.

Jacobs, Jerry, and Kathleen Gerson. 2004. *The Time Divide.* Cambridge, Mass.: Harvard University Press.

Jacoby, Sanford. 2005. "Corporate Governance and Society." *Challenge* 48(4): 69–87.

Jeter, Jon. 1997. "Md. Shields Jobs from Welfare Law." *Washington Post,* May 4, A01.

Jews for Racial and Economic Justice (JFREJ). 2005. Flier, distributed in June 2005, New York City.

Jhabvala, Renana. 1995. "Self-Employed Women's Association: Organizing Women by Struggle and Development." In *Dignity and Daily Bread: New Forms of Economic Organizing among Poor Women from the Third World and the First,* edited by Sheila Rowbotham and Swasti Mitter, 115–38. London: Routledge.

Johnson, Gloria. 1993. "Comments." In *Women and Unions: Forging a Partnership,* edited by Dorothy Sue Cobble, 93–99. Ithaca: ILR Press.

Jones, Charisse. 1989. "Providers of Home Care in Budget Pinch." *Los Angeles Times,* March 22, 2–1.

Jones-Correa, Michael. 1998. "Different Paths: Gender, Immigration and Political Participation." *International Migration Review* 32(2): 326–49.

Juhn, Chinhui, and Kevin M. Murphy. 1997. "Wage Inequality and Family Labor Supply." *Journal of Labor Economics* 15(1): 72–97.

Justice, Dwight. 2002. "Work, Law and the Informality Concept." In special issue on *Unprotected Labor: What Role for Unions in the Informal Economy? Labor Education* 2(127): 1–5.

Katz, Jonathan. 1992. *Gay American History: Lesbians and Gay Men in the U.S.A.: A Documentary History.* Rev. ed. New Haven: Meridian Books.

Kay, Tamara. 2005. "Labor Transnationalism and Global Governance: The Impact of NAFTA on Transnational Labor Relationships in North America." *American Journal of Sociology* 111: 715–56.

———. (2006). Legal Transnationalism: Transnational Law, Governance, and Movement Building Under NAFTA. Unpublished manuscript.

Keck, Margaret E., and Kathryn Sikkink. 1998. *Activists beyond Borders: Advocacy Networks in International Politics*. Ithaca: Cornell University Press.

Kennedy, Elizabeth Lapovsky, and Madeline D. Davis. 1994. *Boots of Leather, Slippers of Gold: The History of a Lesbian Community*. New York: Penguin Books.

Kerchner, Charles. 1999. "Knowledge Workers: Trade Union's New Frontier." *Thought and Action: The NEA Higher Education Journal* 15(2): 11–17.

Kessler-Harris, Alice. 1982. *Out to Work: A History of Wage-Earning Women in the United States*. New York: Oxford University Press.

Kim, Kathleen, and Kusia Hreshchyshyn. 2004. "Human Trafficking Private Rights of Action: Civil Rights for Trafficked Persons in the United States." *Hastings Women's Law Journal* 16: 1–36.

Krueger, Liz, Liz Accles, and Laura Wernick. 1997. *Workfare: The Real Deal II*. New York: Community Food Resource Center.

Krupat, Kitty. 1999. "Out of Labor's Dark Age: Sexual Politics Comes to the Workplace." *Social Text* 17(4): 9–29.

Krupat, Kitty, and Patrick McCreery. 2001. *Out at Work: Building a Gay-Labor Alliance*. Minneapolis: University of Minnesota Press.

Ladd, Deena. 1998. No Easy Recipe: Building the Diversity and Strength of the Labor Movement. Paper presented at Feminist Organizing Models, Canadian Labour Congress Women's Symposium, Ottawa, Canada.

Lake Snell Perry and Associates. 2003. Report on focus group data, prepared for the AFL-CIO, February. Unpublished.

Lang, Sabine. 1997. "The NGOization of Feminism: Institutionalization and Institution Building within the German Women's Movements." In *Transitions, Environments, Translations: Feminisms in International Politics*, edited by Joan W. Scott, Cora Kaplan, and Debra Keates, 101–20. New York: Routledge.

Lapidus, Jane, and Deborah M. Figart. 1998. "Remedying 'Unfair Acts': U.S. Pay Equity by Race and Gender." *Feminist Economics* 4(3): 7–28.

Lardner, James, and David A. Smith, eds. 2005. *Inequality Matters: The Growing Economic Divide in America and Its Poisonous Consequences*. New York: New Press.

Lareau, Annette. 2003. *Unequal Childhoods*. Berkeley: University of California Press.

Leary, Elly. 1998. Keeping a Floor under the Working Class: A New Approach to Welfare Organizing. Paper presented at the American Sociological Association, San Francisco.

Levy, Frank. 1999. *The New Dollars and Dreams: American Incomes and Economic Change*. New York: Russell Sage.

Lichtenstein, Nelson. 1995. *The Most Dangerous Man in Detroit: Walter Reuther and the Fate of American Labor*. New York: Basic Books.

———. 2005. "Wal-Mart and the New World Order: A Template for Twenty-First Century Capitalism?" *New Labor Forum* 14(1): 21–30.

Lim, Lin. 2002. Decent Work and the Informal Economy. Paper presented at the conference on Rethinking Labor Market Informalization: Precarious Jobs, Poverty and Social Protection, Cornell University, October 18–19.

Linder, Marc. 1987. "Farm Workers and the Farm Labor Standards Act: Racial Discrimination in the New Deal." *Texas Law Review* 65: 1335.

———. 1999–2000. "Dependent and Independent Contractors in Recent U.S. Labor Law: An Ambiguous Dichotomy Rooted in Simulated Statutory Purposelessness." *Comparative Labor Law and Policy Journal* 21: 187.

Littman, Mark S. 1998. *A Statistical Portrait of the United States: Social Conditions and Trends.* Lanham, Md.: Bernan Press.

Lobel, Jules. 1995. "Losers, Fools and Prophets: Justice as Struggle." *Cornell Law Review* 80: 1331–421.

Lopez-Claros, Augusto, and Saadia Zahidi. 2005. "Women's Empowerment: Measuring the Global Gender Gap." World Economic Forum, Geneva, Switzerland.

Luce, Stephanie. 2005. "The Role of Community Involvement in Implementing Living Wage Ordinances." *Industrial Relations* 44(1): 32–58.

Luna, Guadalupe T. 1998. "An Infinite Distance?: Agricultural Exceptionalism and Agricultural Labor." *University of Pennsylvania Journal of Labor and Employment Law* 1: 487.

Lynd, Staughton. 1982. *The Fight against Shutdowns: Youngstown's Steel Mill Closings.* San Pedro, Calif.: Singlejack Books.

MacDonald, Diane. 1998. The New Deal Model of Collective Bargaining and the Secondary Labor Market. PhD diss., Northeastern University.

MacLean, Nancy. 2006. *Freedom Is Not Enough: The Opening of the American Workplace.* Cambridge, Mass., and New York: Harvard University Press and Russell Sage Foundation.

Malveaux, Julianne. 1986. "Comparable Worth and Its Impact on Black Women." In *Slipping through the Cracks: The Status of Black Women*, edited by Margaret C. Simms and Julianne Malveaux, 47–62. New Brunswick, N.J.: Transaction Books.

Mankiller, Wilma, Gwendolyn Mink, Maysa Navarro, Barbara Smith, and Gloria Steinem. 1998. *The Reader's Companion to U.S. Women's History.* New York: Houghton Mifflin Company.

May, Martha. 1985. "Bread before Roses: American Workingmen, Labor Unions, and the Family Wage." In *Women, Work, and Protest*, edited by Ruth Milkman, 1–21. Boston: Routledge and Kegan Paul.

McBride, Anne. 2001. *Gender Democracy in Trade Unions.* Aldershot, UK: Ashgate.

McCall, Leslie. 2001. *Complex Inequality: Gender, Class, and Race in the New Economy.* New York: Routledge.

———. 2004. The Inequality Economy: How New Corporate Practices Redistribute Income to the Top. Working paper. Demos: A Network for Ideas and Action. New York.

———. Forthcoming. "What Does Class Inequality among Women Look Like? A Comparison with Men and Families, 1970–2000." In *Social Class: How Does it Work?* edited by Annette Lareau and Dalton Conley.

McCann, Michael W. 1994. *Rights at Work: Pay Equity Reform and the Politics of Legal Mobilization.* Chicago: University of Chicago Press.

McGolrick, Susan J. 2005. "ILA Agrees to Pay $1.65 Million to Settle Discrimination Suit by Female Dockworkers." *Daily Labor Report BNA*, September 26, A-1.

Meyer, Mary K., and Elisabeth Prügl, eds. 1999. *Gender Politics in Global Governance.* Lantham, Md.: Rowman & Littlefield.

Michael, Robert T., Heidi I. Hartmann, and Brigid O'Farell, eds. 1989. *Pay Equity: Empirical Inquiries.* Washington, D.C.: National Academies Press.

Middleton, Jennifer. 1996. "Contingent Workers in a Changing Economy: Endure, Adapt or Organize?" *New York University Review of Law and Social Change* 22: 557–620.

Milkman, Ruth. 1985. "Women Workers, Feminism, and the Labor Movement since the 1960s." In *Women, Work, and Protest*, edited by Ruth Milkman, 300–22. Boston: Routledge & Kegan Paul.

———. 1987. *Gender at Work: The Dynamics of Job Segregation by Sex during World War II.* Urbana: University of Illinois Press.

——. 1990. "Gender and Trade Unionism in Historical Perspective." In *Women, Politics and Change*, edited by Louise A. Tilly and Patricia Gurin, 87–107. New York: Russell Sage Foundation.

——. 1993. "Union Responses to Workforce Feminization in the U.S." In *The Challenge of Restructuring: North American Labor Movements Respond*, edited by Jane Jensen and Rianne Mahon, 226–50. Philadelphia: Temple University Press.

——. 2005. "Labor Unions." In *Readers Companion to U.S. Women's History*. New York: Houghton Mifflin. Online edition: http://college.hmco.com/history/readers com/women (accessed June 10, 2005).

——. 2006. *L.A. Story: Immigrant Workers and the Future of the U.S. Labor Movement*. New York: Russell Sage.

Milkman, Ruth, and Eileen Appelbaum. 2004. Paid Family Leave in California: New Research Findings. UCLA IIR Research Brief, University of California, Los Angeles.

Milkman, Ruth, and Daisy Rooks. 2003. "California Union Membership: A Turn-of-the-Century Portrait." In *The State of California Labor 2003*, edited by Ruth Milkman, 3–37. Berkeley: University of California Press.

Milkman, Ruth, and Kent Wong. 2001. "Organizing Immigrant Workers: Case Studies from Southern California." In *Rekindling the Movement: Labor's Quest for 21st Century Relevance*, edited by Lowell Turner, Harry Katz, and Richard Hurd, 99–128. Ithaca: Cornell University Press.

Mink, Gwendolyn. 1998. *Welfare's End*. Ithaca: Cornell University Press.

Mishel, Lawrence, Jared Bernstein, and Sylvia Allegretto. 2005. *The State of Working America 2004/2005*. Ithaca: Cornell University Press.

Mishel, Lawrence, Jared Bernstein, and Heather Boushey. 2003. *The State of Working America, 2002/2003*. Ithaca: ILR Press.

Mitter, Swasti. 1986. *Common Fate, Common Bond: Women in the Global Economy*. London: Pluto Press.

Moen, Phyllis, and Patricia Roehling. 2004. *Career Mystique: Cracks in the American Dream*. New York: Rowman & Littlefield.

Moghadam, Valerie M. 2000. "Transnational Feminist Networks: Collective Action in an Era of Globalization." *International Sociology* 15(1): 57–85.

Mohanty, Chandra Talpade. 2003. "Women Workers and the Politics of Solidarity." In *Feminism without Borders: Decolonizing Theory, Practicing Solidarity*, edited by Chandra Talpade Mohanty, 139–68. Durham: Duke University Press.

Morgan, Kimberly. 2005. "The 'Production' of Child Care: How Labor Markets Shape Social Policy, and Vice Versa." *Social Politics* 12(2): 243–63.

Morissette, René, Grant Schellenberg, and Anick Johnson. 2005. "Diverging Trends in Unionization." *Perspectives on Labour and Income* 6(4): 5–12.

Moyers, Bill. 2005. Address to Take Back America 2005: The Conference for Americas Future, Washington Hilton Hotel, Washington, D.C., June 3. Transcript available at http://www.ourfuture.org/docUploads/caf060205moyers.pdf (accessed September 6, 2006).

Muenchow, Susan. 2004. Preschool for All: Step by Step. First 5 Commission and American Institutes for Research, Sacramento, Calif.

Mulligan, Casey, and Yona Rubenstein. 2004. The Closing of the Gender Gap as a Roy Model Illusion. Working paper no. 10892. National Bureau of Economic Research, Cambridge, Mass.

Munroe, Ann. 1999. *Women, Work and Trade Unions*. London: Mansell.

Murphy, Evelyn, with E. J. Graff. 2005. *Getting Even: Why Women Don't Get Paid Like Men—and What to Do about It*. New York: Simon and Shuster.

Murphy, Marjorie. 1990. *Blackboard Unions: The AFT and the NEA, 1900–1980*. Ithaca: Cornell University Press.

Nadasen, Premilla. 2005. *Welfare Warriors: the Welfare Rights Movement in the United States*. New York: Routledge.

Namie, Gary, and Ruth Namie. 2004. "Workplace Bullying: How to Address America's Silent Epidemic." *Employee Rights and Employment Policy Journal* 8: 315–33.

Nash, June, and María Patricia Fernández-Kelly. 1983. *Women, Men, and the International Division of Labor*. Albany: State University of New York Press.

National Partnership for Women & Families. 2005. At-Home Infant Care (AHIC): A Side-by-Side Comparison of Federal and State Initiatives [updated 9/05]. Ottawa, Canada: National Partnership for Women & Families.

New York State Assembly. 1975a. Committee Bill Memorandum, Assembly Bill A-4297, Box 1, Folder "Household Workers Collective Bargaining, 1975," Seymour Posner Papers, Collection #70: Tamiment Library and Robert F. Wagner Labor Archives, New York University.

———. 1975b. "Statement Before the Assembly Standing Committee on Labor, Arnold Mauer, Service Employees International Union," April 18, 1975, Box 1, Folder "Household Workers Collective Bargaining, 1975," Seymour Posner Papers, Collection #70: Tamiment Library and Robert F. Wagner Labor Archives, New York University.

———. 1975c. "Testimony from Eleanor Holmes Norton," Assembly Standing Committee on Labor, April 18, 1975, Box 1, Folder "Household Workers Collective Bargaining, 1975," Seymour Posner Papers, Collection #70: Tamiment Library and Robert F. Wagner Labor Archives, New York University.

New York Times, and Bill Keller. 2005. *Class Matters*. New York: New York Times Books.

Nguyen, Tram. 2001. "Real Reforms: State Efforts That Reform, Not Deform, the System for Welfare Recipients." *ColorLines* 4(2): 10.

Northwest Labor Press. 2001. "Home Health Care Workers Vote on Unionization." November 16, n.p.

O'Brien, Robert, Anne Marie Goetz, Jan Aart Scholte, and Marc Williams. 2000. *Contesting Global Governance: Multilateral Economic Institutions and Global Social Movements*. Cambridge, UK: Cambridge University Press.

Ontiveros, Maria. 2002. "Lessons from the Fields: Female Farmworkers and the Law." *Maine Law Review* 55(1): 158–89.

———. 2004. "Immigrant Workers' Rights in a Post-*Hoffman* World—Organizing around the Thirteenth Amendment." *Georgetown Immigration Law Journal* 18: 651–80.

Oppenheim, Lisa. 1991. "Women's Ways of Organizing: A Conversation with AFSCME Organizers Kris Rondeau and Gladys McKenzie." *Labor Research Review* 18: 45–60.

Orleck, Annelise. 1995. *Common Sense and a Little Fire: Women and Working-Class Politics in the US, 1900–1965*. Chapel Hill: University of North Carolina Press.

Osborne, Duncan. 1997. "Lavender Labor: A Brief History." In *Homo Economics: Capitalism, Community, and Lesbian and Gay Life*, edited by Amy Gluckman and Betsy Reed, 223–28. New York: Routledge.

Palmer, Phyllis. 1989. *Domesticity and Dirt: Housewives and Domestic Servants in the United States, 1920–1945*. Philadelphia: Temple University Press.

Parker, Paula. 1980. "Domestics' Union Makes Gains." *Los Angeles Times*, November 22, San Diego County section, A1.

Perlmutter, Emanuel. 1965. "The Welfare Tangle." *New York Times*, January 25, 19.

Phipps, Polly A. 1990. "Industrial and Occupational Change in Pharmacy: Prescription for Feminization." In *Job Queues: Explaining Women's Inroads into Male Occupations*, edited by Barbara F. Reskin and Patricia A. Roos, 111–27. Philadelphia: Temple University Press.

Piven, Frances Fox. 1997. "The New Reserve Army of Labor." In *Audacious Democracy: Labor, Intellectuals, and the Social Reconstruction of America*, edited by Steve Fraser and Joshua B. Freeman, 106–18. Boston: Houghton Mifflin.

Piven, Frances Fox, and Richard A. Cloward. 1977. *Poor People's Movements: Why They Succeed, How They Fail*. New York: Pantheon.

Polaski, Sandra. 2004. "Jobs, Wages, and Household Income." In *NAFTA's Promise and Reality: Lessons from Mexico for the Hemisphere*. Washington, D.C.: Carnegie Endowment for Peace.

Portes, Alejandro, and Saskia Sassen. 1987. "Making It Underground: Comparative Material on the Informal Sector in Western Market Economies." *American Journal of Sociology* 93(1): 30–61.

Posner, Seymour. 1974a. Letter to Edward Bookstein, Box 1, Folder "Household Workers Collective Bargaining, 1974," Seymour Posner Papers, Collection #70: Tamiment Library and Robert F. Wagner Labor Archives, New York University. April 3.

———. 1974b. Letter to Colleague, Box 1, Folder "Household Workers Collective Bargaining, 1974," Seymour Posner Papers, Collection #70: Tamiment Library and Robert F. Wagner Labor Archives, New York University. April 26.

Prashad, Vijay. 2003. *Keeping Up with the Dow Joneses: Debt, Prison, Workfare*. Cambridge, Mass.: South End Press.

Prügl, Elisabeth. 1999. *The Global Construction of Gender: Home-Based Work in the Political Economy of the 20th Century*. New York: Columbia University Press.

Prügl, Elisabeth, and Irene Tinker. 1996. "Micro-Entrepreneurs and Homeworkers: Convergent Categories." *World Development* 25(September): 1471–82.

Public Employee. 1969. "Lindsay Eases Crisis Impact; Pledges Minimum Effect on Jobs." May 2.

Putnam, Robert D., and Lewis Feldstein; with Don Cohen. 2003. "The Harvard Union of Clerical and Technical Workers: 'The Whole Social Thing.'" In *Better Together: Restoring the American Community*, 166–85. New York: Simon & Schuster.

Quan, Katie. 2004. "Global Strategies for Workers: How Class Analysis Clarifies *Us* and *Them* and What We Need to Do." In *What's Class Got to Do with It? American Society in the Twenty-First Century*, edited by Michael Zweig, 94–109. Ithaca: Cornell University Press.

Rathke, Wade. 2005. "Leveraging Labor's Revival: A Proposal to Organize WalMart." *New Labor Forum* 142(summer): 58–66.

Ream, Amanda. 1997. "New York Workfare Workers Vote Union." *Labor Notes* (December): 2.

Reese, Ellen. 2002. "Resisting the Workfare State: Mobilizing General Relief Recipients in Los Angeles." *Race, Gender & Class* 9(1): 72–95.

Reskin, Barbara F. 1993. "Sex Segregation in the Workplace." *Annual Review of Sociology* 19: 241–70.

Reskin, Barbara, and Irene Padavic. 2002. *Women and Men at Work*. 2nd ed. Thousand Oaks, Calif.: Pine Forge Press.

Reskin, Barbara, and Patricia Roos. 1991. *Job Queues, Gender Queues: Explaining Women's Inroads into Male Occupations*. Philadelphia: Temple University Press.

Resnik, Judith. 2004. "The Rights of Remedies: Collective Accountings for and Insuring against the Harms of Sexual Harassment." In *Directions in Sexual Harassment Law*, edited by Catherine A. MacKinnon and Riva B. Siegel, 247–71. New Haven: Yale University Press.

Reza, H. G. 1989. "Organizing Still a Labor of Love." *Los Angeles Times* (San Diego County edition), August 14, 2–1.

Riccardi, Nicholas. 2000. "Post-Welfare Jobs No Cure for Poverty, Study Finds." *Los Angeles Times*, September 7, Metro Section, p. 1.

Ricker-Smith, Katherine. 1978. An Historical and Critical Overview of the Development and Operation of California's In-Home Supportive Services Program. San Francisco Home Health Service, Grant HEW-100–78–0027, December 31, San Francisco, Calif.

Rivas, Lynn May. 2005. A Significant Alliance: The Independent Living Movement, the Service Employees International Union, and the Establishment of the First Public Authorities in California. Draft, March, World Institute on Disability, Oakland, Calif.

Roberts, Dorothy. 2004. "The Collective Injury of Sexual Harassment." In *Directions in Sexual Harassment Law*, edited by Catharine A. MacKinnon and Reva B. Siegel, 365–81. New Haven: Yale University Press.

Roberts, Patti R. 1993. "Comments." In *Women and Unions: Forging a Partnership*, edited by Dorothy S. Cobble, 349–56. Ithaca: ILR Press.

Robles, Betty. 2003. Statement by Betty Robles to shareholders and Sara Lee executives, October 30, 2003, Tampa, Fla. Document from Enlace.

Rollins, Judith. 1985. *Between Women: Domestics and Their Employers*. Philadelphia: Temple University Press.

Romero, Mary. 1992. *Maid in the U.S.A.* New York: Routledge.

Romney, Lee. 2005. "Assembly Bill Targets Forced Labor." *Los Angeles Times*, August 25, California Metro, B1.

Rose, Kalima. 1992. *Where Women Are Leaders: The SEWA Movement in India*. London: Zed Books.

Rose, Nancy E. 1995. *Workfare or Fair Work: Women, Welfare, and Government Work Programs*. New Brunswick, N.J.: Rutgers University Press.

Rose, Stephen J., and Heidi I. Hartmann. 2004. *Still a Man's Labor Market: The Long-Term Earnings Gap*. IWPR Publication #C355. Washington, D.C.: Institute for Women's Policy Research.

Rothenberg, Daniel. 1998. *With These Hands—The Hidden World of Migrant Farmworkers Today*. Berkeley: University of California Press.

Russell, Marta. 1993. "At the ATTENDANT CROSSROADS." Typescript manuscript. Box 7, Folder 36, Edward V. Roberts Papers, Bancroft Library, University of California, Berkeley, Calif. August.

——. 1996. "L.A. County Public Authority: A Zero-Sum Game." *New Mobility*, November 7, 40, 50–52.

Sacramento Union. 1993. "Seniors Fear the New Law Will Send Many to Nursing Homes." Box 36, Folder 7, Edward V. Roberts Papers, Bancroft Library, University of California, Berkeley, Calif. July 27.

Savage, Lydia. 1996. Negotiating Common Ground: The Geography of Organizing Women Workers in the Service Sector. PhD diss., Clark University.

——. 1998. "Geographies of Organizing: Justice for Janitors in Los Angeles." In *Organizing the Landscape: Geographical Perspectives on Labor Unionism*, edited by Andrew Herod, 225–52. Minneapolis: University of Minnesota Press.

——. 2005. Changing Organizing, Organizing Change: SHARE at UMass Memorial. Unpublished manuscript.

Schulman, Karen. 2000. *The High Cost of Child Care Puts Quality Care out of Reach for Many Families*. Washington, D.C.: Children's Defense Fund.

Schultz, Vicki. 1998. "Reconceptualizing Sexual Harassment." *Yale Law Journal* 107: 1683–805.

———. 2000. "Life's Work." *Columbia Law Review* 100: 1881–964.

Schwartz, Christine R., and Robert D. Mare. 2005. Trends in Educational Assortative Marriage from 1940 to 2003. Working paper, California Center for Population Research, University of California, Los Angeles.

Scott, Joan. 1999. *Gender and the Politics of History*. 2nd ed. New York: Columbia University Press.

Seaton-Msemaji, Ken. 1993. " 'He Believed Every Human Being Was Valuable.' " *The Sacramento Observer*, May 27–June 2, n.p.

Selmi, Michael. 2003. "The Price of Discrimination: The Nature of Class Action Employment Discrimination Litigation and Its Effects." *Texas Law Review* 81: 1249–332.

Service Employees International Union (SEIU). 1978. "N.Y. Household Workers Move 'Up from Slavery'." *Service Employee*, September, 2.

———. 1984. Correspondence, Folder "Local 7, 1984," Box 191, President's Office, SEIU Papers, Reuther Library, Wayne State University, Detroit, Mich.

———. 1988. "Program Proposals," attached to Peter Rider to Health Care Organizing Team et al. on 5/25 Meeting Assignment, 2, SEIU Organizing Department, Box 1, Folder "Healthcare Organizing, 1988," SEIU Papers, Reuther Library, Wayne State University, Detroit, Mich.

———. 1992. "Organizing Homecare," 3, SEIU Organizing General 1984–92, Box 42, Folder "Health Care Organizing, 1992," SEIU Papers, Reuther Library, Wayne State University, Detroit, Mich.

———. 1994. "Setting a Precedent." *Health Care Worker Update* 8(winter/spring): 4.

Service Employees International Union (SEIU) 32J-32B. 1977. "Household Workers Say: We Want A Union!!!" *32B-32J SEIU Newsletter* 45(9): 3.

———. 1978a. "Household Workers Organizing Drive under Full Steam" *32B-32J Newsletter* 46(8): 1–2.

———. 1978b. "Household Workers Choose Local 32B-32J." *32B-32J Newsletter* 46(7): 1.

———. 1981a. "Domestic Workers Become Home Attendants." *Home Care Workers News* 3(September): 1.

———. 1981b. "Contract Talks Begin for Home Attendants." *Home Care Workers News* 3(September): 1.

———. 1982. "SEIU Charters Home Attendants Union on Labor Day," *32B-32J Newsletter* 50(7): 1.

Service Employees International Union (SEIU) 32B-32J-144. 1983–1991. *32B-32J-144 News*.

Service Employees International Union (SEIU) Local 144. 1977. "Union Appeals to the State: Nursing Home Crisis—Strike Looms." *Local 144 News* 25(2): 1, 3.

Service Employees International Union (SEIU) 880. 1986–1995. *Local 880 Voice*. SEIU Publications 880. SEIU Papers, Reuther Library, Wayne State University, Detroit, Mich.

Shilts, Randy. 1982. *The Mayor of Castro Street: The Life and Time of Harvey Milk*. New York: St. Martin's Press.

Shipler, David. 2004. *The Working Poor: Invisible in America*. New York: Knopf.

Simmons, Louise. 2002. "Unions and Welfare Reform: Labor's Stake in the Ongoing Struggle over the Welfare State." *Labor Studies Journal* 27(2): 65–83.

Slater, Joseph E. 2004. *Public Workers: Government Employee Unions, the Law, and the State, 1900–1962*. Ithaca: Cornell University Press.

Smith, Pam. 2005. "Bay Area Lawmakers Urge New Human Trafficking Law." *The Recorder*, May 25, 2.

Smith, Peggie R. 2000. "Organizing the Unorganizable: Private Paid Household Workers and Approaches to Employee Representation." *North Carolina Law Review* 79: 1335.

Spitzer, Eliot. 2005. "Eight Employment Agencies to End Discriminatory Practices." Press release from the Office of the New York State Attorney General. May 31, New York.

Stall, Susan, and Randy Stoeker. 1998. "Community Organizing or Organizing Community? Gender and the Crafts of Empowerment." *Gender and Society* 12: 729–56.

Standing, Guy. 1997. "Globalization, Labor Flexibility and Insecurity: The Era of Market Regulation." *European Journal of Industrial Relations* 3(1): 7–37.

Stein, Marc. 2000. *City of Sisterly and Brotherly Loves: Lesbian and Gay Philadelphia, 1945–1972*. Chicago: University of Chicago Press.

Stevens, Joann. 1979. "Domestics Workers Seek Increased Benefits." *Washington Post*, July 19, 1.

Stewart, Brenda. 1997. Public presentation, WEP Forum, New York City, May 28.

Stewart, James. 1997. "Coming Out at Chrysler." *New Yorker* 73(20): 38–49.

Stone, Deborah. 2000. "Caring by the Book." In *Care Work: Gender, Labor, and the Welfare State*, edited by Madonna H. Meyer, 89–111. New York: Routledge.

Stone, Pamela, and Arielle Kuperberg. 2005. "Anti-Discrimination vs. Anti-Poverty? A Comparison of Pay Equity and Living Wage Reforms." *Journal of Women, Politics & Policy* 27(3–4): 23–39.

StreetNet Association. 2002. *Newsletter,* May 4.

Sweeney, John. 1999. "The Growing Alliance between Gay and Union Activists" *Social Text* 17(4): 32–38.

Sweeney, Megan M., and Maria Cancian. 2004. "The Changing Importance of White Women's Economic Prospects for Assortative Mating." *Journal of Marriage and the Family* 66: 1015–28.

Tait, Vanessa. 2005. *Poor Workers' Unions: Rebuilding Labor From Below*. Cambridge, Mass.: South End Press.

Takaki, Ronald. 1983. *Pau Hana: Plantation Life and Labor in Hawaii*. Honolulu: University of Hawaii Press.

Tamayo, William R. 2000. "The Role of the EEOC in Protecting the Civil Rights of Farm Workers." *U.C. Davis Law Review* 33: 1075.

Thompson, Edward P. 1963. *The Making of the English Working Class*. New York: Vintage Books.

Tillmon, Johnnie. 1971. "Insights of a Welfare Mother: A Conversation with Johnnie Tillmon." Interviewed by Hobart A. Burch. *Journal of Social Issues* (January–February): 13–23.

Tinker, Ann. 1999. "Non Governmental Organizations: An Alternative Power Base for Women?" In *Gender Politics in Global Governance*, edited by Mary K. Meyer and Elizabeth Prügl, 88–104. Lantham, Md.: Rowman & Littlefield.

Toy, Alan. 1996. "L.A. County Public Authority: An Empowering Solution." *New Mobility*, November 7, 41, 55–69.

Trager, Brahna. 1973. *Homemaker-Home Health Aide Services in the United States*. Washington, D.C.: U.S. Public Health Service, Department of Health, Education and Welfare.

Treiman, Donald. 1979. *Job Evaluation: An Analytic Review*. Interim Report to the Equal Employment Opportunity Commission. Washington, D.C.: National Academy of Sciences.

Treiman, Donald, and Heidi Hartmann, eds. 1981. *Women, Work, and Wages: Equal Pay for Jobs of Equal Value*. Washington, D.C.: National Academy of Sciences.

Tucker, Eric. 2005. "Star Wars: Newspaper Distribution Workers and the Possibilities and Limits of Collective Bargaining." In *Self-Employed Workers Organize: Law, Policy, and Unions,* edited by Cynthia Cranford, Judy Fudge, Eric Tucker, and Leah F. Vosko, 29–55. Montreal and Kingston: McGill-Queen's University Press.

U.S. Bureau of the Census. 1976. *The Statistical History of the United States from Colonial Times to the Present: Historical Statistics of the United States, Colonial Times to 1970.* New York: Basic Books.

———. 2006. "Section 12: Labor Force, Employment, and Earnings." In *Statistical Abstract of the United States, 2004–2005,* 569–640. Washington, D.C. http://www.census.gov/prod/2004pubs/04statab/labor.pdf (accessed September 9, 2006).

U.S. Bureau of Labor Statistics. 2005. *Highlights of Women's Earnings in 2004.* Report 987. Washington D.C.: U.S. Department of Labor.

U.S. Congress, House of Representatives. 1979. *Independent Contractors.* Hearings before the Subcommittee on Select Revenue Measures of the Committee on Ways and Means, 96th Congress, 1st Session. Washington, D.C.: Government Printing Office.

U.S. Department of Labor. 2002. "Directory of U.S. Labor Organizations." Washington, D.C.: Government Printing Office.

U.S. Department of Labor. Bureau of Labor Statistics. 2005. *Women in the Labor Force: A Databook.* http://www.bls.gov/cps/wlf-databook2005.htm (accessed September 10, 2006).

U.S. General Accounting Office. 2002. "Collective Bargaining Rights: Information on the Number of Workers with and without Bargaining Rights." GAO-02-835, September, Washington, D.C.

Vandervelde, Lea. 2004. "Coercion in At-Will Termination of Employment and Sexual Harassment." In *Directions in Sexual Harassment Law,* edited by Catherine A. MacKinnon and Riva B. Siegel, 496–515. New Haven: Yale University Press.

Verkerke, J. Hoult. 1995. "An Empirical Perspective on Indefinite Term Employment Contracts: Resolving the Just Cause Debate." *Wisconsin Law Review* 1995: 838–918.

Vobejda, Barbara. 1997. "Workfare Must Pay Minimum Wage, White House Says." *Washington Post,* May 17, A06.

Vosko, Leah F. 2000. *Temporary Work: The Gendered Rise of a Precarious Employment Relationship.* Toronto: University of Toronto Press.

———. 2004. *Confronting the Norm: Gender and the International Regulation of Precarious Work.* Ottawa: Law Commission of Canada.

———. 2005. "The Precarious Status of the Artist: Freelance Editors' Struggle for Collective Bargaining Rights." In *Self-Employed Workers Organize: Law, Policy, and Unions,* edited by Cynthia Cranford, Judy Fudge, Eric Tucker, and Leah F. Vosko, 136–69. Montreal and Kingston: McGill-Queen's University Press.

Vosko, Leah F., Nancy Zukewich, and Cynthia Cranford. 2003. "Precarious Jobs: A New Typology of Employment." *Perspectives on Labour and Income* 4(10): 16–26.

Waldfogel, Jane. 1997. "The Effect of Children on Women's Wages." *American Sociological Review* 62: 209–17.

Waldinger, Roger. 2001. *Strangers at the Gates: New Immigrants in Urban America.* Berkeley: University of California Press.

Walsh, Jess. 2001. "Creating Unions, Creating Employers: A Los Angeles Home-Care Campaign." In *Care Work: The Quest for Security,* edited by Mary Daly, 219–33. Geneva: International Labour Organisation.

Ward, Katherine, ed. 1990. *Women Workers and Global Restructuring.* Ithaca: Cornell University Press, ILR Imprint.

Weiler, Paul. 1990. *Governing the Workplace: The Future of Labor and Employment Law.* Cambridge, Mass.: Harvard University Press.

Wertheimer, Richard. 2001. *Poor Families in 2001: Parents Working Less and Children Continue to Lag Behind.* Washington, D.C.: Child Trends.

Whitehouse, Gillian, Di Zetlin, and Jill Earnshaw. 2001. "Prosecuting Pay Equity: Evolving Strategies in Britain and Australia." *Gender, Work, and Organization* 8(4): 365–86.

Wick, Ingeborg. 2000. *Shadow Economy and Trades Unions.* Duisburg: WAZ-Druck.

Wildavsky, Ben. 1997. "Taking Credit: Low-Wage Businesses Love Getting a Tax Credit for Hiring Disadvantaged Workers." *National Journal* 29(13): 610–12.

Williams, Joan. 2000. *Unbending Gender.* New York: Oxford University Press.

Wishnie, Michael J. 2002. "Immigrant Workers and the Domestic Enforcement of International Labor Rights." *University of Pennsylvania Journal of Labor & Employment Law* 4: 529.

Women in Informal Employment Globalizing and Organizing (WIEGO). 2002. "Platform on 'Decent Work in the Informal Economy.'" Unpublished brief, Cambridge, Mass.

——. 2005. "About WIEGO: Origins and Mission." Women in Informal Employment Globalizing and Organizing, http://www.wiego.org/about/ (accessed March 1, 2005).

Worker Rights Consortium (WRC). 2003. Worker Rights Consortium Assessment re: Primo S. A. de C. V. (El Salvador): Preliminary Findings and Recommendations. WRC, Washington, D.C.

——. 2005. Assessment re Confecciones de Monclova S. de R. L. de C. V. (Mexico): Finds, Recommendations, and Status Report. Unpublished report, WRC, Washington, D.C.

Yamada, David C. 2000. "The Phenomenon of 'Workplace Bullying' and the Need for Status-Blind Hostile Work Environment Protection." *Georgetown Law Journal* 88: 475–536.

——. 2004. "Crafting a Legislative Response to Workplace Bullying." *Employee Rights and Employment Policy Journal* 8: 475–521.

Yeager, Patricia. 1993. Letter to Senator David G. Kelley. Box 36, Folder 7, Edward V. Roberts Papers, Bancroft Library, University of California, Berkeley, Calif. June 16.

Yeung, Bernice. 2004. "Enslaved in Palo Alto." *San Francisco Weekly*, February 18, http://www.sfweekly.com/Issues/2004-02-18/news/feature.html (accessed August 20, 2006).

Zweig, Michael. 2000. *Working-Class Majority: America's Best Kept Secret.* Ithaca: Cornell University Press.

ABOUT THE CONTRIBUTORS

Monica Bielski Boris is a labor education specialist for the University of Arkansas, Little Rock. She holds a B.A. from Oberlin College and an M.S. and Ph.D. from Rutgers University. She is currently working on a project examining prospects for unionism in the southern United States.

Eileen Boris is the Hull Professor of Women's Studies and director of the Center for Research on Women and Social Justice at the University of California, Santa Barbara. Among her books are *Home to Work: Motherhood and the Politics of Industrial Homework in the United States* (1994), winner of the Philip Taft Prize in Labor History; *Homeworkers in Global Perspective* (with E. Prügl; 1996); and *Major Problems in the History of American Workers* (with N. Lichtenstein; 2003).

Dorothy Sue Cobble is a professor at Rutgers University, where she teaches labor studies, history, and women's studies. Her books include *Dishing It Out: Waitresses and Their Unions in the Twentieth Century* (1991); *Women and Unions: Forging a Partnership* (1993); and *The Other Women's Movement: Workplace Justice and Social Rights in Modern America* (2004), winner of the 2005 Philip Taft Prize in American Labor History.

Marion Crain is the Paul Eaton Professor of Law at the University of North Carolina, and the deputy director for the Center on Poverty, Work and Opportunity. She is the coauthor of two textbooks published by Lexis Law Publishing, *Labor Relations Law* (with Theodore St. Antoine and Charles Craver;

11th ed., 2005) and *Work Law* (with Pauline Kim and Michael Selmi; 2005), as well as numerous scholarly articles.

Nicola Dones is the program associate at the Labor Project for Working Families. She is the author of numerous articles on work and family issues as well as the coauthor of the Labor Project's new guide, *A Job and a Life, Organizing and Bargaining for Work Family Issues.*

Janice Fine, a political scientist and long-time organizer, is assistant professor of Labor Studies and Employment Relations at the School of Management and Labor Relations, Rutgers University, and senior fellow at the Center for Community Change. She is the author of *Worker Centers: Organizing Communities at the Edge of the Dream* (Cornell University Press, 2006). Her work has been supported by the Open Society Institute, the Neighborhood Funders Group, and the Industrial Performance Center at MIT.

Netsy Firestein is the founder and director of the Labor Project for Working Families, a national nonprofit working with unions for better work and family policies. Netsy has over twenty years experience working with labor on work-family issues, previously at District 65–UAW in New York. She is the coauthor of *A Job and a Life, Organizing and Bargaining for Work Family Issues* (available at http://www.laborproject.org).

Heidi Hartmann is the founder and president of the Washington-based Institute for Women's Policy Research and a research professor at George Washington University. She has published numerous articles in journals and books, and her work has been translated into more than a dozen languages. In 1994, Hartmann was the recipient of a MacArthur Fellowship Award for her work in the field of women and economics.

Gerald Hunt is a professor at Ryerson University, Toronto, where he teaches in the areas of organizational behavior and industrial relations. His research focuses on labor's response to equity, and he is the author of *Laboring for Rights: Unions and Sexual Diversity across Nations.*

Jennifer Klein is assistant professor of history at Yale University. She is the author of *For All These Rights: Business, Labor, and the Shaping of America's Public-Private Welfare State* (Princeton University Press, 2003), awarded the Ellis W. Hawley Prize from the Organization of American Historians and the Hagley Business History Prize from the Business History Conference.

Vicky Lovell received a Ph.D. in public administration and policy from Portland State University and has been the director of Employment and Work/Life Programs at the Institute for Women's Policy Research (IWPR) for seven years. Her work focuses on research and technical assistance on supports for women's economic security, including paid-time-off programs, pay equity, and unionization. Lovell's recent IWPR publications include *Solving the Nursing Shortage through Higher Wages, Valuing Good Health*, and *No Time to Be Sick.*

Leslie McCall is currently associate professor of sociology at Northwestern University. Her book, *Complex Inequality: Gender, Class, and Race in the New Economy* (Routledge, 2001), was the first runner-up for the C. Wright Mills Book Award. Her work has been supported by the National Science Foundation, the Russell Sage Foundation, and Demos: A Network of Ideas and Action.

Ruth Milkman is professor of sociology and director of the Institute of Industrial Relations at University of California, Los Angeles. Her books include *Gender at Work: The Dynamics of Job Segregation during World War II*, which won the 1987 Joan Kelly Prize from the American Historical Association; *Farewell to the Factory: Auto Workers in the Late 20th Century* (1997); and most recently *L.A. Story: Immigrant Workers and the Future of the U.S. Labor Movement* (2006).

Karen Nussbaum was the founder and director of 9to5, National Association of Working Women; the president of District 925, SEIU; and the director of the Women's Bureau of the U.S. Department of Labor. She joined the AFL-CIO in 1996 and now serves as an assistant to the president. She is the author of the books *Solutions for the New Workforce* (with John Sweeney) and *9to5* (with Ellen Cassedy).

Maria L. Ontiveros is professor of law at the University of San Francisco School of Law. In addition to coauthoring a leading casebook on employment discrimination law, she publishes on the topics of workplace harassment of women of color, farmworkers, organizing immigrant workers, and contemporary applications of the Thirteenth Amendment.

Katie Quan, a former union leader for the UNITE, is currently director of the Labor Center at the University of California, Berkeley.

Lydia Savage is an associate professor of geography and chair of the Department of Geography-Anthropology at the University of Southern Maine, where she also is a member of the Women's Studies Council and a founding member of the Labor Studies Minor Program. Her current research examines the ways in which labor unions are reshaping union strategies and transforming institutional cultures in light of contemporary social, cultural, and economic change.

Vanessa Tait received her Ph.D. in sociology from the University of California, Santa Cruz. She is the author of *Poor Workers' Unions: Rebuilding Labor from Below* (South End Press, 2005). Her writings have appeared in *New Labor Forum*, *Critical Sociology*, and on the Pacifica radio network. She is the publications coordinator for University Professional & Technical Employees/CWA 9119 and a reference librarian at University of California, Berkeley.

Leah F. Vosko is associate professor of political science and Canada Research Chair in Feminist Political Economy in the School of Social Sciences at York University, Toronto. She is the author of *Temporary Work: The Gendered*

Rise of a Precarious Employment Relationship (2000) and, most recently, *Self-Employed Workers Organize: Law, Policy and Unions* (with Cynthia Cranford, Judy Fudge, and Eric Tucker; 2005), and she is the editor of *Precarious Employment: Understanding Labour Market Insecurity in Canada* (2006).

Misha Werschkul is currently working as a research associate with SEIU in the District of Columbia. Prior to coming to SEIU, she worked as a researcher with the Institute for Women's Policy Research, where she coauthored publications on women's employment, economic status, and education.

INDEX

Occupational Safety and Health Act (OSHA), 236
occupational sex segregation, 31–32, 35–36, 46–47; male- and female-sector jobs, 50–51; persistence of, 54–55; unions and, 60–61, 67. *See also* low-wage labor market
O'Connor, John, 189
Office of Federal Contract Compliance Programs (OFCCP), 163
office work, 160–61, 165–66
Older Americans Act, 191
Omaha Together One Community (OTOC), 227
One Inc., 85
one-on-one organizing strategies, 120
Ontiveros, Maria L., 231–32
"Opt Out Revolution, The" (Belkin), 170
Orfalea, Paul, 146
Organization of Personal Care and Chore Services, 183
Our Bodies, Ourselves, 162
own account workers, 272, 276–78

Paid Leave Coalition, 148
Parents and Friends of Lesbians and Gays (P-FLAG), 96
part-time employees, 133–34
patient care assistants (PCAs), 122–23
patriarchal family structure, 101
Paycheck Fairness Act, 52, 55
pay equity campaigns, 51–53, 56
pay-for-leave programs, 205–7. *See also* family leave legislation, California
People Organized to Win Employment Rights (POWER), 200, 202, 208–10
People Organizing Workfare Workers, 209
Perkins, Bill, 223
Personal Responsibility and Work Opportunity Reconciliation Act, 195
personal stories, used in campaigns, 146, 149–50
pharmacy profession, 49
Piven, Frances Fox, 201, 202
placement agencies, 217, 219–20, 225
politics of gender equity, 31–34
Poo, Ai Jen, 221, 222
poor, undeserving, 195
poor people's organizing, 197
Posner, Seymour, 184
poverty rates, 44, 46, 195
pregnancy disability, 143
Pregnancy Discrimination Act, 163

preschool programs, 143–44
Pride at Work (PAW), 81, 90, 91, 96
private-care market, 27–28
private-sector unionization, 6, 63–64, 69, 76–77; 1980s, 166–68
problem-solving model, 127–29
professional associations, 6–7
professionalization, 33
Project on Global Working Families, 141
psychological harassment in workplace, 107–8
public sector unionization, 6–7, 67–69, 76–77, 85, 164
public workers, pay equity campaigns, 51–53

Quan, Katie, 232

race: comparable worth and, 53; differences across industry groups, 71–73; discrimination, 107, 111; union anti-discrimination programs, 95; union-busting and, 83; unionization and, 71–73, 84; wage inequality and, 23–24, 37–38
Reagan/Bush years, 165–68
relative progress, 13, 16, 25–26; class-specific factors in, 29–31, *30*
respect, 126
Restaurant Opportunities Center, 221
Retail, Wholesale and Department Store Union (RWDSU), 227
Reuther, Walter, 94
Ricci, Donna, 160
Ricci, Ed, 191
Roberts, Dorothy, 108
Roberts, Ed, 191
Robinson, Lois, 106
Robinson v. Jacksonville, 104, 106
Robles, Betty, 256–59, 269
Rondeau, Kris, 117, 119–22, 125, 129–31, 135–39
Rose, Nancy, 195
Rose, Stephen J., 35, 50
Rosenberg Foundation, 144

San Francisco, 83–84, 88–89
San Francisco General Strike (1934), 83
Sara Lee Corporation, 256–59, 266, 267
Satellite Child Care Program, 149
Savage, Lydia, 117
Schneiderman, Rose, 117
Seaton-Msemaji, Ken, 188
Securitas, 232, 263–68
securities, in labor market regulation era, 275